Palgrave Studies in Political History

The contested nature of legitimacy lies at the heart of modern politics. A continuous tension can be found between the public, demanding to be properly represented, and their representatives, who have their own responsibilities along with their own rules and culture. Political history needs to address this contestation by looking at politics as a broad and yet entangled field rather than as something confined to institutions and politicians only. As political history thus widens into a more integrated study of politics in general, historians are investigating democracy, ideology, civil society, the welfare state, the diverse expressions of opposition, and many other key elements of modern political legitimacy from fresh perspectives. Parliamentary history has begun to study the way rhetoric, culture and media shape representation, while a new social history of politics is uncovering the strategies of popular meetings and political organizations to influence the political system.

Palgrave Studies in Political History analyzes the changing forms and functions of political institutions, movements and actors, as well as the normative orders within which they navigate. Its ambition is to publish monographs, edited volumes and Pivots exploring both political institutions and political life at large, and the interaction between the two. The premise of the series is that the two mutually define each other on local, national, transnational, and even global levels.

More information about this series at
http://www.palgrave.com/gp/series/15603

Ilkka Kärrylä

Democracy and the Economy in Finland and Sweden since 1960

A Nordic Perspective on Neoliberalism

palgrave
macmillan

Ilkka Kärrylä
Faculty of Arts
University of Helsinki
Helsinki, Finland

Palgrave Studies in Political History
ISBN 978-3-030-80630-9   ISBN 978-3-030-80631-6 (eBook)
https://doi.org/10.1007/978-3-030-80631-6

This Palgrave Macmillan imprint is published by the registered company Springer Nature Switzerland AG.
The registered company address is: Gewerbestrasse 11, 6330 Cham, Switzerland

Acknowledgments

This book is based on my doctoral dissertation, which I defended in November 2019. I want to thank all those who have read and commented on the dissertation, especially my supervisors Pauli Kettunen and Jussi Kurunmäki. Pauli was the one who originally proposed that I could study "how working life has been viewed as a domain for applying democracy." The task expanded to concern the economy more broadly, but it was always greatly influenced by Pauli's profound and original style of studying history and politics. Jussi, in turn, gave numerous valuable insights in conceptual history, democratic theory as well as structure and style of writing.

I am grateful to the opponent at my doctoral defense, Hagen Schulz-Forberg, who gave excellent and constructive critique on the dissertation. He also encouraged me to rewrite it into this book. Jenny Andersson and Juha Siltala also provided thorough reviews on the dissertation that helped me improve the text and clarify my arguments.

My dear colleagues at the University of Helsinki, especially in the discipline of Political History and at the Centre for Nordic Studies, also deserve many thanks for commenting on my papers and manuscripts and providing collegial support. Same goes for my colleagues associated with the international History of Concepts Group, the Finnish Society for Labour History and the Finnish Association for Work Life Research.

For the past year, I have been employed in the research program 'Neoliberalism in the Nordics' led by Jenny Andersson and funded by Riksbankens jubileumsfond. I thank my colleagues in the program for offering many new perspectives on neoliberalism, which have influenced the arguments made in this book.

I dedicate this book to my family.

Helsinki, 28 May 2021 Ilkka Kärrylä

Praise for *Democracy and the Economy in Finland and Sweden Since 1960*

"A fascinating work of conceptual history, which analyses the contested political objective of economic democracy to show how the market mechanism has won out as a principle of social organization in the Nordic countries since the 1960s. Kärrylä's meticulous, nuanced and authoritative account sheds new light on the neoliberalization of western societies and is highly relevant for current debates about the relation between democracy and the economy."

—Niklas Olsen, Professor of History, *University of Copenhagen, Denmark* and author of *The Sovereign Consumer: A New Intellectual History of Neoliberalism*

"*Democracy and the Economy* is a well-written, concise account of economic democracy debates in Sweden and Finland from the wage earner funds debates to the neoliberal era. It explains the importance of the wage earner funds idea, of enduring relevance to political economic debates today."

—Jenny Andersson, Professor, *Department of the History of Ideas and Science, Uppsala University, Sweden*

Contents

1 Introduction 1

2 Economic Democracy as a Contested Concept 23

3 Enterprise Democracy: Employee Power or Consultative Cooperation? 75

4 Collective Ownership as a Form of Economic Democracy 119

5 New Economic Paradigm Narrows the Horizon of Democratization 161

6 Last Struggles for Economic Democracy 211

7 From Democratization to Liberalization 251

8 Conclusion 307

References 325

Index 355

About the Author

Ilkka Kärrylä is a postdoctoral researcher at the Centre for Nordic Studies, University of Helsinki. He received his doctorate in the discipline of Political History at the University of Helsinki in 2020.

Abbreviations

ATP	Allmän tilläggspension (General supplementary pension)
EC	European Community
EEC	European Economic Community
EFTA	European Free Trade Association
EMU	European Monetary Union
ESOP	Employee Stock Ownership Plan
EU	European Union
EVA	Elinkeinoelämän valtuuskunta (Finnish Business and Policy Forum)
FP	Folkpartiet (People's Party, Liberals), Sweden
GATT	General Agreement on Tariffs and Trade
IMF	International Monetary Fund
LO	Landsorganisationen i Sverige (Swedish Trade Union Confederation)
MBL	Lagen om medbestämmande i arbetslivet (Codetermination Act), Sweden
NCP	National Coalition Party (Kansallinen kokoomus), Finland
OECD	Organization for Economic Cooperation and Development
SAF	Svenska arbetsgivareföreningen (Swedish Employers Association)
SAK	Suomen ammattiliittojen keskusjärjestö (Central Organization of Finnish Trade Unions)
SAP	Sveriges socialdemokratiska arbetareparti (Social Democratic Party of Sweden)
SDP	Suomen Sosialidemokraattinen Puolue (Social Democratic Party of Finland)
SI	Sveriges Industriförbund (Association of Swedish Industry)
SKDL	Suomen Kansan Demokraattinen Liitto (Finnish People's Democratic League)
SMP	Suomen Maaseudun Puolue (Finnish Rural Party)

STK	Suomen Työnantajain Keskusliitto (Confederation of Finnish Employers)
STTK	Suomen Teknisten Toimihenkilöjärjestöjen Keskusliitto (Finnish Confederation of Salaried Employees)
TCO	Tjänstemännens centralorganisation (Swedish Confederation of Professional Employees)
TKL	Teollisuuden keskusliitto (Central Association of Finnish Industry)
TVK	Toimihenkilö- ja Virkamiesjärjestöjen Keskusliitto (Confederation of functionaries and civil servants), Finland

List of Figures

Fig. 1.1	Number of articles with the terms 'economic democracy' and 'industrial democracy' in the Swedish database of digital newspapers (http://tidningar.kb.se/), 1900–2010. Data retrieved 13 August 2019	5
Fig. 2.1	Number of articles with the terms 'property-owning democracy,' 'owner democracy' and 'ownership dispersion' in the Swedish database of digital newspapers (http://tidningar.kb.se/), 1950–2010. Data retrieved 29 August 2019	57
Fig. 3.1	Number of articles with the terms 'economic democracy,' 'industrial democracy' and 'enterprise democracy' in the Swedish database of digital newspapers (http://tidningar.kb.se/), 1910–2010. Data retrieved 13 August 2019	78
Fig. 4.1	'Wage-earner funds' and concepts of democracy in Swedish newspapers, 1960–2010; number of articles with the terms in the Swedish database of digital newspapers (http://tidningar.kb.se/). Data retrieved 13 August 2019	121

CHAPTER 1

Introduction

Neoliberalization and the Narrowed Meaning of Democracy

Democracy is a key concept in Western political thought and practice. Since the end of World War II, it has been the main principle of legitimizing political power throughout the world. Historians have attempted to explain the rise of an old Greek word into the status of a nearly universal value. For 2000 years, democracy was merely one political system among others. Often the term was forgotten, and at times it was considered an illegitimate, even destructive, form of government. The connotation of democracy turned positive gradually after the French Revolution, as it was associated with the idea of representation.[1] In Nordic political rhetoric, democracy became a central power-legitimating concept after the breakthrough of parliamentarism and universal suffrage in the early twentieth century.[2] Democracy has been questioned by various autocratic regimes, but very few have discarded the term itself. They have usually at least called themselves democratic, as in the cases of communist 'people's democracies' during the Cold War.[3]

The valorization of democracy does not mean that there is a consensus on its meaning. On the contrary, as is common with political concepts, democracy's meaning and reference have always been highly contested. Instead of departing from a fixed definition, this study examines the

I. Kärrylä, *Democracy and the Economy in Finland and Sweden since 1960*, Palgrave Studies in Political History,
https://doi.org/10.1007/978-3-030-80631-6_1

historical meanings of democracy. However, there have been certain key elements historically associated with democracy—especially the ideal that political power should be held by the 'people' instead of a dictator or an elite.[4] Contestation has often concerned interpretations of this principle: It is not at all clear how the 'people' should exercise their power, what should belong to the 'people' in the first place, or what the appropriate scope of democratic power is.[5] At the moment, democracy is a desirable ideal primarily in a certain meaning and usage: States and their political systems have to be 'democratic' in order to legitimize themselves toward their citizens and the international community.[6] But it is not as common to reflect the relation of democracy and the sphere of life we call 'the economy.' Should democracy also be applied to economic organizations such as enterprises?

Although not very common today, the above question has been posed many times in history. During the twentieth century, it was a significant topic of debate in Western and especially Nordic countries. When parliamentary democracy had been achieved, Nordic social democrats began to demand the next steps of democratization in the social and economic spheres. They called for equal distribution of economic power, for example through democratic economic planning, collective ownership and employee decision-making within enterprises. These objectives were commonly called 'economic democracy,' 'industrial democracy' and 'enterprise democracy.'[7] Conservative and Liberal parties devised their own versions of democracy in the economy, such as profit-sharing and cooperative management. Most of the objectives of economic democracy were never realized. Systems of collective bargaining were created and employees gained more rights for participation in workplaces, but as economic ideas and practices have changed, the relationship between democracy and the economy has grown thinner. The terms economic and industrial democracy have almost disappeared from public and political rhetoric, even though they are still used in academic and activist debates.[8]

This book seeks to understand and explain this conceptual and ideational change especially in the Nordic context. It investigates the history of the concepts of 'economic democracy,' 'industrial democracy' and 'enterprise democracy' since the 1960s: what kinds of beliefs, attitudes and concrete practices they have been associated with, how they have been legitimized and criticized, and how their role has changed in political thought and rhetoric. The book aims to explain why these concepts have since the early 1990s mostly disappeared from everyday political language.

It argues that neoliberal beliefs and conceptions that regard democracy and the economy as separate spheres have become dominant, undermining previous ideas of economic democracy. The book's empirical focus is on Sweden and Finland, which gives the work a comparative element. These Nordic countries are geographically and culturally close to each other, with conceptual similarities and transfers, but there are also many differences and discontinuities. Moreover, in the 1970s Sweden was without doubt the most progressive country in promoting economic democracy, which makes it an interesting case study in its own right.

Studies that explicitly deal with economic and industrial democracy have been quite scarce in recent decades. There are contributions in political theory and philosophy,[9] as well as in comparative political and institutional studies.[10] Management and organizational theories also used to discuss the theme before the 1980s,[11] but for historical research these studies represent primary sources rather than secondary literature. Previous research has examined what a democratic economy should look like and what it has looked like in different parts of the world. These studies offer valuable knowledge and interpretations on economic democracy in theory and practice, but their historical perspective is often quite thin. They also have predetermined ideas of what economic democracy means, which narrows their perspective.[12]

Historical research on economic democracy has been more common in Sweden than in Finland. The Swedish tradition of intellectual history is strong and studies on the ideological development of the social democrats are numerous.[13] In Sweden, economic democracy is also linked to one of the country's most contested political issues of the postwar era: wage-earner funds. The original proposal by the trade union confederation LO in the 1970s would have enabled wage-earners significant collective ownership in Swedish enterprises. The funds were eventually established in a moderate form, but the debate has been considered a major factor behind the political mobilization of Swedish business and the breakdown of the coordinated labor market model.[14] In Finland, by contrast, economic democracy has not received as much attention. Research on the political left and the trade union movement has concentrated on organizational and personal history rather than ideological development.[15] However, certain reform processes related to industrial democracy, such as the introduction of production committees in the 1940s and the Act on Cooperation within Undertakings in the 1970s have been studied thoroughly.[16]

In the past, the concept of economic democracy has been connected to various economic systems, including the market economy, planned economy and worker self-governance. A key question has been determining the proper instances of making economic decisions: markets, states, regions, industrial sectors or enterprises? Industrial and enterprise democracy have been common names for democracy on the 'meso' and 'micro' levels of sectors and enterprises, while economic democracy has more often referred to the macro level.[17] However, the historical usage is not as straightforward, and economic democracy has in some cases referred only to the workplace level.[18] Another key question has concerned ownership: What are the appropriate limits of private and public ownership, and should enterprises be owned by employees or their collective associations?[19] Therefore, the concept links strongly to the historical struggle between capitalism and socialism as economic and social orders.

Other variations in the meaning and reference of economic democracy are based on traditional distinctions of the concept of democracy. Recurring problems have been the choice between representative, direct and participatory democracy; collective versus individual decision-making; self-determination versus consultation; and the scope of issues that are decided democratically, for example operational versus strategic decisions in enterprises.[20] The question of power or authority in the economy, that is, how much democratic decision-making should bind owners and managers, has been particularly central in historical debates.[21] Ownership of the means of production has often been viewed as means to gain power, but one distinct meaning of economic democracy has been distribution of economic resources without explicit reference to distribution of power.

Previous research has pointed out three transnational 'waves' of debate on economic and industrial democracy in the twentieth century: immediately after both world wars, and from the mid-1960s until the 1980s.[22] What unites these historical situations, illustrated in Fig. 1.1, is a radical conjuncture where possibilities and hopes for significant societal reforms have been opened. In the 1960s, this kind of politicization was fueled by labor market conflicts and political radicalism, which had a leftist character.[23] A thorough history of the concept of economic democracy from this era has so far remained unwritten. The concepts' decline in the 1990s in particular calls for careful analysis.

Figure 1.1 illustrates the rises and declines of economic and industrial democracy in Swedish public debate. The fluctuation testifies to the historically contested nature of democracy. Unlike in the 1960s and 1970s,

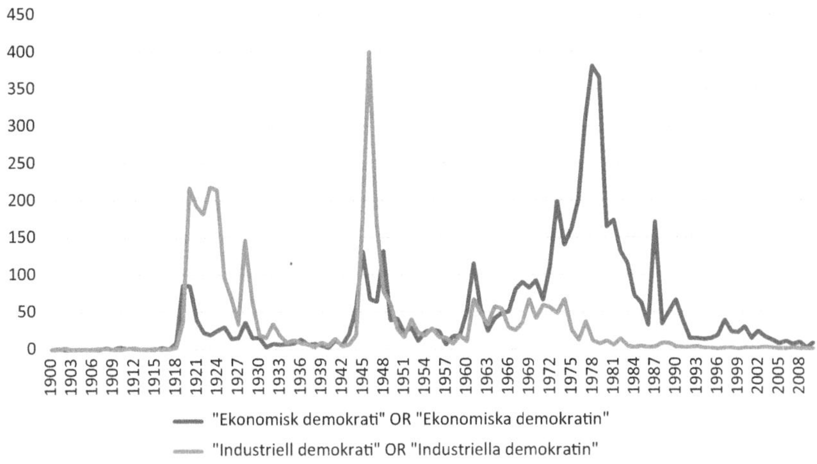

Fig. 1.1 Number of articles with the terms 'economic democracy' and 'industrial democracy' in the Swedish database of digital newspapers (http://tidningar.kb.se/), 1900–2010. Data retrieved 13 August 2019

today's mainstream conception of a democratic society does not include the notion of extending democratic principles and practices into the economy. In the economic sphere, democracy does not have the same function of legitimating power it has in politics. The economy is, at least implicitly, conceived as a private sphere as opposed to the public political sphere, where principles of democracy apply.[24] Democracy in this sense is above all a concept denoting formal practices such as parliamentary representation and universal suffrage, rule of law, and rights such as freedom of speech, press and assembly.[25] This conception of democracy is particularly common in the Western world committed to market economy and representative democracy.[26]

The disappearance of economic democracy from political debate has been explained by social and ideological changes of the past decades. Economic democracy did not fit into a world where economic globalization and free markets have gained ground and been legitimated by 'neoliberal' ideas.[27] Many historians and social scientists use the concept of neoliberalism to name the political and economic modes of thought that have since the 1970s influenced the transition from interventionist Keynesian economic policy to liberalization of economic activity and marketization of societies. The intellectual history of neoliberalism has been studied thoroughly during the past couple of decades. Neoliberalism is usually portrayed as a new phase of economic liberalism, whose advocates were marginalized during and after the Great Depression and World War II, as economic planning, redistributive welfare states and Keynesianism became political norms. However, liberal ideas lived on especially in the Mont Pèlerin society (MPS) founded by Friedrich von Hayek and other liberal philosophers and economists. The society's task was to uphold liberalism against totalitarianism and collectivism of both fascist and socialist varieties.[28] In the 1950s and 1960s, free markets and limited state intervention gained strong advocates in the monetarist theories of the Chicago School of economics, which had intimate ties with the MPS. With Milton Friedman as its most prominent figure, the school challenged Keynesian policy and prioritized battle against inflation instead of the goal of full employment.[29] In the wake of the economic crises of the 1970s, neoliberal ideas gained foothold in economic policy, especially in the governments of Margaret Thatcher and Ronald Reagan in United Kingdom and the United States. International organizations, such as the International Monetary Fund (IMF) and Organization for Economic Cooperation and Development (OECD) also began advocating neoliberally oriented policies promoting free markets.[30]

Some scholars have found the term 'neoliberalism' problematic, because it is used in everyday political debate without proper definition and because few people today identify themselves as neoliberals.[31] The term was used in networks aiming to renew liberalism in the 1930s and 1940s, but since the 1950s they have called themselves more often 'classical liberals.' When the ideas of the MPS and the Chicago School gained political currency, neoliberalism became mostly a pejorative word used by their opponents.[32] There are nevertheless viable criteria for using 'neoliberalism' as an analytical concept for ideas that are connected to the liberal 'thought collective' identified by intellectual historians. Historian Niklas Olsen defines neoliberalism as "the ideological product of processes in which self-identified liberals have attempted to renew liberalism as an ideology that claims to promote societal orders based on free markets and individual freedom."[33] The political scientist Thomas Biebricher, in turn, argues that neoliberalism is characterized by a shared problematic, which "concerns the political and social conditions of possibility for functioning markets, the latter being characterized by the integrity of the price system, which must operate unperturbed."[34] In other words, neoliberalism is interested in designing social and political institutions that would allow maximal use of the market mechanism. It does not mean minimizing the state's role but retasking it to support and extend markets.[35]

The political economist Jamie Peck has pointed out how neoliberal ideas have produced various forms of regulation and state intervention that aim to create and uphold market-like rule. According to Peck, a macro concept is needed to highlight the connections of different 'local neoliberalisms.' As the phenomenon is not about realizing a well-defined political model but some generally shared objectives and tendencies toward freer markets and commodification of new spheres of life, Peck argues that it is more appropriate to talk about 'neoliberalization' than 'neoliberalism.'[36] Therefore, I will also use neoliberalization in this study as a general label for the tendency of promoting the market mechanism as a principle of social organization, often by utilizing the state's capacities.

This book provides a new perspective on the neoliberalization of the Nordic countries, which have not yet been very well covered in international literature on neoliberalism. They have rather been portrayed as resistant to neoliberalization with their strong welfare states,[37] but this interpretation underestimates the changes the countries have gone through since the 1970s. Some Nordic historians have already argued that ideas of economic democracy were incompatible with emerging neoliberal ideas and practices, but the reasons for this conceptual incompatibility have not been thoroughly analyzed.[38] This book complements the interpretation with a more rigorous analysis of neoliberal conceptions of democracy and society. I argue that there indeed are elements in neoliberal thought that rule out democracy in the economic sphere, such as defining the economy as a domain of individual choices rather than collective decisions. Ideas of this variety have gained currency in the Nordic countries since the 1970s.

Many scholars have already argued that neoliberalism is an antidemocratic intellectual tradition.[39] Central neoliberal thinkers, such as Hayek and Friedman, advocated a limited democracy and a firm rule of law. According to them, democracy, especially as majority rule, needs to be kept in check so that it cannot initiate a turn toward de-marketization and thus threaten individual freedom.[40] Hayek is known to have distinguished liberalism from democracy and prioritized the former. According to him, a democratic government can be totalitarian, while an authoritarian one can be liberal.[41] Liberals of all varieties have of course portrayed democracy and free markets as necessary preconditions for each other, and many neoliberal thinkers have even portrayed market choices as analogous to voting.[42] However, a 'market democracy' of one dollar, one vote, differs substantially from a political democracy of one person, one vote. Placing decisions in the hands of individual consumers in the market excludes many historical key elements of democracy, such as political equality and collective decision-making.[43]

Besides neoliberalism as a mode of thought, many scholars have suggested that capitalism as an economic and social system restricts democracy both ideologically and materially.[44] This book focuses on the historical use of concepts, but it also utilizes 'capitalism' as an analytical concept. Capitalism means an economic system based on private ownership of capital and the aim of its constant accumulation. Capitalism should be distinguished from a market economy, neither of which is a necessary condition for the other.[45] The relation between capitalism and democracy has often been found problematic in social, political and economic research. Democratic institutions have of course legitimate power to regulate the economy in capitalist democracies, but their possibilities to do so have decreased as globalized capital has been able to escape national borders.[46] Instead of democracy, the legitimacy of economic power is based on the principle of private ownership, the free market as the most efficient allocator of resources, and apolitical expertise that can govern the market.[47]

In recent years, many scholars have been worried about the increasing separation of capitalism and democracy and the growing dominance of narrow economic elites and transnational firms, which has been blamed for citizens' increasing alienation from democratic politics.[48] Part of the blame has been put onto the political parties, which have turned from interest representation to 'catch-all' parties and moved from democracy toward technocracy that prioritizes economic imperatives. According to the political scientist Peter Mair, 'constitutional democracy' has been replacing 'popular democracy,' which was based on rule by the people through mass parties.[49] The sociologist Colin Crouch is even more pessimistic and calls the post-Cold War era 'post-democracy.'[50]

Problematizations of this variety have since the financial crisis of 2008 received growing attention in history and the social sciences. In these debates, democracy is connected to broader questions of social justice and a good society. Many scholars have been concerned about the power of economic elites, as it has been noted that the people responsible for creating debt and asset bubbles keep getting richer, while states and ordinary citizens pay the bill for financial meltdowns.[51] The state of democracy has also been a concern due to growing populism and nationalism, which questions liberal democracy and may gain its momentum partly from economic inequality.[52] Research on inequality has become topical in economics, as well, as scholars have noted a drastic increase in income and wealth differences over several decades within advanced capitalist countries, as well as the persistence of differences between developed and developing countries.[53] These studies often reflect whether the current economic system is fair or even efficient. They are not always conceptualized as being about economic democracy, but growing inequalities are often portrayed as undemocratic or at least as undermining the preconditions of democracy.[54] Economists like Thomas Piketty and Joseph Stiglitz have openly advocated stronger democratic control of capital to deal with these problems.[55]

Explaining Conceptual Change with Changing Ideational Constellations and Dilemmas

The relation between democracy and the economy—or the prevailing economic system of capitalism—seems ambiguous and ridden with tensions. The aim of this book is to analyze and clarify this historical relationship in Sweden and Finland as well as its broader implications in political thought and practice in the latter half of the twentieth century. The study relates to several fields of research: the history of democracy, the history of the economy and working life, and the history of political thought and ideologies. It is necessary to use many perspectives in order to give a thorough account of the relation that is condensed in composite concepts like economic and industrial democracy. Rather than examining economic and social structures as objectively existing entities, my focus is on the history of concepts and ideas. I look at historical agents' contested ways of conceiving and conceptualizing democracy and the economic order. In a sense, this study combines conceptual and social history, as well as political and economic history, as suggested by historian Reinhart Koselleck.[56]

Along with the concepts of economic and industrial democracy, alternatives to capitalism as an economic order have also been marginalized in recent decades. These debates are closely linked to ideological contestation, especially the battle between two grand social and economic orders of the twentieth century—capitalism and socialism.[57] However, when studying the history of thought and concepts, one must go beyond such dichotomous frameworks and look for variations and nuances. By concentrating on the relatively marginalized themes of economic and industrial democracy, we can find new viewpoints on contemporary society and its long-term development. In this sense, the book also represents 'history of the present,' as coined by Michel Foucault.[58] This does not mean tracing some teleological origins of the present. In the words of historian Quentin Skinner, historical research can bring to light foreign or forgotten ideas and possibilities, thus revealing the historicity and contingency of dominant beliefs and values of our time.[59] With this aim in mind, the book provides a critical perspective on the political, economic and intellectual history of the postwar era by examining the relationship between democracy and the economy in Finland and Sweden.

To analyze the relationship between democracy and the economy and to explain its changes, I utilize an analytical framework based on conceptual history, intellectual history and rhetorical analysis. Following the tradition of conceptual history, I see political concepts as highly contested and historically contingent. They are used as tools in political struggles, which shape their meanings and valuations as well as contribute to constituting reality.[60] I will therefore examine how different agents used and defined the concepts of economic, industrial and enterprise democracy, and how they legitimized their views. This way I can uncover the most important similarities and differences, continuities and discontinuities in the concepts' meaning and usage. I can also determine whether the concepts had any historically stable core elements that made them something more than empty signifiers. Following Quentin Skinner, I look especially at three aspects of concepts, which can all be contested politically: their criteria of application, their range of reference and the range of attitudes they can express. The first aspect means the necessary criteria for a concept's application, the second the set of concrete phenomena that can fulfill these criteria and the third the concept's normative role and implications.[61]

To explain the different meanings of concepts, their change and disappearance, I move toward broader intellectual history and sketch out the ideational constellations historical actors have held and expressed. Key elements in these constellations include different beliefs about the workings of society, democracy and the economy, as well as beliefs about relevant problems and their potential solutions. Following the approach of Mark Bevir, I explain conceptual and ideational change with 'dilemmas' that historical actors have faced and that have prompted them to modify their beliefs and concepts.[62] I pay special attention to value hierarchies that could legitimize and delegitimize different conceptions of economic democracy and that determined the concepts' importance in an ideational constellation.[63] In this respect, tensions between concepts like democracy, efficiency and economic growth are of special interest. Swedish historian Jenny Andersson has claimed that growth has been a priority in the social democratic ideology in Sweden. It has been viewed as an inescapable precondition to other objectives, such as equality and security.[64] Among Finnish scholars, the interpretation of economic necessities dictating the common interest and the scope of politics and democracy has been even more common.[65] Economic democracy, too, had to be legitimized against the values of economic efficiency and growth that often represented the common good in political thought and rhetoric.

Structure and Scope of the Book

This study examines the relation of democracy and the economy by beginning the analysis from explicit usages of the terms economic, industrial and enterprise democracy. It maps the most common elements of these concepts and traces their use in relevant political debates. Therefore, the analysis is not restricted to the use of individual words, but neither is the aim to examine everything that has been said about democracy and the economy. The empirical focus is on debates between the 1960s and 1990s, while earlier debates and reforms in the 1920s and 1940s form a background for the research. I provide a brief account on these developments at the beginning of Chap. 2. During the 1960s and 1970s, debates and legislative processes connected to economic democracy were intense, and they took place almost simultaneously in Finland and Sweden. In the 1980s, the most vivid debate formed around wage-earner funds, until the visions of economic democracy faded toward the end of the decade. I conclude by examining the decline of the concept in conjunction with the economic crises and ideological and political changes of the 1980s and 1990s. This gives grounds for assessing the concept's role in twenty-first-century political thought and language.

The structure of the empirical chapters is based on my findings. The work focuses especially on three concrete themes, around which the main debates on economic and industrial democracy revolved in the 1960s–1980s: (1) public steering and planning of the economy (active industrial policy), (2) democracy in workplaces and enterprises, and (3) collective ownership (especially wage-earner funds). There are many overlaps between these themes, but the debates are distinct enough to be analyzed separately. The same division has sometimes been made in previous research.[66] Some themes that have been connected to economic and industrial democracy in other temporal and spatial contexts, such as collective bargaining, consumer influence and taxation do not play significant roles in this book. Taxation was practically never associated with economic and industrial democracy in Finland and Sweden during the research period. Collective bargaining is an important background to enterprise democracy, and consumer influence also figures in the historical debates, but the main thrust of democratization as a future-oriented activity was not aimed toward these issues in my research period.

The chapters of this book examine ideological and theoretical debate and concrete political reforms. The first empirical chapter begins with a look at the history of economic and industrial democracy in Sweden and Finland before the 1960s, mostly drawing on previous literature. Then it moves on to ideological debate in pamphlets, party programs and congresses in the 1960s, during which democratization of the economy began to reemerge as a political objective. The focus is on the debates on economic planning and active industrial policy. Chapters 3 and 4 deal with two important thematic questions during the 1960s and 1970s: enterprise democracy and wage-earner funds. These 'case studies' look at the day-to-day political debate, conceptual struggles and rhetorical moves in more detail, using for example newspaper and archival material in addition to party programs and pamphlets. In the cases of enterprise democracy and wage-earner funds, labor market organizations become key protagonists alongside political parties. Chapter 5 moves a little back in time from the resolutions of enterprise democracy and wage-earner fund debates, placing them in the context of the crisis of postwar capitalism. It looks at the changing economic policy of the Social Democrats and the political mobilization of business, and how these affected the ideas and rhetoric of economic democracy. Chapter 6 examines how debates on principles and concrete applications of economic and industrial democracy developed in the 1980s in the context of economic liberalization. The final empirical chapter analyzes changing thought and rhetoric since the early 1990s, in the context of the Finnish and Swedish economic crises and the collapse of 'real and existing' socialism. It takes a more general look at programs and debates in the 1990s and 2000s, tracing the concepts and beliefs that remained and emerged after the rapid decline of economic democracy as a key political concept. The final chapter sheds light on currently prevailing conceptions of democracy and the economy.

The concepts of economic and industrial democracy were defined and evaluated by many actors in Finland and Sweden, which makes the number of potential primary sources enormous. To sketch out the wider landscape of thought and rhetoric and to unveil conceptual struggles, I examine significant parties from different ends of the political spectrum. The primary focus is on Social Democratic (SAP, SDP) and Conservative parties (*Högerpartiet/Moderata Samlingspartiet*, *Kansallinen kokoomus*) from Sweden and Finland. I do not treat the parties as representatives of strictly defined ideologies like conservatism and social democracy. Instead, I offer an account of the ideological evolution of these organizations and examine how the actors have related themselves to different ideologies. Other parties are examined on a more cursory level. The roles of agrarian/center parties and the liberal People's Party (*Folkpartiet*) in Sweden are important, as they all became strong advocates of enterprise democracy in the 1970s.

Similarities in party structure between Finland and Sweden make comparative analysis easier: from the 1960s to the 1990s in both countries the key parties in the parliament were Conservatives, Liberals, Agrarians, Social Democrats and Communists.[67] In addition, green, populist and Christian democratic parties emerged at different points in time, but they are excluded from the present research. Power relations between the parties were different in Sweden and Finland. In Sweden, the Social Democrats were able to rule alone for decades, whereas in Finland they had to form coalition governments. In Sweden, the Liberals had quite strong support, but in Finland it was weak. Conversely, the Finnish Communists were strong but the Swedish rather weak.

In addition to political parties, I examine trade unions (LO, SAK) and employer confederations (SAF, STK). The Swedish LO was intimately connected to the Social Democratic Party: Until 1992, its members automatically became members of SAP.[68] In the Finnish SAK, Communists also played a significant role. This made SAK more independent but also more divided than LO. I have also taken selective glimpses at material by white-collar confederations (TCO, TVK, STTK) and business think tanks, such as the Finnish EVA and Swedish Timbro, which were founded in the 1970s and became visible in public debate.

Social Democrats and the trade union movement figure as main characters in a large part of the book. They were the groups that produced the most material and statements about economic and industrial democracy. Especially in Sweden, the Social Democrats were the most significant power-holders for most of my research period. As historian of the Swedish conservatives, Torbjörn Nilsson, has criticized, it is easy to focus on the decision-makers and 'winners' of history. In some parts of this study I repeat this unfortunate tendency, but also conservatives and employer organizations eventually play a key role—especially in struggles over concrete reforms and toward the end of the book, as they in turn become power-holders and 'winners.'

The most important primary sources of the study are, on the one hand, documents representing ideological and theoretical debate, such as programs and manifestos of parties and labor market organizations, as well as political and academic books on economic and industrial democracy. These are used to uncover the diachronic changes in concepts and beliefs. On the other hand, I examine debates on concrete reform and legislation initiatives, using sources like committee reports, parliamentary records, archival material as well as newspaper and journal articles. In this way I get closer to the daily struggles over concepts, which brings a synchronic perspective to the study. By examining several synchronic struggles at different points in time, the diachronic analysis and understanding of conceptual change are deepened.[69]

I focus on debates in Finland and Sweden, while other countries are not directly part of the research setting. However, I briefly describe some debates and practices in other European countries and the United States to better explain and situate the Finnish and Swedish cases, which drew much inspiration from international comparison.[70] Transnational connections between Finland and Sweden are of special interest. Swedish legislative reforms and other initiatives worked as examples for neighboring Finland, where the issues of economic and industrial democracy took longer to manifest in concrete reforms. Finnish actors often leaned on Swedish examples when arguing for and against economic and enterprise democracy, while the movement of influences in the other direction was less frequent.

The analysis moves between Finland and Sweden in different ways depending on what kind of narration has seemed appropriate. I analyze and explain differences and similarities in political thought and rhetoric in the light of local political contexts. Sometimes Finnish and Swedish cases are more tightly interwoven; sometimes they are examined in separate subchapters. The findings of this comparative analysis provide new insights on the changing relation between democracy and the economy, as well as the general development of political thought and rhetoric in Sweden and Finland in the postwar era.

Notes

1. John Dunn, *Setting People Free: The Story of Democracy* (London: Atlantic Books, 2005), 15–20; Jussi Kurunmäki, Jeppe Nevers and Henk te Velde, "Introduction," in *Democracy in Modern Europe: A Conceptual History*, eds. Jussi Kurunmäki, Jeppe Nevers and Henk te Velde (New York: Berghahn, 2018), 1–11; Martin Conway, "Democracy in Western Europe after 1945," in *Democracy in Modern Europe: A Conceptual History*, eds. Jussi Kurunmäki, Jeppe Nevers and Henk te Velde. (New York: Berghahn, 2018), 234–235; Jan-Werner Müller, *Contesting Democracy: Political Ideas in Twentieth Century Europe* (New Haven and London: Yale University Press, 2011), 3–5.
2. Jussi Kurunmäki and Johan Strang, "Introduction: 'Nordic Democracy' in a World of Tensions," in *Rhetorics of Nordic Democracy*, eds. Jussi Kurunmäki and Johan Strang (Helsinki: Finnish Literature Society, 2010), 9–11.
3. Dunn, *Setting the People Free*, 15–20.
4. Norberto Bobbio, *Democracy and Dictatorship: The Nature and Limits of State Power* (Cambridge: Polity Press, 1989), 133–135; John S. Dryzek, *Democracy in Capitalist Times* (New York and Oxford: Oxford University Press, 1996), 4.
5. David Held, *Models of Democracy*, 2nd edition (Stanford: Stanford University Press, 1996), 2–3; Dryzek, *Democracy in Capitalist Times*, 5–7.
6. Dunn, *Setting the People Free*, 19.
7. For example, Anna Friberg, *Demokrati bortom politiken: En begreppshistorisk analys av demokratibegreppet inom Sveriges socialdemokratiska arbetareparti 1919–1939* (Stockholm: Atlas, 2012), 256–265.
8. Bo Rothstein, "Ekonomisk demokrati? Reflexioner kring en borttappad diskussion," in *Tillsammans: En fungerande ekonomisk demokrati*, ed. Bo Rothstein (Stockholm: SNS förlag, 2012), 9–23.
9. Most explicitly in Rothstein, "Ekonomisk demokrati?"; David Schweickart, *After Capitalism* (Lanham: Rowman & Littlefield, 2002); Robin Archer, *Economic Democracy: The Politics of Feasible Socialism* (Oxford: Oxford University Press, 1995); Robert A. Dahl, *Preface to Economic Democracy* (Cambridge: Polity Press, 1985).
10. For example, Rothstein, "Ekonomisk demokrati?"; Herman Knudsen, *Employee Participation in Europe* (London: Sage, 1995); Joel Rogers and

Wolfgang Streeck, eds., *Works Councils: Consultation, Representation, and Cooperation in Industrial Relations* (Chicago and London: University of Chicago Press, 1995); M. Donald Hancock, John Logue and Bernt Schiller, eds., *Managing Modern Capitalism: Industrial Renewal and Workplace Democracy in the United States and Western Europe* (New York: Praeger, 1991).

11. A key work is Eric Rhenman, *Företagsdemokrati och företagsorganisation* (Stockholm: P. A. Norstedt & Söners Förlag, 1964).
12. For example, Ilja Viktorov, *Fordismens kris och löntagarfonder i Sverige* (Stockholm: Stockholm University, 2006), 115–117.
13. For example, Friberg, *Demokrati bortom politiken*; Lars Ekdahl, *Mot en tredje väg: En biografi över Rudolf Meidner. II. Facklig expert och demokratisk socialist.* (Lund: Arkiv, 2005); J. Magnus Ryner, *Capitalist Restructuring, Globalisation and the Third Way: Lessons from the Swedish Model* (London and New York: Routledge, 2002); Bo Stråth, *Mellan två fonder: LO och den svenska modellen* (Stockholm: Atlas, 1998); Tim Tilton, *The Political Theory of Swedish Social Democracy* (Oxford: Oxford University Press, 1990); Leif Lewin, *Planhushållningsdebatten* (Stockholm: Almqvist & Wiksell, 1967).
14. On the wage-earner fund debate, see Viktorov, *Fordismens kris*; Ekdahl, *Mot en tredje väg II*; Ryner, *Capitalist Restructuring*; Stråth, *Mellan två fonder*; Stefan Sjöberg, *Löntagarfondsfrågan – En hegemonisk vändpunkt: En marxistisk analys* (Uppsala: Universitetstryckeriet, 2003); Mark Blyth, *Great Transformations: Economic Ideas and Institutional Change in the Twentieth Century* (Cambridge: Cambridge University Press, 2002); Jonas Pontusson, *The Limits of Social Democracy: Investment Politics in Sweden* (Ithaca: Cornell University Press, 1992); Gregg M. Olsen, *The Struggle for Economic Democracy in Sweden* (Aldershot and Brookfield: Avebury, 1992); Mikael Gilljam, *Svenska folket och löntagarfonderna: En studie i politisk åsiktsbildning* (Lund: Studentlitteratur, 1988); Erik Åsard, *LO och löntagarfondsfrågan: En studie i facklig politik och strategi* (Stockholm: Rabén & Sjögren, 1978); Erik Åsard, *Kampen om löntagarfonderna: Fondutredningen från samtal till sammanbrott* (Stockholm: Norstedt, 1985).
15. For example, Hannu Soikkanen, *Kohti kansanvaltaa 1: Suomen Sosialidemokraattinen puolue 75 vuotta, 1899–1937* (Helsinki: Suomen Sosialidemokraattinen puolue, 1975); Hannu Soikkanen, *Kohti kansanvaltaa 3: SDP 1944–1952* (Helsinki: Suomen Sosialidemokraattinen puolue, 1991); Tapio Bergholm, *Sopimusyhteiskunnan synty I: Työehtosopimusten läpimurrosta yleislakkoon. Suomen Ammattiyhdistysten Keskusliitto 1944–1956* (Helsinki: Otava, 2005); Tapio Bergholm, *Sopimusyhteiskunnan synty II: Hajaannuksesta tulopolitiikkaan. SAK 1956–1969* (Helsinki:

Otava, 2007); Tapio Bergholm, *Kohti tasa-arvoa: Tulopolitiikan aika I* (Helsinki: Otava, 2012); Tapio Bergholm, *Laatua ja vapaa-aikaa. Tulopolitiikan aika II: Suomen ammattiliittojen keskusjärjestö vuodesta 1977* (Helsinki: Suomalaisen kirjallisuuden seura, 2018). As exceptions to the trend see Pauli Kettunen, *Poliittinen liike ja sosiaalinen kollektiivisuus: Tutkimus sosialidemokratiasta ja ammattiyhdistysliikkeestä Suomessa 1918–1930* (Helsinki: Suomen historiallinen seura, 1986); Pauli Kettunen, *Suojelu, suoritus, subjekti: Työsuojelu teollistuvan Suomen yhteiskunnallisissa ajattelu- ja toimintatavoissa* (Helsinki: Suomen historiallinen seura, 1994).

16. On production committees see Bergholm, *Sopimusyhteiskunnan synty I*, 77–82; Ilkka Turunen, "Arbete, produktion och demokrati: De finländska produktionskommittéernas historia," in *Industriell demokrati i norden*, ed. Daniel Fleming (Lund: Arkiv, 1990), 197–217; Markku Mansner, *Suomalaista yhteiskuntaa rakentamassa: Suomen Työnantajain Keskusliitto 1940–1956* (Helsinki: Teollisuuden kustannus, 1984), 250–267. On enterprise democracy and cooperation see Bergholm, *Laatua ja vapaa-aikaa*, 19–49; Ilkka Kärrylä, "Kansallinen etu demokratian rajoituksena: Suomalaisten työnantajien retoriikka 1960- ja 1970-lukujen yritysdemokratiakeskustelussa," *Historiallinen aikakauskirja* 114, 4 (2016): 445–457; Markku Mansner, *Suomalaista yhteiskuntaa rakentamassa: Suomen työnantajain keskusliitto 1980–1992* (Helsinki: Elinkeinoelämän keskusliitto EK, 2005), 316–345; Markku Mansner, *Suomalaista yhteiskuntaa rakentamassa: Suomen Työnantajain Keskusliitto 1956–1982* (Helsinki: Teollisuuden kustannus, 1990), 431–446.
17. Rothstein, "Ekonomisk demokrati?", 26–27; Olsen, *The Struggle for Economic Democracy*, 11; Donald Sassoon, *One Hundred Years of Socialism: The West European Left in the Twentieth Century* (London: Fontana Press, 1996), 481, 706–707.
18. Christer Lundh, *Den svenska debatten om industriell demokrati 1919–1924: 1. Debatten i Sverige* (Lund: Studentlitteratur, 1987), 26.
19. Rothstein, "Ekonomisk demokrati?", 26–28; Sassoon, *One Hundred Years of Socialism*, 481, 528–533, 706–713; Lundh, *Den svenska debatten om industriell demokrati 1*, 475–484.
20. Joel Rogers and Wolfgang Streeck, "The Study of Works Councils: Concepts and Problems," in *Works Councils: Consultation, Representation, and Cooperation in Industrial Relations*, eds. Joel Rogers and Wolfgang Streeck (Chicago and London: University of Chicago Press, 1995), 6–10; Knudsen, *Employee Participation in Europe*, 5–21; Lundh, *Den svenska debatten om industriell demokrati 1*, 19–23.
21. Lundh, *Den svenska debatten om industriell demokrati 1*, 21–23.
22. Niels Dalgaard, *Ved demokratiets grænse: Demokratisering af arbejdslivet i Danmark 1919–1994* (Copenhagen: Selskabet til Forskning i

Arbejderbevægelsens Historie, 1995); Niklas Bruun, Pauli Kettunen and Ilkka Turunen, "Industriell demokrati i Norden: Introduktion till det finska delprojektet," in *Industriell demokrati i norden*, ed. Daniel Fleming (Lund: Arkiv, 1990), 120–121; Bernt Schiller, *"Det förödande 70-talet": SAF och medbestämmandet 1965–1982* (Stockholm: Arbetsmiljöfonden, 1988), 17–19; Birger Simonson, *Arbetarmakt och näringspolitik: LO och inflytandefrågorna 1961–1982* (Stockholm: Arbetsmiljöfonden, 1988), 9–12; Mansner, *Suomen Työnantajain Keskusliitto 1956–1982*, 431.

23. Ingrid Gilcher-Holtey, "Political Participation and Democratization in the 1960s: The Concept of Participatory Democracy and its Repercussions," in *Democracy in Modern Europe: A Conceptual History*, eds. Jussi Kurunmäki, Jeppe Nevers and Henk te Velde (New York: Berghahn, 2018), 257–273; Luc Boltanski and Ève Chiapello, *The New Spirit of Capitalism* (London and New York: Verso, 2005), 167–172; Sassoon, *One Hundred Years of Socialism*, 362–376; Stråth, *Mellan två fonder*, 108–122, 130–136.
24. Teivo Teivainen, *Enter Economism, Exit Politics: Experts, Economic Policy and the Damage to Democracy* (London and New York: Zed Books, 2002), 1–4, 19–21; Dryzek, *Democracy in Capitalist Times*, 35–36.
25. Larry Diamond, *The Spirit of Democracy* (New York: Times Books, 2008), 21–23; Freedom House. https://freedomhouse.org/.
26. With this generalization I refer to all conceptions of democracy that do not find it necessary to apply democracy to the sphere understood as 'economic.' Within this broad framework there can of course be numerous other theoretical and practical disagreements regarding democracy.
27. Jenny Andersson, *Between Growth and Security: Swedish Social Democracy from a Strong Society to a Third Way* (Manchester: Manchester University Press, 2006), 20–21; Kristina Boréus, *Högervåg: Nyliberalism och kampen om språket i svensk offentlig debatt 1969–1989* (Stockholm: Tiden, 1994), 321–324.
28. Dieter Plehwe, "Introduction," in *The Road from Mont Pèlerin: The Making of the Neoliberal Thought Collective*, eds. Dieter Plehwe and Philip Mirowski (Cambridge, MA and London: Harvard University Press, 2009), 10–26; Philip Mirowski, *Never Let a Serious Crisis Go to Waste: How Neoliberalism Survived the Financial Meltdown* (London and New York: Verso, 2013), 42–49; Daniel Stedman Jones, *Masters of the Universe: Hayek, Friedman, and the Birth of Neoliberal Politics* (Princeton: Princeton University Press, 2012), 30–36, 73–84; Jamie Peck, *Constructions of Neoliberal Reason* (Oxford: Oxford University Press, 2010), 3–4; David Harvey, *A Brief History of Neoliberalism* (Oxford and New York: Oxford University Press, 2005), 19–23.

29. Rob Van Horn and Philip Mirowski, "The Rise of the Chicago School of Economics and the Birth of Neoliberalism," in *The Road from Mont Pèlerin: The Making of the Neoliberal Thought Collective*, eds. Dieter Plehwe and Philip Mirowski (Cambridge, MA and London: Harvard University Press, 2009), 139–178; Daniel T. Rodgers, *Age of Fracture* (Cambridge, MA & London: Belknap Press of Harvard University Press, 2011), 50–52; Stedman Jones, *Masters of the Universe*, 88–100, 201–212.
30. Stedman Jones, *Masters of the Universe*, 7–9, 18–19, 136–137, 254–270; Harvey, *A Brief History of Neoliberalism*, 1–4, 22–27, 55–63; Sassoon, *One Hundred Years of Socialism*, 452–457.
31. For example, Rajesh Venugopal, "Neoliberalism as a Concept," *Economy and Society* 14, 2 (2015): 165–187.
32. Thomas Biebricher, *The Political Theory of Neoliberalism* (Stanford: Stanford University Press, 2019), 13–18; Taylor C. Boas and Jordan Gans-Morse, "Neoliberalism: from New Liberal Philosophy to Anti-Liberal Slogan," *Studies in Comparative International Development* 44, 2 (2009): 145–152; Hagen Schulz-Forberg, "Laying the Groundwork: The Semantics of Neoliberalism in the 1930s," in *Re-inventing Western Civilisation: Transnational Reconstructions of Liberalism in Europe in the Twentieth Century*, eds. Hagen Schulz-Forberg and Niklas Olsen (Newcastle upon Tyne: Cambridge Scholars Publishing, 2014), 29–39; Mirowski, *Never Let a Serious Crisis Go to Waste*, 26–29, 37–41.
33. Niklas Olsen, *The Sovereign Consumer: A New Intellectual History of Neoliberalism* (Cham: Palgrave Macmillan, 2019), 6.
34. Biebricher, *The Political Theory of Neoliberalism*, 26.
35. Philip Mirowski, "Postface: Defining Neoliberalism," in *The Road from Mont Pèlerin: The Making of the Neoliberal Thought Collective*, eds. Dieter Plehwe and Philip Mirowski (Cambridge, MA and London: Harvard University Press, 2009), 433–436.
36. Jamie Peck, "Explaining (with) Neoliberalism," *Territory, Politics, Governance* 1, 2 (2013): 132–154; Peck, *Constructions of Neoliberal Reason*, xii–xiii, 7–8, 19–20.
37. For example, Torsten Svensson, *Marknadsanpassningens politik: Den svenska modellens förändring 1980–2000* (Uppsala: Statsvetenskapliga föreningen, 2001), 280–285.
38. Andersson, *Between Growth and Security*, 20–21; Boréus, *Högervåg*, 321–324.
39. For example, Wendy Brown, *Undoing the Demos: Neoliberalism's Stealth Revolution* (New York: Zone Books, 2015).
40. Quinn Slobodian, *Globalists: The End of Empire and the Birth of Neoliberalism* (Cambridge, MA: Harvard University Press, 2018), 13–18; Sean Irving, "Limiting Democracy and Framing the Economy: Hayek,

Schmitt and Ordoliberalism," *History of European Ideas* 44, 1 (2018): 113–127; Lars Cornelissen, "'How can the People be Restricted?': The Mont Pèlerin Society and the Problem of Democracy, 1947–1998," *History of European Ideas* 43, 5 (2017): 507–524; Thomas Biebricher, "Neoliberalism and Democracy," *Constellations* 22, 2 (2015): 255–266; Stedman Jones, *Masters of the Universe*, 62–65.

41. Friedrich Hayek, *Studies in Philosophy, Politics and Economics* (New York: Simon & Schuster, 1967), 161; Mirowski, "Postface," 443–446.
42. Olsen, *The Sovereign Consumer*, 7–11, 260–264; Stedman Jones, *Masters of the Universe*, 56–59.
43. Tom Christiano, "Democracy," in *The Stanford Encyclopedia of Philosophy*, ed. Edward N. Zalta (Spring 2015 Edition). https://plato.stanford.edu/archives/spr2015/entries/democracy/; Bobbio, *Democracy and Dictatorship*, 133–135.
44. Dryzek, *Democracy in Capitalist Times*, vii, 24–33.
45. For more elaborate definitions along the same lines, see Jürgen Kocka, "Introduction," in *Capitalism: The Reemergence of a Historical Concept*, eds. Jürgen Kocka and Marcel van der Linden (London and New York: Bloomsbury Academic, 2016), 1–7; Boltanski and Chiapello, *The New Spirit of Capitalism*, 4–8; Schweickart, *After Capitalism*, 22–24.
46. Bob Jessop, *The State: Past, Present, Future* (Cambridge: Polity Press, 2015), 199–200; Boltanski and Chiapello, *The New Spirit of Capitalism*, 365–372.
47. Cf. Nikolas Rose, *Powers of Freedom: Reframing Political Thought* (Cambridge: Cambridge University Press, 1999); Francis Sejersted, "Capitalism and Democracy: A Comparison between Norway and Sweden," in *The Democratic Challenge to Capitalism: Management and Democracy in the Nordic Countries*, eds. Haldor Byrkjeflot, Sissel Myklebust, Christine Myrvang and Francis Sejersted (Bergen: Fagbokforlaget, 2001), 88–89, 115–116.
48. Wolfgang Streeck, *Buying Time: The Delayed Crisis of Democratic Capitalism* (London and New York: Verso, 2014), 4–6, 76–96; Andrew Sayer, *Why We Can't Afford the Rich* (Bristol: Policy Press, 2015), 237–253; Jessop, *The State*, 211–216.
49. Peter Mair. *Ruling the Void: The Hollowing of Western Democracy* (London and New York: Verso, 2013), 1–16.
50. Colin Crouch, *Post-Democracy* (Cambridge: Polity Press, 2004), 1–28.
51. Colin Crouch, *The Strange Non-Death of Neoliberalism* (Cambridge: Polity Press, 2011); Göran Therborn, *The Killing Fields of Inequality* (Cambridge: Polity Press, 2013); Göran Therborn, *Kapitalet, överheten och alla vi andra: Klassamhället i Sverige – Det rådande och det kommande* (Lund:

Arkiv, 2018); Mirowski, *Never Let a Serious Crisis Go to Waste*; Sayer, *Why We Can't Afford the Rich.*

52. For example, Jan-Werner Müller, *What is Populism?* (Philadelphia: University of Pennsylvania Press, 2016); Cas Mudde and Cristóbal Rovira Kaltwasser, "Populism: Corrective *and* Threat to Democracy," in *Populism in Europe and the Americas: Threat or Corrective for Democracy?* eds. Cas Mudde and Cristóbal Rovira Kaltwasser (Cambridge: Cambridge University Press, 2012).
53. Thomas Piketty, *Capital in the Twenty-First Century* (Cambridge, MA: Belknap Press of Harvard University Press, 2014); Anthony Atkinson, *Inequality: What can be Done?* (Cambridge, MA: Harvard University Press, 2015); Joseph Stiglitz, *The Price of Inequality* (New York and London: W.W. Norton, 2012); Branko Milanovic, *Global Inequality: A New Approach for the age of Globalization* (Cambridge, MA: Belknap Press of Harvard University Press, 2016); Matti Tuomala, *Markkinat, valtio ja eri-arvoisuus* (Tampere: Vastapaino, 2019).
54. For example, Piketty, *Capital in the Twenty-First Century*, 1–2, 569–570; Stiglitz, *The Price of Inequality*, 2012, 148–182; Therborn, *Kapitalet, överheten och alla vi andra*, 131–141; Bo Stråth, "När var demokratin?" *Historisk tidsskrift* 95, 2 (2016): 290–291.
55. Piketty, *Capital in the Twenty-First Century*, 470–570; Stiglitz, *The Price of Inequality*, 332–343.
56. Reinhart Koselleck, "Introduction and Prefaces to the Geschichtliche Grundbegriffe," *Contributions to the History of Concepts* 6, 1 (2011) [1972]: 16–19; Reinhart Koselleck, "Social History and Begriffsge schichte," in *History of Concepts: Comparative Perspectives*, eds. Iain Hampsher-Monk, Karin Tilmans and Frank van Vree (Amsterdam: Amsterdam University Press, 1998), 25–28.
57. Steven Lukes, "The Grand Dichotomy of the Twentieth Century," in *Cambridge History of 20th Century Political Thought*, eds. Terence Ball and Richard Bellamy (Cambridge: Cambridge University Press, 2003).
58. Michel Foucault, *Discipline and Punish: The Birth of the Prison* (New York: Pantheon Books, 1977), 30–31.
59. Quentin Skinner, *Visions of Politics I: Regarding Method* (Cambridge: Cambridge University Press, 2002), 6.
60. Koselleck, "Introduction and Prefaces"; Skinner, *Visions of Politics I*, 145–150.
61. Skinner, *Visions of Politics I*, 160–172.
62. Mark Bevir, *The Logic of the History of Ideas* (Cambridge: Cambridge University Press, 1999); Ilkka Kärrylä, "Concepts, Beliefs and their Constellations: A Proposal for Analytical Categories in the Study of Human Thought," *Contributions to the History of Concepts* 17 (2022) [forthcoming].

63. Chaïm Perelman, and Lucie Olbrechts-Tyteca, *The New Rhetoric: A Treatise on Argumentation* (Notre Dame and London: University of Notre Dame Press, 1969), 80–83.
64. Andersson, *Between Growth and Security*.
65. Risto Alapuro, "Ulkoinen ja sisäinen: Suomen poliittisen kulttuurin pitkä linja," *Yhteiskuntapolitiikka* 75, 5 (2010): 528–537; Pauli Kettunen, *Globalisaatio ja kansallinen me: Kansallisen katseen historiallinen kritiikki* (Tampere: Vastapaino, 2008), 88–89; Jukka Pekkarinen and Juhana Vartiainen, *Suomen talouspolitiikan pitkä linja* (Helsinki: WSOY, 1993), 51–57.
66. Most notably in Pontusson, *The Limits of Social Democracy*, which is one of the few studies that deals extensively with all three topics. However, Pontusson's umbrella term is not 'economic democracy' but 'investment politics.'
67. I sometimes refer to parties with umbrella terms that place them in larger groups but do not contain claims on their ideology and policy. The terms 'Left' and 'Socialist' refer to Social Democrats and Communists. 'Right' refers to conservatives, while 'Center' refers to liberals and agrarian/center parties. I will also use the term 'bourgeois parties' (*porvaripuolueet/borgerliga partier*), which is commonly used in Finland and Sweden to label all center and right parties. In my own use it has a purely descriptive and nonnormative function.
68. Kjell Östberg, "När ingen längre kokar kaffe – eller vad har hänt folkrörelsepartierna?" in *Demokratins drivkrafter: Kontext och särdrag i Finlands och Sveriges demokratier 1890–2020*, eds. Henrik Meinander, Petri Karonen and Kjell Östberg (Helsinki: Svenska litteratursällskapet i Finland, 2018), 403–404, 413–414.
69. On synchronic and diachronic analysis see Koselleck, "Introduction and Prefaces," 18; Koselleck, "Social History and Begriffsgeschichte," 30–34; Jan Ifversen, "About Key Concepts and How to Study Them," *Contributions to the History of Concepts* 6, 1 (2011): 82–85.
70. Finnish and Swedish debates on economic and industrial democracy have been very Euro- and Western-centric, which is inevitably mirrored in the perspective of this book. However, some Asian and Eastern European countries, especially Japan and Yugoslavia, were also used as models.

CHAPTER 2

Economic Democracy as a Contested Concept

The Origins of Economic Democracy

Extending democracy to the sphere of life called 'the economy' was a key objective for social democratic parties from the early twentieth century, but its meaning and reference have varied throughout the years. Even the origin of the idea is not entirely clear. The most common composite concepts that combine democracy and the economy, economic democracy and industrial democracy, are often associated with Ernst Wigforss, the important theoretician of the Swedish Social Democratic Party (SAP). He served as MP and minister of finance from the 1920s until the 1950s.[1] However, the terms predate the writings of Wigforss. Apparently, the Swedish Social Democrats appropriated and translated them from socialists in other European countries. 'Industrial democracy' had already been coined in the first half of the nineteenth century, probably by the anarchist Pierre-Joseph Proudhon. It was later used, for example, by the English Fabians Sidney and Beatrice Webb, as well as many American trade unionists. Industrial democracy usually meant democracy within factories and workplaces or in labor market relations in general. Especially in the United States, it was often synonymous with collective bargaining.[2]

Employers and nonsocialist parties had also since the nineteenth century advocated ideas and practices that could be called industrial democracy. However, the actual use of the term democracy in these contexts is

I. Kärrylä, *Democracy and the Economy in Finland and Sweden since 1960*, Palgrave Studies in Political History,
https://doi.org/10.1007/978-3-030-80631-6_2

dubious. Usually, the practices in question were linked to social liberal and paternalistic ideas of worker welfare. They were restricted to the workplace level and preferred individual instead of collective solutions. Different strands of management and organization theory have advocated taking care of employees with pension and healthcare plans, profit-sharing and consultation. These ideas were put into practice especially in France, United Kingdom and United States. The main aim has been to make employees better attached to the company and its goals and therefore to enhance industrial peace and productivity.[3] This was also a counterstrategy to the socialist trade union movement. Some (social) liberal politicians and thinkers also advocated collective bargaining and employee-owned cooperative enterprises. John Stuart Mill predicted in his 1848 book *Principles of Political Economy* that in the future, capitalists might be replaced by "associations of labourers."[4]

Apart from industrial paternalism, the above practices were not widely adopted in the Nordic countries.[5] In Finland, liberal thinkers and progressive corporate managers as early as in the nineteenth century introduced democracy-related terms such as 'industrial constitutionalism' and 'industrial parliamentarism,' which referred to welfare schemes, profit-sharing, or even bargaining systems.[6] Cooperatives have figured as potential organizations for democratization also in socialist thought, but their role has remained limited. The Finnish and Swedish labor movements established strong chains of consumer cooperatives to distribute consumer goods, but worker cooperatives have been rare. Nordic cooperative movements were initially nonsocialist and often legitimized as ways of reforming capitalism without the need for state intervention. The labor movement was for a long time suspicious toward consumer cooperatives, as they were considered as potentially eroding workers' class consciousness.[7] The historian Mary Hilson has concluded that cooperation was "both a social movement and a business; motivated by ideological principle and steered by commercial pragmatism; opposed to capitalism but forced to compete for market share and willing to learn practical lessons from capitalist businesses."[8]

Economic democracy is a parallel concept to industrial democracy, but its origins are harder to trace. The first usages of the English term and its German counterpart *Wirtschaftsdemokratie* took place in the nineteenth century. In Swedish daily newspapers, *ekonomisk demokrati* first appeared as a translation in a 1901 article that discussed French initiatives for local labor councils.[9] Previous research on economic and industrial democracy has not always been very careful to distinguish analytical concepts from historical ones. The sociologist Gregg Olsen has referred to SAP's Gothenburg program, written by Wigforss in 1919, as an early demand for economic democracy.[10] This interpretation postulates economic democracy as a concept, while the term is missing from the program. It did, however, include ideational elements that were or became main features of economic democracy, such as state-led, democratic economic planning, and worker councils in workplaces.[11] Therefore, Olsen's postulation may be justified based on the program's ideational elements and the fact that at least soon after its publication in 1919, Wigforss did begin to use the terms economic and industrial democracy.[12]

Industrial democracy became a central topic of debate in many European countries and the United States around the end of World War I. Revolutionary movements, social turmoil and food shortages spurred the creation of workers councils, guilds and other self-governing economic bodies. In some countries, Weimar Germany being the most notable example, councils were later given an official, albeit consultative, status.[13] 'Economic democracy' also became a prominent concept for German Social Democrats and trade unions during the 1920s. It referred to controlling the economy more broadly in addition to democracy at the workplace level.[14] However, not all the diverse socialist, communist and anarchist movements in Britain, Central Europe and Russia used the terms industrial and economic democracy. This makes, for example, Christer Lundh's treatment of these as parts of one and the same phenomenon potentially problematic, even though they did share many elements, such as the aspiration for worker self-governance. In Sweden, terminology was more established by 1920, when the Social Democratic minority government appointed a committee, led by Wigforss, to investigate industrial democracy. However, its proposal of establishing consultative works councils (*driftsnämnder*) in companies was not implemented by the bourgeois parties who returned to office in 1921.[15]

At this point, the term economic democracy was also used more consistently. Looking at the largest Swedish newspapers, the term's breakthrough took place in 1919, when Erik Palmstierna's proposal for economic democracy was discussed.[16] Palmstierna was a right-wing Social Democrat who presented economic democracy as an alternative to socialization.[17] In his use, economic democracy was a synonym for industrial democracy, but soon it gained broader meanings. Economic democracy was efficient for highlighting the importance of other core concepts, especially democracy, equality, and economic redistribution, in socialist thought. Mainstream Swedish Social Democrats had already before World War I turned to a 'reformist' line that sought to transform society through democratic and parliamentary means. As the revisionist socialist Eduard Bernstein had stated, democracy was for socialists both a means and an end.[18] SAP adopted the meaning of economic democracy as democratic control over the whole economy and utilized economic oligarchy as its counter-concept. In the famous 'people's home speech' held in the Swedish Parliament in 1928, the SAP leader Per Albin Hansson expressed very explicitly the idea of extending democracy to the economic sphere and its importance in decreasing inequalities in society.[19]

The people's home did not become a core concept for the Swedish Social Democrats, even though historians have often treated it as such.[20] In contrast, using the approach of the political scientist Michael Freeden, one could say that the concept of economic democracy quickly became situated close to the core of social democratic ideology in Sweden.[21] The often voiced demand for economic democracy meant a slight reconceptualization of the labor movement's traditional demands for socialism, collective ownership and eradication of the class society. Economic democracy shifted the viewpoint from material issues such as ownership and production toward more abstract notions of democracy and power. Old demands for placing means of production under the control of 'society,'[22] which in the Nordic countries has often been a synonym for the state,[23] began to be rephrased as 'democratic control of the economy.' This could be taken as the main criterion for the concept of economic democracy in social democratic thought and rhetoric. It entailed the idea that economic decisions should not be made by a few owners of capital (economic oligarchy), but by regular people. In this context the state was, at least after the breakthrough of parliamentarism, considered the most important democratic entity through which the people expressed its will.

Economic democracy was a strongly future-oriented concept, placed into a modernist narrative of linearly progressing democratization that would reach different spheres of society. After the introduction of universal suffrage in Sweden in 1919, there was a lively debate on the meaning of democracy. A three-tier conception of democracy became common in social democratic thought and rhetoric. The party called for expanding *political democracy* and increasing also *social* and economic democracy in order to create a fully democratic society. In this context, social democracy meant social rights, security and services for all citizens, while economic democracy referred to determination over economic decisions. However, although the Swedish Social Democrats gained governmental power in 1932, no notable progress toward economic and industrial democracy was made, and the party also began to use the concepts less frequently. Demands for the self-governance (*självbestämmande*) or codetermination (*medbestämmande*) of workers were toned down to influence (*inflytande*) and insight (*insyn*).[24] Instead, the Social Democrats concentrated on expansive fiscal policy and job creation to get out of the Great Depression and took the first steps toward a welfare state by building social security. SAP's agreement with the Peasant Union entailed that they would abstain from any nationalization plans. According to a common interpretation, SAP turned at this point from a class-based rhetoric to a perspective of the nation as whole.[25] The party continued to advocate democracy, especially the concept of 'Nordic democracy,' in the context of emerging fascist regimes across Europe. At this point, the conservatives also toned down their earlier critique of representative democracy in order not to come across as supporters of authoritarianism.[26]

Historical research sees the Saltsjöbaden agreement of 1938 as the cornerstone of the 'Swedish model' of class compromise and consensual cooperation between labor and capital. In this model, the state mostly stayed in the background and let the labor market parties negotiate between themselves on the terms and conditions of employment. The employers accepted social reforms and the rights of organized workforce, while the employee side accepted the employers' right to manage and organize work as well as hire and fire personnel. Instead of class conflict, Swedish labor market relations became characterized by a search for common interests in the 'virtuous circle' of economic growth and increasing democracy and social rights. The state contributed to the regime's stability by exercising macroeconomic management and an active labor market policy, as well as granting tax exemptions to private profits if they were used for investment. In this way, Sweden's strong industrial and financial capitalists were integrated into the system.[27] The Saltsjöbaden agreement and strengthening of collective bargaining were often conceptualized as economic democratization and considered a distinct feature of 'Nordic democracy.'[28] However, this did not have a significant democratizing effect at the workplace level, but the greatest power was exercised by the state, labor market organizations, as well as corporate owners and managers. Centralized collective bargaining and/or company-level works councils became the norm in many European countries like Germany, Austria, the Netherlands and the Nordic countries. This tradition of 'democratic corporatism' has often been viewed as a distinct model of ordering capitalism and contrasted, for example, with the more liberal, decentralized and adversarial models of the Anglo-Saxon countries.[29]

Finland had been part of Sweden for some 600 years, and it retained its Swedish institutions, traditions and elites as an autonomous grand duchy of Russia in 1809–1917 and as an independent republic from 1917 onward.[30] Research on Finnish political culture has often suggested that the national interest or the common good has been the most important value in the country's political rhetoric. Usually, this common interest has been portrayed as a matter of objective and rational knowledge rather than a compromise between conflicting interests and values. A phrase associated with Finland's former president J. K. Paasikivi, in office 1946–1956, crystallizes the idea: "The beginning of all wisdom is acknowledging the facts." The belief entails that national interest is best guarded by possessing objective knowledge on the facts and necessities of our surroundings and acting accordingly. This mentality has prevailed especially in Finnish foreign policy, where the key 'fact' has been Finland's position between great powers and as the neighbor of Russia and the Soviet Union. The sociologist Risto Alapuro has argued that a certain 'defensive ethos' is a key component of the Finnish identity. To a large extent, this is rooted in Finland's experiences in the Civil War of 1918, World War II and the Cold War era.[31] Another source of perceived facts and necessities has been the economy, which has created tensions with the aim of developing economic democracy.

Economic and industrial democracy were introduced into Finnish political language around the same time as in Sweden, but due to the lack of previous research it is difficult to give as comprehensive an account of their early history. Digitized Finnish newspapers show that there were occasional uses since 1901—usually in news from abroad—while more consistent use began in the first wave of debate from 1919 onward.[32] In the interwar period, the concepts of economic and industrial democracy were less prominent in comparison to Sweden, which may be explained by differences in the political situation and labor market relations. In spring 1918, some months after gaining independence, Finland went through a civil war between socialist 'reds' and bourgeois 'whites.' The reds occupied the southern part of the country and attempted to carry out socializations and establish worker control over production. These measures were not called economic democracy, and their scope remained limited during the three-month war.[33] After the victory of the 'whites,' the Finnish Social Democrats were relatively weak while communist organizations were made illegal and had to operate underground. However, in the 1920s, communists participated in elections under the Socialist Workers' Party of Finland. Communists also became influential in the trade union movement, which had a unified organization despite ideological struggles.[34] The new Social Democratic leadership was more revisionist, but communist pressure created tensions within the party. During the 1930s, control of communist activities became stricter, and in 1937 the first center-left coalition between the Social Democrats and the Agrarian Party gave the former a stronger position in the Finnish government.[35]

For the Finnish labor movement, concepts that signified linear extension of democracy from 'political' to other spheres mostly figured in programmatic rhetoric that lacked anchoring to the local context. There were demands for socialization, control of production, workers' councils and collective bargaining, but many of these were expressions of ideological long-term objectives and did not lead to anything concrete during the interwar period.[36] A system of collective bargaining was formally accepted by Finnish employers only in 1944. As in Sweden, the conceptual distinction between general economic planning and employee influence in workplaces was made, even though the distinction of the terms economic and industrial democracy was not always clear. The trade union movement stressed the development of collective bargaining and shop steward systems as realizations of economic or industrial democracy.[37] The Social Democrats also used economic democracy in the context of state-led economic planning, which could have included new corporatist institutions with representation of most important experts and interest groups.[38]

After World War II, new meanings and ideational constellations of economic democracy made their way into SAP's programs in Sweden. In SAP's 1944 platform and the labor movement's postwar program, democracy and the economy were explicitly connected. The program called for more democracy in "economic life" and "economic organizations." As concrete reforms, it demanded societal planning of investments and increased influence of employees over production.[39] In Social Democratic rhetoric, economic democracy meant placing at least the most significant parts of economic activity under democratic control. The term's range of reference usually encompassed economic planning, and even socializing or nationalizing means of production, which made the democratic state the most important democratic entity. These concepts were central in the economic thought of most European left-wing parties. However, the views differed within and between Social Democrats and Communists, for example, regarding the extent of maintaining capitalist institutions and whether socializing property was necessary in order to meet the central criterion for economic democracy: distributing economic power more equally.[40]

In the first half of the twentieth century, support for economic planning and social reforms grew even among liberal and conservative parties. Belief in free markets was harmed by the Great Depression, and Keynesian economics gained many followers who were ready to increase the state's role in the economy. Economic planning was not a necessary part of Keynesianism, but it became more widely implemented in the postwar period, largely thanks to the experiences of the war economy. Even public ownership of the means of production became a more viable political option, as politicians began to restrict capitalism in the name of security and welfare. In many countries, the main objectives of economic policy were stability and full employment, which would be achieved through planning and social policy reforms, such as the Beveridge plan in Britain. State intervention in the economy became stronger via the regulation of prices, interest rates and movement of capital. The Bretton Woods system regulated and stabilized monetary policy and currency trade globally.[41] However, detailed economic planning was not established in any Western country and the market mechanism retained a significant role. Even in countries with substantial nationalizations, such as France and Britain, state-owned companies were mostly left to operate independently in the market.[42]

In Sweden, the roles and relations of socialization and economic planning in social democratic thought and policy have been much debated and researched. The questions of private versus collective ownership and markets versus planning have been considered some of the greatest ideological divides within the party.[43] Social democratic theoreticians Ernst Wigforss and Nils Karleby both argued as early as in the 1920s that socialization was not necessary for the fundamental aims of socialism: centralized ownership did not guarantee that freedom, equality and democracy would increase. What was more important was economic planning and democratization.[44] It became a mainstream view for the Swedish Social Democrats that socialization had only instrumental value and was not a necessary part of socialism. It has been considered SAP's official line at least since the interwar period, when the party switched from pursuing radical changes in the economic system to piecemeal reforms. However, within the party there was usually some support for extensive nationalization, and the issue was raised and discussed on several occasions.[45]

The postwar 'planned economy debate' in Sweden has been studied extensively. At this time, a wide consensus had been reached on state intervention in the economy in order to even out business cycles and reach full employment. Social democratic ideas of large-scale economic planning and the socialization of industry were left unrealized due to strong political opposition and a lack of concrete plans. However, finance markets were extensively regulated by the state, as in most other Western countries.[46] According to Jonas Pontusson, planning remained an important element of social democratic ideology, but it "came to be identified with long-term economic forecasting and with public infrastructure and services rather than with industrial development."[47]

Similar debates on economic planning and socialization took place in other Nordic countries with similar results.[48] In Finland, the economy became tightly regulated and restrictions on prices, wages, interests and capital flows were in place for a long time, as in most European countries. However, economic planning and Keynesian counter-cyclical policy were mostly excluded from the toolbox. Finland was more focused on budget balance and the competitiveness of the export industry, using currency devaluations as a central policy tool. These measures were advocated by the strongest interest groups, especially the industry. They influenced economic policy and portrayed their interests as economic necessity, whereas the advocates of full employment were weaker. The Bank of Finland and civil servants also had considerable power over economic policy, while governments were usually weak and short-lived until the late 1970s. When in government, center-right parties and the Social Democrats alike practiced similar economic policy. The Finnish constitution gave the president great powers in foreign as well as domestic policy, especially in government formation. President Urho Kekkonen, who represented the Agrarian/Center Party, utilized these powers to the maximum during his long term in office from 1956 to 1981.[49] The Finnish state put a lot of effort into industrialization, making state-owned industry an important player in the economy. Unlike in Sweden, where the state-owned sector was rather small, most of Finland's largest metal industry companies as well as many chemical and forest industry companies were state-owned. However, they operated independently under professional managers and were market-oriented.[50] Foreign trade was also heavily regulated after the war, but Finland took its first steps toward economic cooperation and European integration by joining the IMF and World Bank in 1948, GATT in 1949, and signing a free trade agreement with EFTA in 1961.[51]

The use of the concepts of economic and industrial democracy increased in Finland in the immediate postwar era. As in Sweden, there was debate on works councils and planned economy. The trade union movement's primary focus was still on collective bargaining and stabilizing its position vis-à-vis the employer organizations. The Social Democrats advocated state-led economic planning in the fashion of their Swedish counterparts, which made promoting democracy in workplaces a minor objective. The Communists, whose operations were now legalized, also began to emphasize actions at the levels of the state and civic organizations instead of workplaces. A socialization committee was appointed in 1946, partly inspired by nationalizations done by the British Labour Party. However, this did not lead to reforms, as leading Social Democrats turned against large-scale socializations and the bourgeois parties turned down the idea completely. Finland's constitution and its protection of ownership also made it practically impossible to socialize private property. The objectives of economic planning were toned down to stabilization of wages and prices, which also proved difficult.[52]

In the 1950s, unprecedented economic growth, the increasing affluence of citizens and the spread of the consumer society in Western countries seemed to prove that capitalism was a functional economic system. Broad consensus on the symbiosis of regulated capitalism and social reforms sparked interpretations of 'the end of ideology.'[53] At the same time, support for left-wing parties stagnated in many countries. Socialist and social democratic parties throughout Europe had settled for pursuing reformist politics and supporting the capitalist status quo, which was given new names like 'mixed economy' and 'social market economy.' Profitable industry was needed in order to maintain full employment and fund social reforms, while the pursuit of the 'end-state' of socialism became vague. Socialists had clear short-term goals and continued to see socialism somewhere in the future, but they did not quite know how to connect these two temporal layers.[54] As Jenny Andersson has pointed out, the tension between utopian critique and pragmatic improvement of capitalism has been a fundamental dilemma for social democracy, which was the most influential strand of leftism in most of Western Europe.[55]

Demands for the democratization of workplaces also weakened in most of Western Europe, and the role of existing works councils soon diminished.[56] The trend was similar in Sweden: Demands for planning, socialization and democratization of the economy weakened, and right-wing critique of social policy increased. The 1950s were characterized by collaboration between labor and capital, which was made easier by steady economic growth. In this context, the Social Democrats concentrated on social reforms and reaching the combination of full employment and low inflation through labor market policy that came to be named the 'Rehn-Meidner model' after two trade union economists. Social Democratic rule in Sweden lasted throughout the decade, but in many elections their position was anything but certain, and in 1951–1957 they formed a coalition government with the Peasant Union.[57] The debate on values was toned down, and politics was increasingly viewed as a question of instrumental social engineering.[58]

Growing Demands for Democratization in the 1960s

In the 1960s, the Swedish and Finnish Social Democrats were reserved toward socialization of ownership, but economic planning and cooperation between capital and labor were portrayed as necessary features in the ongoing economic and technological development. Modernity was viewed as progressing on a benign and inevitable course, bringing a better standard of living and more freedom to everyone. This positive view was common in the Western world. A new emphasis on economic democratization fit well into this progress narrative, which often gained even teleological qualities. The need for economic planning and coordination became a more pressing theme in the second half of the 1960s, especially because economies were going through rapid structural changes. Planning was believed to counteract their negative consequences, such as the forced mobility of people from the countryside into cities and unemployment due to automatization and disappearance of occupations.[59]

In Sweden, the 1960s marked a change in the economic policy orientation of the Social Democrats, whose cornerstone had been the Rehn-Meidner model's solidaristic wage policy and active labor market policy. It hindered the wages in most profitable enterprises and allowed the destruction of unprofitable firms. People were provided support in changing jobs and reeducating themselves for new professions in order to maintain full employment.[60] Jonas Pontusson has emphasized that in effect this model meant accepting the workings of the market mechanism within the industry and included restraint from state intervention in the allocation of investment. Altering the market allocation of investment was not a significant motivation even behind Swedish public investment funds and ATP pension funds.[61] However, the fact that Swedish corporate taxation encouraged investment instead of consumption of private profits was a key factor in maintaining full employment.[62] This model had been in the interests of both capital and labor during the period of strong economic growth in the 1950s and early 1960s, but now the situation was changing.

Many Social Democrats took a more outspoken stance on economic planning in the mid-1960s. They claimed that there was not enough planning in Sweden. Inspiration was taken from the *dirigiste* economic policy in France, with the emphasis that there should be stronger democratic control of planning institutions.[63] The well-established emphasis on the instrumentality of socialization also got a new theorist in the Social Democrat economist Gunnar Adler-Karlsson, who named his way of thinking 'functional socialism.'[64] With reference to judicial definitions by Nils Karleby and Östen Undén, he argued that ownership was a combination of multiple functions related to production, distribution and harmonization. With regulation, it was possible to divide the functions in different ways between individuals and society, but the form of ownership did not dictate any of this—for example, employees did not necessarily have any more influence in state-owned enterprises.[65] Adler-Karlsson found that in Sweden ownership functions had already been 'socialized' to a large extent without socializing ownership itself. Owners could not use their profits as they pleased due to taxation, and the public sector contributed to a significant part of production and investments.[66] Adler-Karlsson argued that there was no 'pure' socialism or capitalism, but all countries were mixed economies with different divisions of the ownership function. He suggested that the problems of bureaucracy, economic development and environmental degradation would be solved by altering the distribution of the functions between the private and public sector.[67]

Many contemporaries considered functional socialism a good summary of the mainstream Social Democratic policy. Presenting one had also been Adler-Karlsson's intention. The term became frequently used in Social Democratic rhetoric both by its supporters[68] and especially critics, who advocated more far-reaching socialization measures. Functional socialism has also been used as an analytical concept in many scholarly works,[69] and I find it useful in this study. If one wants to condense the mainstream Social Democratic stance on the economic system and the role of the state into one concept, functional socialism is better than, for example, market socialism or welfare capitalism,[70] which were rarely used by social democrats themselves. Another way to conceptualize the ideological stance of SAP could be the traditional notion of reformism.[71] However, functional socialism refers to economic policy and excludes socialization more clearly than reformism does. It is most important to be aware of the intellectual origins of the concept, which even its scholarly users sometimes leave unclear.

In the mid-1960s, the traditional ideational structures of the social democrats became challenged by the emerging 'New Left,' which criticized the bureaucracy and alienation produced by modern industrial societies, old rigid norms and power politics, especially the Vietnam War. The New Left was a heterogeneous phenomenon, consisting of movements for pacifism and cultural and sexual liberation. Most of these were situated to the left of the social democrats. Many of the new movements, often led by students and intellectuals, also took up the theme of democratization. They called for participation in everyday life instead of centralized control by the state. The welfare state gained its share of the critique. As the standard of living had risen and poverty was not a significant problem for the working class, the New Left turned its critique toward alienating and materialistic working life and consumer society.[72] In its individualist ethos, calls for authenticity and critique of the state apparatus, the New Left had certain ideational touching points with the liberal right.[73] Luc Boltanski and Ève Chiapello call this the 'artistic critique' of capitalism as distinct from the 'social critique,' which concentrated on poverty and exploitation. The New Left combined both types of critique, but the artistic was more prominent among student movements and easier for capitalism to appropriate as an ingredient of its 'new spirit.'[74]

The New Left was a transnational phenomenon, but it gained indigenous features in every country. In Sweden, structural rationalization and reliance on the market mechanism were questioned. They had created insecurity and produced problems in the emptying countryside as well as in large cities struggling with a housing shortage. It has been argued that the Swedish New Left sought to change the existing left rather than replace it, and drew more on traditional Marxist thought than the movements in other European countries.[75] New ideas gained visibility especially after the publication of the pamphlet *En ny vänster* (A New Left), edited by sociologist Göran Therborn in 1966. The pamphlet emphasized democracy as an intrinsic value and demanded 'true' democracy in workplaces, which required disposing of the employers' right to manage and organize work.[76] Some radicals raised demands for nationalizations, but more often they talked about bringing equality back as the most important value. This created a broader awareness of the shortcomings of the welfare state and its excluded groups who had not benefited from the increasing standard of living.[77] It could hence be interpreted that the Swedish New Left expressed a 'social critique' of capitalism often more strongly than the 'artistic' one. The Swedish Social Democrats replied that they were fighting on the same side against inequality and for increasing welfare.[78] The challenge from the left, as well as a major setback in the 1966 municipal elections, prompted SAP to take concrete measures, such as appointing a working group on equality, led by Alva Myrdal, at the 1967 party congress.[79] A concrete example of the changing discourse is that the number of usages of the word equality at party congresses multiplied by 10 between 1940 and 1969.[80]

In Finland, the culmination of left-wing radicalism took place slightly later than in most other European countries. The first leftist movements were more preoccupied with themes like pacifism, humanitarian aid and criminal policy than the economy. The rise of the left was channeled through traditional political parties along with new student and civic movements. In 1966, the Social Democrats gained a landslide victory in the parliamentary elections, after spending seven years in opposition and suffering from severe internal contradictions. The election brought about a left-wing parliamentary majority for the third and thus far the last time in Finnish history. Radical left-wing ideas gained currency among SDP's young members, and the party leadership had to take them seriously. The Communist Party and their Soviet-minded minority also attracted many young radicals toward the end of the decade, and their activity became more institutionalized. In general, Finnish New Left movements mirrored the country's official foreign policy in their uncritical attitude toward the Soviet Union, despite the shock caused by the occupation of Czechoslovakia in 1968.[81]

The 1960s meant increasing contestation over the meanings and hierarchies of political concepts, especially over the meaning of democracy.[82] The New Left and other movements advocated democratization of different walks of life, which became a slogan of the 1960s. Besides economic democracy, there were demands for school, hospital and prison democracy. Belief in the growing demands of citizens and employees was also central for social scientists, who saw democratization as an intrinsic part of social modernization.[83] Democratization was justified with what in democratic theory is called the principle of affected interests. It means that everyone who is affected by decisions made in different arenas should also participate in making them. In practice, it is often impossible to determine who is affected by a given decision and where to draw the boundaries of participation, but the principle of affected interests can serve as a critical starting point for considering economic and industrial democracy. Why should not people who are affected by economic decisions, for example workers of private enterprises, also participate in making them?[84]

A significant topic of discussion in the 1960s was the concentration of wealth and power, which were taken up as problems for democracy. The leftist belief that the power of capital restricted democracy gained new viability. In Sweden, the Communist C. H. Hermansson had already published in 1959 a book on the concentration of industrial ownership into a few camps controlled by the largest commercial banks. He coined the notion of the '15 families' that controlled a large share of Swedish wealth.[85] Concentration of wealth and ownership was conceived as a problem also outside the political left and investigated by a state committee.[86] Reports on concentration of wealth in banks and owner families were also made in Finland, and social scientists of the time found the phenomenon problematic.[87] In Nordic comparison, the economies of Sweden and Finland had more concentrated ownership structures and relied more heavily on industrial capitalism than those of Norway and Denmark.[88] This may explain the prominence of this debate in the former countries.

A theme that particularly increased in importance throughout Europe, after a relative silence, was the democratization of working life. This was partly inspired by the New Left and its demands for participation, partly by record numbers of strikes that were witnessed in many countries during the 1960s. Even though many of these protests were about wages, there were also grievances against monotonous and dangerous industrial work as well as lack of influence in the workplace. Demands for industrial democracy emerged especially in countries with a strong and unified trade union movement, and they were political responses to the growing unrest.[89] In Sweden and Finland, too, strike waves prompted politicians to prepare labor market and working-life reforms.[90] The left considered democratization of working life a vital part of economic democracy. Conceptual struggles over enterprise democracy were vivid and resulted in legislation toward the end of the 1970s, which makes them good synchronic and comparative case studies. They deserve a detailed analysis of their own, which is provided in Chap. 3.

Active Industrial Policy and Economic Planning as Social Democratic Strategies

While demands for enterprise democracy increased in the 1960s, the Swedish Social Democrats continued to direct their attention toward macroeconomic regulation. This was manifested especially in the debate on industrial policy (*näringspolitik*),[91] which gained an increasingly state-interventionist tone.[92] Jonas Pontusson has interpreted this development as resurgence of anticapitalist aspirations in investment politics.[93] In fact, all of the lines of thought and action emerging in the 1960s—industrial policy, enterprise democracy and equality—shared a more anticapitalist sentiment, which had its roots in the changing ideological and social circumstances. The New Left criticized SAP for an overly market-oriented and bureaucratic government, and many experienced structural renewal as growing uncertainty. Economic growth began to slow down and, more importantly, private-sector savings were no longer channeled as effectively into investments to sustain full employment and social reforms.[94] The stances of the SAP and LO leaders remained moderate and adhered to principles of class compromise, but economic and enterprise democracy were firmly on the agenda after 1965.

Demands for active industrial policy intensified in Sweden in the mid-1960s. LO and the Metalworkers' Union, as well as the Social Democratic Youth Organization (SSU) began to call for more determined economic planning and steering, even nationalization of the finance, energy and pharmaceutical sectors.[95] After its loss in the 1966 municipal elections—especially in regions suffering from structural change—SAP found it viable to listen to these demands and began to form a new industrial policy.[96] It was discussed at the party congresses of the late 1960s and early 1970s. At the congress of 1968, SAP ratified the *Program for Active Industrial Policy*, which emphasized the role of society in steering and controlling the economy. Democratic influence over the economy was a central notion in the program and taking its place at the core of SAP's economic thought. The traditional goal was stated clearly: "We must continue to extend political democracy toward economic democracy."[97] As core problems regarding both industrial policy and economic democracy, the program named income differences that were due to privileges and power positions outside democratic control.[98] Thus the concept of economic democracy was connected to the distribution of both wealth and power. The program gave a rather precise definition for economic democracy, which it viewed as primarily representative, and realized through the parliament and state apparatus: "It means that elected representatives gain a decisive influence on decisions that determine the country's economic development, and along with that the working and living conditions of a great majority of citizens."[99]

The Industrial Policy Program argued for wide-ranging economic planning and coordination of investments.[100] This meant developing new planning institutions, increasing the role of public credit institutions and creating investment funds for structural renewal. Strengthening the state-owned sector was also considered important.[101] Individual enterprises were considered too small units to conduct extensive planning: For example, laying off employees often improved the profitability of a company, but then the people became a cost for society.[102] Planning meant controlling the process of structural change, stabilizing the economy, maintaining full employment and creating preconditions for fast growth and efficient use of resources. Central planning was to be a continuous process, which adapted to changing situations and leaned on close coordination between state and regional level. One objective was to combine the ministries of industry, trade and employment into a large ministry of the economy.[103] Another proposed reform was political representation on the boards of important private companies.[104]

Public control and steering of credit and investment was an important concrete dimension of industrial policy and economic democracy. Sweden's credit market had expanded quickly, especially due to the establishment of public institutions such as the ATP pension funds in the early 1960s and the State Investment Bank in 1967. They provided loans for private enterprises and reduced the need of their own savings to finance investment.[105] However, the industrial policy report argued that increased public financing was still needed, for example in housing and high-risk projects. It was ultimately society's task to channel capital to the most profitable projects and the most productive sectors in an effective way, which would avoid the 'irrationalities' of the private credit market and its concentrated corporate and banking sectors. This required strengthening the role of public credit institutions, which was justified also by increasing competition in the credit market.[106]

In the early 1970s, the economic situation deteriorated in Sweden. Structural renewal, unemployment and decline in industrial investments were major concerns. Even though the unemployment rate was only 2.5%, 100,000 unemployed made up a significant group and fell short of the ideal of full employment.[107] At SAP's 1972 congress, democracy was somewhat less significant a concept in the context of industrial policy. Concrete proposals took a more technical direction, seeking remedies to the deteriorating economic situation. A new Industrial Policy Program concentrated especially on investments and capital formation. It was suggested that the ATP pension funds could use a small part of their assets for risk investments. At the moment, they invested only in state, enterprise and housing obligations. The program emphasized the increased role of collective saving since the establishment of the pension system. It was pointed out that in the 1960s, Sweden had experienced stronger growth with less private savings than for example the United States and Britain. According to the program, the rising importance of collective savings had to mean that the owners of pension assets—wage-earners—would get influence over investments, for example by participating in the governance of ATP funds. It was believed that wealth and income differences could be further diminished with efficient use of the pension funds.[108] It had also been noted in other Western countries that pension funds were becoming major sources of credit and investment, and hence offered a possibility for democratic influence on the economy. A few years later, the American management guru Peter Drucker coined a slightly pejorative term, 'pension fund socialism,' referring to growing pension assets that had become important players in finance markets.[109]

SAP's active stance on industrial policy paid off and contributed to the party's victory in the 1968 parliamentary election. The center-right opposition had not succeeded in convincing the electorate that perceived social problems had resulted from Social Democratic policy. The Social Democrats alone gained a parliamentary majority with 50.1% of the vote. SAP could therefore form a government without the usual support from the small Communist Party, which had lost almost half of its support. At SAP's 1969 congress, the party elected a new leader, who would also replace Tage Erlander as Prime Minister. The choice fell on Olof Palme, a young but experienced and cosmopolitan Social Democrat, who had worked as Erlander's assistant, MP and Minister of Education. He immediately grasped the key issues of the time and stated that to avoid growing social tensions and polarization in the coming decade, the Social Democrats needed to determinedly promote equality and the extension of democracy.[110]

SAP governed for only two years after 1968. The next election was held in autumn 1970, and this time Sweden elected a unicameral parliament for the first time after the constitutional reform. SAP lost their majority but remained the largest party with 45.3% of the vote. They formed a new government but depended again on Communist support, who in the new election system increased their mandate from 3 to 17 MPs despite still getting only 4.8% of the vote. The 1973 parliamentary election was a second consecutive loss for SAP, which received 43.6% of the vote and lost seven seats. Particularly middle-class and young voters seemed to be turning for the center-right parties. The most popular among these was the Center Party, which reached its best result ever with 25.1%. The election resulted in an extraordinary tie of mandates between the socialist and bourgeois blocs. This was something the designers of constitutional reform had not taken into account. It meant that the Social Democrats could form a government, but they had to rely on bourgeois support on individual questions. Economic policy was determined with the support of Center and Liberals in the so-called Haga Agreements, but the most difficult issues had to be resolved in the parliament by drawing lots.[111] This made reforms more difficult and, along with the economic situation, partly explains SAP's dropping ambition level in industrial policy and economic democracy.

In Finland, enterprise democracy was the main element of democratization rhetoric in the late 1960s, but the Social Democrats increasingly also spoke about democratizing the economy more broadly. Their concepts and beliefs shared many features with Swedish ones. Even though the term economic democracy was not always used, the ideational element of democratic control over the economy was central to Social Democratic thought and rhetoric in Finland, too. As before, its practical references included the concepts of economic planning and societal ownership. These concepts formed a strong and rather stable constellation in social democratic thought and rhetoric, even though their mutual relations and hierarchies varied.

As in Sweden, SDP's concept of economic democracy did not always include ideas on new forms of democratic participation, but democracy was considered to function through the existing parliamentary system. Representatives elected by the people would steer the economy to the benefit of the whole of society. Emphasis on the parliamentary system was complemented with enterprise and workplace democracy, which were apparently considered as sufficient forms of local-level participation. However, unlike in Sweden, the relation of these two levels, their respective rights and responsibilities in large investment and production decisions, was not very explicitly problematized. Unlike enterprise or workplace democracy, the objectives of economic planning and steering did not lead to concrete reform initiatives in Finland as in the Swedish industrial policy debate but were mostly restricted to program-level rhetoric. It seems that economic democracy was a longer-term objective for the Finnish Social Democrats, whereas enterprise democracy included elements that were fit for short-term goals. Again, one explanation for these differences is the different political position of the Finnish Social Democrats, who had returned to power only in 1966. They were no longer in the disfavor of the president and the Soviet Union but had to rely on coalition governments with the Center Party and Communists.[112]

The space of economic policy was perceived as rather narrow in Finland and thus counter-cyclical policy and an active labor market policy of the Swedish type were usually out of the question. Mauno Koivisto, the Social Democratic Finance Minister from 1966 to 1968 and Prime Minister from 1968 to 1970, emphasized budget-balancing and aimed at decreasing public debt, which he argued also made economic planning easier. Koivisto wanted to avoid devaluations, but in October 1967, Finland devalued its currency by 30%. This was followed by extensive stabilization measures and a moderate wage agreement, which paved the way for a more permanent tripartite incomes policy.[113] In the 1960s, economic growth was strong and Finland industrialized rapidly, with state-owned enterprises an important sector. The postwar strategy of promoting rural smallholders reached a dead end as agriculture and forestry became more efficient and automatized, resulting in massive migration to cities. As the increase in industrial and service jobs could not keep up, some 200,000 people migrated to Sweden over the course of the decade. Rapid structural change raised similar grievances among the people as it did in Sweden.[114]

Like the Swedish SAP, the Finnish Social Democrats usually portrayed the state rather as a regulator than an owner of the means of production. However, many party members also talked about partial nationalization of production, and the party council (*puolueneuvosto*) stressed it before the election of 1966. According to its statement, the new society would build on increasing collective ownership, and beside private entrepreneurship and cooperatives, the state-owned sector was also to be systematically expanded. This was legitimized by both historical necessity and economic concerns. It was argued that the power of private capital belonged to a receding society, and the rise in the living standard was not to be left dependent on the interest calculations of narrow elites.[115]

The party secretary Erkki Raatikainen, who belonged to SDP's leftist fraction, discussed the topics of economic democracy and industrial policy several times in editorials he wrote for the party journal *Sosialistinen aikakauslehti* (Socialist periodical). Raatikainen borrowed from the Swedish Social Democrats the concept of 'societal rationalization,' which meant extensive economic planning not limited to individual industrial sectors. According to him, this required increasing both state-owned business and "control of capital flows."[116] The latter was one of the new Social Democratic buzzwords and conceptually close to economic democracy. Many other Finnish Social Democrats put forward the theme of rational economic planning and considered it beneficial for economic growth. However, as in Sweden, the question of nationalization divided party members. Jermu Laine, who in the 1970s became MP and Minister of Trade and Industry, gave a historical interpretation of linear progress where urbanization and changing social structure made industrialization an important national mission. According to Laine, there was a relatively strong consensus across ideological divides that economic planning was a necessity, in which other industrial countries were ahead of Finland.[117] In Laine's rhetoric, economic democracy was essential for social reforms and closely linked to economic planning, not so much to ownership or altering the foundations of the economic order. However, Laine found that socialization was also to be included in the toolbox, at least if it was needed to secure the market mechanism. Like Raatikainen, Laine followed the beliefs of the Swedish Social Democrats, but he situated himself as a defender of the market economy, defining economic democracy as correcting the deficiencies and injustices of the system.[118]

The goals of economic and enterprise democracy were expressed at SDP's congress of 1969. The party voiced the familiar demand for democratizing society and removing the deficiencies of the oligarchic economic system. Critics claimed that the economic policy of the Social Democrat-led government concentrated too much on growth, stabilization and correcting the current account balance, while supporters considered it a necessary basis for a more leftist policy.[119] SDP set out for the parliamentary election in spring 1970 to defend their position as the largest party and took economic and enterprise democracy as central themes.[120] To justify the objective of economic democratization, SDP presented figures on the concentration of wealth: 10 families controlled 30% of the industrial national product of Finland. SDP called for investigation of this concentration comparable to the report that had been done in Sweden.[121]

Macro-level objectives of economic democracy—industrial policy and steering capital flows—continued to figure in the Social Democratic agenda. The new party secretary Kalevi Sorsa emphasized the need for the democratic steering of capital to productive investments in order to secure employment. However, there also had to be room for private economic activity, as a centralized economy could not answer changing consumption needs.[122] The tension of planning and markets thus became explicit: The former was better for full employment, but the latter better for free consumption.

The parliamentary election of 1970 turned out to be a protest against the structural renewal of the economy and the supporters of President Kekkonen. The opposition parties, conservative National Coalition Party (NCP) and the populist Finnish Rural Party (SMP), collected the bulk of the protest, increasing their mandates by 11 and 17, respectively. The ruling Social Democrats suffered a defeat and lost three seats but retained their place as the largest party. After difficult negotiations and a short-term caretaker government, SDP formed again a majority government with the Center Party and the Communists. They had lost 13 and 6 mandates, respectively, mostly by losing rural votes to SMP. Despite this defeat, Center's Ahti Karjalainen became Prime Minister. At first, the president had allowed NCP to attempt to form a government, but the other parties' unwillingness to cooperate with the Conservatives guaranteed that the winners of the election did not make it into government. The shift to the right in the parliament did not immediately move the direction of Finnish politics, as the entry of left-wing representatives into legal and administrative positions continued. However, since 1970 socialists have not reached a majority in the Finnish parliament or government.[123]

The next parliamentary election was held as early as in January 1972, as President Kekkonen disbanded parliament after the government had resigned due to internal disputes. The premature election did not change the distribution of mandates very much, and Rafael Paasio formed a Social Democratic minority government.[124] The intensity of demands for economic and enterprise democracy decreased slightly in Finland in the early 1970s. At SDP's congress of 1972, economic and enterprise democracy played smaller roles than in the previous two congresses. However, the party secretary Kalevi Sorsa gave a long speech, in which he connected democratization especially to the concept of equality. Sorsa argued that societal control of the economy was a conclusion drawn from the nature of economic development. Large companies had already become "social institutions," which had little to do with private entrepreneurship. Belief in the social nature of economic activity was expressed often in socialist rhetoric and already in the writings of Marx. It was a powerful justification for politicization and democratization of the economy. Despite this point, Sorsa was more moderate than his predecessor Erkki Raatikainen regarding the democratic steering of the economy and expanding state-owned business. Sorsa expressed the belief that nationalization and economic steering were not to be taken too far in order to avoid restraining people's economic initiative. According to Sorsa, social democracy considered private entrepreneurship a vital part of the economy, provided that the relations between the employer and the employee were equal.[125] In its middle-of-the-road pragmatism, Sorsa's thought and rhetoric was close to the functional socialism of Olof Palme and other notable Swedish Social Democrats.

Markets Against Planning and Socialization

The debate on industrial policy exemplifies the Social Democrats' old problem of defining the boundaries of planning and markets in their ideal economic system. SAP perceived the markets as important for efficiency as well as for legitimizing economic reforms. The 1968 Industrial Policy Program argued for the belief that societal influence and planning of the economy did not mean replacing the market economy, but merely strove to make it work better and to fulfill people's needs by securing full employment, social security and distribution of income. It was emphasized that the social democratic movement was 'dogmatic' only regarding its core values of equality, security and democracy, but not regarding the means of achieving them. This statement intended to downplay the possibility of socializing the means of production.[126] In congresses and public debate, however, SAP members often expressed desires for more 'socialist' politics. This exemplifies traditional ideological cleavages in the party, which gained new importance as the new generation came to the fore in the 1960s. The sociologist Sten Johansson claimed in the Social Democratic journal *Tiden* that SAP had begun to rely too much on the belief that markets would produce rational results. However, structural rationalization and the ensuing loss of jobs created insecurity for people, especially in rural areas. According to Johansson, this was greatly altering the party's role as the representative of the 'little people.'[127]

Promoting the market economy and private ownership was not a unanimously shared goal within SAP, especially not after the rise of radical demands for equality and democracy. SAP's 1967 and 1968 congresses received over 30 motions on industrial policy, which called for greater societal control or supervision of the economy in the form of steering or even nationalizing financial institutions, credit and investments. These reforms were believed to promote development toward economic democracy, and many were justified with the same aim that the party leadership expressed: improving security in the midst of structural and technological change. Many speakers were critical toward the Industrial Policy Program, which they considered too moderate or lacking concrete proposals.[128] At SAP's 1972 congress, many motions expressed disappointment in the industrial policy and called for stronger influence and planning of investments.[129] Demands for socializing banks, other financial institutions and the pharmaceutical industry multiplied from previous congresses.[130] The demands were based on the belief that socialization was necessary for establishing true control over investments and hence secure full employment and security in structural change.[131]

The party leadership's response to too far-reaching proposals had traditionally been dismissive. SAP's Executive Committee always reminded about the instrumental value of socialization: There were other means for achieving the party's aims. At the congress of 1969, the committee stated that socialization was a question that "lacks actuality." It argued that societal influence on the economy had already increased considerably through the ATP pension funds, the State Investment Bank and other public institutions.[132] In 1972, the party leadership admitted that there had not been enough resources for general planning and appealed to the difficult economic conjuncture, which had made it harder to solve structural problems.[133] However, highlighting the tension with SAP's strong rhetoric of planning, they stressed that the foundation for industrial policy was "that our economy chiefly functions according to the principles of market economy."[134] Prime Minister and party leader Olof Palme argued in the same congress that socialization was an unpragmatic policy that could cost SAP many votes in future elections.[135] Instead, he stressed democratization through better planning and steering mechanisms, and industrial democracy, which meant "the individual's influence on their immediate surroundings at a company."[136] Palme thus carried on the Social Democratic ideological tradition of moderate reformism and 'functional socialism' that had dominated the party since the 1920s, although even at this point, internal critique of the line was strong. According to Kjell Östberg's interpretation, Palme was a firm advocate of the market economy and free entrepreneurship, which just needed to be balanced with social policy and extended democracy.[137]

Even though equality and democracy were strongly emerging themes in the late 1960s, the legitimation of SAP's industrial policy had many traditional elements. Democracy often figured in SAP's rhetoric as means to other goals, such as economic growth and equality, but the compatibility and mutual support of these values were key concerns. This was evident also in the 1968 Industrial Policy Report. The aims of industrial policy were to "combine economic progress with security and equity of individuals," to "create security within change" and to "be a functioning tool for increased equality."[138] The necessity of change was emphasized together with the need for security (*trygghet*). It was argued that it would be shortsighted to step aside from the rapid international development driven by technological change. Instead, the insecurities created by the changing economy and production were to be countered with active policymaking.[139] In the report, however, democratic influence was legitimized rather as necessary for economic efficiency, not as a way of extending democracy in and for itself. Societal control was seen as a way to use economic resources in the best possible way.[140]

This dual legitimation of reforms by both democracy and efficiency was a recurring feature of social democratic thought and rhetoric. The aim was to portray different values as mutually supportive, which exemplifies the idea of 'virtuous circles' in Nordic political thought. It is based on the belief of growing economic success, democracy, equality and social justice reinforcing each other.[141] Jenny Andersson has argued that despite this synergetic picture, SAP's ideology was "inherently economistic." Social policy and full employment were considered 'productive investment,' but they were subordinated to the hegemonic goal of economic growth, and participation in productive work was the basis of social citizenship.[142] Michael Freeden and Tim Tilton have also argued that efficiency played a larger role for Swedish Social Democrats than for most other strands of socialism. Its connection to equality was a key feature of Swedish social democracy.[143] As Stephanie Mudge has shown, this kind of economistic rhetoric was also common to the major center-left parties of Germany, Britain and the United States in the 1960s.[144]

Growth of the national economy and welfare along with it were of course important political goals throughout the twentieth century, shared by both left and right.[145] They were inherently connected to the modern linear conception of time and the belief in progress. Pauli Kettunen has described the appropriation of this growth ideology as a part of the development of labor movement's self-understanding. The movement wanted to differentiate itself from the progress-dreading Luddites and accepted the role of growing production forces in the process of working-class emancipation. Growth was to strengthen the working class, which eventually would throw down the old social order. Kettunen argues that taking this belief for granted limited the horizon of possibilities for social and economic reforms. They were often approached primarily from the viewpoint of their benefits to economic efficiency.[146]

At the same time, efficiency itself was defined in a new way, following beliefs often attributed to the Austrian Marxist Otto Bauer, who portrayed socialist planned economy as true societal rationalization, which would replace the false and inhuman capitalist rationalization. The basic idea came from Marx, who had already argued against capitalism on the basis of its inefficiency in addition to its social injustice. The same beliefs were shared by Swedish Social Democrats like Ernst Wigforss.[147] Economic efficiency was therefore an important issue to be considered in conjunction with economic democracy. In right-wing rhetoric, a wrong kind of democracy based on a large state was portrayed as a counter-concept for efficiency. For the left, state-led planning contrariwise supported 'true' efficiency. In both cases, democracy was often left behind efficiency in conceptual hierarchy in an instrumental role along the road toward national interest, defined as economic growth and material welfare. In this respect, the thought and rhetoric of the Finnish and Swedish Social Democrats were not markedly different.

In the end, SAP's industrial policy reforms were rather moderate. The party dismissed demands for socialization and strengthened the idea of economic democracy as societal steering, which would retain the market economy and private ownership. The concept of 'functional socialism' is apt for describing SAP's industrial policy. However, research has shown that SAP's reforms did not even have a notable steering impact on the allocation of investment in Sweden. New institutions, such as the Ministry of Industry and tripartite Industrial Policy Council (*Näringspolitiska rådet*), were primarily consultative. They conducted research and forecasting for different industry sectors but did not draw up binding economic plans. The State Investment Bank was supposed to finance long-term development projects in advanced sectors and help create competitive firms in basic industries, but it faced similar problems as state-owned enterprises: There were no clear guidelines for weighing employment and other social aspects against profitability, and therefore professional managers hired for the companies usually prioritized profitability. The same factors also came to limit the role of the fourth ATP pension fund, which was established in 1974 and allowed to make direct investments in enterprises. In general, steering of investments was light in Sweden, and the market retained its significant role as allocator of resources. The prevailing system, which encouraged private investments with tax exemptions and loans from the pension funds, did not markedly change in the 1970s.[148] Minor reforms, such as the possibility to appoint public representatives to boards of commercial banks, did not change the big picture.[149] Socializations were carried out only as a last resort to save certain companies. Defensive, selective measures were used especially as the economic situation deteriorated after 1974 and declining enterprises needed aid.[150] The rhetoric also shifted from principled demands for democratic control over the economy to discussing the technicalities of new organizational structures and subsidies to enterprises and regions. During the 1970s, economic democracy's explicit range of reference moved gradually from general industrial policy and macroeconomic steering to issues where the state did not necessarily play such a large role: collective capital formation and employee influence at workplaces.

The ideological discussion regarding the means and ends of politics was more explicit in Sweden than in Finland. This has probably much to do with the fact that the Finnish Social Democrats were not in such a dominant political position. In addition, they concentrated more on economic constraints and Finland's need to catch other Western countries in the modernization process. Of course, SDP also had ideological contemplations on the relationship between markets and economic planning, but a principled debate regarding the relations and hierarchies of core values such as democracy, equality and economic growth was almost nonexistent.[151] In the early 1970s, the constraints of the international economy and the oil crisis, such as inflation and current account problems began to occupy a central place in the ideational constellations related to economic policy in Finland, too. Economic planning and steering were often portrayed as the best way to deal with these constraints, but competitiveness and growth were inescapable policy objectives. Jermu Laine wrote that the government had to pursue investment policy that would improve the competitiveness of enterprises and economic growth. Laine appealed to international economic dependencies as constraints of the social democratic economic policy. He spoke about the "historical reality" and "objective circumstances" in an almost deterministic manner but nevertheless saw some prospects for intentional political action that would advance a democratic planned economy.[152]

The emerging global economic crisis brought up strong concerns, but the Social Democrats nevertheless often pointed out that economic growth and material welfare were not the fundamental aims of policy. Echoing rising environmental concerns and growth criticism, which the Club of Rome report *Limits of Growth* had fueled, they often expressed the belief that better material standards were no good if environmental degradation advanced and psychological problems increased at the same time.[153] Kalevi Sorsa declared in a 1973 article: "The exploitation of nature, including the human, has its limits. The sooner we understand this, the better."[154] Often democracy occupied a central place on the horizon of expectation, as a remedy to the adverse consequences of growth. Despite these statements, the economic situation was usually perceived as so pressing that growth and efficiency had to be taken as political priorities, at least in the short term. Same considerations may have hindered the introduction of ambitious steering mechanisms envisioned by the Finnish Social Democrats, but more immediate reasons for their non-realization were political opposition by other parties and constitutional barriers. The Finnish constitution had strong limits to majority decisions, such as protection of ownership. Constitutional reforms required two-third or five-sixth qualified majorities in the parliament.[155] In Sweden, the constitution allowed more room for majority decisions. Protection of ownership was weaker, and constitutional changes could be made with simple majorities in two consecutive parliamentary terms.[156]

The Dream of Decentralization

The concept of democracy and the goal of its extension were major themes of political debate in the late 1960s and early 1970s. Transnational debates and the 'spirit of 1968' inspired ideas of local and participatory democracy that would challenge state-centered bureaucracy. In the late 1960s, the Swedish Liberal Party contributed to the debate by introducing a conceptual innovation, 'near democracy' (*närdemokrati*). It crystallized the ideas of decentralization and local governance that had been prevalent in the party's thought and rhetoric for long. It essentially meant local democracy, but in Scandinavian languages the word *near* has a very positive connotation, linking to ideas of communitarianism, tradition and down-to-earth lifestyles. The Liberals wanted to reform representative democracy and decrease the gap between decision-makers and citizens.[157] Enterprise democracy was defined as one form of near democracy, but the term economic democracy was absent from Liberal rhetoric. The party advocated certain forms of economic planning, but in general democracy through the state did not have a positive flare in liberal constellations. The concept of near democracy was based on the intention of highlighting (civil) society, which the party did not want to equate with the state.[158] This rhetoric was close to that of the Center Party's, which also increasingly emphasized planning and active involvement of the state, but stated that planning had to lead to "as decentralized a society as possible." The state was only to make general framework planning and modify it based on actual experiences. In contrast, the Center Party argued that "socialist detail regulation" only led to inefficiency and bad economic judgment.[159]

The Social Democrats also had to take a stance on decentralization. In 1968, *Tiden* called for new forms of democracy against the centralization of local administration and private companies. It considered essential that the debate focused on people's true possibilities of influence. Tenant democracy and school democracy were mentioned as potential new forms of participation, the latter also having the capability to foster skills needed in a democratic society.[160] However, an even more prominent concept was enterprise democracy, which gradually increased its role as a key element of economic democracy in the late 1960s. At SAP's 1972 congress, Olof Palme highlighted the importance of working life democratization and stated that renewal had to begin from there.[161] Palme connected enterprise democracy to the broader democratization of the economy, describing it with the prestigious concept of decentralization. The rhetoric of decentralization and citizen participation was already common for Palme, which shows that he utilized the constellations of the new left-wing critique and sought to accommodate them in SAP's policy. This may be an example of Palme's capability of reading his time, as Kjell Östberg has argued in his biography of the party leader.[162]

In an interview with *Tiden* before the congress, Palme argued that participation was necessary in order to avoid bureaucratization and to increase people's satisfaction at work. The interviewer took up a key problem of economic democratization by asking was there not a contradiction within SAP between the demand for individual influence and strong centralized organizations. Palme did not see a conflict but argued that wage-earners needed their own organizations against private centers of economic power. He believed that democracy could be strengthened within these organizations as well as in people's everyday environments. According to Palme, it was a misconception that some issues were too difficult for regular people to decide.[163]

Despite its editors' sympathies to the ideas of the New Left, *Tiden* was not a channel for a single truth but also gave room for critical views on the new conceptions of democracy. In 1969, political scientist Olof Ruin argued that the traditional, institutional macro perspective had been replaced with a micro perspective, which considered all roles people could take in society: employee, consumer, tenant and so forth. The possibility of participation was now demanded in all these spheres where it had often been hard to influence decision-makers. Terms like 'near democracy' and 'grassroots democracy' had been introduced. Ruin wrote that there were many positive aspects to this debate, but it also created potential conflicts with the old definition of democracy: majority rule. Spatially restricted communities would have the possibility to block the will of the majority. If, for example, school or hospital democracy was introduced, it was not evident why only students, teachers or patients could participate in decisions that affected other people. This was why Ruin considered majority decision a better option in these cases. He also suspected that if decisions were made in 'general assemblies,' only the most active people would be making the decisions. Therefore, Ruin found it most desirable to improve participation through the representative system, making it easier for citizens to meet their representatives and influence them.[164] This was a rather traditional and procedural view of democracy, which differed from the ideas advocated by many Social Democrats and Liberals at the time.

In Sweden, questions on the relation between representative and participatory democracy, or central and local decision-making often attracted more attention than in Finland. They did so especially when enterprise democracy advanced in political decision-making, and center-right parties advocated their ideas of decentralization and near democracy. For example, Social Democratic MP Mats Hellström argued that the challenge of democratic socialism was to find a balance between "overarching economic planning and locally anchored, true influence of people."[165] Olof Palme reflected on the roles of central and local in an article before the election of 1973. According to Palme, labor reforms that were taking place in Sweden, such as codetermination and work environment legislation, constituted "the biggest process of democratization and decentralization in Swedish society since universal suffrage."[166] Economic democracy was therefore the main element of Social Democratic visions of the future. The third step of democratization after political and social democracy seemed to be well underway. In order to avoid bureaucratization, it was important to create democratization, "which is close to people's everyday experiences in working life," Palme wrote.[167] This meant altering local economic power relations and giving wage-earners both new rights and responsibilities. Palme's rhetoric exemplifies the Social Democratic problem of finding balance between local and central levels of democracy. In this case, he tried to accommodate the left-wing critique of bureaucracy. Kjell Östberg has argued that despite his rhetoric, Palme was in favor of a strong state, even at the expense of local influence if they were in conflict. This can be seen, for example, in his uneasy relation with new grassroots movements.[168]

There was a constant tension and struggle between the strengthening rhetoric of decentralization and the will to coordinate the economy as a whole and defend traditional Social Democratic institutions. The latter goals were stressed by *Tiden*, which argued that in some cases moving decision-making to 'local' settings could even decrease the influence of weaker groups. They benefited from central, public decision-making, which made them less dependent on holders of economic power. Therefore, the cure for bureaucratization was not moving power to equally uncontrolled local bodies, but establishing 'true' democratic insight and control in the central ones. The editorial portrayed this as analogous to trade unions, which in fact increased the freedom of weaker employee groups against employees.[169] Sociologist Berndt Öhman also pointed out the question's difficulty in the process of preparing SAP's new platform and connected it to the dichotomy of markets and planning. He argued that decentralizing power to employee-governed enterprises did not solve all problems. "It must be complemented with a strong central authority, which solves problems on the macro level. One of the difficult points in the program debate is therefore finding a viable reconciliation between centralization and decentralization, between plan and market."[170]

Economic Democracy Anchored to the Market Economy and Local Communities

To find views that challenged the Social Democrats and the New Left in arranging democracy and the economic system we can turn to conservative and liberal parties. In Finland, a prominent party of the political right was the National Coalition Party (*Kansallinen kokoomus*). It was the successor of the earlier Finnish party, which had a conservative heritage and originally supported making Finland a monarchy after the country gained independence. However, the Finnish conservatives also had a long social conservative tradition, and in the 1960s NCP increasingly adopted liberal ideas. It portrayed itself as a people's party claiming that other parties were tied to the class interests of workers, farmers and minority groups. Most of NCP's voters belonged to the upper and middle classes but it also had support among workers and farmers who supported the conservative values of home, religion and fatherland. Politically NCP was not a very significant party in the 1960s. It formed two center-right governments with the Agrarian League between 1962 and 1966, but in the 1966 election its support was less than 15%. The most powerful nonsocialist party in Finland was the Agrarian League (from 1965 onward the Center Party) with over 25% support at best.[171]

In Sweden, the conservative party *Högerpartiet* (Right Party) represented a fusion of social, cultural and liberal conservatism.[172] It competed for the position of the biggest bourgeois party with the liberal *Folkpartiet* (People's Party, FP) in the 1950s and early 1960s. Both parties had electoral support of between 15 and 20. The third bourgeois party, the Center Party (until 1957 the Peasant Union), was usually slightly behind the Conservatives with 10–15% of the vote. The Swedish bourgeois parties were constantly in opposition despite narrow margins in parliamentary elections. The only exception was the Peasant Union's coalition with the Social Democrats during 1951–1957.[173] Like NCP, the Right Party portrayed itself as a people's party, but most of its voters belonged to the upper and middle classes. In course of the twentieth century, the support base moved from religious rural areas to cities.[174] In 1969, the party changed its name to *Moderata samlingspartiet* (the Moderate Coalition Party). This was a result of declining electoral support and the belief that the term 'Right' had antisocial and antiprogressive connotations.[175] Despite this move, the party's support continued its decline that had been fueled by internal disputes and leadership problems during the 1960s. In the election of 1970, the Moderates gained only 11.5% of the vote, which left it behind both the Liberal and Center Parties.[176]

Conservative parties have often been pragmatic and adapted their policy to the ideas and demands of their time.[177] However, this does not mean that conservatives lack a distinct ideology. Conservatives in both Finland and Sweden turned to support social policy reforms after World War II and adopted liberal economic and cultural ideas in the course of the twentieth century. They hence fused a 'liberal-conservative' ideology with social elements.[178] It is not difficult to find a relatively stable ideational core from conservative programs, especially regarding the economy. Both the Swedish Right/Moderates and Finnish NCP held on to liberal economic beliefs. In the postwar era, their rhetoric on economic policy was based on the conflict of rivalling economic and political systems. They supported private ownership, market economy and individual freedom while firmly opposing socialism and state-owned and state-controlled economy.[179] However, Swedish and Finnish conservatives had different domestic antagonists: The Swedish Right challenged the governing Social Democrats, while NCP's identity was defined especially by anticommunism. In certain questions, NCP could cooperate with the Social Democrats against the Communists and the reigning Agrarian/Center Party.[180] Despite increasing acceptance of the welfare state, opposition to many social reforms was strong among Finnish Conservatives for a long time. This became tangible in the question of universal basic education in the 1960s and 1970s.[181]

The conservative parties' conceptions of economic democracy were close to each other and drew on the core principles described above. They were reluctant to increase centralized coordination and the state's role in the economy, even though they had accepted a certain degree of steering and planning in the postwar Keynesian regime.[182] However, the concept of economic democracy was close to inescapable in the sense that all parties had to take a stance on its key elements: economic planning, workplace democracy, and the fundamental criterion of giving more economic power to citizens. The solution of all nonsocialist parties was emphasizing democracy through the civil society and against the state, while the Left's vision of democracy was often realized through the state and against 'economic oligarchy'. Nonsocialists advocated a 'decentralized' model based on free market economy and the Nordic tradition of local self-governance, where private ownership would be dispersed more widely among citizens.

They were firm opponents of socialism and emphasized responsibilities along with rights and liberties.[183]

Conservatives named their economic models with terms of Anglo-American origin. The Swedish Right Party appropriated the British conservatives' concept of 'property-owning democracy' (*egendomsägande demokrati*) and later shortened it to 'owner democracy' (*ägardemokrati*).[184] In Finland, the NCP appropriated 'people's capitalism', which had been invented by Republicans in the United States.[185] They also utilized the German concept of 'social market economy,' which combined market economy with social policy and represented a middle way between laissez-faire and planned economies, which conservatives and liberals across Europe were seeking.[186]

In the early 1970s, the NCP introduced the conceptual innovation of 'social choice economy' (*sosiaalinen valintatalous*),[187] which does not really have equivalents in other countries. Instead of a free market as an end in itself, it emphasized freedom of individual choice, which could be realized only with the help of social reforms. With the new concept, progressive reformers of the party aimed to find a certain synthesis between socialism and capitalism and gain the acceptance of President Kekkonen. The NCP had to stay in opposition despite a major victory in the 1970 election, as it was considered untrustworthy on Finland's Soviet-friendly foreign policy.[188] Social choice economy marked a shift from negative to positive freedom in NCP's ideology: All freedom was not necessarily *from* the state but it could also be realized *through* the state. NCP also intended to change its image from a party of capital toward being a middle-class and wage-earner party.[189] According to historian Vesa Vares, social choice economy was close to Keynesian social liberalism and the concept of the welfare state, but allowed NCP to avoid these concepts, which traditional conservatives might have opposed.[190] However, social choice economy was ultimately devised to oppose socialism. An essential ideological difference between NCP and the left was still the role of the state. Instead of expanding the state's functions, the NCP emphasized actions in the spheres of the market and what is nowadays called civil society.

Swedish conservatives rarely used the concept of economic democracy, but their Finnish counterparts appropriated it as a synonym to people's capitalism.[191] The Swedish Right believed that politicizing economic decisions would create inefficiencies and criticized social democratic visions of economic democracy that aimed at increasing the state's economic power and were based on 'forced saving' via taxes and the ATP pension funds.[192]

However, the concepts of 'owner democracy' and 'people's capitalism' were clear attempts to occupy the semantic field of economic democratization and present a liberal conservative vision of the future. The key element in these concepts was making all citizens owners of capital, which would have increased their freedom and independence. In its simplest form, capital meant houses, cars, and household appliances, but also corporate shares. They were to be made more easily available to all citizens for example by tax exemptions and deregulation of finance markets. In the rhetoric of the Swedish Right, owner democracy was even argued to decrease class differences. As the party's newspaper *Medborgaren* stated in a 1964 editorial: In owner democracy, ownership becomes "everyone's right and no-one's privilege."[193] For some time, owner democracy occupied a place close to the core of the party's ideational and rhetorical constellations and even became a main theme in the 1964 election.[194] However, as we can see from Fig. 2.1, the use of owner democracy and property-owning democracy declined rather quickly in the 1970s.

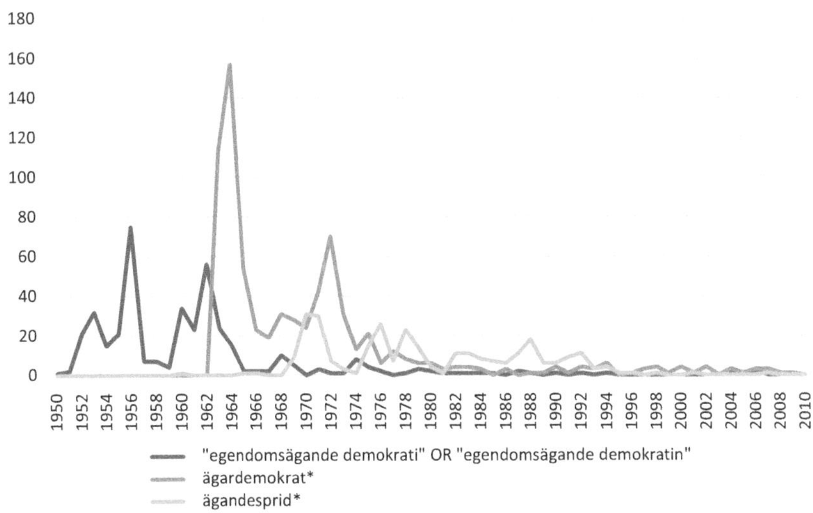

Fig. 2.1 Number of articles with the terms 'property-owning democracy,' 'owner democracy' and 'ownership dispersion' in the Swedish database of digital newspapers (http://tidningar.kb.se/), 1950–2010. Data retrieved 29 August 2019

The visions of property-owning democracy and people's capitalism had clear continuities with older ideas of smallholder society and self-governance.[195] However, they did not include ideas on new forms of democratic participation. It was not clear whether the concepts were intended to signify novel models of democracy or rather private ownership combined with the existing political democracy on national and local levels. In conservatism and early liberalism, ownership and economic independence were often considered preconditions for democratic participation.[196] Alternatively, if ownership and economic freedom were directly identified with democracy, it would entail a conception rather different from traditional political democracy of 'one person, one vote'—rather market democracy of 'one dollar, one vote.'[197] According to the Left's standard critique on owner democracy, accumulating notable amounts of capital and economic influence through saving was possible only for people with relatively high income. Moreover, dispersed share ownership allowed large owners to retain their power in companies with smaller amounts of shares.[198]

The Right/Moderate Party was an active critic of Social Democratic industrial policy in Sweden. They argued that state-owned companies and the State Investment Bank would create inefficiencies and market disturbances if they did not operate according to the principle of profitability. The use of public money was believed to obscure responsibilities. It was implied that economic democracy was not desirable if it meant public steering of the economy. Often all economic intervention was placed under the concept of socialism, which was claimed to threaten both efficiency and democracy, as in the postwar planned economy debate. To secure efficiency, political actors were not to make too many economic decisions—or as Moderate vice-chair Gösta Bohman put it, economic questions ought to be de-ideologized.[199] The economy was thus considered a realm of objective knowledge instead of political choices—a belief that was central to the right-wing ideational constellations.

After facing their worst result ever in the 1970 parliamentary election, the Moderates voted Gösta Bohman to replace Yngve Holmberg as party leader. Bohman, a nearly 60-year-old experienced lawyer and politician, began to take the Moderates in a more market liberal direction and sharpened the party's critique of the welfare state. This was done even at the cost of endangering cooperation with the Center Party and Liberals. Bohman found that all the bourgeois parties had moved too far to the left, along with the Social Democrats. The Moderates were to break this trend by decisively promoting values of 'liberal conservatism,' especially individual freedom and responsibility.[200] However, Bohman continued to dissociate his party from extreme economic liberalism and accepted the state's role in social policy and creating the economic framework.[201] Torbjörn Nilsson has argued that in Bohman's conception of democracy, the concepts of liberty and legal state were conflated so as to form a conception of democracy's substance. This differed especially from the conception of earlier party leader Gunnar Heckscher, who as a political scientist had advocated a strictly procedural definition of democracy as rule by the people.[202]

Unlike the Left, Conservatives did not find it problematic to call a society based on market economy and private ownership democratic as long as it had political leaders chosen by the people in free and regular elections. The tendency of separating political and economic spheres was often implicit in these constellations of ideas. However, conservatives also implied the idea that economic democracy could be realized through civil society or the market rather than through the state.[203] The term 'civil society' was not used explicitly at the time, but Conservatives rather conflated all activities that were free from state intervention, such as market exchanges and voluntary associations. This thinking mirrors the traditional liberal ideal of free markets, which draws on beliefs of a decentralized system guided by a benign invisible hand and restricted by free competition where any harmful concentration of power and resources becomes impossible. Even though Conservatives in both Sweden and Finland admitted that a certain level of state regulation was necessary, in their vision of democratic society the most important subject was the individual, while the roles of the state and interest groups were to be restricted as much as possible.[204] This ideational constellation represents traditional right-wing ideas but has also strong affinity with neoliberal ideas. Familiarity with Hayek or other neoliberal prophets was not necessary for promoting similar ideas.[205] However, Hayek had already become well-known at least in Sweden in the late 1940s, thanks to the employers' campaign against social democratic ideas of economic planning.[206]

Notes

1. Donald Sassoon, *One Hundred Years of Socialism: The West European Left in the Twentieth Century* (London: Fontana Press, 1996), 706–707.

2. Christer Lundh, *Den svenska debatten om industriell demokrati 1919–1924: 1. Debatten i Sverige* (Lund: Studentlitteratur, 1987), 26; Bernt Schiller, "Workplace Democracy: The Dual Roots of Worker Participation," in *Managing Modern Capitalism: Industrial Renewal and Workplace Democracy in the United States and Western Europe*, eds. M. Donald Hancock, John Logue and Bernt Schiller (New York: Praeger, 1991), 112–113; Nelson Lichtenstein and Howell John Harris (eds.), *Industrial Democracy in America: The Ambiguous Promise* (New York: Woodrow Wilson Center Press, 1993).
3. Joel Rogers and Wolfgang Streeck, "The Study of Works Councils: Concepts and Problems," in *Works Councils: Consultation, Representation, and Cooperation in Industrial Relations*, eds. Joel Rogers and Wolfgang Streeck (Chicago and London: University of Chicago Press, 1995), 16–19; Herman Knudsen, *Employee Participation in Europe* (London: Sage, 1995), 14–21; Howell John Harris, "Industrial Democracy and Liberal Capitalism, 1890–1925," in *Industrial Democracy in America: The Ambiguous Promise*, eds. Nelson Lichtenstein and Howell John Harris (New York: Woodrow Wilson Center Press, 1993), 43–66; Daniel T. Rodgers, *Work Ethic in Industrial America 1850–1920* (Chicago and London: University of Chicago Press, 1978), 45–50, 57–62; Lundh, *Den svenska debatten om industriell demokrati 1*, 47–54.
4. John Stuart Mill, *Principles of Political Economy with Some of their Applications to Social Philosophy* (Kitchener: Batoche, 2001 [1848]); Michael Freeden, *Ideologies and Political Theory: A Conceptual Approach* (Oxford: Oxford University Press, 1996), 459–461; Schiller, "Workplace Democracy," 109–111; Rodgers, *Work Ethic in Industrial America*, 40–50, 57–62.
5. Lundh, *Den svenska debatten om industriell demokrati 1*, 48, 52–54. On Nordic paternalism see also Susanna Fellman, "Academic Patriots or Individualistic Entrepreneurs? Finnish Management in a Nordic Perspective," in *The Democratic Challenge to Capitalism: Management and Democracy in the Nordic Countries*, eds. Haldor Byrkjeflot, Sissel Myklebust, Christine Myrvang and Francis Sejersted (Bergen: Fagbokforlaget, 2001), 195–200.
6. Ilkka Turunen, "Ammattiyhdistysutopia," in *Kansa liikkeessä*, eds. Risto Alapuro, Ilkka Liikanen, Kerstin Smeds and Henrik Stenius (Helsinki: Kirjayhtymä, 1987), 202–205.
7. Mary Hilson, *The International Co-operative Alliance and the Consumer Co-operative Movement in Northern Europe, c. 1860–1939* (Manchester: Manchester University Press, 2018), 150–153, 162–167; Lundh, *Den svenska debatten om industriell demokrati 1*, 75–81.
8. Hilson, *The International Co-operative Alliance*, 165.

9. *Dagens Nyheter* 8 May 1901, 3. Digitala svenska dagstidningar. http://tidningar.kb.se/.
10. Gregg M. Olsen, *The Struggle for Economic Democracy in Sweden* (Aldershot and Brookfield: Avebury, 1992), 20–21.
11. Ernst Wigforss, "Göteborgsprogrammet," in Ernst Wigforss, *Vision och verklighet* (Stockholm: Prisma, 1967), 19–25; Tim Tilton, *The Political Theory of Swedish Social Democracy* (Oxford: Oxford University Press, 1990), 45.
12. For example, Ernst Wigforss, "Utgångspunkter för industriell demokrati," in Ernst Wigforss, *Vision och verklighet* (Stockholm: Prisma, 1967), 26–32.
13. Christer Lundh, *Den svenska debatten om industriell demokrati 1919–1924: 2. Utländska inspirationskällor* (Lund: Studentlitteratur, 1989), 64–82, 229–233; Niels Dalgaard, *Ved demokratiets grænse. Demokratisering af arbejdslivet i Danmark 1919–1994* (Copenhagen: Selskabet til Forskning i Arbejderbevægelsens Historie, 1995), 21–88; Rodgers, *Work Ethic in Industrial America*, 57–62.
14. Sheri Berman, *The Social Democratic Moment: Ideas and Politics in the Making of Interwar Europe* (Cambridge, MA: Harvard University Press, 1998), 185–186; Pauli Kettunen, *Poliittinen liike ja sosiaalinen kollektiivisuus: Tutkimus sosialidemokratiasta ja ammattiyhdistysliikkeestä Suomessa 1918–1930* (Helsinki: Suomen historiallinen seura, 1986), 265–269.
15. Lundh, *Den svenska debatten om industriell demokrati 1*, 471–474, 493–495; Tilton, *The Political Theory of Swedish Social Democracy*, 45–46.
16. *Dagens Nyheter* 29 April 1919, 5; *Dagens Nyheter* 4 May 1919, 11.
17. Lundh, *Den svenska debatten om industriell demokrati 1*, 156–159.
18. Sheri Berman, *The Primacy of Politics: Social Democracy and the Making of Europe's Twentieth Century* (Cambridge: Cambridge University Press, 2006), 38–42; Anna Friberg, *Demokrati bortom politiken: En begreppshistorisk analys av demokratibegreppet inom Sveriges socialdemokratiska arbetareparti 1919–1939* (Stockholm: Atlas, 2012), 48–53. On the problems of a simple reformist–revolutionary dichotomy, see Kettunen, *Poliittinen liike ja sosiaalinen kollektiivisuus*, 9–26.
19. Per Albin Hansson, Speech in the parliament's second chamber, 18 January 1928 (Folkhemstalet). http://www.svenskatal.se/1928011-per-albin-hansson-folkhemstalet/.
20. Apart from Hansson's use of the term, 'people's home' was not widely used in Social Democratic rhetoric, until it was appropriated in the 1980s as a symbol for defending the welfare state. See Nils Edling, "The Primacy of Welfare Politics: Notes on the Language of the Swedish Social Democrats and their Adversaries in the 1930s," in *Multi-layered Historicity of the Present*, eds. Heidi Haggrén, Johanna Rainio-Niemi and

Jussi Vauhkonen (Helsinki: Publications of the Department of Political and Economic Studies 8, 2013), 125–135.

21. Freeden, *Ideologies and Political Theory*, 75–85. Freeden analyzes ideologies by distinguishing their core, adjacent and peripheral concepts. In this book I apply the same typology to the thought and rhetoric of political parties without implying broader ideologies, such as socialism or liberalism.
22. For example, SAP (Sveriges socialdemokratiska arbetareparti). *Program för Sveriges socialdemokratiska arbetareparti* (1897). https://snd.gu.se/sv/vivill/party/s/p/1897.
23. In the Swedish and Finnish languages, the word society (*samhälle*, *yhteiskunta*) is often synonymous with the state (*stat*, *valtio*). The concept of the state, hence, has had a more positive connotation in Nordic languages and 'civil society' has not been as prominent a counter-concept as it is in many other European traditions. See Pauli Kettunen, "Yhteiskunta," in *Käsitteet liikkeessä: Suomen poliittisen kulttuurin käsitehistoria*, eds. Matti Hyvärinen, Jussi Kurunmäki, Kari Palonen, Tuija Pulkkinen and Henrik Stenius (Tampere: Vastapaino, 2003).
24. Friberg, *Demokrati bortom politiken*, 256–257, 273–276.
25. Edling, "The Primacy of Welfare Politics," 138–142; Jussi Kurunmäki and Johan Strang, "Introduction: 'Nordic Democracy' in a World of Tensions," in *Rhetorics of Nordic Democracy*, eds. Jussi Kurunmäki and Johan Strang (Helsinki: Finnish Literature Society, 2010), 9–11.
26. Jussi Kurunmäki, "'Nordic Democracy' in 1935: On the Finnish and Swedish Rhetoric of Democracy," in *Rhetorics of Nordic Democracy*, eds. Jussi Kurunmäki and Johan Strang (Helsinki: Finnish Literature Society, 2010), 45–47, 74–76.
27. Lars Magnusson, *Sveriges ekonomiska historia* (Stockholm: Norstedts, 2010), 401–404; Jonas Pontusson, *The Limits of Social Democracy: Investment Politics in Sweden* (Ithaca: Cornell University Press, 1992), 43–47; Walter Korpi, *The Working Class in Welfare Capitalism: Work, Unions and Politics in Sweden* (London: Routledge & Kegan Paul, 1978), 80–86.
28. Carl Marklund, "Sharing Values and Shaping Values: Sweden, 'Nordic Democracy' and the American Crisis of Democracy," in *Rhetorics of Nordic Democracy*, eds. Jussi Kurunmäki and Johan Strang (Helsinki: Finnish Literature Society, 2010), 120–123; Francis Sejersted, "Capitalism and Democracy: A Comparison between Norway and Sweden," in *The Democratic Challenge to Capitalism: Management and Democracy in the Nordic Countries*, eds. Haldor Byrkjeflot, Sissel Myklebust, Christine Myrvang and Francis Sejersted (Bergen: Fagbokforlaget, 2001), 100–101; Marquis W. Childs, *This is Democracy: Collective Bargaining in*

Scandinavia (New Haven: Yale University Press, 1938); Ernst Wigforss, *Ekonomisk demokrati* (Stockholm: Natur och kultur, 1948).

29. David Montgomery, "Industrial Democracy or Democracy in Industry? The Theory and Practice of the Labor Movement, 1870–1925," in *Industrial Democracy in America: The Ambiguous Promise*, eds. Nelson Lichtenstein and Howell John Harris (New York: Woodrow Wilson Center Press, 1993), 20–42; Ilkka Turunen, "Arbete, produktion och demokrati: De finländska produktionskommittéernas historia," in *Industriell demokrati i norden*, ed. Daniel Fleming, 197–217 (Lund: Arkiv, 1990) 197–200, 209–217; Niklas Bruun, Pauli Kettunen and Ilkka Turunen, "Industriell demokrati i Norden: Introduktion till det finska delprojektet," in *Industriell demokrati i norden*, ed. Daniel Fleming (Lund: Arkiv, 1990), 115–116, 124–127.
30. Henrik Meinander, "Det långa 1900-talet," in *Demokratins drivkrafter: Kontext och särdrag i Finlands och Sveriges demokratier 1890–2020*, eds. Henrik Meinander, Petri Karonen and Kjell Östberg (Helsinki: Svenska litteratursällskapet i Finland, 2018), 28–30; Risto Alapuro, "Ulkoinen ja sisäinen: Suomen poliittisen kulttuurin pitkä linja," *Yhteiskuntapolitiikka* 75, 5 (2010): 529–530.
31. Alapuro, "Ulkoinen ja sisäinen," 534–536.
32. Searches with terms "taloudellinen demokratia," "teollinen demokratia," "taloudellinen kansanvalta," "teollinen kansanvalta," "ekonomisk demokrati," "industriell demokrati" between 1750 and 1929. Finnish National library's archive of digitized newspapers. https://digi.kansalliskirjasto.fi/sanomalehti/.
33. Osmo Rinta-Tassi, *Kansanvaltuuskunta punaisen Suomen hallituksena* (Helsinki: Opetusministeriö, 1986), 363–378.
34. Kettunen, *Poliittinen liike ja sosiaalinen kollektiivisuus*, 90–104, 122–128, 163–173.
35. Pauli Kettunen, "The Tension between the Social and the Economic," in *The Road to Prosperity: An Economic History of Finland*, eds. Jari Eloranta, Jukka Jalava and Jari Ojala (Helsinki: Suomalaisen Kirjallisuuden Seura, 2006), 294.
36. Kettunen, *Poliittinen liike ja sosiaalinen kollektiivisuus*, 272–280, 344–350, 484; Hannu Soikkanen, *Kohti kansanvaltaa 1: Suomen Sosialidemokraattinen puolue 75 vuotta, 1899–1937* (Helsinki: Suomen Sosialidemokraattinen puolue, 1975), 400–403.
37. Turunen, "Arbete, produktion och demokrati," 197–200; Pauli Kettunen, *Suojelu, suoritus, subjekti: Työsuojelu teollistuvan Suomen yhteiskunnallisissa ajattelu- ja toimintatavoissa* (Helsinki: Suomen historiallinen seura, 1994), 332–334.

38. Turunen, "Arbete, produktion och demokrati," 209–217; '"Taloudellinen kansanvalta" ja "talouden kansanvaltaistuttaminen."' *Suomen sosialidemokraatti* 21 October 1928, 10.
39. SAP, LO, SSKF and SSU. *Arbetarrörelsens efterkrigsprogram* (1944), 1, 7–10; Tilton, *The Political Theory of Swedish Social Democracy*, 48; Leif Lewin, *Planhushållningsdebatten* (Stockholm: Almqvist & Wiksell, 1967), 213–234.
40. On the tension between economic planning and socialization in the interwar period see Sassoon, *One Hundred Years of Socialism*, 60–69.
41. Tony Judt, *Postwar: A History of Europe since 1945* (London: Penguin, 2005), 67–77; Eric Hobsbawm, *Age of Extremes: The Short Twentieth Century 1914–1991* (London: Abacus, 1995), 267–275; Berman, *The Primacy of Politics*, 5–8, 177–187; Magnusson, *Sveriges ekonomiska historia*, 374–378, 418–422.
42. Sassoon, *One Hundred Years of Socialism*, 150–166.
43. For example, Lars Ekdahl, *Mot en tredje väg: En biografi över Rudolf Meidner. II. Facklig expert och demokratisk socialist* (Lund: Arkiv förlag, 2005), 13–14.
44. Pontusson, *Limits of Social Democracy*, 2–3, 37–39; Tilton, *The Political Theory of Swedish Social Democracy*, 1990, 66–69, 71–72; Lewin, *Planhushållningsdebatten*, 32–41, 69–77.
45. Francis Sejersted, *The Age of Social Democracy: Norway and Sweden in the Twentieth Century* (Princeton: Princeton University Press, 2011), 293–296; Andersson, *Between Growth and Security*, 5–8; Tilton *The Political Theory of Swedish Social Democracy*, 6–8.
46. Torsten Svensson, *Marknadsanpassningens politik: Den svenska modellens förändring 1980–2000* (Uppsala: Statsvetenskapliga föreningen, 2001), 74–79; Pontusson, *Limits of Social Democracy*, 11, 47–56; Lewin, *Planhushållningsdebatten*, 263–347.
47. Pontusson, *Limits of Social Democracy*, 40.
48. Sejersted, "Capitalism and Democracy," 102–105.
49. Jukka Pekkarinen and Juhana Vartiainen, *Suomen talouspolitiikan pitkä linja* (Helsinki: WSOY, 1993), 49–57; Jukka Pekkarinen, "Keynesianism and the Scandinavian Models of Economic Policy," in *The Political Power of Economic Ideas: Keynesianism across Nations*, ed. Peter A. Hall (Princeton: Princeton University Press, 1989), 322–332; Hannu Soikkanen, *Kohti kansanvaltaa 3: SDP 1944–1952* (Helsinki: Suomen Sosialidemokraattinen puolue, 1991), 483–489.
50. Pasi Nevalainen and Ville Yliaska, "From State-owned Smokestacks to Post-industrial Dreams: The Finnish Government in Business, 1970–2010," *Business History* 62 (2020). https://doi.org/10.1080/00076791.2020.1842874; Tapani Paavonen, "Talouden kehitys ja

talouspolitiikka hyvinvointivaltion kaudella," in *Eduskunta hyvinvointivaltion rakentajana. Suomen eduskunta 100 vuotta*, eds. Tapani Paavonen and Olli Kangas (Helsinki: Edita, 2006), 40–42, 46–49; Markku Kuisma, *Kylmä sota, kuuma öljy: Neste, Suomi ja kaksi Eurooppaa 1948–1979* (Porvoo: WSOY, 1997), 28, 99–101, 103, 106, 108.

51. Juhana Aunesluoma, *Vapaakaupan tiellä: Suomen kauppa- ja integraatiopolitiikka maailmansodista EU-aikaan* (Helsinki: Suomalaisen kirjallisuuden seura, 2011), 130–135, 141–148; Tapani Paavonen, *Vapaakauppaintegraation kausi: Suomen suhde Länsi-Euroopan integraatioon FINN-EFTAsta EC-vapaakauppaan* (Helsinki: Suomalaisen kirjallisuuden seura, 2008), 298–299.
52. Paavonen, "Talouden kehitys ja talouspolitiikka," 36–38; Soikkanen, *Kohti kansanvaltaa 3*, 487–489.
53. Stephanie L. Mudge, *Leftism Reinvented: Western Parties from Socialism to Neoliberalism* (Cambridge, MA: Harvard University Press, 2018), 53–55; Jan-Werner Müller, *Contesting Democracy: Political Ideas in Twentieth Century Europe* (New Haven and London: Yale University Press, 2011), 143–146; Daniel Bell, *The End of Ideology: On the Exhaustion of Political Ideas in the Fifties* (New York: The Free Press, 1965); Herbert Tingsten, *Från idéer till idyll: Den lyckliga demokratien* (Stockholm: Norstedts, 1966).
54. Sassoon, *One Hundred Years of Socialism*, 150–151, 190–199.
55. Jenny Andersson, *The Library and the Workshop: Social Democracy and Capitalism in the Knowledge Age* (Stanford: Stanford University Press, 2010), 7–10.
56. Wolfgang Streeck, "Works Councils in Western Europe: From Consultation to Participation," in *Works Councils: Consultation, Representation, and Cooperation in Industrial Relations*, eds. Joel Rogers and Wolfgang Streeck (Chicago and London: University of Chicago Press, 1995), 317–318.
57. Ekdahl, *Mot en tredje väg II*, 53–63; Sassoon, *One Hundred Years of Socialism*, 203–207; Pontusson, *Limits of Social Democracy*, 50–53, 59–69, 93–96.
58. Johan Strang, "Why 'Nordic Democracy?': The Scandinavian Value Nihilists and the Crisis of Democracy," in *Rhetorics of Nordic Democracy*, eds. Jussi Kurunmäki and Johan Strang (Helsinki: Finnish Literature Society, 2010), 108–110.
59. Pentti Puoskari, *Väärää politiikkaa suuren muuton vuosina? Virolaisen ja Paasion hallitusten elinkeino- ja rakennepolitiikka 1964–1968* (Joensuu: University of Eastern Finland, 2013), 36–41; Magnusson, *Sveriges ekonomiska historia*, 379–384, 392–397; Pontusson, *Limits of Social Democracy*, 97–111, 129–130.

60. Magnusson, *Sveriges ekonomiska historia*, 405–410; Sassoon, *One Hundred Years of Socialism*, 203–207.
61. Pontusson, *Limits of Social Democracy*, 11–14, 57–96.
62. Adam Przeworski, *Capitalism and Social Democracy* (Cambridge: Cambridge University Press, 1985), 211–217.
63. Maj-Britt Sandlund, "Sverige borde kunna planera," *Tiden* 1/1965, 34–38; Ingvar Carlsson, "Handlingsviljan socialdemokratins främsta garanti," *Tiden* 2/1966, 82–83.
64. Gunnar Adler-Karlsson, *Funktionssocialism: Ett alternativ till kommunism och kapitalism* (Stockholm: Prisma, 1967); Berman, *The Primacy of Politics*, 196; Tilton, *The Political Theory of Swedish Social Democracy*, 262–267.
65. Adler-Karlsson, *Funktionssocialism*, 59–74.
66. Ibid., 23–37.
67. Ibid., 92–98.
68. For example, Jan Bergqvist, "Arbetarrörelsen och den ekonomiska makten," *Tiden* 9/1973, 546–555.
69. For example, Ekdahl, *Mot en tredje väg II*; Magnusson, *Sveriges ekonomiska historia*, 418; Svensson, *Marknadsanpassningens politik*, 13–14.
70. For example, Korpi, *The Working Class in Welfare Capitalism*; Olsen, *The Struggle for Economic Democracy*, 9–11.
71. For example, Adam Przeworski, "How Many Ways Can Be Third?" in *Social Democracy in Neoliberal Times*, ed. Andrew Glyn (Oxford: Oxford University Press, 2002), 318–320.
72. Ingrid Gilcher-Holtey, "Political Participation and Democratization in the 1960s: The Concept of Participatory Democracy and its Repercussions," in *Democracy in Modern Europe: A Conceptual History*, edited by Jussi Kurunmäki, Jeppe Nevers and Henk te Velde (New York: Berghahn, 2018), 257–273; Luc Boltanski and Ève Chiapello, *The New Spirit of Capitalism* (London and New York: Verso, 2005 [1999]), 169–178; Thomas Ekman Jørgensen, *Transformations and Crises: The Left and the Nation in Denmark and Sweden, 1956–1980* (New York and Oxford: Berghahn, 2008), 180–184; Sassoon, *One Hundred Years of Socialism*, 383–391.
73. Boltanski and Chiapello, *The New Spirit of Capitalism*, 169–178.
74. Boltanski and Chiapello, *The New Spirit of Capitalism*, 32–41, 169–172.
75. Kjell Östberg, *1968 – när allting var i rörelse* (Stockholm: Prisma, 2002), 10, 23–25, 61–72, 120–122; Bo Stråth, *Mellan två fonder: LO och den svenska modellen* (Stockholm: Atlas, 1998), 108–122, 130–136, 302–303; Sassoon, *One Hundred Years of Socialism*, 383–385.
76. Göran Therborn, (ed.), *En ny vänster* (Stockholm: Rabén & Sjögren, 1966), 169–182; Östberg, *1968*, 113–114.

77. Andersson, *Between Growth and Security*, 46–51.
78. For example, "Vänstern i teori och praktik." *Tiden* 4/1967.
79. Andersson, *Between Growth and Security*, 56–58.
80. Bengt Lundberg, *Jämlikhet? Socialdemokratin och jämlikhetsbegreppet* (Lund: Dialog, 1979); Stråth, *Mellan två fonder*, 97–98.
81. Kimmo Rentola, *Vallankumouksen aave: Vasemmisto, Beljakov ja Kekkonen 1970* (Helsinki: Otava, 2005), 146–147, 169–173; Martti Siisiäinen, *Suomalainen protesti ja yhdistykset*. (Helsinki: Tutkijaliitto, 1990), 104–108, 113–118, 127–130, 135–138.
82. Stråth, *Mellan två fonder*, 299–301.
83. Gilcher-Holtey, "Political Participation and Democratization," 257–267; Boltanski and Chiapello, *The New Spirit of Capitalism*, 62–67 169–172; Paavo Kärenlampi, *Taistelu kouludemokratiasta: Kouludemokratian aalto Suomessa* (Helsinki: Suomen Historiallinen Seura, 1999), 9–15, 238–239.
84. Gustaf Arrhenius, "Politisk och ekonomisk demokrati," in *Tillsammans: En fungerande ekonomisk demokrati*, ed. Bo Rothstein (Stockholm: SNS förlag, 2012), 71–77; Robert A. Dahl, *Democracy and its Critics* (New Haven and London: Yale University Press, 1989), 119, 207.
85. C.H. Hermansson, *Monopol och storfinans: De 15 familjerna*. 3rd edition (Stockholm: Rabén & Sjögren, 1971); Ilja Viktorov, *Fordismens kris och löntagarfonder i Sverige* (Stockholm: Stockholm University, 2006), 65–69, 80–82.
86. SOU 1968: 7. *Ägande och inflytande inom det privata näringslivet* (Stockholm: Finansdepartementet, 1968); Magnusson, *Sveriges ekonomiska historia*, 385–390; Ekman Jørgensen, *Transformations and Crises*, 28–29.
87. Committee report 1972: A6. *Keskittymiskomitean mietintö* (Helsinki, 1972); Kettil Bruun and Antti Eskola (eds.), *Taloudellinen valta Suomessa*. Helsinki: Tammi, 1969; Matti Hyvärinen, "Valta," in *Käsitteet liikkeessä: Suomen poliittisen kulttuurin käsitehistoria*, eds. Matti Hyvärinen, Jussi Kurunmäki, Kari Palonen, Tuija Pulkkinen and Henrik Stenius (Tampere: Vastapaino, 2003), 92–94, 108–112.
88. Bo Stråth, "Nordic Capitalism and Democratisation," in *The Democratic Challenge to Capitalism: Management and Democracy in the Nordic Countries*, eds. Haldor Byrkjeflot, Sissel Myklebust, Christine Myrvang and Francis Sejersted (Bergen: Fagbokforlaget, 2001), 67–72, 75–77; Sejersted, "Capitalism and Democracy," 92–95.
89. Sejersted, *The Age of Social Democracy*, 366–369; Sassoon, *One Hundred Years of Socialism*, 375–376.
90. Ritva Savtschenko, *Kompuroiden korporatismissa: Eheytyneen SAK:n ristipaineet suomalaisessa korporatismissa 1968–1978* (Doctoral dissertation, University of Helsinki 2015), 73–76, 91–92, 123–136, 247–248; Kjell

Östberg, *När vinden vände: Olof Palme 1969–1986* (Stockholm: Leopard, 2009), 31–40; Rentola, *Vallankumouksen aave*, 116–118.

91. The Swedish term *näringspolitik* refers to policies that regulate and create preconditions for economic activities. It relates to the term *näringsliv*, which Jonas Pontusson has defined as the "corporate, commodity producing sector of the economy" (Pontusson, *Limits of Social Democracy*, 2). *Näringspolitik* is differentiated from economic policy, as it does not include for example monetary policy. Here I use the common translation of industrial policy, even though *näringspolitik* also encompasses other economic sectors, and sometimes even other traditional policy sectors, such as labor market and regional policy. I translate the term *näringsliv* itself as 'the economic life' or simply 'the economy.' In Finland, industrial policy (*teollisuuspolitiikka*) was a more common term, but translations of *näringsliv* and *näringspolitik* also exist: *elinkeinoelämä* and *elinkeinopolitiikka*.
92. Joachim Schäfer, *Från tillväxt till trygghet: Tio års debatt om strukturpolitikens mål och medel* (Stockholm: Almqvist & Wiksell, 1984), 9–10; Pontusson, *Limits of Social Democracy*, 129–131.
93. Pontusson, *Limits of Social Democracy*, 16.
94. Pontusson, *Limits of Social Democracy*, 97–99, 104–109.
95. For example, *Expressen* 3 May 1966, 10; *Dagens Nyheter* 27 May 1967, 6; *Svenska Dagbladet* 29 May 1967, 4.
96. Pontusson, *Limits of Social Democracy*, 128–129.
97. SAP and LO, *Program för aktiv näringspolitik* (1968), 18.
98. Ibid., 7–8, 22–23.
99. Ibid., 22.
100. Ibid., 7–8.
101. Ibid., 10–11; Schäfer, *Från tillväxt till trygghet*, 48–50.
102. SAP and LO, *Program för aktiv näringspolitik*, 19, 54.
103. Ibid., 55–62.
104. Ibid., 66–67.
105. Pontusson, *Limits of Social Democracy*, 134.
106. SAP and LO, *Program för aktiv näringspolitik*, 95–101.
107. Magnusson, *Sveriges ekonomiska historia*, 427–429; Östberg, *När vinden vände*, 60–61; "Planhushållning för arbete åt alla," *Tiden* 9/1972, 481–484.
108. SAP and LO, *Näringspolitiskt program* (1972), 33–41, 107–108; Schäfer, *Från tillväxt till trgghet*, 124–126; Pontusson, *Limits of Social Democracy*, 103–104.
109. Peter F. Drucker, *The Unseen Revolution: How Pension Fund Socialism Came to America* (New York: Harper & Row, 1976).
110. Östberg, *När vinden vände*, 9–12.

111. Östberg, *När vinden vände*, 63–68; Torbjörn Nilsson, *Hundra år av svensk politik* (Malmö: Gleerups, 2009), 118.
112. Rentola, *Vallankumouksen aave*, 121–123.
113. Puoskari, *Väärää politiikkaa suuren muuton vuosina?*, 200–220, 292–295; Sakari Heikkinen and Seppo Tiihonen, *Hyvinvoinnin turvaaja: Valtiovarainministeriön historia 3* (Helsinki: Edita, 2010), 124–133.
114. Puoskari, *Väärää politiikkaa suuren muuton vuosina?*, 14–15, 45–56; Heikkinen and Tiihonen, *Hyvinvoinnin turvaaja*, 122–123.
115. "Nyt on käännekohta. Sosdem. puolueneuvoston julkilausuma 16.2.1966," *Sosialistinen Aikakauslehti* 2/1966, 4–6.
116. Erkki Raatikainen, "Asenteista," *Sosialistinen aikakauslehti* 2/1967, 3–5.
117. Jermu Laine, "Kohti aktiivista elinkeinopolitiikkaa," *Sosialistinen aikakauslehti* 2/1968, 38. See also Olavi Jäminki, "Pääomien ohjaus – yhdentekevääkö?" *Sosialistinen aikakauslehti* 2/1967, 43.
118. Laine, "Kohti aktiivista elinkeinopolitiikkaa," 40–41.
119. For example, SDP congress protocol 1969, 51–52, 57–58, 100–101.
120. Memo: Towards the decisive election 1970. Campaign plans for parliamentary election. HDA 57 Parliamentary election 1970. 329.5 Parliamentary elections. SDP Archive, The Labor Archives, Helsinki.
121. SDP Election book I. HDA 58 Parliamentary election 1970. 329.5 Parliamentary elections. SDP archive, The Labor Archives, Helsinki.
122. Kalevi Sorsa, "Pääomavirtoja ohjattava – tuloja tasattava," *Sosialistinen aikakauslehti* 2/1970, 3–4; Kalevi Sorsa, "Tasa-arvo sosialidemokratian tavoitteena ja mittapuuna," *Sosialistinen aikakauslehti* 4/1970, 3–4.
123. Vesa Vares, *Korpivaellukselta vallankahvaan: Kansallisen kokoomuspuolueen historia 1966–1987* (Jyväskylä: Docendo, 2017), 90–98; Seppo Kääriäinen, *Sitä niittää, mitä kylvää: Keskustan strategiset valinnat 1964–2001* (Jyväskylä: Gummerus, 2002), 131–135, 143–144; Rentola, *Vallankumouksen aave*, 101–103.
124. Vares, *Korpivaellukselta vallankahvaan*, 120–121, 126.
125. SDP Congress protocol 1972, 37.
126. SAP and LO, *Program för aktiv näringspolitik*, 50–52.
127. Sten Johansson, "En plädering för jämlikhetspolitik," *Tiden* 9/1967, 541–553; Sten Johansson, "Socialdemokratins roll i samhällsstrukturen," *Tiden* 3/1968, 144–152.
128. SAP congress protocol 1967, 119–195; SAP congress protocol 1968, 55–57, 63–64, 78–79, 107–108.
129. SAP congress motions 1972, 133–147.
130. SAP congress motions 1972, 80–109; Schäfer, *Från tillväxt till trygghet*, 134–138.
131. SAP congress protocol 1972, 582–593.
132. SAP congress motions 1969, 226–228, 261–263.

133. SAP congress motions 1972, 173–175.
134. Ibid., 176.
135. SAP congress protocol 1972, 608.
136. Ibid., 607.
137. Östberg, *När vinden vände*, 237–246.
138. SAP and LO, *Program för aktiv näringspolitik*, 1968, 5–7.
139. Ibid., 18.
140. Ibid., 64–65.
141. Pauli Kettunen, *Kansallinen työ: Suomalaisen suorituskyvyn vaalimisesta* (Helsinki: Yliopistopaino, 2001), 144–146; Pekka Kosonen, *Pohjoismaiset mallit murroksessa* (Tampere: Vastapaino, 1998), 33–35.
142. Andersson, *Between Growth and Security*, 9–11, 28–44.
143. Freeden, *Ideologies and Political Theory*, 454–455; Tilton, *The Political Theory of Swedish Social Democracy*, 56, 149–153, 260.
144. Mudge, *Leftism Reinvented*, 50–53.
145. On welfare as a synonym to the common good see Nils Edling, "Multiple Welfare States: Histories of a Keyword," in *Changing Meanings of the Welfare State: Histories of a Key Concept in the Nordic Countries*, ed. Nils Edling (New York and Oxford: Berghahn, 2019), 28–29.
146. Kettunen, *Suojelu, suoritus, subjekti*, 92–97.
147. Kettunen, *Suojelu, suoritus, subjekti*, 277–283; Tilton, *The Political Theory of Swedish Social Democracy*, 55–56; Sassoon, *One Hundred Years of Socialism*, 70.
148. Pontusson, *Limits of Social Democracy*, 131–134, 152–154, 158–159; Sejersted, *The Age of Social Democracy*, 326–328.
149. Svensson, *Marknadsanpassningens politik*, 77–78.
150. Pontusson, *Limits of Social Democracy*, 151–160; Schäfer, *Från tillväxt till trygghet*, 139–141, 215–216.
151. As exceptions see Erkki Raatikainen, "Järjellä ja sydämellä," *Sosialistinen aikakauslehti* 4/1968, 3–4; Erkki Raatikainen, "Aatteellisuuden paluu," *Sosialistinen aikakauslehti* 1/1969, 3–4.
152. Jermu Laine, "1970-luvun talouspolitiikan ydinkysymyksiä," in *Talouspolitiikan ydinkysymyksiä*, ed. Martti Koivisto (Helsinki: Tammi, 1974), 16–19.
153. Kalevi Sorsa, "Sosialidemokratia 1970-luvulla," in *Käytännön sosialidemokratiaa*, ed. Pentti Holappa. (Helsinki: Tammi, 1973), 103–115.
154. Ibid., 104.
155. Antero Jyränki, "Kansanedustuslaitos ja valtiosääntö 1906–2005," in *Eduskunnan muuttuva asema: Suomen eduskunta 100 vuotta*, eds. Antero Jyränki and Jaakko Nousiainen (Helsinki: Edita, 2006), 41–65.
156. For example, Barry Holmström, "The Judicialization of Politics in Sweden," *International Political Science Review* 15, 2 (1994): 153–164.

157. On the concept of near democracy and similar debates in Denmark see Jesper Vestermark Køber, *Et spørgsmål om nærhed: Nærdemokratibegrebets historie i 1970'ernes Danmark* (Doctoral dissertation, University of Copenhagen 2017).
158. Folkpartiet. *Socialliberal kurs* (1972). http://snd.gu.se/sv/vivill/party/fp/p/1972.
159. Center Party of Sweden. *Valprogram för Centerpartiet.* Antaget vid Centerpartiets riksstämma i Visby 17–19 Juni 1968. https://snd.gu.se/sv/vivill/party/c/v/1968; Schäfer, *Från tillväxt till trygghet*, 97–102.
160. "Fördjupad demokrati," *Tiden* 10/1968, 577–582; "Skoldemokrati," *Tiden* 10/1969, 577–579.
161. The strike wave a couple of years earlier had made Palme aware of the topic's importance. See Östberg, *När vinden vände*, 37–42.
162. Östberg, *När vinden vände*, 415.
163. "Socialdemokratin i Europa starkare än någonsin," *Tiden* 7–8/1972, 397–398.
164. Olof Ruin, "Dagens demokratidebatt," *Tiden* 7/1969, 413–419.
165. Mats Hellström, "Finns det en väg ut ur kapitalismen?" *Tiden* 4/1973, 213–214.
166. Olof Palme, "Ett demokratiskt genombrott." *Tiden* 7/1973, 396–397.
167. Ibid., 393.
168. Östberg, *När vinden vände*, 231–237.
169. "Decentralisering (c) eller medborgarmakt (s)," *Tiden* 9/1973, 513–516.
170. Berndt Öhman, "Tiden är mogen för industriell demokrati," *Tiden* 3/1974, 175.
171. Jyrki Smolander, *Suomalainen oikeisto ja "kansankoti": Kansallisen Kokoomuksen suhtautuminen pohjoismaiseen hyvinvointivaltiomalliin jälleenrakennuskaudelta konsensusajan alkuun* (Helsinki: Suomalaisen kirjallisuuden seura, 2000), 16–27; Vesa Vares, *Suomalaiskansallinen kokoomus: Kansallisen kokoomuspuolueen historia 1944–1966* (Helsinki: Edita, 2008), 528–534; Vares, *Korpivaellukselta vallankahvaan*, 12–14.
172. Stig-Björn Ljunggren, *Folkhemskapitalismen: Högerns programutveckling under efterkrigstiden* (Stockholm: Tidens förlag, 1992), 30–37.
173. Nilsson, *Hundra år av svensk politik*, 176.
174. Torbjörn Nilsson, *Mellan arv och utopi: Moderata vägval under hundra år, 1904–2004* (Stockholm: Santérus, 2004), 315–318.
175. Ibid., 92–93.
176. The Right changed its leader in 1961, 1965 and 1970. Ibid., 228–231.
177. Smolander, *Suomalainen oikeisto ja "kansankoti"*, 44–45.
178. Ljunggren, *Folkhemskapitalismen*, 407–408, 412–417; Nilsson, *Mellan arv och utopi*, 16–17, 85–88, 307–310; Smolander, *Suomalainen oikeisto ja "kansankoti"*, 99–105.

179. Vares, *Korpivaellukselta vallankahvaan*, 42–43, 99, 157–158, 184–185; Nilsson, *Mellan arv och utopi*, 347–348.
180. Smolander, *Suomalainen oikeisto ja "kansankoti"*, 310–311.
181. Ville Okkonen, *Peruskoulua vastaan: Yksityisoppikoulut ja yhteiskuntajärjestys 1966–1975* (Turku: University of Turku, 2017). 323–325.
182. Berman, *The Primacy of Politics*, 5–8, 177–187; Judt, *Postwar*, 67–77; Magnusson, *Sveriges ekonomiska historia*, 374–378, 418–422.
183. Högerpartiet, *Högerpartiets principprogram*. Fastställt av Högerpartiets riksstämma den 4 juni 1956. http://snd.gu.se/sv/vivill/party/m/p/1956; Center Party of Sweden, *Centerpartiets program*. Fastställt av centerpartiets riksstämma den 30 juni 1959. https://snd.gu.se/sv/vivill/party/c/p/1959; Folkpartiet, *Folkpartiets program*. Antaget vid landsmötet i Göteborg 1962. http://snd.gu.se/sv/vivill/party/fp/p/1962. On the ideal of self-governance see Sejersted, *The Age of Social Democracy*, 314–315; Stråth, *Mellan två fonder*, 37–39.
184. Högerpartiet, *Högerpartiets principprogram*; Högerpartiet, *Egendomsägande demokrati* (1962); Daniel Stedman Jones, *Masters of the Universe: Hayek, Friedman, and the Birth of Neoliberal Politics* (Princeton: Princeton University Press, 2012), 297–298; Nilsson, *Mellan arv och utopi*, 193–194; Smolander, *Suomalainen oikeisto ja "kansankoti"*, 150; Ljunggren, *Folkhemskapitalismen*, 130–132.
185. Greg Castillo, *Cold War on the Home Front: The Soft Power of Midcentury Design* (Minneapolis: University of Minnesota Press, 2010), 122–130; Smolander, *Suomalainen oikeisto ja "kansankoti"*, 118–119.
186. Stedman Jones, *Masters of the Universe*, 122–125; Müller, *Contesting Democracy*, 153–154; Smolander, *Suomalainen oikeisto ja "kansankoti,"* 119–121.
187. National Coalition Party. *Kokoomuksen lähiajan tavoiteohjelma*. Hyväksytty Kokoomuksen puoluevaltuuston kokouksessa Tuusulassa 6.8.1972. https://www.fsd.uta.fi/pohtiva/ohjelmalistat/KOK/80. The English translation is a bit cumbersome but highlights the important affinity with the 'social market economy.'
188. Smolander, *Suomalainen oikeisto ja "kansankoti,"* 244–249.
189. Ibid., 268–275, 312–313.
190. Vares, *Korpivaellukselta vallankahvaan*, 110–114.
191. National Coalition Party, *Me luotamme ihmiseen ja vapauteen* (1956). https://www.fsd.uta.fi/pohtiva/ohjelmalistat/KOK/115; National Coalition Party, *Kohti huomispäivän yhteiskuntaa*. Kansallisen kokoomuksen poliittinen toimintaohjelma 1966. https://www.fsd.uta.fi/pohtiva/ohjelmalistat/KOK/90.
192. Ljunggren, *Folkhemskapitalismen*, 132–135; Schäfer, *Från tillväxt till trygghet*, 59.

193. "Allas rätt – ingens privilegium," *Medborgaren* 9/1964, 4.
194. Högerpartiet, *Konsten att fånga en miljon* (1964). https://snd.gu.se/sv/vivill/party/m/v/1964.
195. Ljunggren, *Folkhemskapitalismen*, 408–409.
196. Cf. Ljunggren, *Folkhemskapitalismen*, 409.
197. Cf. Przeworski, *Capitalism and Social Democracy*, 218–219.
198. Nils Carlshamre, "Ernst Wigforss: Den osäkre ägardemokraten," *Medborgaren* 16/1964, 8; Mauno Koivisto, (ed.). *Laajempaan kansanvaltaan* (Helsinki: Akateeminen sos.dem. yhdistys, 1960), 50–55.
199. Moderata samlingspartiet, *Partiprogram i sammandrag* (1969). http://snd.gu.se/sv/vivill/party/m/p/1969; Schäfer, *Från tillväxt till trygghet*, 61–70, 205–209.
200. Ljunggren, *Folkhemskapitalismen*, 277–279, 287–293; Smolander, *Suomalainen oikeisto ja "kansankoti"*, 299–301.
201. Ljunggren, *Folkhemskapitalismen*, 305–306.
202. Nilsson, *Mellan arv och utopi*, 239–240.
203. For example, David Held, *Models of Democracy*, 2nd edition (Stanford: Stanford University Press, 1996), 74–75.
204. For these arguments see also Kari Palonen, "Sosialistien demokratiasta," *Nykypäivä* 4/1967, 35–36.
205. Torbjörn Nilsson, "Nyliberalismens spöke och Moderaternas politik," in *Det långa 1990-talet: När Sverige förändrades*, eds. Anders Ivarsson Westerberg, Ylva Waldemarson and Kjell Östberg (Umeå: Boréa, 2014), 45–50.
206. Rikard Westerberg, "The Alternative: How Nordic Business Interest Associations Attempted to Formulate an Ideological Programme, 1945–1975," *Scandinavian Journal of History* 2018, https://doi.org/10.1080/03468755.2018.1532316; Lewin, *Planhushållningsdebatten*, 267–273.

CHAPTER 3

Enterprise Democracy: Employee Power or Consultative Cooperation?

This chapter examines how political parties and labor market confederations struggled over the meaning and valuation of the concept 'enterprise democracy' in Finland and Sweden in the 1960s and 1970s.[1] In Finland, enterprise democracy was the most debated issue of economic democratization in the late 1960s, and it also received increasing attention in Sweden, especially after Olof Palme became the leader of the Social Democrats in 1969. Labor market organizations were the most important stakeholders in the issue and had considerable power in shaping the implementation and practices of enterprise democracy. Hence, their thought and rhetoric gain more attention here than in Chap. 2. Concentrating on official statements of labor market confederations may make employees and employers seem too united internally. It is worth noting that trade and employer unions often had considerable differences of opinion. Within the Finnish trade union movement, the power struggle between Communists and Social Democrats was a significant factor.[2] The negotiation and legislation processes related to enterprise democracy have been well mapped in previous research, but the focus has usually been on narrating events instead of analyzing concepts, beliefs and rhetoric.[3] Therefore, in the following I will concentrate on struggles over the meaning and value of enterprise democracy, and ways of relating it to broader hierarchies and constellations of concepts and beliefs.

I. Kärrylä, *Democracy and the Economy in Finland and Sweden since 1960*, Palgrave Studies in Political History,
https://doi.org/10.1007/978-3-030-80631-6_3

The Origins of Enterprise Democracy

The concept of enterprise democracy has normally referred to the 'micro' and 'meso' levels of economic activity—democratization of workplaces and enterprises. In many European countries the concept 'industrial democracy' has been used for the same purpose.[4] I have chosen 'enterprise democracy' as the translation for Finnish and Swedish terms that do not have established equivalents in English. Finnish *yritysdemokratia* and Swedish *företagsdemokrati* meant democracy in all enterprises and were often distinguished from 'industrial democracy,' which was criticized for only implying heavy industry.[5] Enterprise democracy is sometimes used in English literature,[6] and is a more appropriate translation than 'corporate democracy,' which might imply only large corporations. 'Enterprise democracy' began to substitute for 'industrial democracy' in Sweden after the World War II. Judging by newspaper material, it was appropriated especially by the white-collar trade unions, with the intention of stressing that their workplaces also needed to be democratized—not exclusively the industry.[7] However, in the 1940s, enterprise democracy was not a very common term. In Finland it substituted for 'industrial democracy' only in the 1960s. In the keywords of parliamentary proceedings, *yritysdemokratia* was included in 1967. Before that the same topics are found under keywords like *teollinen demokratia* (industrial democracy) and *tuotantokomiteat* (production committees/works councils).[8] The Nordic term 'enterprise democracy' was not widely adopted and translated, which creates potential translation problems. For example, enterprise democracy did not usually refer to collective bargaining on the national level like industrial democracy did in many countries. Enterprise democracy and 'workplace democracy' were often used synonymously, but according to a common distinction, the former could also refer to large consolidated companies as opposed to single workplaces.[9]

Democracy in workplaces and enterprises was discussed during all three 'waves' of debate on economic democratization in Europe. Concrete results were reached after World War II, as works councils and codetermination were introduced in many European countries.[10] The German system of codetermination (*mitbestimmung*), established in 1952, is probably the best-known example of postwar industrial democracy. In large corporations of the coal and steel industry, employees gained 50% representation in supervisory boards, which are the highest bodies of governance in German enterprises. In 1976, codetermination was extended to all companies with supervisory boards. Moreover, all German companies with more than five employees had since the 1920s works councils as employee representation bodies. Like Finnish and Swedish shop stewards, they supervised that the company followed laws and agreements. The councils also took part in decision-making on social issues and company rules. German works councils were not necessarily connected to trade unions, although in the postwar decades they increasingly became so.[11]

Swedish Social Democrats demanded employee influence within companies in their 1944 platform and postwar program, but its content was left quite vague.[12] In 1946, labor market organizations reached an agreement on works councils, which were bodies of cooperative consultation in the fashion proposed by the committee of the 1920s.[13] The use of the concepts economic and industrial democracy also increased in Finland. There was debate on economic planning, and works councils or 'production committees' were established in 1946 by legislation. Finnish employers insisted they should remain bodies of cooperative consultation that contributed to increasing the efficiency of industrial production. Unlike German works councils, the Finnish and Swedish ones had also employer representatives.[14] In the 1950s, demands for democratization of workplaces became weaker, and the role of existing works councils diminished in many countries.[15] In Sweden, the decade was characterized by collaboration between labor and capital, which was facilitated by steady economic growth.[16] In Finland, the situation was more conflictual, but demands for democratization were not voiced even during the general strike of 1956.

In the 1960s, ideas of democratizing working life reemerged around Europe. Worker protests against monotonous industrial work and lack of influence increased. Demands for democratization were strengthened by new transnational movements, such as the New Left.[17] In Sweden, the confederation of trade unions (LO) at first retained a moderate stance, as workplace democracy could potentially conflict with collective bargaining and solidaristic wage policy.[18] The debate on enterprise democracy, which had now replaced the term industrial democracy, was intensified by center-right parties and employer organizations. In the mid-1960s, the Confederation of Swedish Employers (SAF) began to promote its own version of enterprise democracy.[19] Employers and center-right parties advocated enterprise democracy based on their traditional policy of cooperation at workplaces, aiming to increase work satisfaction and the sense of a common interest. This echoed older paternalistic and social liberal principles of management.

In Sweden, some of the new ideas were brought into the renewed agreement on works councils in 1966, which stayed within the traditional bounds of cooperation. LO was still reserved toward democracy in workplaces while calls for more substantial employee influence were increasing. In 1969, a growing number of parliamentary motions on enterprise democracy were given by different parties. LO took a more critical stance toward the works council agreement and began to prepare a report on enterprise democracy. After a major wildcat strike at the state-owned LKAB mine at the turn of 1970, enterprise democracy became a top theme in Swedish public debate. In the following year, a state committee on labour law (*Arbetsrättskommittéen*) was appointed to investigate enterprise democracy and codetermination.[20] By early 1970s, enterprise democracy had become a major topic of public debate. It was mentioned in Swedish press much more often than economic or industrial democracy, but the use declined within a decade and other terms, such as 'codetermination' (*medbestämmande*), substituted it (Fig. 3.1).

In Finland, there was some discussion on industrial or enterprise democracy since the early 1960s, but it mostly dealt with extending the mandate of production committees. A more intense debate began in 1966

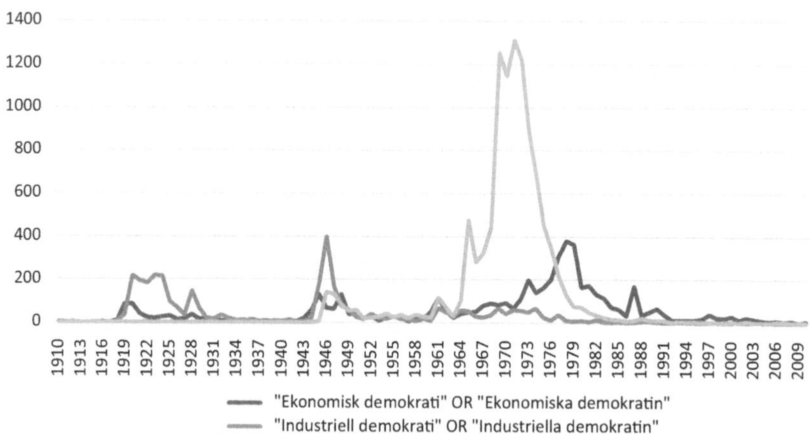

Fig. 3.1 Number of articles with the terms 'economic democracy,' 'industrial democracy' and 'enterprise democracy' in the Swedish database of digital newspapers (http://tidningar.kb.se/), 1910–2010. Data retrieved 13 August 2019

when the Social Democrats gained a landslide victory in parliamentary elections, after seven years in opposition and severe internal contradictions. This resulted in a left-wing parliamentary majority, and Communists participated in the government with the Social Democrats and the Center Party, which at the time was exceptional in Western countries.[21] Due to the active stance of the Social Democrats, a state committee on enterprise democracy was appointed, and a legislation process initiated in 1967, four years before Sweden. The committee finished its work in March 1970 without very concrete proposals. Labor market confederations had attempted an agreement along consultative lines in 1969, but it was buried due to trade union opposition. Negotiation continued within a second state committee, and finding a satisfactory solution took several years.[22]

Power, Codetermination or Cooperation?

In the Finnish and Swedish debates on enterprise democracy, there was a wide agreement over a fundamental criterion of democracy and enterprise democracy, namely, the possibility of citizens to influence decisions concerning their own life. In democratic theory, this ideal is called the 'principle of affected interests.' It was a true slogan of the 1960s and aspirations to democratize different walks of life, which were advocated in Western countries especially by the New Left.[23] Belief in the growing demands of citizens and employees was also central for social scientists, who were developing ways of reforming working life. Worker protests in the 1960s were explained for example by the 'hierarchy of needs' introduced by sociologist Abraham Maslow: when basic material needs have been fulfilled, mental or spiritual needs become the most important. These include self-fulfillment and influence over one's own life, instead of monotonous work under someone else's control.[24] One potential solution for worker discontent was found in Ralf Dahrendorf's theory of managing social conflicts, which called for making conflicts explicit instead of suppressing them.[25] The theory was promoted by Finnish and Swedish sociologists such as Erik Allardt and Edmund Dahlström.[26]

Belief in the inevitability of linearly progressing democratization as a part of modernization was often expressed by Finnish and Swedish intellectuals. Finnish sociologist Seppo Randell, who was appointed Chair of the State Committee on Enterprise Democracy, spoke about the theme in the business magazine *Tehostaja* in autumn 1968: "Even though I hardly believe in any 'zeitgeists', it's impossible to deny the pursuit of democratization in many spheres of life."[27] According to Randell, youth activism in Finland and especially the Prague Spring signified that the movement was important and could not be easily suppressed. Therefore, in due time, it was crucial to answer the demands for extended democracy.

Employer ideas on enterprise democracy were influenced especially by the approaches of the human relations school of management, which were compatible with the democratization ideas of the time. In Finland, the 1970s marked the consolidation of Human Relations (HR) as a standard corporate function, for example with the aid of a vast amount of educational material published by the Finnish employer confederation STK.[28] Like all management approaches, human relations aimed at increasing the efficiency of work organizations. As opposed to technical rationalization, which was believed to cause alienation and mental problems, HR emphasized the importance, even the psychological necessity of influence and participation in the workplace. It was widely believed that contemporary workers demanded more autonomy, participation and responsibility, especially in matters concerning their everyday work.[29] Therefore, antiquated authoritarian management styles were to be replaced with democratic ones. Many theorists and managers believed that the only way to make organizations more efficient was listening to the employees.[30] They shared the belief of democratization being an intrinsic trait of a modernizing society, which legitimized the democratization of working life.[31]

Despite the widely shared belief in the inevitable democratization of societies, a disagreement over the criteria of enterprise democracy came up. It concerned the extent to which ordinary employees could take part in decision-making within companies: Would they have actual power to make decisions or would they only be consulted beforehand? The question was essentially about the division of power in companies. Swedish historian Lars Ekdahl has described power over the economy as a latent issue in Swedish politics. The 'Swedish model' was based on a historical compromise between capital and labour, which approved private ownership and the employers' right to manage and organize work. When these principles were questioned, such as in the planned economy debate after World War II, the employer side and center-right parties reacted with a counter-campaign.[32] To apply a distinction used in working life studies, employers viewed enterprise democracy as a question of human relations management. It was considered a technical problem in achieving predetermined goals, and it meant efficient management for the benefit of the company rather than distribution of power or managing conflicts. The employee side's viewpoint, in contrast, was 'industrial relations,' which included questions of power relations and conflicting interests.[33]

Employers and employees in both Finland and Sweden leaned toward a similar classificatory scheme of enterprise democracy, based on international 'models' that gave a different amount of power to the employees. The same typology is used in most sociological and management-theoretical research on employee participation.[34] The most common terms delineating the meaning of enterprise democracy in this respect were (1) information and communication, (2) consultation or 'co-influence' (medinflytande/myötävaikuttaminen), (3) codetermination (medbestämmande/myötämäärääminen) and (4) employee self-governance.[35] The second level after information referred to cooperative consultation, which took place, for example, in Finnish and Swedish production committees and works councils. Employee self-governance usually referred to the Yugoslavian model, where employees governed companies through workers' councils and elected the board and managers amongst themselves.[36]

Codetermination was situated between these ideal types and meant that employees had power in some decisions, for example through a German-style parity representation or by requiring mutual agreement before decision-making. However, in practical rhetoric the distinction between codetermination and consultation was often unclear. A key feature of the debate was disagreement as to which of these models would represent 'true' or desirable enterprise democracy. Employees demanded codetermination and even self-management, whereas employers spoke for consultation and communication. The parties stuck to their rivaling definitions for several years. In Finland, they came closer only after the second committee report was completed in 1974. In Sweden, the employer side opposed some features of the 1976 codetermination legislation but was ready to use it as a framework for future negotiations.

In its definitions of enterprise democracy, the employer side focused on improving cooperation and communication at the workplace, which had been the dominant employer line of industrial democracy since the nineteenth century. Employers called these practices democratic but did not support employee claims for decision-making rights or control of managers. They thus put forward different criteria for enterprise democracy—and for democracy in general—than the employee side. In a way, employers also tried to portray the question as only concerning the range of reference of democracy: The essential criterion of employee influence or participation could also be fulfilled through consultation.

The employer side was aware of the contested nature of enterprise democracy. This is evident in the 1964 book *Industrial Democracy and Industrial Management* (*Företagsdemokrati och företagsorganisation*) by the Swedish management theorist Eric Rhenman.[37] The study was commissioned by SAF and became the most influential theoretical work defining employer position on enterprise democracy.[38] It presented the idea of employers and managers as mediators whose task was to find a balance of interests between different stakeholders, such as employees, customers and society. Rhenman's book has in fact been considered one of the first contributions to the stakeholder approach to corporate management.[39] Rhenman's starting point was the contested meaning of enterprise democracy, which he wanted to clarify with a "common frame of reference" based on modern organization theory. Rhenman argued that although everyone would agree on the basic principle of employee participation in management, people were "considering very different practical steps and aiming at different goals."[40] Employers argued that even though democratization of enterprises was desirable in principle, the meaning of enterprise democracy could not be analogous to political democracy. In 1965, SAF's report *Cooperation in the Enterprise of the Future* (*Samarbetet i framtidens företag*) expressed reservations toward combining democracy and working life, as politics and enterprises were very different environments:

> The concept of democracy has its natural area of use within analyses of the political life. In this context the term also gains its ideological content. When one talks about 'industrial democracy and 'enterprise democracy' it means transferring the terminology to the circumstances of enterprises, which creates risks of misunderstanding and false analogies.[41]

Employer representatives often continued by arguing that if enterprise democracy was understood as different from political democracy, it had actually been realized to a large extent, for example through balancing the interests of employers and employees in the collective bargaining system.[42] Many employer representatives argued that in modern organizations power was already delegated and decentralized, which made claims of oligarchic decision-making misguided.[43] This kind of argumentation is at the core of conceptual struggles, because it implies that the other party has defined a concept in a wrong way, and even has a false picture of the social problems at stake. I call this argument a 'false diagnosis thesis.'

The rhetoric of Finnish employers followed similar paths, and explicit references to Rhenman and SAF were often made. STK representative Osmo A. Wiio expressed a belief resembling Rhenman's: Employers and employees had a shared meaning for enterprise democracy but pursued different means and goals. Wiio quoted Norwegian management theorist Einar Thorsrud, who had defined enterprise democracy as "distributing the possibility to social influence to all participating in working life as opposed to concentrating influence to only a few people."[44] In Wiio's view, this meant that employee self-management, codetermination, consultation and communication could all be considered forms of enterprise democracy. Its counter-concept was patriarchal, authoritarian leadership. Wiio argued that enterprise democracy should not be linked exclusively to one model, but the most appropriate models should be tested in different companies.[45] Thus, he implied that the employers' definition of enterprise democracy was more encompassing than the employee side's. However, the potential scope of enterprise democracy was practically narrowed by making consultation the most appropriate model.[46] In this version, the concepts of participation, cooperation and communication delineated the field of acceptable democratization, which was adapted to the objectives of enterprises.

In the rhetoric of the employee side, in turn, real decision-making power and the possibility of democratic control over managers represented 'true' democracy, which would defuse the conflict between capital and labor and make social power relations more equal. In Sweden, a radical conception of enterprise democracy was advocated especially by the New Left. Its ideas gained visibility after the publication of the pamphlet *En ny vänster* (A New Left), edited by the sociologist Göran Therborn.[47] The book criticized the employer and 'bourgeois' version of enterprise democracy for the attempt to play down the power relations and contradictions of capitalism by using the stakeholder model. The writers argued that Eric Rhenman confused interest conflicts with each other on different levels inside as well as outside the company. In reality, these conflicts were separate and did not create a balance of interests. Furthermore, managers could not act as neutral mediators, as they represented the interest of capital.[48] The New Left made the contestation over the meaning of democracy explicit and criticized Rhenman for ignoring some of the concept's basic features.

> The method is therefore to first give an unreasonable definition of democracy (in fact a definition of anarchy), reject it as unreasonable and then 'define' democracy by pointing out what in the conservative direction are considered its most important goals. In this way the rhetoric loses what is distinctive for democracy, concretely put that leaders are appointed by, responsible for and withdrawable by those they govern. What is gained is that the watchword democracy can be used to signify even non-democratic power structures.[49]

The New Left thus portrayed enterprise democracy as analogous to political democracy through the principle of leaders' accountability to the people, which was completely against what the employer side was arguing. The New Left maintained, for example, that true enterprise democracy could only be achieved if the employers' right to manage and organize work (paragraph 32/23 in SAF's statutes) was disposed of. In a radical manner, they related enterprise democracy to broader democratic control of the economy, which required for example societal ownership relations, planning, and definitive influence for the employees in company boards.[50]

Despite growing demands for democratization, LO and SAP maintained a moderate stance on the issue. The Swedish trade union movement remained committed to class compromise and the imperatives of efficiency and productivity that would guarantee rising standards and wages. LO's magazine *Fackföreningsrörelsen* (Trade union movement) published a positive review of Eric Rhenman's book, which found that his ideas were compatible with LO's 1961 report on enterprise democracy and could facilitate experimenting with enterprise democracy on an enterprise level.[51] The 1966 works council agreement between LO and SAF did not introduce major changes. At that point, LO's most far-reaching demands were increasing employers' obligation to negotiate and share information with works councils. The agreement gave the employer side an obligation to negotiate on new issues, such as the principles of personnel policy.[52] Two years after the agreement, surveys showed that in many enterprises works councils had been given new tasks, especially in social issues. However, many also reported that the flow of information between management and the council had not greatly improved.[53]

After SAP's loss in the 1966 municipal election, demands for enterprise democracy gradually intensified in Sweden along with the debates on equality and active industrial policy. SAP's Executive Committee remained cautious about the issue. In the party congress of 1967 it stated that democratization was not simple: There were many dimensions to be considered, such as the rightful interests of society, consumers and other groups. The committee preferred promoting the issue through labor market agreements instead of legislation, and it found that the new agreement on works councils included some positive reforms.[54]

SAP and LO's stance on enterprise democracy began to change toward the end of the 1960s. Criticism toward bureaucratic welfare state and alienating working life increased, and enterprise democracy also became a central topic for other groups. As part of their demands for decentralization and near democracy, the Center Party and the Liberals called for enterprise democracy in a form that came close to the employer side's definitions.[55] In 1969, a growing number of parliamentary motions on enterprise democracy were made by different parties. LO took a more critical stance toward the works council agreement and appointed a working group to write a report on enterprise democracy.[56] At the SAP congress of 1969, the tone of voice was quite sharp. The LO Secretary Olle Gunnarsson stated that the most important demand was stronger equality between labor and capital. He argued that employer proposals of consultation were not a step forward from the current works councils. Instead of formal influence, Gunnarsson called for "true influence," which meant, for example, the ability to influence decisions already in the planning phase.[57]

In its 1971 report *Demokrati i företagen* (Democracy within Enterprises), LO wanted substantial reforms as soon as possible. The report demanded employee influence on different levels of the company, from everyday work to corporate management. It stressed enterprise democracy as part of the democratization of the whole of society.[58] Equality between capital and labor was an important theme, and it was to mean equal influence in the management of enterprises. The employers' right to manage and organize work, as well as their interpretation privilege of laws and collective agreements were strongly criticized. They were called serious obstacles to the democratization of working life.[59]

Equal standing and influence of the employers and employees was a common definition for the concept of codetermination, although in LO's report it was somewhat unclear whether codetermination meant joint decisions and agreements or merely mandatory negotiation without requiring mutual agreement. LO's rhetoric vacillated between radical and moderate concepts and demands: It called for restrictions to the employers' right to manage and organize work, but often it emphasized consultation and negotiation rather than final decision-making power. The report used the concepts of cooperation and insight (*insyn*) rather than codetermination or control.[60] It did not specify which matters should be subject to agreement or even employee decision and which only to negotiation with the final decision left for the employer.[61] High LO officers were keen to point out the practical obstacles of radical reforms. The LO lawyer Sten Edlund argued that it was difficult to attack SAF's paragraph 32, because it would have had many side effects and required a major reform of Swedish labor legislation. The best road forward was extending the right to negotiate collectively, as the report suggested.[62] Pragmatic beliefs on what was politically possible thus played a key role in LO's constellations.

In Finland, the report of SAK's enterprise democracy working group, published in 1969, was closer to the Swedish New Left than LO. Its demands and arguments were repeated in many employee side's statements in the following years. The report expressed the belief that class conflict was permanent, which was why the position of employees was to be secured by changing the prevailing power and ownership relations.[63] 'Economic oligarchy' was used as a counter-concept of economic and enterprise democracy. SAK's working group was aware of the emerging struggle over the concept of enterprise democracy. The report commented different definitions and hinted that the employer version was an attempt to conceal class conflict:

> The conception of capital owners, according to which enterprise democracy means increasing HR and information activities on their terms without allowing employees to participate in the company's decision making makes it seem they have identified manipulation with democracy. The trade union movement's conception of democracy is different.[64]

The report's key message was distinguishing between preconditions of enterprise democracy and actual democratic reforms. Preconditions, like developing information services and strengthening the position of shop stewards created a foundation for reforms without changing the power structure within companies. Democratic reforms, in contrast, were defined as changes that enabled the participation of employees in decision-making. Without 'true' power of employees, enterprise democracy would not qualify as democracy.[65] SAK's second chair, Communist Arvo Hautala later phrased this criterion in a way that was clearly distinguished from the employer ideas of consultation and communication:

> Enterprise democracy means that employees are given the right to participate in setting objectives, approving plans, and making decisions on workplace- and enterprise-levels and that the implementation of decisions is placed under the supervision of the entire personnel.[66]

Although employers sometimes used the term enterprise democracy in a positive sense, especially in Finland, they were more comfortable with the term cooperation (*yhteistoiminta/samarbete*). In Sweden, the employer side had traditionally preferred this term over industrial or enterprise democracy.[67] This tendency continued in the 1960s. Eric Rhenman suggested that it was best to forget the ambiguous term enterprise democracy, which was "overloaded with time-worn emotions and evaluations."[68]

The title of SAF's report *Samarbetet i framtidens företag* also reveals which term the employers favored. In the report, the words industrial and enterprise democracy were only used to describe previous debates. Actual practices at workplaces were called cooperation. SAF continued this line until the early 1970s and often abstained from using the terms industrial and enterprise democracy. Finnish employers, in contrast, used the terms more explicitly but ascribed their own meaning to them. As enterprise democracy and codetermination became key terms describing the aspired scope of democratization, the Swedish employers also began to use them more frequently. This suggests that the labour movement at this point had a strong agenda-setting power, and the employers had to modify their language. However, employers still tried to replace enterprise democracy with cooperation, and especially codetermination with the milder term 'co-influence,' which effectively meant consultation. In the second half of the 1970s, cooperation again became the dominant term.[69]

It seems that SAF considered the word democracy threatening because of its layers of meaning that pointed to the distribution of power and workers' control over managers. Employers rather portrayed economic activities as harmonious and apolitical, for which the term cooperation suited well. SAF's uncomfortable relation with enterprise democracy was made explicit by CEO Curt-Steffan Giesecke, who stated that in order to avoid conceptual confusion, the term democracy should be reserved to political democracy and terms like cooperation and co-influence used in the area of working life.[70] The policy of the Finnish employers regarding the criteria and terminology of enterprise democracy was similar to their Swedish counterparts, and SAF's material was used as a source of definitions and arguments. STK's Eero Voutilainen argued that because the concept of cooperation, "clearly expresses what is fundamentally at stake, using it is rather recommendable." This implied a desire to leave the concept of democracy in the background. Instead of being a democratic reform, Voutilainen defined cooperation as a necessity in all corporate activity: "Enterprise democracy does not exist without an enterprise, and no enterprise can survive without functioning cooperation."[71]

Strategic Management or Influence in Everyday Work?

The potential range of reference of enterprise democracy was also contested, but was more open than the concept's necessary criteria. Both employers and employees considered that enterprise democracy could be manifested in many different practices and organizational models as long as the criteria were fulfilled. Different emphases came up especially on the axes of direct /representative democracy and influence in everyday work/ in strategic management. These disagreements also drew on different classifications of democracy and their desirability. For example, the employer side's argument that companies were not analogous to societies was used to justify the incompatibility of representative democracy as a model of decision-making.

Instead of a universal model of representation, Swedish employers preferred local cooperation with employees, where companies themselves could determine the most suitable practices.[72] The SAF stressed that the same model of cooperation could not be applied in every enterprise and emphasized adaptation to their specific needs. Employers often turned enterprise democracy into a question of management techniques and organization design rather than employee influence. In this line of thought, managers became the central actors of democratization. The concept 'democratic management' was often pitted against 'authoritarian' management styles that were deemed outdated.[73] Despite emphasizing direct relations between managers and employees, the SAF was generally pleased with the existing representative works councils and stated that although they were less important than democratic management, in many companies they provided a suitable model of cooperation.[74]

When the debate on enterprise democracy heated up in the late 1960s, the SAF continued to oppose new regulation but spoke for experimentation in companies to find the most appropriate forms of cooperation.

Employers emphasized employee influence in everyday work through new organizational forms like project groups. These gave employees power in operational matters—their own work methods and the work environment—but did not intervene with the strategic power of managers.[75] Especially, the results of Norwegian experiments on 'self-managed groups' were viewed positively. The experiments seemed to confirm that shop floor influence, where groups of employees could independently organize their work to reach production goals, was more efficient and created more satisfaction than representative models.[76] The Norwegian example was so influential that in 1969 Swedish labour market parties agreed on voluntary experiments of self-managing groups and other new forms of cooperation.[77]

Finnish employers were also keener to introduce influence in everyday work through self-managed workgroups and other new forms of work, and less keen to establish new representative bodies.[78] Like its Swedish counterpart, the STK encouraged its member companies to initiate their own experiments of enterprise democracy, and in 1971 there were almost 500 experiments underway. In this way the employer side's definitions and practices were implemented before any official enactments. Voluntary experiments increased the consultation and information rights of the employees, and existing production committees were often turned into 'cooperation committees' with slightly extended mandates. Agreements between central labor market organizations also increased cooperation in rationalization and training issues in the early 1970s.[79] This may have been largely a strategy for rebutting the most radical demands on the employee side and the left, but it was also based on proactive efforts to find more efficient organizational practices.

In Finland, the employee side focused more on representative practices although it did not turn down shop floor influence, either. SAK's 1969 report on enterprise democracy took the latter into account by suggesting that employee influence was to be increased first in matters close to them. According to the report, reforms were to be carried out gradually as the employee side often pragmatically emphasized.[80] The most important form of democracy was representative: developing enterprise democracy should start from companies that already had a production committee, but the compositions of the committees were to be changed as more beneficial to the employees. In the longer term, employees should gain representation in corporate governance. SAK wished for an equal representation with the employers, although in the early phase also employee minority representation might have been acceptable.[81]

Even though the employee side in principle supported employee representation in management, it also expressed reservations toward these kinds of organizational reforms. Trade union confederations emphasized that the roles of collective bargaining and the shop steward system were to be secured. Enterprise democracy was to complement these existing practices by bringing new issues to the sphere of mandatory negotiation. In other words, enterprise democracy did not mean moving matters from centralized or union-level bargaining to the workplace level. In spring 1971, SAK chair Niilo Hämäläinen formulated this principle as follows: "Enterprise democracy does not aim at wrecking collective bargaining but to complement it by guaranteeing employees possibilities of influence in company-specific matters that are not included in the scope of collective agreements and which are rigid and slow to be influenced through centralized and sectoral agreements."[82] This also explains SAK's emphasis on representation: The trade union movement was considered better aware of the interests of the employees than single employees. Therefore, trade union representatives were the ones who should primarily participate also in new enterprise democracy practices.[83]

Like SAK in Finland, LO supported both direct and representative forms of enterprise democracy. This was implied in the common demand for "influence on all levels." Sometimes LO representatives criticized the employer side for putting the two models against each other.[84] For LO, however, the coordination between the local and national level had traditionally appeared problematic. If local works councils had significant power to make decisions, it might clash with the general goals of the trade union movement, such as solidaristic wage policy and macroeconomic stability. LO was also suspicious of employee representation in corporate governance, which might create a 'double loyalty' for employees between the interests of their company and the wage-earner collective.[85] This had been a main reason for their traditional reservations toward democracy at the workplace level. LO's rhetoric differed slightly from SAK's in putting stronger emphasis on issues close to everyday work rather than representation and influence on management. LO's magazine *Fackföreningsrörelsen* stated in 1968 that the development of enterprise democracy was to take place primarily on the shop floor, as the role of representative works councils had never been considered as anything more than contact and consultation.[86] In LO's 1971 report, direct influence was not the only solution but gained much attention. Like the employer side, LO was positive toward "partly self-managed" groups, where employees could take on tasks of managing and organizing their own work.[87] LO had a similar gradualist model as SAK, starting from influence on everyday work, increasing communication and negotiation in the works councils, and then moving on to stronger codetermination. As LO official Inge Janérus argued, the development of democracy had to begin in the concrete work situation and grow upward from there.[88]

Discussion on direct and representative forms of enterprise democracy was closely connected to the question of issues handled within enterprise democracy. In both Finland and Sweden, the employer side was clear on its aim to restrict these issues to job design, organization and other matters close to everyday work. This has been a common employer stance in past debates of working life democratization.[89] In Finland, the STK stated that they would not negotiate on employee participation in top management or on profit sharing. Instead, they welcomed procedures that improved the possibility of employee participation in work safety and satisfaction issues.[90] In Sweden, the SAF determined that in addition to planning and organization of work in project groups, works councils could discuss issues like personnel policy, long-term planning, and rationalization. However, it was always stressed that the councils were bodies of consultation and information.[91] SAF spoke for experimentation in companies to find the most appropriate forms of cooperation, like the Norwegian model of 'self-managing groups.'[92] Experiments on them seemed to confirm the belief Eric Rhenman had already expressed. Shop floor influence was more efficient and created more satisfaction than representative models.[93] This meant giving employees more operational power but did not intervene with the strategic power of managers.

The employee side's goals were again more ambitious. SAK's report from 1969 stated that employee representatives should be granted power in social affairs, work planning, safety and HR. Longer-term goals included creating profit-sharing systems.[94] SAK's platform of 1971 presented even more far-reaching demands, such as the right to participate in the appointment of company management, in decisions on the development of companies as well as the equitable distribution of outcomes.[95] For LO, personnel policy, including recruitment, lay-offs and training, was the first area where codetermination was to be introduced. Employees were also to have a "true right of codetermination" on the organization and supervision of work. In addition, the work environment and rationalization were important areas where employees were already gaining influence via separate agreements.[96] According to the rationalization agreement between SAF and LO in 1972, employee influence was to be increased by better information and negotiation through local trade unions, works councils and safety councils before deciding on rationalization measures. The use of project groups in planning and implementing rationalizations was encouraged.[97]

In Finnish committee reports, profit sharing and employee representation in corporate governance were eventually left outside the discussion. The committees proposed an organizational model for enterprise democracy with two representative bodies: personnel councils and cooperation committees. The cooperation committees would have consisted of both employer and employee representatives and would have made decisions unanimously or by vote, with a veto right reserved for the employer side. The personnel council would have had only wage-earner representatives, and its role would have been consultative. Employers were against this model and continued to emphasize direct influence in everyday work.[98]

In Sweden, there was no serious discussion on councils consisting exclusively of wage-earner representatives. The most significant representative sites would have been the board of directors and the works council, where employers were also represented.[99] Like SAK, LO emphasized the role of existing trade union organizations in developing enterprise democracy throughout the debate. The 1971 report suggested that board representatives would have been chosen by the trade union.[100] In this sense, the fear of double loyalty persisted, as independent employee representatives might more easily have sided with the employer. LO stressed that reforms were to be realized so that the trade union organizations could "maintain and strengthen their free and independent position."[101]

Perhaps the greatest institutional difference between Sweden and Finland was that in Sweden employee representation in corporate governance was established by legislation in 1972. Trade unions gained the right to appoint two representatives in the boards of directors of companies with 25 or more employees. Similar reforms were carried out in Denmark and Norway. Bernt Schiller and Birger Simonson have interpreted that LO shifted from its fear of double loyalty to advocating employee representation because the Liberals and the Center Party, as well as the white-collar confederation TCO, were in favor of it. The reform was also technically easy to carry through compared to codetermination. The Social Democratic government was ready to legislate on the issue when the labor market organizations did not reach agreement.[102] The attitude of SAF and its member companies was negative at first. SAF argued that proper results from the different company-level experiments should have been gathered before issuing new legislation.[103] In the end, however, employers did not find employee minority representation harmful to private companies.[104]

The Value of Enterprise Democracy: National Interest as a Limit to Democracy

Disagreement over the desirability of enterprise democracy and its relations to other values were central parts of the Finnish and Swedish debates.[105] In the following, I analyze what were the most potent concepts for legitimizing and criticizing enterprise democracy, and what kind of conceptual hierarchies can be discerned from employer and employee rhetoric. I also examine what kind of conceptions of working life and society different versions of enterprise democracy entailed. Especially the construction of 'political' and 'economic' spheres of knowledge and action was a key aspect of these conceptualizations.

The debate on enterprise democracy is an illustrative example of struggles over concepts and their valuation. It is worth noting that even the employer side did not usually portray enterprise democracy as undesirable, even though especially in Sweden they avoided using the term. Instead, the employee side's definitions were heavily criticized. Employer statements show that they believed some reforms to be necessary in working life. Developing new forms of participation and cooperation was not only a reaction to the demands for democratization, but it also stemmed from the internal need to make the organizations and practices of enterprises more efficient in the context of structural change and international competition. This is visible in the emphasis of enterprise-level experiments.[106]

Even though democracy, equality and work satisfaction were important values in political debate, employer representatives did not begin their argumentation from them, but from a fundamental economic belief: the necessity of economic efficiency in a competitive and increasingly internationalized market economy. Due to the centrality of this belief, a major tension was formed between the concepts of democracy and efficiency. This dichotomy has been one of the recurring problems of working life democratization.[107] However, we can paint a more nuanced picture of the conceptual struggle by including other values and their hierarchies in employer thought and rhetoric.

In his influential book, Eric Rhenman did not mention the extension of democracy as the goal of enterprise democracy. Instead, he specified two main objectives: (1) increasing productivity; (2) balancing different interests and decreasing conflict within the company. Rhenman's conclusion was that most models did not fulfill these aims, and therefore he proposed a new approach based on business economy.[108] SAF's Cooperation Report took efficiency as its starting point, but acknowledged that there were also relevant sociological and political viewpoints. However, the report argued that the demand for efficiency could not be overridden. It was "totally alien to reality" to question efficiency or productivity as dominant demands for enterprises. This concerned especially the prevailing situation of Swedish companies: "Their possibilities of survival in the long run are highly dependent on their capability to hold off international competition."[109] On the employer side, employee influence was not an end in and for itself, as it conflicted with the employer's freedom of action. Better goals were balance of interests and job satisfaction. However, the "all-encompassing demand for a company" was improving its productivity.[110] This constellation of values was also used in the Swedish works council agreement in 1966: The task of the councils was to promote productivity and work satisfaction.[111]

According to Albert O. Hirschman, one of the recurring strategies and tropes of reactionary rhetoric is to argue that a reform jeopardizes something valuable that already exists or is pursued in society.[112] In employer rhetoric, a 'jeopardy thesis' was a common way to question the desirability of enterprise democracy. At least when defined and implemented in a wrong way, enterprise democracy was claimed to jeopardize not only efficiency but even more important values. These included the growth of welfare, which was portrayed as a common interest for companies, their employees and the entire society. Enterprises were portrayed as guardians of the national interest rather than as organizations pursuing their particular interests. Instead of maximizing profits, their objective was to secure their own continuity and employment.[113] This belief was a cornerstone of employer rhetoric in both Sweden and Finland. It was often expressed in the debate on the social responsibility of companies, which was already being discussed in the 1960s.[114]

A logical derivative of this belief was that if efficiency was jeopardized, so too was the national interest. Päiviö Hetemäki, the CEO of Finnish STK, stressed that the welfare of the whole society was dependent on the efficient realization of corporate objectives. Therefore, it was crucial to find means of employee influence that would not disturb the development of welfare. Hetemäki argued that there was in fact very little room for choices in economic activity. Democratic decision-making thus inevitably jeopardized economic efficiency. "The national economy could not bear such a hindrance, which will be formed when corporate management is subjected to collective vote," Hetemäki stated.[115] This kind of argumentation was not a novelty in Finland. Historically, it has been common to legitimize different objectives and actions, such as rationalization of production by appealing to national interests and giving them a very economic nature.[116] Some scholars have argued that the role of economic necessities as policy legitimation and as a means to depoliticize certain issues has been a fundamental characteristic of Finnish political culture, even more central than in other Nordic countries.[117]

In the rhetoric of Finnish employers, national interest, which often figured in the more tangible form of increasing welfare, was a more common legitimation concept than private ownership or economic freedom. Even though enterprise democracy challenged traditional rights based on private ownership, it was defended only occasionally.[118] It seems that the right of ownership was a rarely used legitimation strategy also in the Swedish debate. It is possible, however, that appealing to ownership was not considered necessary, as enterprise democracy challenged only part of the power based on ownership, not private ownership as a principle. In this way, enterprise democracy was a 'functional socialist' reform proposal.

Despite their critical tone, employers valued enterprise democracy positively if it was adapted to the necessities of economic efficiency and competitiveness. This meant defining enterprise democracy as cooperation and consultation. Employers argued that efficiency was best guaranteed by competent management and a certain organizational hierarchy, complemented with flexible practices of cooperation. Taking the employees' interests into account and improving their work satisfaction were considered productivity factors, especially in new management theories. Eric Rhenman even suggested a new definition of efficiency that would include work satisfaction. However, satisfaction increases were not desirable if they resulted in decreasing profitability.[119] By contrast, enterprise democracy in the sense of employee participation in final decision-making—especially via representative models—was portrayed as an inflexible and bureaucratic practice that threatened crucial components of national interest such as competitiveness and welfare.

The Distinction Between Political and Economic Issues

One of the key distinctions in employer rhetoric was the fundamental difference of political and economic issues and practices. The employers agreed that enterprises and workplaces should be democratized, but not in a way analogous to political democracy. They argued that political goals were always a matter of debate, but companies could not be organized on the basis of political ideologies. They had one primary goal, survival in competition by operating efficiently.[120] This was strictly a matter of economic facts, not political choices. Facts and values, knowledge and ideology, were to be separated. SAF director Karl-Olof Faxén expressed this belief, which determined the appropriate limits of enterprise democracy, as follows:

> It is thus the surrounding world that sets the demand to constantly strive for increased profitability. An ideologically grounded development towards enterprise democracy does not interest customers. It cannot last in the long run if it does not fulfill other demands at the same time.[121]

Employer representatives often continued this line of thought by arguing that employees—or politicians—did not have the necessary knowledge on economic affairs. Therefore, decisions had to be left to managers and other experts. SAF newspaper *Arbetsgivaren* made this argument, albeit with a reservation, in its editorial: "A company cannot be managed through a collective vote—some must have the right to make decisions. This is still the task of experts, which of course need to have power, but should also have a small possibility to misuse this power."[122] Finnish STK official Heikki Pärnänen argued in a similar vein that the objective of economic efficiency and the means to achieve it were "not matters of vote but matters of expertise."[123] The possibility of participation at work was essentially dependent on expertise, and the operations had to be, to some extent, based on hierarchy in order to secure efficiency.[124] Hierarchy was therefore legitimized by appealing to a common interest and to differences in competence, which has historically been a common strategy for many critics of democracy.[125] Another way to argue for the apolitical nature of corporate activity and cooperation was insisting that they were strictly matters between the labor market parties not to be 'politicized' by state intervention, and certainly not by issuing legislation.[126]

Sometimes, employer representatives explicitly claimed that in overlooking economic facts, advocates of employee decision-making prioritized their group interests over a broader, even national interest. STK's Heikki Pärnänen stated: "A company, while working as an instrument in society's economic activity, may come into conflict with individual members or a group of their personnel, the objective of whom is especially to improve their own security and living standards."[127] Eric Rhenman's stakeholder model had influenced Pärnänen, who also saw managers as the best people to mediate these conflicting interests. It is worth noting that the employers refrained from appealing to their group interests in public, which gave their arguments and expert position more credibility. Group interests may very well have been a significant motive for them, but this cannot be verified by rhetorical analysis. Employee representatives, in turn, often appealed to the security, autonomy and rights of the workers rather than to common interests. This may have made it easier to accuse them of advocating particular interests.

To strengthen their argument that ultimately rested on the concept of national interest, employers argued that the conflict between labor and capital was mostly illusory. Instead, the common interest of both parties and the foundation of enterprise democracy were found in the continuity and success of the enterprise. Cooperation between employers and employees would help in perceiving this 'true' state of affairs.[128] Stig H. Hästö, Finnish CEO and later chair of STK, argued that cooperation in the sense of consultation and communication helped perceive the interest of the company. This required setting aside all sources of conflict.

> While acting in this spirit, we will understand things better on every level, we will realize the inevitability of measures and changes. ... Taking a step of this nature would require a harmonious, balanced view of society, not by any means a quarrelsome society.[129]

This kind of functional view of working life, which portrays it as completely void of harmful or asymmetric power relations and struggles, has been common to employers and business representatives in Finland and elsewhere.[130] It also goes back to the different layers of meaning of the concepts cooperation and enterprise democracy. Cooperation presupposes only one common interest—that of the company's—which is objective and can be achieved with sufficient knowledge. Hierarchical decision-making is therefore conceived as natural and necessary, not coercive or authoritarian. The concept of cooperation seems to have been an attempt to conceptually isolate the employee side's perspective, which emphasized the conflict and asymmetric power relation between capital and labor, from the economic life. Critical scholars have pointed out that also human relations theories of management mostly assumed the inherent functionality and common interests of work organizations instead of considering their potential structural conflicts. New models of employee participation appropriated some demands for autonomy and work satisfaction but did not redistribute strategic power to the employees or give them the power to control and supervise their managers, which had been core features of the leftist visions of working life democratization.[131]

The Primacy of Efficiency Over Democracy and Security

The employee side did not have strong means to question the primacy of national economic interest, which was anchored in concepts like efficiency and competitiveness. Trade union representatives in both Finland and Sweden acknowledged the necessity of economic efficiency in creating growth and welfare.[132] There was, however, some effort to promote rivaling conceptions of national interest based on immaterial values such as democracy, equality and security. Many employee representatives put forward security as the ultimate objective of enterprise democracy. This is natural, as the mission of the trade union movement has always been guarding the interests of wage-earners, especially upholding security of employment and subsistence.[133] The employer objective of making their business more effective and the employee objective of securing their livelihood were not believed to be always compatible. The power of employers was a major source of uncertainty, which could be remedied with enterprise democracy. Therefore, traditional objectives of the trade union movement, such as full employment, strengthening protection against dismissal and improving the organization rights of employees were emphasized in enterprise democracy rhetoric since the beginning.[134]

LO's 1971 report found increasing material security not only an objective but a crucial precondition for democratic participation.[135] Lack of security due to unsafe work environments, rationalization and piecework was taken up as a justification for developing enterprise democracy. The LO economist Anna Hedborg connected security especially to employment: "Enterprise democracy, influence on the terms of one's own work, has naturally an intrinsic value, but it is also significant in spreading employment opportunities to ever more people. The right to work includes not only the right to get a job, but also to keep it."[136] With this kind of emphasis, the central subject whose rights and autonomy were to be improved became the working class, whereas in the justifications emphasizing freedom and equality the central subject was the individual citizen. The employee side also argued that, unlike the employers often claimed, employees were competent enough for democratic participation, and democratic practices were in fact the only means to build the competence and autonomy needed in a democratic society.[137]

The rhetorical strategy of placing democracy highest in the conceptual hierarchy as an intrinsic value was mostly limited to the New Left and more radical wings of the labor movement. In their pamphlet, Göran Therborn et al. argued that Eric Rhenman's goal for enterprise democracy—balance of interests—described the prevailing situation where employees were content with their role in the production process and legitimized those power relations. But instead of guarding the prevailing norms, enterprise democracy was to mean the creation of new, democratic norms.[138]

> For socialists, democracy is not primarily a means—a fluent way to choose government every fourth year—but an end, a value in itself. And we demand enterprise democracy not least because we believe that power within enterprises and over their vast resources should be based on democratic institutions, not on money (control of capital). Simply and briefly put, the socialist demand for enterprise democracy can be said to aim at abolishing the alienation of wage-earners in their work.[139]

Finnish trade union representatives could similarly claim that the common interest was unreachable in the prevailing reality of conflicting class interests and asymmetric economic power relations.[140] According to a common belief of the employee side, especially of communists, the models of enterprise democracy advocated by the employer side would have been mere instruments of manipulation, which were used to conceal true power relations. Consultation and cooperation created a false picture of influence and autonomy, even though decisions had already been made elsewhere. Employees could be given actual power to make decisions only on insignificant matters. SAK lawyer, Communist Olavi Sulkunen emphasized the severity of conflict and criticized its disregarding in the enterprise democracy debate: “From the viewpoint of the labor movement and the trade union movement, realizing enterprise democracy is not a separate phenomenon but a part of the democratization of the entire society.”[141]

Work satisfaction was an additional value and objective that legitimized enterprise democracy and employee influence. Its counter-concept was alienation caused by repetitive industrial work, emphasized especially in the rhetoric of the New Left and the sociological literature.[142] However, both ‘true democracy’ and ‘humanization of work’ could be portrayed as increasing satisfaction and preventing alienation. In LO’s magazine it was pointed out that research and experiments had spurred new organizational practices, such as enrichment of work, job rotation and self-managed work groups. They gave employees more variation and autonomy, and enabled them to develop their skills and see a broader meaning for their work.[143] Work satisfaction was a more central theme in the Swedish debate than in Finland, perhaps because in Sweden the security of employees and the rights of trade unions were already on a higher level. As the LO Chair Arne Geijer wrote in 1971, improved social security and material standards had prepared the ground for new demands.[144]

What united the debates of the two countries, however, was the importance of economic efficiency and growth as objectives and legitimation concepts. The employee side did not have strong means to challenge the conception of economic activity as fulfilling the national interest, which was anchored in the concept economic efficiency. Especially trade union leadership acknowledged the necessity of economic efficiency in creating growth and welfare. SAK chair Niilo Hämäläinen, summarized the growth-oriented reality of the 1960s and 1970s: “The trade union movement has had to adapt to [economic] competition, because its alternative is unemployment and lowering standard of living.”[145] The employees mostly adopted the strategy of arguing that their view on enterprise democracy would promote economic efficiency in a capitalist economy.[146] Another statement from SAK chair Hämäläinen illustrates this tendency:

> Developing enterprise democracy must not jeopardize the preconditions for efficient and flexible economic activity. My understanding is that by developing the matter rationally we can improve the operational preconditions of companies while securing the justified claims and interests of the employees.[147]

One potential strategy was not to deny the primacy of efficiency but argue that the capitalist mode of production was, in fact, less efficient than its socialist alternatives.[148] Also these beliefs portrayed economic life as a realm of factual knowledge, where it was possible to find the most efficient solutions with close scientific scrutiny. However, when trade union representatives argued that enterprise democracy would increase economic efficiency, it was not always clear whether they were advocating altered power structures or consultation and cooperation. In the end, many adopted the strategy of arguing that enterprise democracy would promote economic efficiency in a capitalist society instead of prioritizing democracy or security over efficiency in their hierarchy of values.[149] The Swedish Social Democratic economist and labor market researcher Olle Hammarström wrote that enterprise democracy could be a solution to the dynamism capitalism had partially lost due to regulation. He argued that enterprise democracy might help to utilize unused resources as employees took more responsibility for the enterprise's future and development.[150]

When rhetorically combining democracy and efficiency, the employee side did not question the value hierarchies of the employers. This had also been a common strategy in other debates on labor market policy.[151] Therefore, the agenda of the debate was defined, either intentionally or inadvertently, as reconciling democracy with efficiency, not the other way around. This hierarchy was codified in the assignment of the first Finnish state committee investigating enterprise democracy. The committee had to "draw up suggestions which could be used to develop enterprise and workplace democracy without efficiency losses."[152] It stated in its final report that it was useful to examine if democracy could in some cases be prioritized over efficiency, but also confirmed the status of efficiency as an overarching value: "Regardless of their closer definition, within the market economy the goals of an enterprise must be adapted to the frame of profitable operations and retaining competitiveness."[153]

However, the downsides of efficiency and growth became widely acknowledged in the 1960s and 1970s. These included not only decreasing work satisfaction but also environmental degradation. Besides material welfare, mental welfare was also taken as an objective, although it was usually left in the shadow of the necessity for efficiency. The prevalence of the critique of economic growth may explain why efficiency, or even rising living standards, were not clear-cut objectives in the rhetoric on the employer side, either. The Finnish business magazine *Yritystalous* stated in 1970 that the "immaterial aspect of welfare" could no longer be ignored in the debate on economic growth, but it might rather be a precondition to growth in the long term.[154] In this kind of rhetoric the hierarchy of values seems to twist into a circle, forming yet another vision of a 'virtuous circle' common in welfare state rhetoric. The mutually reinforcing nature of efficiency and welfare gained familiar features of necessity.[155] In his reply to trade union journalist Kimmo Kevätsalo, STK's Heikki Pärnänen expressed a belief in the indispensable nature of efficiency as a step to greater good:

> I fully agree with Kevätsalo on the fact that efficiency is not a meaningful objective for people in itself (...) personally, I enjoy summer holidays, free Saturdays, good food etc. much more than a stressful day of efficiency. Unfortunately, however, no one has yet invented a magic lantern to fulfill my wishes better than efficiency.[156]

Enterprise Democracy Turns into Cooperation and Codetermination

In both Sweden and Finland, the debate on enterprise democracy led to new legislation, albeit along different paths. In Sweden, the process began later, but there was the political will to realize the Labor Law Committee's law proposal even if labor market parties disagreed. The Codetermination Act of 1976 (*medbestämmandelagen*, "MBL") became part of the 'labor law offensive' in Sweden, which included new legislation on shop stewards, the work environment, and employment protection. SAP and LO were willing to improve the conditions of Swedish employees even at the expense of harmonious labor market relations. In Finland, by contrast, the governments did not want to push legislation without an agreement between labor market parties. Relations were already conflictual enough with extensive local strikes and difficult incomes policy solutions.

In Sweden, the employee side wanted to push through radical reforms, while employer representatives wanted to stay on a cooperative line. LO and the white-collar confederation TCO demanded decision-making power and veto rights for employees on many questions, especially the work environment. They wanted interpretation privilege of laws and agreements for the employee side and the possibility to demand agreements with the management even on strategic issues. Employer representatives could not accept the demands, which made it impossible for the committee to reach a unanimous result. SAF appealed to the government that this far-reaching reform would render the management of enterprises extremely difficult. The committee's final report, however, incorporated most of the employee side's demands but proposed they had the right to veto only on the use of external workforce.[157]

The MBL became a framework law that was to be supplemented through labor market agreements. It obliged employers to negotiate on significant changes affecting the employees. Employees gained the right to interpret laws and agreements in the case of a disagreement, and a right to make agreements on issues concerning the management of companies. It became possible to abolish works councils and arrange cooperation between shop stewards and managers.[158] Despite these reforms, the law did not really change power relations but extended the cooperation practice that works councils already represented.

In the negotiations on the MBL's implementation, the LO continued to call for more influence, especially on changes in the work organization or introduction of new technology.[159] However, the Social Democrats' loss in the 1976 parliamentary election and the formation of Sweden's first bourgeois government in 44 years took away the 'legislation threat' from the employee side's weaponry. Sweden was also suffering from economic stagnation after the oil crisis, which turned attention away from working life issues. At this point, the initiative in the codetermination question moved to the employer side.[160] The negotiations were difficult, and it took until 1982 to reach a solution, named the "Development agreement" (*utvecklingsavtal*).[161] The Agreement marked a retreat from most of LO's objectives. It emphasized competitiveness and cooperation, did not give codetermination an intrinsic value, and focused on technical development and rationalization rather than personnel issues. The Agreement did not give the employee side determination or veto rights in any issues but confirmed the employers' obligation to share information and negotiate with employees.[162]

According to Bernt Schiller, the Development Agreement continued the same tradition of labor market cooperation as the 1946 agreement on works councils. Fundamental power relations did not change, but the agreement gave employees some new rights and did not exclusively follow employer lines.[163] Jonas Pontusson has emphasized more the power of employers. Despite growing influence on work design and organization in some companies, employees continued to have little power in strategic decisions, such as the internationalization of Swedish firms. The employer side was unwilling to negotiate on major issues if it was not forced to. In other words, the boundaries of class compromise determined the room to maneuver in enterprise democracy.[164] This was also the perception of many contemporaries, and critique on the lack of 'true' codetermination continued after the Development Agreement's signing.[165]

In Finland, an agreement on enterprise democracy became possible when the SAK left aside demands for far-reaching employee decision-making. This was due to slow progress, employer resistance and the small role reserved for employee representation. Trade unions began to fear that representative bodies could be used to circumvent existing trade union institutions, such as shop stewards and safety delegates, which had strengthened their role during the 1970s.[166] Pauli Kettunen has pointed out that the Finnish aim toward enterprise democracy ran dry after the new institutions of work safety and local negotiation had been created in the 1970s.[167] The employer and employee confederations came to an agreement on the outlines of the enterprise democracy legislation in autumn 1977. Instead of new representative bodies, enterprise democracy was to be realized through the existing workplace negotiation system, in which shop stewards played a key role. This strengthened the collective organization of the trade union movement by giving it new workplace-level tasks in HR and social matters. The name of the practice was changed to the employer-favored term 'cooperation.'[168]

The agreement on enterprise democracy was reached at the same time as the Social Democrats and Finnish business had reached a consensus on a new, more market-oriented economic policy to end economic stagnation. It was coded in the program of the new SDP-led government in spring 1977 and symbolized especially by the major conference held at Hotel Korpilampi in September the same year.[169] Enterprise democracy was not explicitly linked to the new economic policy, which is examined more closely in Chap. 5, but the cooperative atmosphere may have encouraged the labor market parties to seek solutions to this question.

Inspiration from Sweden is evident in the Finnish legislation.[170] Both laws were based on fitting enterprise democracy to the existing organizations rather than creating new systems of representation. The explicit objectives of the Finnish 'Act on Cooperation within Undertakings' from 1978 were cooperation and efficiency.[171] The law required negotiations on issues that significantly affected the position of employees, such as lay-offs and changes in work methods. They were to take place between the employer and individual workers or trade union representatives. In cases of disagreement the employer retained the right to make the final decision. The only exceptions were certain social issues, such as employee meal and housing benefits.[172] Like in Sweden, the Finnish law was not named the Enterprise Democracy Act, but it was based on the employer-favored concept of cooperation, which implied a less conflictual conception of working life.

Extending the practice of negotiation between trade union and employer representatives at the workplace level thus became the primary model of enterprise democracy in both countries. Finnish employees used the Swedish MBL as a model to justify the organizational solution. In contrast, Swedish labor market parties did not take very much inspiration from Finland during the debate, but they looked more closely at the development in Denmark, Norway and West Germany. Finnish employers welcomed the reform that was close to their objectives and did not require organizational changes. It improved cooperation but did not change the power relations in companies. Trade unions and Social Democrats were not entirely happy but considered the law a first step toward enterprise democracy. It realized the preconditions of enterprise democracy by strengthening the position of local trade unions, shop stewards, and the significance of collective bargaining.[173]

When the implementation of the Cooperation Act began in Finland, many employees found that their influence had not notably increased and some of them even preferred the old production committees with their regular meetings. Employees felt that the legislation was not implemented correctly: Many companies did not negotiate with their employees and shop stewards as the legislation required, or if they did, the decisions had already been made before the negotiations. In the rhetoric of the left-wing parties and trade union movement, all this meant that 'true' enterprise democracy had not yet been realized.[174] SDP's and SAK's new goal was developing enterprise democracy and the Cooperation Act by increasing the rights and influence of the employee side. A key objective was giving the interpretation privilege of laws and agreements to the employees like the Swedish MBL had done. The term enterprise democracy remained widely in use, even though the employer-favored term 'cooperation' had been accepted as a general title for legislation and the practice it established.[175] However, the trade union movement's explicit criteria for enterprise democracy were gradually moving from employee decision-making and power to vaguer notions such as increased influence.

Swedish and Finnish employers did not share the trade union view that the implementation of cooperation and codetermination had been disappointing. Göran Skogh stated in his report for SAF's 1980 congress that the MBL had not really changed anything but confirmed existing practices. Employers had negotiated with their employees before, but now they had also formal obligations to do so.[176] SAF's outlook became positive, especially after the Development Agreement had been signed in 1982. The SAF director Lars-Gunnar Albåge stated that it could form the basis for a new "spirit of Saltsjöbaden." The agreement entailed a broad consensus on efficiency and competitiveness and stressed the influence of individual employees while avoiding confrontation and bureaucratization.[177] Finnish employers also found The Cooperation Act successful and argued its criticism was unjustified.[178]

The definitions of enterprise democracy by Finnish and Swedish employer organizations drew on similar conceptions of democracy and had many shared features. Employers advocated consultation and communication with employees, focusing on issues close to individual employees and the work process. To turn down the employee side's demands for stronger codetermination, the employers argued that representative democracy and employee control over corporate management would jeopardize the efficient operations of enterprises. During the debate, employers in both countries favored the term cooperation instead of enterprise democracy and codetermination, but in Sweden the reluctance to use the latter terms was higher. The tendency to replace the word 'democracy' with 'cooperation' may have been a way to downplay questions of power relations central to the concept of democracy and promote a harmonious and apolitical image of working life, where the success of companies was based on objective knowledge and was ultimately a common interest.

The employee side and the Social Democrats in both Finland and Sweden saw the legislation of the 1970s as a first step toward enterprise democracy. However, with the benefit of hindsight it can be argued that the Finnish Cooperation Act and the Swedish MBL and Development Agreement were instead first steps toward the hegemony of employer thought. In the 1980s, the rhetoric and practice of working life reforms continued to emphasize cooperation and employee participation, but the idea of redistributing power and the term 'enterprise democracy' was marginalized. Even the Swedish concept of codetermination, implying an equal relationship between employees and employers, has lost much of its meaning. In Finland, the practice of 'cooperative negotiations,' became notorious because it was primarily connected to collective lay-offs. It thus became a symbol of the era of economic recession and mass unemployment. These developments are examined more closely in Chaps. 5 and 6.

Debates on enterprise democracy exemplify the gradual consolidation of ideas that view working life as an essentially economic sphere of activity, which should be kept apart from the 'political.' In areas defined as 'economic,' power and decision-making are not based on democratic rights but on objective knowledge, expertise and merit. Social relations are conceptualized as functional and as aiming for the common good, not as asymmetric power relations and conflicts of interest. Beliefs in the latter are dismissed as false consciousness, which only obscures economic facts. Within this kind of ideational constellation, employees can participate in decisions on issues close to their everyday work, but strategic decision-making is reserved for managers who possess the required competence. Economic efficiency and growth are treated as inescapable components of the national interest, which other values need to serve.

National economic interest was in effect an overriding cultural norm that conditioned the whole debate. This is what previous research on Finnish political culture has suggested, and it also seems to apply to Sweden to a major extent, even though there was more space for legitimations based on democracy and equality. The necessity of efficiency was based on convincing evidence and shared beliefs, which gave it a lawlike quality. Representatives of the trade union movement sought to justify enterprise democracy by appealing to citizens' and workers' right to democratic self-determination and security, but it was hard to prioritize these values over efficiency. Most employees adopted the strategy of arguing that their version of enterprise democracy would promote economic efficiency in a capitalist society. To legitimize their objectives, they had to prove that increasing democracy would not undermine the self-evident foundation of welfare and the common good. In the end, they rarely ventured beyond employer ideas of consultative cooperation and participation in everyday work. This may have also been a strategy of guarding the centralized power of trade unions and the state, which were perceived as necessary for considering economic interests and equality on the national scale. This tension sometimes hindered the will to pursue strong local employee influence.

Notes

1. Some sections of this chapter are reproduced, with the publisher's kind permission, from Ilkka Kärrylä, "National Interest as a Limit to Democracy: The Rhetoric of Finnish and Swedish Employers in the Debates on 'Enterprise Democracy' during the 1960s and 1970s," in *Nationalism and Democracy in the Welfare State*, eds. Pauli Kettunen, Saara Pellander and Miika Tervonen (Cheltenham: Edward Elgar, 2022) (forthcoming). On Finnish employer rhetoric see also Ilkka Kärrylä, "Kansallinen etu demokratian rajoituksena: Suomalaisten työnantajien retoriikka 1960- ja 1970-lukujen yritysdemokratiakeskustelussa," *Historiallinen aikakauskirja* 114, 4 (2016): 445–457.
2. Tapio Bergholm, *Sopimusyhteiskunnan synty II: Hajaannuksesta tulopolitiikkaan. SAK 1956–1969* (Helsinki: Otava, 2007), 12–14.
3. Tapio Bergholm, *Laatua ja vapaa-aikaa. Tulopolitiikan aika II. Suomen ammattiliittojen keskusjärjestö vuodesta 1977* (Helsinki: Suomalaisen kirjallisuuden seura, 2018); Markku Mansner, *Suomalaista yhteiskuntaa rakentamassa: Suomen Työnantajain Keskusliitto 1956–1982* (Helsinki: Teollisuuden kustannus, 1990); Bernt Schiller, *"Det förödande 70-talet": SAF och medbestämmandet 1965–1982* (Stockholm: Arbetsmiljöfonden, 1988); Birger Simonson, *Arbetarmakt och näringspolitik: LO och inflytandefrågorna 1961–1982* (Stockholm: Arbetsmiljöfonden, 1988); Axel Hadenius, *Medbestämmandereformen* (Stockholm: Almqvist & Wiksell, 1983).
4. Christer Lundh, *Den svenska debatten om industriell demokrati 1919–1924: 1. Debatten i Sverige* (Lund: Studentlitteratur, 1987), 26; Schiller, *"Det förödande 70-talet"*, 17. On Danish debates and reforms see Niels Dalgaard, *Ved demokratiets grænse: Demokratisering af arbejdslivet i Danmark 1919–1994* (Copenhagen: Selskabet til Forskning i Arbejderbevægelsens Historie, 1995).
5. Committee report 1970: A3 *Yritysdemokratiakomitean mietintö*. Helsinki (1970), 8; SAK, *SAK:n yritysdemokratiatyöryhmän mietintö* (1969), 8.
6. For example, John Logue, "Democratic Theory and Atheoretical Democracy: Reflections on Building Democratic Enterprises in the American Economy," in *Managing Modern Capitalism: Industrial Renewal and Workplace Democracy in the United States and Western Europe*, eds. M. Donald Hancock, John Logue and Bernt Schiller (New York: Praeger, 1991), 313–336.
7. For example, *Dagens Nyheter* 9 January 1946, 34; *Aftonbladet* 17 January 1946, 4; *Aftonbladet* 9 April 1946, 4.
8. Finnish parliamentary proceedings 1960–1969, indexes.
9. Committee report 1970: A3, 9.

10. Wolfgang Streeck, "Works Councils in Western Europe: From Consultation to Participation," in *Works Councils: Consultation, Representation, and Cooperation in Industrial Relations*, eds. Joel Rogers and Wolfgang Streeck (Chicago and London: University of Chicago Press, 1995), 313–316; Herman Knudsen, *Employee Participation in Europe* (London: Sage, 1995), 31–50.
11. Walther Müller-Jentsch, "Formation, Development and Current State of Industrial Democracy in Germany," *Transfer: European Review of Labour and Research* 22, 1 (2016): 49–54; Knudsen, *Employee Participation in Europe*, 31–50; Streeck, "Works Councils in Western Europe", 313–316.
12. SAP, LO, SSKF and SSU, *Arbetarrörelsens efterkrigsprogram* (1944), 10.
13. Simonson, *Arbetarmakt och näringspolitik*, 29–31.
14. Tapio Bergholm, *Sopimusyhteiskunnan synty I: Työehtosopimusten läpimurrosta yleislakkoon. Suomen Ammattiyhdistysten Keskusliitto 1944–1956* (Helsinki: Otava, 2005), 77–82; Ilkka Turunen, "Arbete, produktion och demokrati: De finländska produktionskommittéernas historia," in *Industriell demokrati i norden*, ed. Daniel Fleming (Lund: Arkiv, 1990), 197–217; Markku Mansner, *Suomalaista yhteiskuntaa rakentamassa: Suomen Työnantajain Keskusliitto 1940–1956* (Helsinki: Teollisuuden kustannus, 1984), 250–267.
15. Streeck, "Works Councils in Western Europe," 317–318.
16. Donald Sassoon, *One Hundred Years of Socialism: The West European Left in the Twentieth Century* (London: Fontana Press, 1996), 150–151, 190–199.
17. Wolfgang Streeck, *Buying Time: The Delayed Crisis of Democratic Capitalism* (London and New York: Verso, 2014), 12–18; Streeck, "Works Councils in Western Europe," 321–322; Luc Boltanski and Ève Chiapello, *The New Spirit of Capitalism* (London and New York: Verso, 2005), 169–172.
18. LO, *Fackföreningsrörelsen och företagsdemokratin* (1961); Bo Stråth, *Mellan två fonder: LO och den svenska modellen* (Stockholm: Atlas, 1998), 79–81; Simonson, *Arbetarmakt och näringspolitik*, 34–38.
19. Eric Rhenman, *Företagsdemokrati och företagsorganization* (Stockholm: P. A. Norstedt & Söners Förlag, 1964); SAF, *Samarbetet i framtidens företag* (1965).
20. Jonas Pontusson, *The Limits of Social Democracy: Investment Politics in Sweden* (Ithaca: Cornell University Press, 1992), 161–167; Stråth, *Mellan två fonder*, 81–91, 120–122.
21. Mansner, *Suomen Työnantajain Keskusliitto 1956–1982*, 431.
22. Bergholm, *Laatua ja vapaa-aikaa*, 36–44; Mansner, *Suomen Työnantajain Keskusliitto 1956–1982*, 431–443.

23. Ingrid Gilcher-Holtey, "Political Participation and Democratization in the 1960s: The Concept of Participatory Democracy and its Repercussions," in *Democracy in Modern Europe: A Conceptual History*, eds. Jussi Kurunmäki, Jeppe Nevers and Henk te Velde (New York: Berghahn, 2018); Janne Holmén, "Den demokratiska skolan: Om likvärdighet och delaktighet 1960–2020," in *Demokratins drivkrafter: Kontext och särdrag i Finlands och Sveriges demokratier 1890–2020*, eds. Henrik Meinander, Petri Karonen and Kjell Östberg (Helsinki: Svenska litteratursällskapet i Finland, 2018), 264–266.
24. Boltanski and Chiapello, *The New Spirit of Capitalism*, 62–67, 169–172; Paavo Kärenlampi, *Taistelu kouludemokratiasta: Kouludemokratian aalto Suomessa* (Helsinki: Suomen Historiallinen Seura, 1999), 9–15, 238–239; Raija Julkunen, *Työprosessi ja pitkät aallot* (Tampere: Vastapaino, 1987), 37–42.
25. Ralf Dahrendorf, *Class and Class Conflict in Industrial Society* (London: Routledge & Kegan, 1959).
26. Antti Eskola, "Sosiologian uudistuminen 1950-luvulla," in *Suomalaisen sosiologian historia*, eds. Risto Alapuro, Matti Alestalo and Elina Haavio-Mannila (Helsinki: WSOY, 1992), 284–285; Edmund Dahlström, *Klasser och samhällen: Teorier om social skiktning och social integration* (Stockholm: Prisma, 1971).
27. *Tehostaja* 8/1968, 45.
28. Kari Lilja, "Henkilöstöhallinnon ammattikäytännön kehityspiirteitä Suomessa," *Hallinnon tutkimus* 16, 3 (1987): 185–194.
29. Hannele Seeck, *Johtamisopit Suomessa* (Helsinki: Gaudeamus, 2008), 103–105, 151–153; Anna Kuokkanen, *Johtamisen ihmissuhdekoulukunta Suomessa: Työntekijäkeskeiset johtamisopit suomalaisen työelämän muutoksessa* (Helsinki: Työterveyslaitos, 2015), 13–16.
30. For example, *Yritystalous* 13/1969, 36; *Yritystalous* 13/1970, 29.
31. Bergholm, *Laatua ja vapaa-aikaa*, 36–44; Kärenlampi, *Taistelu kouludemokratiasta*, 50–51.
32. Lars Ekdahl, "Svensk arbetarrörelse på den tredje vägen? Socialdemokratiska vägval under det "korta 1900-talet"," in *Kommunismen hot och löfte: Arbetarrörelsen i skuggan av Sovjetunionen 1917–1991*, eds. Håkan Blomqvist and Lars Ekdahl (Stockholm: Carlsson, 2002), 24–26.
33. Pauli Kettunen, *Historia petollisena liittolaisena: Näkökulmia työväen, työelämän ja hyvinvointivaltion historiaan* (Helsinki: Työväen historian ja perinteen tutkimuksen seura, 2015), 107–109.
34. Knudsen, *Employee Participation in Europe*, 8–10; Lundh, *Den svenska debatten om industriell demokrati 1*, 19–21.

35. LO, *Fackföreningsrörelsen och företagsdemokratin*, 110; SAF, *Samarbetet i framtidens företag*, 50; Niilo Koljonen, *Työntekijä ja yritysdemokratia* (Helsinki: Tammi, 1966), 164–225; Osmo A. Wiio, *Yritysdemokratia ja muuttuva organisaatio* (Helsinki: Weilin + Göös, 1970), 134–171.
36. Frank Georgi, *L'autogestion en chantier: Les gauches françaises et le « modèle » yougoslave (1948–1981)* (Nancy: Arbre bleu, 2018); Bengt Abrahamsson, *Exemplet Jugoslavien och den svenska debatten om löntagarstyre* (Stockholm: Almqvist & Wiksell, 1976).
37. Eric Rhenman, *Industrial Democracy and Industrial Management* (London: Tavistock, 1968). I have used the English translation here. Translation problems are highlighted by the fact that *företagsdemokrati* is translated as industrial democracy.
38. Schiller, *"Det förödande 70-talet"*, 21–23.
39. Wim Vandekerckhove, "What Managers Do: Comparing Rhenman and Freeman," *Philosophy of Management* 8, 3 (2009), 25–35.
40. Rhenman, *Industrial Democracy and Industrial Management*, 3–4.
41. SAF, *Samarbetet i framtidens företag*, 15–16.
42. Ibid.
43. For example, Axel Enström, "Hur beslut kommer till i ett storföretag," *Tiden* 10/1965, 603–608.
44. Osmo A. Wiio, "Yritysdemokratiasta," *Teollisuuslehti* 5/1967, 108.
45. The same typology of enterprise democracy was used in management guidebooks. See, for example, Arvo Saarikko and Eero Voutilainen, *Johtaminen, yhteistoiminta ja yritysdemokratia* (Helsinki: Weilin + Göös, 1977), 18–20.
46. See also SAF, *Samarbetet i framtidens företag*, 194.
47. Göran Therborn (ed.), *En ny vänster* (Stockholm: Rabén & Sjögren, 1966); Kjell Östberg, *1968 – när allting var i rörelse* (Stockholm: Prisma, 2002), 113–114.
48. Therborn, *En ny vänster*, 169–173.
49. Ibid., 174.
50. Ibid., 182.
51. Eric Pettersson, "Demokratin i företagen," *Fackförensingsrörelsen* 6/1964, 186–189.
52. Stråth, *Mellan två fonder*, 81–84; Simonson, *Arbetarmakt och näringspolitik*, 42–43. On LO's objectives see, for example, "LO vill stärka nämndernas ställning: 20-punktsprogram presenterat för SAF," *Fackföreningsrörelsen* 11/1965, 378–379, 410.
53. Inge Janérus, "Företagsnämndsarbetet – något bättre," *Fackföreningsrörelsen* 26/1968, 385–387.
54. SAP congress protocol 1967, 430–432.

55. Folkpartiet, *Företagsdemokrati i utveckling* (1967); Folkpartiet, *Demokrati och medinflytande* (1969), 46–51; Center Party of Sweden, *Handlingsprogram för en utbyggd företagsdemokrati* (1969); Hadenius, *Medbestämmandereformen*, 43–50.
56. Schiller, *"Det förödande 70-talet"*, 24–33; Simonson, *Arbetarmakt och näringspolitik*, 58–65, 87–89.
57. SAP congress protocol 1969, 43–46.
58. LO, *Demokrati i företagen* (1971), 24–30, 49–52.
59. Ibid., 58–61, 67–68, 71–75; Sten Edlund, "Både lagstiftning och avtal behövs för att lösa § 32-problemen," *Fackföreningsrörelsen* 13/1971, 408–411.
60. For example, LO, *Demokrati i företagen*, 14.
61. Ibid., 77–78, 97.
62. LO congress protocol 1971, 480–481.
63. SAK, *Yritysdemokratiatyöryhmän mietintö* (1969), 5–6, 9.
64. Ibid., 8.
65. Ibid., 7, 9.
66. Arvo Hautala, "Yritysdemokratiakomitean mietintö SAK:n näkökulmasta," in *Yritysdemokratia: Demokratian yritys*, ed. Matti Parjanen (Helsinki: Kirjayhtymä, 1970), 62–64.
67. Lundh, *Den svenska debatten om industriell demokrati 1*, 479–481.
68. Rhenman, *Industrial Democracy and Industrial Management*, 136.
69. Schiller, *"Det förödande 70-talet"*, 12–13,
70. "Ett ökat medinflytande i företagen måste baseras på fortsatt snabb utveckling av produktiviteten," *Arbetsgivaren* 10 September 1971, 7.
71. Eero Voutilainen, *Yritysdemokratia: Yhteistoimintaa yrityksessä* (Helsinki: Tietomies, 1974), 3.
72. Stråth, *Mellan två fonder*, 226–228.
73. Rhenman, *Industrial Democracy and Industrial Management*, 131; SAF, *Samarbetet i framtidens företag*, 175–177.
74. SAF, *Samarbetet i framtidens företag*, 180–184.
75. Julkunen, *Työprosessi ja pitkät aallot*, 58–60.
76. "Självstyrande grupper kan öka produktivitet och arbetstillfredsställelse," *Arbetsgivaren* 7 February 1969, 5; "Självstyrande grupper skapar ny mentalitet i företag," *Arbetsgivaren* 18 April 1969, 4.
77. The experiments were reported in employer newspapers in order to show that employee influence was increasing. See Gunnar Westermark, ""Målstyrning i samverkan": Plan för ökat medinflytande," *Arbetsgivaren* 17 October 1969, 3; "Projektgrupper ger medinflytande," *Arbetsgivaren* 14 April 1972; Schiller, *"Det förödande 70-talet"*, 49–51.
78. Heikki Pärnänen, "Yritysdemokratia yrityksen teorian valossa," *Ekonomia* 8/1968, 286; Wiio, *Yritysdemokratia ja muuttuva organisaatio*,

138–139, 188–189; Saarikko and Voutilainen, *Johtaminen, yhteistoiminta ja yritysdemokratia*, 7.
79. Mansner, *Suomen Työnantajain Keskusliitto 1956–1982*, 440–443.
80. SAK, *Yritysdemokratiatyöryhmän mietintö*, 19–20.
81. SAK congress protocol 1971, 334–335; Committee Report 1974: 99, *Yritysdemokratian sovellutuskomitean mietintö*, 19–20.
82. *Palkkatyöläinen* 22 April 1971, 4.
83. Kettunen, *Historia petollisena liittolaisena*, 73–75.
84. For example, "De anställdas inflytande – individen och kollektivet," *Fackföreningsrörelsen* 3/1965, 76.
85. Janérus, Inge: "Vildvuxen debatt om företagsdemokrati borde hyfsas från fackligt håll," *Fackföreningsrörelsen* 5/1966, 177; Simonson, *Arbetarmakt och näringspolitik*, 34–41; Stråth, *Mellan två fonder*, 130–136.
86. "Företagsdemokrati på nya vägar," *Fackföreningsrörelsen* 15–16/1968, 364.
87. LO, *Demokrati i företagen*, 66, 84–87.
88. Janérus, Inge: "Demokrati i företagen," *Fackföreningsrörelsen* 13/1971, 406–407.
89. Knudsen, *Employee Participation in Europe*, 10–12.
90. Meeting of STK's Board of directors, 28 April 1969, STK archive, Central Archive of Finnish Business Records, Mikkeli (ELKA); Mansner, *Suomen Työnantajain Keskusliitto 1956–1982*, 435.
91. For example, "SAF-skrift diskuterar samarbetet i företagen," *Arbetsgivaren* 9/1971.
92. As a report of the Norwegian experiments see Einar Thorsrud and Fred E. Emery, *Mot en ny bedriftsorganisasjon: Eksperimenter i industrielt demokrati: fra samarbeidsprosjektet LO/NAF* (Oslo: Tanum, 1969).
93. For example, "Självstyrande grupper kan öka produktivitet och arbetstillfredsställelse," *Arbetsgivaren* 7 February 1969, 5; Francis Sejersted, *The Age of Social Democracy: Norway and Sweden in the Twentieth Century* (Princeton: Princeton University Press, 2011), 369–370.
94. SAK, *Yritysdemokratiatyöryhmän mietintö*, 19–20.
95. SAK congress protocol 1971, 312.
96. LO, *Demokrati i företagen*, 6, 14–15, 64–65.
97. "Nya rationaliseringsavtalet understryker vikten av god utbildning och information," *Arbetsgivaren* 2 June 1972; Schiller, *"Det förödande 70-talet"*, 89–92; Simonson, *Arbetarmakt och näringspolitik*, 106–109.
98. Committee Report 1970:A3, 443–445; Committee Report 1974:99, 28.
99. LO, *Demokrati i företagen*, 14–15; Simonson, *Arbetarmakt och näringspolitik*, 71–82.
100. LO, *Demokrati i företagen*, 128–129.
101. Ibid., 118.

102. Schiller, *"Det förödande 70-talet"*, 67–87; Simonson, *Arbetarmakt och näringspolitik*, 91–103. Norway legislated on employee representation in the same year. This reform was also largely driven by nonsocialist parties and meant creating supervisory boards with one-third employee representation in all companies. See Sejersted, *The Age of Social Democracy*, 367–368. Denmark followed in 1973 by establishing a nearly identical system as in Sweden. See Dalgaard, *Ved demokratiets grænse*, 222–224.
103. "Forcerat samarbetsförslag," *Arbetsgivaren* 11 August 1972, 2.
104. "Nya styrelseledamöter," *Arbetsgivaren* 15 December 1972, 2.
105. Cf. Quentin Skinner, *Visions of Politics I: Regarding Method* (Cambridge: Cambridge University Press, 2002), 169–171.
106. Boltanski and Chiapello, *The New Spirit of Capitalism*, 70–75; Julkunen, *Työprosessi ja pitkät aallot*; "Klarsignal för experiment," *Arbetsgivaren* 3 October 1969, 2.
107. John S. Dryzek, *Democracy in Capitalist Times* (New York and Oxford: Oxford University Press, 1996), 60–61; Julkunen, *Työprosessi ja pitkät aallot*, 46.
108. Rhenman, *Industrial Democracy and Industrial Management*, 133–134.
109. SAF, *Samarbetet i framtidens företag*, 57
110. Ibid., 81–82, 86–87.
111. "Nya samarbetsavtal SAF–LO och SAF–TCO," *Arbetsgivaren* 6 May 1966, 5.
112. Albert O. Hirschman, *The Rhetoric of Reaction: Perversity, Futility, Jeopardy* (Cambridge, MA and London: Belknap/Harvard University Press, 1991), 7–8.
113. Heikki Pärnänen, "Onko voiton maksimointi yrityksen päätavoite?" *Yritystalous* 13/1969, 22–23.
114. "Sagt på SAF-konferens i Karlstad om människan i arbetslivet," *Arbetsgivaren* 16 May 1969.
115. *Tehostaja* 8/1968, 50–51; Wiio, *Yritysdemokratia ja muuttuva organisaatio*, 179–180.
116. Pauli Kettunen, *Suojelu, suoritus, subjekti: Työsuojelu teollistuvan Suomen yhteiskunnallisissa ajattelu- ja toimintatavoissa* (Helsinki: Suomen historiallinen seura, 1994), 261–264; Kuokkanen, *Johtamisen ihmissuhdekoulukunta Suomessa*, 73–77.
117. Risto Alapuro, "Ulkoinen ja sisäinen: Suomen poliittisen kulttuurin pitkä linja," *Yhteiskuntapolitiikka* 75, 5 (2010): 534–536; Pauli Kettunen, *Globalisaatio ja kansallinen me: Kansallisen katseen historiallinen kritiikki* (Tampere: Vastapaino, 2008), 88–89; Timo Kyntäjä, *Tulopolitiikka Suomessa: Tulopoliittinen diskurssi ja instituutiot 1960-luvulta 1990-luvun kynnykselle* (Helsinki: Gaudeamus, 1993), 260–265.
118. For example, *Tehostaja* 8/1968, 48.

119. Rhenman, *Industrial Democracy and Industrial Management*, 127–128; SAF, *Samarbetet i framtidens företag*, 97–107.
120. SAF, *Samarbetet i framtidens företag*, 58–59, 66–67, 86–87.
121. Karl-Olof Faxén, "Produktivitet och företagsdemokrati," *Arbetsgivaren* 27 August 1971, 4.
122. "Makt och koncentration," *Arbetsgivaren* 23 February 1968, 2.
123. Heikki Pärnänen, "Yritysdemokratia," *Teollisuuslehti* 6–7/1969, 166; Heikki Pärnänen, "Yritysdemokratia: Kenen osallistumista ja mihin?" in *Yritysdemokratia – demokratian yritys*, ed. Matti Parjanen. Helsinki: Kirjayhtymä, 1970, 80.
124. Pärnänen, "Yritysdemokratia," 167.
125. John Dunn, *Setting the People Free: The Story of Democracy* (London: Atlantic Books, 2005), 46–52, 76–80; David Held, *Models of Democracy*, 2nd edition (Stanford: Stanford University Press, 1996), 105–110.
126. For example, "Företagsnämnder behöver arbetsro," *Arbetsgivaren* 20 October 1967, 2.
127. Pärnänen, "Yritysdemokratia yrityksen teorian valossa," 284.
128. Wiio, *Yritysdemokratia ja muuttuva organisaatio*, 19–25.
129. *Työnantaja* 2 June 1977, 4.
130. Kettunen, *Suojelu, suoritus, subjekti*, 294–300; Knudsen, *Employee Participation in Europe*, 14–18.
131. Boltanski and Chiapello, *The New Spirit of Capitalism*; Kuokkanen, *Johtamisen ihmissuhdekoulukunta Suomessa*, 13–16, 26–29; Julkunen, *Työprosessi ja pitkät aallot*, 52–54.
132. For example, *Palkkatyöläinen* 23 April 1970, 1; *Arbetsgivaren* 3 October 1969, 4.
133. Tapio Bergholm, *Kohti tasa-arvoa: Tulopolitiikan aika I* (Helsinki: Otava, 2012), 13.
134. For example, SAK, *Yritysdemokratiatyöryhmän mietintö*, 15–18.
135. LO, *Demokrati i företagen*, 50–51.
136. Anna Hedborg, "Jämlikhetsgruppens andra rapport," *Fackföreningsrörelsen* 20/1972, 8.
137. Koljonen, *Työntekijä ja yritysdemokratia*, 26–27, 265–266.
138. Therborn, *En ny vänster*, 175.
139. Therborn, *En ny vänster*, 179.
140. SAK, *Yritysdemokratiatyöryhmän mietintö*, 5–6; Hautala, "Yritysdemokratiakomitean mietintö SAK:n näkökulmasta," 62–64.
141. Olavi Sulkunen, "Yritysdemokratiasta yhäkin selkiytymättömiä käsityksiä," *Palkkatyöläinen* 17 June 1971, 14.
142. Therborn, *En ny vänster*, 179; Bertil Gardell, "Starka krav på ökat inflytande från de anställda," *Fackföreningsrörelsen* 11/1967, 397–399.

143. Elving Herrman, "Arbetsorganisation och företagsdemokrati," *Fackföreningsrörelsen* 13/1971, 412–415.
144. Arne Geijer, "Företagsdemokratin under 1970-talet," *Fackföreningsrörelsen* 4/1971, 100.
145. *Palkkatyöläinen* 23 April 1970, 1.
146. For example, Koljonen, *Työntekijä ja yritysdemokratia*, 103, 117–118, 127.
147. *Palkkatyöläinen* 22 April 1971, 4.
148. For example, Koljonen, *Työntekijä ja yritysdemokratia*, 71, 79; Kettunen, *Suojelu, suoritus, subjekti*, 277–283.
149. For example, Koljonen, *Työntekijä ja yritysdemokratia*.
150. Olle Hammarström, "Vad den företagsdemokratiska försöksverksamheten gett – och vad den kan ge," *Tiden* 5/1973, 290–292.
151. Kettunen, *Suojelu, suoritus, subjekti*, 397–398.
152. Committee Report 1970:A3, preface.
153. Ibid., 104.
154. "Hyvinvoinnista pahoinvointia?" *Yritystalous* 2/1970.
155. See also Maiju Wuokko, *Markkinatalouden etujoukot: Elinkeinoelämän valtuuskunta, Teollisuuden keskusliitto ja liike-elämän poliittinen toiminta 1970–1980-lukujen Suomessa* (Helsinki: University of Helsinki, 2016), 105–107.
156. Heikki Pärnänen, "Heikki Pärnänen vastaa: STK:n yritysdemokratia-ajattelun arvostelua," *Teollisuuslehti* 4/1970, 128.
157. SOU 1975: 1. *Demokrati på arbetsplatsen: Förslag till ny lagstiftning om förhandlingsrätt och kollektivavtal*; Schiller, *"Det förödande 70-talet"*, 118–123; Simonson, *Arbetarmakt och näringspolitik*, 132–137. On wage-earner demands see also Inge Janérus, "Sopas §32 under mattan – eller avskaffas den?" *Fackföreningsrörelsen* 4/1975, 8–9; Sten Edlund, "Nej, vi kompromissade inte…" *Fackföreningsrörelsen* 6/1975, 16–17.
158. Lag (1976:580) om medbestämmande i arbetslivet https://www.riksdagen.se/sv/dokument-lagar/dokument/svensk-forfattningssamling/lag-1976580-om-medbestammande-i-arbetslivet_sfs-1976-580; Simonson, *Arbetarmakt och näringspolitik*, 132–137; Schiller, *"Det förödande 70-talet"*, 128–133.
159. Simonson, *Arbetarmakt och näringspolitik*, 157–167; Schiller, *"Det förödande 70-talet"*, 172–177; LO, *Solidariskt medbestämmande* (1976), 37–62.
160. Simonson, *Arbetarmakt och näringspolitik*, 151–157, 187–189.
161. Simonson, *Arbetarmakt och näringspolitik*, 167–180; Schiller, *"Det förödande 70-talet"*, 177–194.
162. Simonson, *Arbetarmakt och näringspolitik*, 180–185; Schiller, *"Det förödande 70-talet"*, 194–202.
163. Schiller, *"Det förödande 70-talet"*, 215–217.

164. Pontusson, *Limits of Social Democracy*, 183–185.
165. For example, Bengt Sandkull, "Medbestämmande utan inflytande," *Tiden* 9/1984, 545–551.
166. Heikki Lappalainen, "Yritysdemokratiasta YT-lakiin: Yritysdemokratiakeskustelu Suomessa 1970-luvulla," *Työelämän tutkimus* 1, 2 (2003): 158–159; Mansner, *Suomen Työnantajain Keskusliitto 1956–1982*, 446.
167. Kettunen, *Suojelu, suoritus, subjekti*, 414.
168. Mansner, *Suomen Työnantajain Keskusliitto 1956–1982*, 446–448. In the public sector and especially in municipalities, representative councils became a more common practice, although voluntary. See Aarne Mattila, *Kunnat työmarkkinapolitiikassa: Kunnallinen työmarkkinalaitos 1970–2000* (Helsinki: Kunnallinen työmarkkinalaitos, 2000), 203–206.
169. Juho Saari, "Suomalainen konsensus: Korpilammen konferenssi (-77) käännekohtana," *Yhteiskuntapolitiikka* 75, 5 (2010): 469–471.
170. Lappalainen, "Yritysdemokratiasta YT-lakiin," 160–161.
171. Act on Cooperation within Undertakings. Säädös 725/1978, *Laki yhteistoiminnasta yrityksissä*. http://www.finlex.fi/fi/laki/alkup/1978/19780725?search%5Btype%5D=pika&search%5Bpika%5D=laki%20yhteistoiminnasta%20yrityksiss%C3%A4.
172. Act on Cooperation within Undertakings; Mansner, *Suomen Työnantajain Keskusliitto 1956–1982*, 446–448.
173. Heikki Lappalainen, "Mitä "yritysdemokratiauudistus" merkitsee?" *Ahjo* 27 September 1978, 8–9.
174. For example, *Palkkatyöläinen* 2 July 1979, 5; 1 October 1979, 1; 10 March 1980, 3; 25 May 1981, 3; 3 May 1982, 6; Mansner, *Suomen Työnantajain Keskusliitto 1956–1982*, 449–454.
175. Markku Mansner, *Suomalaista yhteiskuntaa rakentamassa: Suomen työnantajain keskusliitto 1980–1992* (Helsinki: Elinkeinoelämän keskusliitto EK, 2005), 142–149, 207–208.
176. SAF, *SAF Congress 1980: Reports, summaries*, 11.
177. Kalle Karlsson, "Bred uppslutning viktig för ny saltsjöbadsanda," *SAF-tidningen* 13/1982, 3; "Utvecklingsavtalet," *SAF-tidningen* 14/1982, 2.
178. Meeting of STK's managing group 29 May 1980. 1992 Managing group minutes 1978–1980. STK Archive, ELKA; *Teollisuusviikko* 27 August 1981, 2.

CHAPTER 4

Collective Ownership as a Form of Economic Democracy

Perhaps the most well-known reference point for the concept of economic democracy in the 1960s and 1970s was collective ownership and capital formation, which was discussed in many countries throughout Europe, for example in Germany, France and Denmark. The envisioned institutions were slightly different, but all plans shared the idea of capital formation under the ownership and control of wage-earners.[1] Usually, this would have meant establishing collective funds owned by trade unions or employees of individual enterprises. They would have collected a share of profits and invested them back in the companies, thus providing a way to even out business cycles and sectoral differences and give employees power based on their ownership.[2] In Sweden, collective ownership through wage-earner funds (*löntagarfonder*) became an important part of the range of reference of economic democracy in the 1970s, although the idea had its roots in earlier debates. In most countries, wage-earner funds and other similar proposals were never realized. Sweden was a significant exception to this trend, and the funds became one of the country's most conflictual political issues of the postwar era.

In this chapter, I examine what kinds of meanings and valuations were given to economic democracy in conjunction with the wage-earner fund debate in Sweden and its reception in Finland. Swedish literature has charted well the political debate and negotiations on wage-earner funds, the viewpoints of different groups, as well as the differences of the

I. Kärrylä, *Democracy and the Economy in Finland and Sweden since 1960*, Palgrave Studies in Political History,
https://doi.org/10.1007/978-3-030-80631-6_4

numerous practical models. Some scholars have also analyzed the concepts and argumentation of the debate.[3] Therefore, the criteria and range of reference of economic democracy in the form of wage-earner funds are already well-known. Here, I will shed more light on two aspects of the debate, which have not been discussed so much in previous research. The first is the valuation and legitimation of wage-earner funds. Previous research has shown that wage-earner funds were often justified not only by their contribution to economic democratization, but also by their potential to support capital formation and economic growth. In the course of the debate, the latter legitimation became more common as the economic situation in Sweden deteriorated.[4] Besides this change, it is important to look more closely at different legitimation or opposition strategies, as well as the beliefs and hierarchies they utilized or implied. It is also important to bear in mind which models of the funds were being defended or criticized at given times. This brings out cleavages within the labor movement and the nonsocialist groups.

The second aspect I will focus on is the actual rhetorical relation of economic democracy and wage-earner funds. How commonly was the latter conceptualized as a manifestation of the former, by whom, and did the rhetoric change to emphasize other concepts instead of economic democracy? Previous research has not been very systematic in this respect. The meaning of economic democracy has often been taken for granted or treated too narrowly. For example, Ilja Viktorov has defined economic democracy exclusively as collectivization of ownership,[5] even though its historical meaning was much broader, as I have already shown. The relation between economic democracy and wage-earner funds was not self-evident but contested and fluctuating. Based on newspaper data, wage-earner funds were mentioned during the debate even a hundred times more frequently than concepts of democracy (Fig. 4.1). The Social Democrats did regularly associate the two concepts but, as seen in previous chapters, the employers and center-right parties always had a problematic relationship with applying the concept of democracy to economic relations.

Power and Ownership for Wage-Earners?

The debate on collective wage-earner funds truly began in Sweden after a report by the LO economists Rudolf Meidner, Anna Hedborg and Gunnar Fond was published in 1975. The report had been commissioned by the

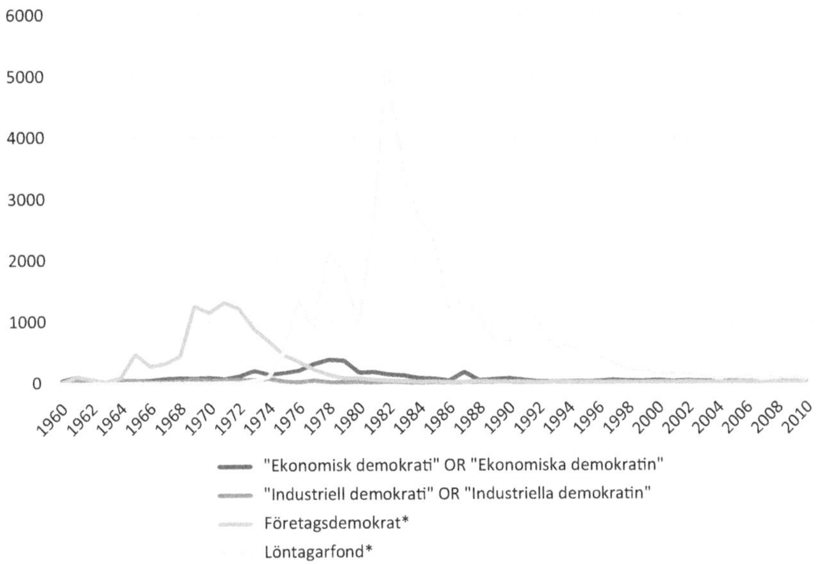

Fig. 4.1 'Wage-earner funds' and concepts of democracy in Swedish newspapers, 1960–2010; number of articles with the terms in the Swedish database of digital newspapers (http://tidningar.kb.se/). Data retrieved 13 August 2019

LO congress of 1971, and the next congress of 1976 accepted it in a slightly revised form as an official program. The idea of wage-earner funds had been raised from time to time in LO reports of the 1950s and 1960s under the name 'branch funds' (*branschfonder*). The main rationale behind the concept was supporting the Swedish labor market model (Rehn-Meidner model) and especially the solidaristic wage policy, which had the tendency of creating large profits for the owners of Sweden's most profitable companies. Trade union economists believed that collecting a share of profits into branch funds governed by the trade unions would ease the wage pressure in an equitable way and provide capital for future investments. Inspiration came from international debates, and it had its roots already in the labor movement's postwar program and earlier visions of the planned economy. They had presented, for example, the idea of branch councils as important bodies taking on the tasks of planning.[6]

In 1959, Ernst Wigforss wrote a pamphlet in which he reflected on the possibility of collective ownership, where private enterprises would become "foundations without owners," governed for example by trade unions. Profits would stay in the company for productive investments. This would secure sufficient investments without concentration of wealth with a few private owners. For decades, Wigforss had been interested in guild socialism and its ideas of socialization through trade unions and other collectivities below the state, but this text written in his retirement in particular worked as inspiration for later theorists, Rudolf Meidner among them.[7]

Democratization of ownership and economic power was used as a legitimation for branch and wage-earner funds, especially by Rudolf Meidner, who became the main advocate of these practices. Lars Ekdahl has interpreted Meidner's interest in the fund idea as a wish to find a third way between Soviet communism and Western state capitalism; a model that would restrict the power of capital and increase the power of workers and citizens in a democratic and decentralized manner.[8] However, in discussions regarding branch funds, the strongest emphasis was usually on economic objectives, especially supporting economic growth, rationalization and the Swedish labor market model. LO was not eager to go forward with the idea in the early 1960s. Economic growth was stable and the labor market model seemed to work well, providing full employment and steadily rising wages for most employees.[9] The LO leaders supported cooperation with employers, and the chair Arne Geijer suspected that interfering with private ownership could have threatened the Swedish model.[10] However, the developments of the late 1960s paved the way for a stronger interest in collective ownership. As discussed in previous chapters, the perceived problems of wealth and income differences, structural change, concentrated ownership and economic power as well as alienating work environments led to increasing calls for the democratization of economic relations. In this context, wage-earner ownership was viewed as a potential solution, which LO took seriously in its 1971 congress.[11]

From 1975 until the realization of wage-earner funds in 1983, a number of different proposals for the organizational model of the funds came from the Social Democrats, LO, center-right parties and employer organizations alike. In leftist proposals, wage-earner funds differed from pension funds in that they would have been able to make direct investments into corporate shares and gain control, even majority ownership, in them. A central point of contestation was whether they would make individual payments to beneficiaries like pension funds did or use the assets and profits only for collective purposes. Different proposals and their complex technicalities have been examined thoroughly in previous research, which I will lean on to give a summary of the different options without going too much into technical details.

The first fund proposal by the LO economists Meidner, Hedborg and Fond in 1975 resembled more a pamphlet than a full research report. It was meant to function as a basis for discussion before the final report was presented at the LO congress the following year.[12] The authors suggested that a 10–20% share of corporate profits that exceeded a certain limit would be collected to wage-earner funds in the form of new share emissions by the companies taking part in the system.[13] In order to not hinder the growth of any company, and to ensure the system's cost and price neutrality, the share capital was to stay in the home company and be used for its development.[14] To promote the collective interests of wage-earners, the profits of the funds were to be collected into a central 'clearance fund' (*utjämningsfond*). This meant that even though share capital would stay in the original company, its profit could be used collectively, for example for education, research, developing work environments and services for job seekers. The authors found that some issues were best handled on branch level by branch councils, but they were not to have too much control over the funds. To avoid centralization, the authors suggested that the central fund could appoint board members in the companies owned by wage-earner funds, based on the proposal of a local trade union.[15]

Meidner and his colleagues opposed the ideas of company-specific funds and profit-sharing to individuals, as they would have benefited only the employees of most profitable companies, whereas the less profitable would have very little profits to place in their funds. They argued that this kind of profit-sharing would have worked against solidaristic wage policy and would not have strengthened employee power and influence.[16] LO had opposed these practices for the same reasons when the center-right parties suggested them earlier. In Germany, where Meidner drew a lot of inspiration, trade union economists had already argued for the benefits of collective funds without individual shares, but these were never realized even though the Social Democratic party and confederation of trade unions accepted the proposal in principle.[17] The proposal's most controversial feature was that depending on profit rate, the wage-earner funds would have been able to become majority owners of the largest Swedish companies in 20–75 years.[18] Meidner later explained that the table presenting different scenarios for the wage-earner fund 'takeover' was intended merely as a mathematical illustration. The political decision on limiting the funds' ownership in individual enterprises was to be made later, but LO did not really discuss the matter during the first years of debate, which Meidner considered a strategic mistake.[19]

Both the content and legitimation of Meidner's report differed significantly from previous LO proposals on branch funds. Meidner and his colleagues appealed strongly to democracy in the form of wage-earner power and influence. They took class conflict, concentration of wealth and economic power as starting points when defining their objectives.[20] They emphasized the importance of economic power as the main motivation for wage-earner funds.[21] Wage-earner funds were explicitly connected to democracy by stating that they had to have "true democratic content," build a "democratic control apparatus" and be considered "part of a democratization process." Their most important motivation lay in "the labor movement's general pursuit for equality and democratization."[22] Meidner and his colleagues took up the theme of power also in interviews, and the editors of LO's newspaper emphasized it with headlines like, "It is power that matters" and "This is how we shall take POWER from the owners of capital!"[23] Meidner commented that according to all experience, influence and control in the workplace were not enough. "Ownership plays a decisive role," he stated.[24]

It is worth noting that the authors acknowledged that wage-earner funds had to fulfill certain economic objectives, such as employment, sufficient capital formation and price stability. They believed this was possible, and redistribution of ownership into collective funds could be carried out without the threat of capital flight or investment strike.[25] It seems that the authors had to argue for the economic soundness and feasibility of the wage-earner funds in order to pursue the more important value of democracy. On the other hand, economic growth was a precondition for the funds' existence—without it, there would be no profits and hence no wage-earner capital.[26] This testifies to the inescapability of economic legitimation in political rhetoric.

Social Democratic Doubts About Collective Ownership

The most controversial aspect of wage-earner funds, also among the labor movement, was collective ownership. As discussed earlier, the mainstream of social democrats had already in the 1920s and 1930s begun to emphasize economic planning and social reforms instead of socialization of the means of production. According to the principle of 'functional socialism,' rights based on ownership could be restricted by legal regulations, and by introducing new rights based on work and social citizenship. The visions of active industrial policy and enterprise democracy of the 1960s both followed this line of economic democracy, which was distinct from that based on collective ownership. The dichotomy between rights deriving from work and rights deriving from ownership was a common conceptualization in debates of the time. As witnessed in previous chapters, Social Democratic leaders like Olof Palme usually defined economic democracy in terms of economic planning, active industrial policy and enterprise democracy, but not as redistributing economic power by redistributing ownership. The Social Democrats' experience was that when private ownership had been questioned, as in the postwar planned economy debate, they had usually suffered defeat.[27]

SAP's leaders were not very well-informed of the content of Meidner's report, and its nature came as a surprise to some.[28] There was certain support for collective ownership among party members, and it was discussed as a potential form of economic democracy at the party congress in October 1975. Economic democracy was a central concept in the new platform that was ratified in the congress, and party members placed high hopes on finally taking the 'third step' in the democratization of society.[29] However, the attitude of most leading Social Democrats was reserved toward wage-earner funds. The difficult tie situation in the parliament may have hindered radical openings, but ideological adherence to functional socialism also played a role. Economic democracy defined in these terms mostly excluded collective ownership of the means of production. This exemplifies the old ideological division within SAP that was again becoming actual.[30] For the Social Democrats, it was also important to emphasize that authority over economic decisions should be in the hands of the people, not just the working people. These aspects were evident in Olof Palme's speech on the new platform.[31] Palme did not think there would be enough support among voters and party members for the wage-earner fund proposal, but also acknowledged that the debate on ownership and capital formation had become significant. The party leader adopted a wait and see strategy in anticipation of the decisions of the 1976 LO congress and the state committee that had been appointed at the beginning of 1975.[32]

LO announced its official support for wage-earner funds in March 1976, when Meidner's revised proposal was made public.[33] LO was encouraged by the strong support wage-earner funds got from study circles, although these represented only a small portion of LO members.[34] The revised report on wage-earner funds did not significantly differ from the initial proposal, but it was more concrete and technical.[35] The rhetoric of power and democracy had been somewhat toned down, and now the objectives of wage-earner funds were defined as supporting solidaristic wage policy, preventing concentration of wealth and increasing wage-earner influence in the economic process.[36] The LO congress of 1976 accepted the wage-earner fund report as an official program, and many unions announced their support for it, which came as a surprise for the SAP leadership.[37] Many participants expressed the belief that collective ownership through wage-earner funds was a significant step toward economic democracy. Very few found the report radical. Instead, there was much discussion on how to make the system more encompassing by including smaller firms, cooperatives and public institutions.[38] However, LO was not demanding the funds to be created right away but was ready to wait for the report of the state committee.[39]

The Social Democratic Party still avoided taking a clear stance on wage-earner funds and their effects on private ownership. LO considered the funds primarily a trade union matter and SAP did not want to make them an electoral theme.[40] Center-right parties had already criticized the funds quite harshly, and the issue contributed to the election result that ended SAP's 44-year mandate in government in September 1976. Wage-earner funds were the biggest question that divided the socialist and center-right blocs, but the number one theme of the election was nuclear power, which also created divisions among the center-right. The Center Party in particular gained support with its antinuclear campaign. It became the largest bourgeois party and its chair Thorbjörn Fälldin the new prime minister. The result was quite narrow: The bourgeois bloc had 180 seats against the 169 of SAP and the communists.[41]

SAP and LO published their new wage-earner fund proposal in 1978. Its significance remained limited, as the SAP leadership wanted to keep a low profile before the next election. The economic crisis had truly hit Sweden, and perceived economic necessities took a larger role in the debate on wage-earner funds. Capital formation for industrial investments was now included as a central objective. Excessive corporate profits were no longer a concern, as many Swedish companies were faring badly. Declining savings and investment figures were viewed as facts that set the agenda for reform. Capital formation was considered essential for productive investments, and a revitalized industry a prerequisite of democratization, employment and the Swedish standard of living. The new objective was a certain compromise between LO and SAP, who wanted to make the proposal more acceptable to the public.[42]

The previous objectives of wage-earner influence, distribution of wealth and supporting solidaristic wage policy were retained, but the concepts of power and ownership were toned down. The fact that Sweden now had a bourgeois government and the electorate's unclear stance on wage-earner funds most likely hindered demands. The report emphasized that wage-earner funds would not change the economic system and that the proposal could not determine in advance how democratic enterprises should be organized.[43] Most significant technical changes were driven through by SAP representatives.[44] Profit-sharing would have only concerned companies with more than 500 employees, which were the most significant power centers in the Swedish economy. In addition, the system would have included a nationwide "codetermination fund" and at least two "development funds," which would be financed with small payroll taxes and support education, productive investments and the technical development of Swedish companies.[45] The new proposal was legitimized with economic arguments, although many democratic aspects of Meidner's model remained. The funds were still collective and based on profit-sharing through share emissions. In theory they were able to become majority owners of large companies in a few decades. However, the current shareowners' asset values and dividends would be protected with tax exemptions and other tools.[46]

The idea of wage-earner funds was further modified in a second proposal by LO and SAP in 1981. The report was part of SAP's broader policy change to end the persistent economic crisis and return to political power, which is examined in Chap. 5. The wage-earner funds were to be connected to the ATP pension system by transferring a share of the fund profits to pension funds. This was meant to support future pension payments and brought an element of personal shares, which Meidner had criticized. The main objective was helping Sweden out of the crisis by strengthening capital formation for investment. The rationale was not about transforming the market economy but supporting it. The previous primary objectives of employee influence and equal distribution of wealth remained, and it was stated that wage-earner funds could be a "limited but significant part of a program for developing economic democracy."[47]

SAP's crisis rhetoric determined an objectified roadmap to the future, which constructed strict boundaries for wage-earner funds. MP Kjell-Olof Feldt exemplified SAP's view on the limits of economic democracy. He argued that political democracy and economic democracy were fundamentally different: In politics, the guiding norm was the will of the majority, and objectives could be determined freely; in economic life, by contrast, profitability was a predetermined objective that ultimately dictated what was right or wrong. According to Feldt, this created a tension between democracy and economy in the concept of economic democracy.[48] For the writers of the new fund report, competitiveness and profitability were not ends in themselves. But as was common in social democratic thought and rhetoric, in order to reach more important values, economic ones had to be prioritized, and their potential conflicts with the actual ends had to be resolved. The changing economic environment, declining savings and investment and increasing pension expenses were emphasized and presented as objective reality in the report, which constituted a problem to be solved.[49]

The most important concrete novelty in the 1981 report was that the fund capital would no longer be required to stay in the original company, but it would be possible to invest it in the stock market.[50] The proposal had a narrower conception of the use of profits, as the ideas of education and research to support wage-earners were not expressed this time. The funds' ability to invest in the stock market would also change the dynamics of the system. The investments might have been concentrated in a few most attractive companies, but it was not automatically the most profitable firms that would be taken over first. Moreover, without mandatory share emissions, current shareholders had the possibility to decline to sell to the wage-earner funds. The report did not propose a limit to wage-earner fund ownership in individual companies, so even though the accumulation of assets would have been slower, in theory it was still possible to gain command in enterprises owned by the funds, if their board and/or shareholders agreed. Therefore, the proposal retained some potential to reform the economic system and its ownership structure.[51] Lars Ekdahl has concluded that at this point the SAP leaders were pursuing wage-earner funds, as letting go of them might have been taken as a sign of weakness and at least angered the fund supporters within the party. However, they were not pursuing Meidner's and LO's original version. The objective of capital formation had surpassed democratization and wage-earner influence, and the party leaders were taking the funds in a 'functional socialist' direction.[52]

Business and Center-Right Mobilization Against 'Fund Socialism'

The employers and center-right parties had had their own ideas of sharing profits with wage-earners since the nineteenth century. This was a part of the traditions of industrial paternalism and social liberalism discussed earlier. It entailed that employees were not considered as expenses but as productivity factors that need to be treated well and motivated. The idea was also presented as an answer to the rise of socialism. Profit-sharing belonged to the ideational constellations of many (social) liberals and it was used already in the nineteenth century by some private companies, especially in France, Britain and the United States. Sometimes liberals in Europe and the United States even promoted employee-owned companies.[53] In particular in the United States there has long been a small but significant sector of worker cooperatives. Since 1974, there has also been a system called the Employee Stock Ownership Plan (ESOP), which has enabled employee ownership in many companies in different sectors.[54]

In Sweden, the liberal *Folkpartiet* (FP) in particular talked about profit-sharing and employee ownership. In the 1950s, they raised several parliamentary motions on the issue, but other parties found that it should be handled by the labor market parties. The conservative concept of 'owner democracy' had equal distribution of wealth as a major element but was not connected to profit-sharing. The conservatives, as well as most employers, opposed the idea, and it was not realized in Sweden to any significant extent.[55] The main difference between liberal and socialist ideas was that in the former, profit-shares would have been given to individuals instead of trade unions or other collectives. This was compatible with the ideas of owner democracy and people's capitalism. Trade union ownership seldom figured positively in liberal visions, whereas trade unions themselves believed individual shares would undermine solidarity and turn workers into 'little capitalists.' The reasoning was similar to that behind their reservations about enterprise democracy—fear of 'dual loyalties' toward the enterprise, on the one hand, and the worker collective, on the other hand.[56]

Swedish Liberals took up the ideas of profit-sharing and collective capital formation again in 1968, legitimizing them with economic benefits, but also democratization and wealth distribution. Employers and other bourgeois parties now responded more actively in order to avoid collective fund models. The former Moderate Party leader Yngve Holmberg drafted a proposal for SAF. He suggested a combination of profit-sharing and wage-based saving for individual employees. SAF found that this was the only acceptable option but did not publish the proposal as the time was not considered ripe for it.[57] In their 1972 program, Liberals toned down their beliefs in free markets and started to consider collective capital formation in addition to profit-sharing to individuals. After the so-called Haga agreement between SAP and FP on economic policy in spring 1974, the government appointed a parliamentary committee to investigate measures for supporting capital formation and solidaristic wage policy. Excess profits were a major problem the committee was supposed to tackle, as the economic situation had remained favorable despite the oil crisis. The committee's starting point was not in LO's proposal, but in broad examination of international examples.[58]

Employer organizations were informed of Meidner's work at LO, and in order to steer the debate to more acceptable lines, SAF and the Confederation of Swedish Industry (SI) began drafting their own proposal. The working group was led by Erland Waldenström, an experienced corporate executive and chair of SI. The group kept a low profile, and experimentation with profit-sharing and fund systems was not encouraged in order to avoid conflict with LO.[59] The report came out in May 1976, when LO's final wage-earner fund report for the congress had also been published. Waldenström's group criticized LO's proposal and presented the outlines of their own fund model, which resembled earlier proposals by center-right parties: It was voluntary, company-specific and based on individual instead of collective ownership. Investments could be made freely in the stock market, and individual shares could be withdrawn after a certain period. The assets would be collected by a payroll tax instead of profit-sharing, even though Waldenström himself favored the latter.[60] Like LO, Waldenström's group had examined models and debates in other countries, as well as some Swedish examples that were mostly company-specific pension funds.[61]

In the early phase of the debate, employer representatives were constructive in proposing alternatives. They could even call Meidner's proposal well-written and thought-provoking,[62] while offering to replace it with voluntary stock-saving for individual employees. Employer representatives claimed that "distant" collective funds would not give any tangible benefit to individuals.[63] At the core of the debate was a struggle over the concepts of centralization and decentralization and their meaning: The employer side argued that collective funds would result in a new concentration of power in the hands of the trade union elite. Concentration and centralization were also in this context very negative terms, so all parties used them for labeling undesirable models, while their own model always represented 'decentralization.'[64] Employer beliefs suggesting that wage-earner funds would not fulfill their objectives of wage-earner influence, but possibly even work against it, resembled those expressed against representative and too far-reaching enterprise democracy.

SAF did not launch an all-out attack against wage-earner funds right away.[65] After 1976, however, they chose a harder line and increased activity on other political issues as well. SAF's new chair, Curt Nicolin, CEO of Asea Group, began changing SAF's role into a more active proponent of the market economy and took a strict stance on wage-earner funds. Nicolin was firmly against them and believed they would be a step toward a socialist economy.[66] SAF's public relations department, along with its chief Sture Eskilsson and employee Danne Nordling, was also in favor of a harder line. By the end of 1977 SAF had decided to abandon the idea of a counter-proposal for wage-earner funds, as it would have meant admitting that some change in economic power relations was needed.[67]

SAF's PR department prepared an ideological campaign to promote the belief that the current economic system was good and efficient, and that no wage-earner funds were needed. The belief in wage-earner funds being a weapon of a systemic battle between socialism and the market economy was constantly stressed in employer rhetoric.[68] SAF portrayed the market economy as a guarantee of democracy in Western society, but implicitly retained the distinction between political and economic democracy without stressing the latter. SAF also launched a general PR campaign for the market economy like business organizations in many other Western countries at the time.[69] The background and broader implications of this mobilization are examined more closely in Chap. 5. In the late 1970s, however, the wage-earner fund debate was the main arena for manifestations of SAF's new harder and more politicized line.[70]

A dominant feature in the employer side's rhetoric against wage-earner funds, like in many other debates, were arguments based on economic legitimations. A common rhetorical figure was the claim that wage-earner funds would jeopardize the efficient functioning of enterprises and markets. The report by Waldenström's group expressed many beliefs about the economic problems Meidner's proposal would create. It was argued that mandatory share emissions into wage-earner funds would make share prices decline and thus hurt current shareowners, many of whom were small investors. Meidner's model would therefore not be neutral regarding capital formation but would seriously impair the market for private risk capital. As a result, it would have to be compensated with public alternatives.[71] The evident centralization of economic steering and adoption of social objectives alongside or as substitutes to profitability would lead to efficiency losses resembling those of socialist economies. The interests of consumers would also be hurt in a centralized economy.[72]

As in the enterprise democracy debate, another dominant employer strategy was promoting the belief that democracy did not belong to the economic sphere. As previously described, the employer conception of democracy entailed that the economy was a private sphere of objective laws that was restricted by the imperatives of efficiency and competitiveness; therefore, it mostly lay outside the scope of democracy. The employers were not comfortable with applying the concept of democracy in the economic sphere. Its common meanings had the potential to open the door for demands for a new distribution of power and politicization of economic issues. These beliefs were expressed in an explicit discussion on the conceptual struggle over economic democracy by SAF's Hans-Göran Myrdal. He stated that the choice of concepts had a major impact on opinion-building and pointed out that sometimes it was possible to change the content or valuation of a concept. Myrdal found that SAF had succeeded in "de-ideologizing" the concept of enterprise democracy, but he suspected that the same was not possible for economic democracy, which already had a very stable meaning: collective ownership as opposed to individual ownership.[73]

Myrdal was perhaps unaware that the meaning of economic democracy was multifaceted for social democrats and trade unionists, many of whom said that collective ownership was not a necessary component of economic democracy. It is interesting that Myrdal found SAF had succeeded in promoting such a meaning in the case of enterprise democracy, even though in light of my analysis, Swedish employers also avoided using this term, substituting it with 'cooperation.' This may have been a way to promote alternative conceptual content while the term itself was of secondary importance. By contrast, the strategy regarding economic democracy soon turned into a more open opposition of the term and concept. On the occasions the employers did use it, it was usually not given any concrete content,[74] portrayed as something the Social Democrats and LO pursued but could not quite define,[75] or associated exclusively with employee co-ownership of enterprises like Myrdal had done.[76] The last-mentioned usage narrowed the range of reference of economic democracy. Association with wage-earner funds gave economic democracy a negative connotation, despite the universally valued word democracy as its component.

A distinctive feature of employer critique was the frequent use of socialism and socialization as threats and negative images of the future. This was largely absent from the enterprise democracy debate but familiar from general ideological debate and the question of industrial policy examined in Chap. 2. On the question of wage-earner funds, however, claims that socialism would jeopardize not only economic efficiency, but also freedom, political democracy and the entire Western lifestyle, were especially strong. The Waldenström group's report stated outright that preservation of the prevailing economic system and private ownership were preconditions for the proposal. The new system was not to result in confiscation of current shareowners' assets or depreciation of their value. According to the report, LO's proposal of collective funds would mean a system change to "corporatist socialism." As the market for private risk capital would collapse, either the state or trade unions would be forced to take it over. Neither wage-earner managed companies nor 'fund socialism' were therefore desirable institutions.[77]

Danne Nordling, an economist from SAF's public relations department and an active figure in the anti-fund campaign,[78] expressed the 'threat of socialism' belief more bluntly than Waldenström's group, but using the same dual-jeopardy thesis. He wrote that wage-earner funds would clearly mean a system change into "market socialism" or to something even more centralized. He argued that trade union ownership would lead to the same efficiency problems as nationalization. In addition, it would be undemocratic if trade union representatives retained their power in funds regardless of the results of national elections.[79] In 1977, Nordling presented the main arguments against wage-earner funds in SAF's pamphlet named *Fritt näringsliv eller fondsocialism* (Free Economy or Fund Socialism). It consolidated 'fund socialism' as the employer side's pejorative name for wage-earner funds. The pamphlet argued that the wage-earner funds would take Sweden from a mixed to a planned economy, which meant less pluralism, democracy and freedom, as well as a sinking standard of living.[80]

The employer side apparently found socialism an effective scare word that a large part of the rhetoric's audience would instinctively oppose. At times, the employers defended private ownership and market economy so adamantly as to make them appear intrinsic values, but usually they were legitimized with appeals to other values higher up in the hierarchy. Private ownership and the market economy figured as guarantees of the even more precious efficiency and competitiveness as well as of freedom and democracy. Ultimately, all of these contributed to the 'common good.' While applying the jeopardy thesis to several values at the same time, employer rhetoric against wage-earner funds was more varied than their rhetoric against enterprise democracy. The latter leaned mostly on belief in jeopardized efficiency and competitiveness, while rhetoric drawing on freedom and democracy was less frequent in that debate.

In a sense, the struggle over wage-earner funds became more openly political than that over enterprise democracy. This time it was rather the Social Democrats trying to direct the debate into a depoliticized course with their crisis rhetoric, while the employers and center-right parties framed the debate as a struggle between conflicting ideologies and economic systems. There were multiple values at stake instead of a technical disagreement over means of improving economic efficiency and promoting the national interest. For the employers, efficiency had become almost a secondary concern compared to freedom, democracy and the frictionless image of a 'Western society' that, according to them, was jeopardized by the wage-earner funds.

Swedish center-right parties took different stances on wage-earner funds. As noted, the Liberals advocated profit-sharing and even turned positive toward certain forms of collective ownership and mandatory share emissions to employees. This was due to the party's pursuit of more wage-earner voters, but also the ideological inclination toward social liberalism and a middle way between capitalism and socialism.[81] The Moderates, by contrast, were completely opposed to any mandatory funds and even individual profit-sharing. The party portrayed the funds exclusively as a means to bring socialism to Sweden, which had to be opposed by all means.[82] The Center Party and its leader Thorbjörn Fälldin also opposed collective wage-earner funds. However, they were open to some forms of capital formation for wage-earners, and Fälldin was later the first to propose connecting wage-earner funds to the pension system. In general, the Center Party was positive to the objectives of increased capital formation and more equal distribution of wealth but saw the threat of trade union power in collective funds.[83] As the Liberals also took a negative stance on LO's first fund proposal, the center-right parties had a common front against collective funds in the 1976 election, which they won and formed a cabinet led by Fälldin.[84]

A compromise between different groups was being sought in the state committee on wage-earner funds. Rudolf Meidner interpreted in his last book that in the autumn of 1978, the possibility of a compromise between SAP, LO, FP and the white-collar confederation TCO was at its highest. However, opposition toward the funds was growing within FP, and SAP was passive due to the strong opposition and meager public support for funds, which made them cautious before the 1979 parliamentary election.[85] The center-right bloc won the election by only one seat, and Fälldin again became Prime Minister after FP's minority government.[86] The committee had already published four volumes of background analyses on collective capital formation but a broad agreement on any proposals of its own was impossible as the Moderates remained opposed to all kinds of mandatory systems and FP was moving closer to the same position.[87] As there were no preconditions for compromise, the committee's work was wrapped up in 1981 without any proposals for concrete fund models.[88] The employers' PR work and the rise of the Moderates to the position of the largest bourgeois party clearly contributed to this outcome. FP noticed that public opinion was moving to the right and adjusted its own policy accordingly. Cooperation with the Social Democrats became a less attractive option. The Center Party moved in the same direction, although it had been more critical of collective funds from the start. SAP and LO were left alone with their collective fund model.

In the early 1980s, the employer and center-right campaign against wage-earner funds became fiercer.[89] SAF wanted to raise its profile and turn unsure citizens and especially the white-collar confederations against wage-earner funds, so it poured a lot of money into PR work and succeeded in turning public opinion more unfavorable to the funds.[90] There were only few internal critics to this strategy, but some of them were notable. Volvo's CEO Pehr G. Gyllenhammar would have rather stayed out of politics and suspected that the PR campaigns might also turn public opinion against business.[91] SAF's campaign inspired especially owners of small and medium-sized firms. A key argument was that small enterprises would suffer without getting anything in return, because they had to pay fees for the wage-earner funds but were unlikely to get their investment money.[92]

The Modest Realization of Wage-Earner Funds

The Social Democrats returned to power in the fall of 1982. The election result was again narrow, but SAP and the Communists achieved a parliamentary majority with 186 seats against the bourgeois bloc's 163. Wage-earner funds were not the most important election theme despite bourgeois counter-campaigning. However, afterward, polls showed that right-wing voters in particular considered the funds a decisive question. Rising unemployment was the biggest concern, and the majority of voters now counted on the Social Democrats to solve the crisis instead of the bourgeois parties, whose cooperation had turned out difficult. After their victory, SAP wanted to get the issue of funds quickly off the agenda, but otherwise they found that they needed to concentrate on the competitiveness of Swedish industry.[93]

It took until autumn 1983 to finalize the legislation on wage-earner funds. The government's proposal was drafted by the ministry of finance and the LO economist Per-Olof Edin. Now the funds were definitively stripped of all their radical potential. This was a final attempt to reach a compromise with the bourgeois parties and employers, but they did not grab the "outreached hand" offered by Prime Minister Olof Palme. Instead, the bourgeois parties promised to close down the funds as soon as they were able to form a government again. The counter-campaign and declining enthusiasm of voters and party members worried SAP's leadership, and even after the election Palme considered burying the fund question. However, the funds had to be carried through or the party would have suffered a loss of authority.[94]

When it became clear that the Social Democrats would prepare legislation for wage-earner funds, SAF's PR director Sture Eskilsson came up with the idea of a large demonstration in Stockholm. The date of the event was set at 4 October 1983, when the parliament began its autumn term. The 'October 4 committee' managed to organize a true mass movement that was not limited to businesspeople and entrepreneurs. Thousands of participants from around the country were transported to Stockholm by plane, train and bus. The scale of the demonstration surprised many, including the organizers, who had expected maybe 5000 people. There were very different estimates of the final number of participants. The committee itself announced that there were 100,000 people; the police talked about 50,000 and the social democrats about 27,000.[95] Rudolf Meidner later pointed out that there was a hint of irony in the fact that Swedish business used the labor movement's traditional method of political influence.[96]

The proposal for wage-earner funds was accepted in parliament on 21 December. The Communists, who opposed this model of funds, abstained from voting; 108 people spoke at the plenary, but no new arguments were heard. Finance Minister Kjell-Olof Feldt stated that the tradition of reforms that benefited all interests was now continued and the welfare society was strengthened, but the Moderates argued that they were witnessing the most socialistic reform in any Western mixed economy.[97]

The most notable new features of the final proposal restricted the funds' growth and level of control in single companies. The funds could collect their assets only until the year 1990, after which they could only grow with the profits of existing capital. The assets for the funds were to be collected by a 'profit-sharing tax' of 20% from profits exceeding one million SEK (about $150,000) or 6% of a firm's total payroll costs, whichever was higher. This profit-sharing tax was paid by all Swedish companies. Another financing source was a 0.2% tax on the total payroll costs of all corporations, private and public. However, small enterprises and family foundations were left outside the system. The fund organization was changed from 24 to five regional funds, where the majority of the boards were trade union representatives and the minority appointed by the government. The funds were to operate like the fourth ATP pension fund, which invested in corporate shares. They acquired shares from the open market and could also provide risk capital for unlisted companies. A limit to the total share of ownership of each of the funds in a company was set to a maximum of 10% of shares and 8% of votes. In theory, together with the fourth ATP fund, they could control 50% of shares in a single company. The funds had to contribute to the pension system a sum corresponding to 3% of the inflation-adjusted value of their revenues. This meant that they had to obtain a more than 3% return on their investments annually in order to grow. There was no stipulation on using the profits for education, research or other collective purposes. The funds were now primarily legitimized as a solution to the economic crisis. They supported production and employment by providing new capital and maintaining wage stability.[98]

The wage-earner funds were established in 1984, and it soon became clear that they did not mark a radical change in the economic system. They operated independently from the state and were rather passive portfolio investors that pursued healthy profits instead of steering investment toward social and structural goals. The funds invested mostly in large enterprises in manufacturing industry but also made some risk investments in unlisted companies. They had to acquire their shares from the stock market instead of new offerings, which made their contribution to new capital formation limited. Restricting the funds' share of ownership in single enterprises to 10% efficiently held back their influence over the economy.[99] Many LO representatives were disappointed in this limitation and wondered why private ownership was allowed to concentrate much more. However, some considered the funds a viable first step toward stronger influence, for example in ethical investment.[100] People involved in the administration of funds usually viewed them more positively. The fund director Lennart Låftman and board member Villy Bergström argued in 1987 that the funds were steadily becoming bigger players in the capital market and helped in holding back wage demands. They also contributed to curbing the inequalities caused by currency devaluations and record profits in certain industries.[101]

Center-right parties and business representatives continued their critique of wage-earner funds and made the October 4 manifestation an annual tradition. The Moderate, Liberal and Center Parties promised that if they formed a government, wage-earner funds would be abolished and their assets used for education and R&D.[102] The main arguments against the funds remained the same: The payroll tax was viewed as an extra burden for Swedish enterprises, which jeopardized their economic performance as well as the national economy.[103] A new argument criticized the fund administration for its lack of transparency, which had even concealed some bad investment decisions.[104] This belief in the funds operating undemocratically can be taken as a Hirschmanian perversity thesis. At the same time, it implied the traditional claim that collective funds were too distant for individual wage-earners.[105]

Center-right commentators also argued that if more wage-earners had participated individually in new mutual funds, they would have benefited from the rising stock prices, which would have dispersed ownership.[106] Wage-earner funds were of course collective and hence portrayed as concentration of ownership, but they did allow wage-earners to participate in the stock market boom of the 1980s. Leftist commentators pointed out that new stock-saving models had increased the wealth of many regular citizens but not increased economic democracy.[107] Later analyses on the performance of wage-earner funds have made similar conclusions. The funds' profitability was good, on average even better than development in the Stockholm Stock Exchange, but they did not fulfill the goals of economic influence and democracy very well. Moreover, wage-earner funds did not have notable effects on macroeconomic stability or supporting solidaristic wage policy, which had been among the initial objectives. Instead, wage differences increased throughout the 1980s, and after a period of steady growth and low inflation, liberalization of finance overheated the Swedish economy. According to the economist Philip Whyman, the modest size of the fund system curbed its significance: In 1991, the funds' assets amounted to 2.6% of Sweden's total stock market value, which nevertheless made them the 8th largest stock owner in the country.[108]

Wage-Earner Funds Turn Into Cooperation Funds in Finland[109]

The debate on wage-earner funds was much more intensive in Sweden, but it was also in Finland the most obvious case of channeling a concept of economic democracy into a concrete policy proposal. Many began to consider new fund systems even a necessity for the democratization of ownership. At the same time, ideas of other forms of democratic steering of capital and investment were gradually left in the background. Economic liberalization, which began in the 1970s after the dissolution of the Bretton Woods currency regime and the first oil crisis, restricted the possibilities to steer and plan national economies. The development prompted social democrats to adopt more market-oriented Third Way policies, which focused on competitiveness and inflation containment rather than full employment.[110]

In Finland, the debate on wage-earner funds began after the question of enterprise democracy had been momentarily solved. In their 1978 party congress, the Social Democratic Party presented a roadmap for the 1980s. It stated the party's traditional objective of extending democracy into the economy. The diffusion of power and ownership was an important democratic reform, and wage-earner funds were now portrayed as a viable tool for this goal. The SDP decided to investigate the fund idea, leaving open the possibility for a collective model that was discussed in Sweden.[111] After this, interest toward wage-earner funds gradually increased in Finland. They were viewed, for example, as answers to the problems of technological development. If wage-earners gained more influence over automatization, it could be harnessed to serve their interests instead of increasing unemployment and monotonous work.[112]

In 1981, SDP's congress received a report on wage-earner funds, concentrating especially on the developments in other European countries.[113] Instead of the Swedish model of nationwide or regional trade-union-governed funds, the party decided to advocate company-specific 'cooperation funds.' Funds of this type had the risk of undermining wage-earner solidarity by favoring those working in profitable firms. They were nevertheless believed to increase employee influence if they were collectively owned by the employees and their assets used only for job-creation investments as well as research and development. The report argued that individual stock-saving schemes and bonus systems advocated by employers would only increase inequality and undermine collective wage agreements.[114]

The replacement of 'wage-earner funds' with a new term was based on strategic considerations. The developments in Sweden and other Western European countries were closely followed,[115] and when the fund issue took wind in Finland, the Swedish initiatives had already been geared in a more moderate direction. Opposition to the LO's proposal of wage-earner funds made the Finnish Social Democrats want to maneuver the issue into a scheme that could be negotiated with the employer side. As the ruling party in Finland, the SDP wanted to safeguard a consensus and cooperation with the private sector on economic policy, which was based on export sector competitiveness.[116] SAK, in turn, wanted to secure labour market cooperation, which had been damaged in Sweden when the SAF began to withdraw from centralized bargaining and tripartite bodies during the 1980s. Tripartite cooperation provided a significant means for the SAK to exercise its power, and was not to be risked for short-term gains.[117]

The objective of avoiding conflict is evident in the SDP's statements. Prime Minister Kalevi Sorsa gave a conciliatory speech at the Finnish Business and Policy Forum EVA's meeting in 1983. Sorsa said that good relations between interest groups and the government should not be ruined as had happened in Sweden, but wage-earner funds should not be made taboo, either. According to Sorsa, the SDP's cooperation funds aimed at a model of capital formation within the market economy, which would promote employee influence as well as economic redistribution. Sorsa tried to legitimize cooperation funds to business representatives with their economic benefits by arguing that dispersed ownership would give wage-earners an incentive to increase profitability instead of demanding immediate wage increases. He concluded by stating that fund solutions could be built only on a consensual basis.[118] This shows that the SDP wanted to avoid confrontation, even if it meant stepping back from their initial objectives and advocating a less ambitious model than had been realised in Sweden.

The SAK was not persuaded immediately to get behind the SDP's idea of cooperation funds. At its congress of 1981, the SAK did not advocate any specific fund model but commissioned a report on different options. Communist members criticized the wage-earner funds in general as a lukewarm version of people's capitalism, which did not represent 'true' democracy.[119] In general, however, Finnish communists were rather silent on wage-earner funds. It took the SAK's working group nearly four years, until February 1985, to prepare a report on wage-earner funds.[120] The report also discussed other means of promoting economic democracy, such as nationalizations and codetermination practices.[121] The SAK's research secretary Peter J. Boldt explained to the SAK's board that this was an attempt to avoid the polarization of the debate by pushing one specific model of wage-earner funds. Sweden was viewed as an alarming example in this respect, and the SAK wanted to initiate a broader debate on economic democracy.[122] The strategy was in line with that of the SDP, which was evident in the report itself, despite the radical calls for the redistribution of power and wealth.

The SAK's report echoed the principle of functional socialism by arguing that work, not ownership, should be the ultimate source of democratic rights. In Norway, the trade union movement had even refused to promote wage-earner funds because it would have meant accepting ownership as a source of rights. However, since working life democratization was progressing slowly, the SAK was willing to utilize the right of ownership to improve the status of wage-earners. As with the SDP's programs, the report stated that ownership was an unevenly distributed and concentrated source of power. Its redistribution was justified by the values of equality, security and the right to participate in decisions concerning oneself.[123] However, the SAK emphasized that it did not propose a transition to socialism or replacing the market economy but advocated a mixed economy.[124] The SAK acknowledged the importance of economic efficiency but distinguished its concept of efficiency from a capitalist one. Wage-earner funds were viewed as a means of channeling profits to productive investments instead of financial speculation, therefore promoting 'true' efficiency.[125]

The SAK refrained from advocating any specific model of wage-earner funds; it merely presented different options to inspire further debate. The SAK acknowledged that the SDP had endorsed company-specific funds, but the report emphasized the benefits of trade-union-governed funds, especially their better contribution to employment and solidaristic wage policy.[126] The SAK showed an ideological inclination toward the Swedish model of wage-earner funds, but overall focused pragmatically on what was considered achievable. The most viable method was to reach a collective agreement on the funds, which, due to employer opposition, significantly restricted the possible models.[127] Peter Boldt also explained this to the SAK's board: company-specific funds were not considered the best option, but they were "from certain points of departure the only option."[128]

Economic legitimation for the funds and the practical obstacles in their realization continued to play a large role in the SAK's rhetoric.[129] In the SAK congress of 1986, many participants were willing to pursue an extensive reform more in tune with the Swedish model. They pointed out that company-specific funds could lead to wage-earners turning against each other.[130] Instead of concrete actions, the congress statement obliged the SAK to "develop and promote economic democracy through collective agreements and legislation."[131] The proposals of the SDP and trade unions had now consolidated around the idea of company-specific but collectively owned cooperation funds. The SAK also came up with a new idea of nationwide education and training funds, but the employer side did not welcome this proposal.[132]

Finnish white-collar confederations were also in favor of creating new funds, and they suggested concrete models earlier than the SAK. In 1981, the Finnish Confederation of Professionals STTK advocated company-specific cooperation funds as proposed by the SDP.[133] The Confederation of Salaried Employees TVK, which represented, for example, public officials, was more radical and strongly supported the Swedish fund proposals. In 1984, the TVK accepted company-specific funds, but a nationwide or regional model was considered a more desirable option. The TVK stated that company-specific funds were not solidaristic and placed employees of different companies in different positions.[134]

"Funds Would Not Solve the Problem"

Many Finnish employers and center-right politicians in the early 1980s remained favorable toward certain forms of economic democracy, but they generally opposed wage-earner funds.[135] As in Sweden, they strongly disliked the idea of modifying ownership structures in private companies and equated this with socialism. The Employer Confederation STK's stance on wage-earner funds was based on the principle: "[W]e do not negotiate on the ownership of our member companies."[136] In public debate, employers had certain standard criticisms against too extensive or wrongly implemented employee influence: It would either fail to motivate employees and increase their efficiency, or it would in fact be detrimental to efficiency. The rhetoric resembled that of Swedish employers but lacked their strong appeal to the threat of socialism and their ideological defense of Western liberal democracy. In 1978, the STK's chair Stig Hästö argued that motivation and efficiency were the main objectives of economic democracy. Hästö wondered why wage-earner funds had become the main solution in public debate, as they would be remote for individual employees and thus poor for motivation.[137]

Instead of binding legislation on economic democracy, employers' strategy was to emphasize flexible and company-specific solutions. Hästö believed that these were the best ways to increase both profitability and individual motivation. According to him, new organizational arrangements were not necessary, but "by making communication and participation more efficient, the personnel would learn to understand better economic causes and effects."[138] This was the broader strategy of Finnish businesses: focusing the debate on the good objectives of the funds and proposing already existing means for achieving them. For example, motivation for work could be more efficiently promoted with performance-based remuneration, and corporate finance by developing the stock markets.[139]

Finnish employers and their publications followed closely the development of wage-earner funds in Sweden. In employer rhetoric, Sweden was not the ideal society but a cautionary tale of the overstretched aspirations of trade union power, which had damaged labor market relations.[140] The articles pointed out that Swedish employers believed the funds made the country unattractive to private investments and would, thus, be destructive to Sweden's economy and employment. They also referred to survey results showing that only a minority of Swedish people in general and even members of trade unions and the Social Democratic Party supported wage-earner funds.[141] Employers criticized Swedish plans by contrasting wage-earner funds with 'economic facts.' The STK newspaper *Teollisuusviikko* talked about the "Swedish disease" and argued that wage-earner funds were an example of tightening norms and expanding the public sector in a way that ignored economic realities.[142] When the Swedish Social Democrats had returned to office and were about to realize the wage-earner funds in autumn 1983, *Teollisuusviikko* reported on employers' demonstrations on October 4.[143]

Finnish center-right parties assumed a positive attitude to solutions along the lines of 'people's capitalism'. Key words in their models were voluntary basis and individualism, and they resembled the proposals of the Swedish center-right parties and the Waldenström report. The National Coalition Party (NCP) first suggested share issues to company-specific funds where employees could acquire personal holdings.[144] The Center Party also called for company-specific and voluntary economic participation systems for employees. The party explicitly denied support for collective wage-earner funds.[145] The economic viewpoint was the standard legitimation for funds in the rhetoric of the center-right parties. Employee participation and motivation were usually mentioned but appeals to democracy were scarce.

"Productive Participation" Through Voluntary Personnel Funds

In March 1986, Kalevi Sorsa's government appointed a committee to examine "new forms of cooperation to promote economic democracy and competitive production." The committee named itself the Participation Systems Committee (*Osallistumisjärjestelmäkomitea*).[146] The committee was chaired by Matti Pekkanen, an experienced employer union leader. Members included corporate CEOs and managers as well as social democratic economists.[147] The STK initially opposed appointing a "wage-earner fund committee" but found it better to participate than remain outside.[148] It soon became clear that the committee would not pose a threat to the employers. The STK's board was informed that the committee chair Pekkanen would emphasize voluntary basis and treat the participation systems as an issue broader than wage-earner funds.[149]

The Participation Systems Committee favoured the concepts of participation and cooperation instead of economic democracy. In line with the ongoing structural change debate, the committee was supposed to consider the effects of technological change, which required improved cooperation in workplaces to promote adaptation.[150] As usual, international comparison was central in the committee's work, and the common beliefs of Finland being a latecomer in employee participation were expressed.[151] The committee's first report was entitled *Productive Participation in a Renewing Working Life*.[152] The committee concentrated on the 'micro level' of economic democracy, participation in the workplace. This had become dominant during the 1980s, when calls for democratic macroeconomic steering were fading. The committee assessed different fund and profit-sharing models mostly with regard to their effects on economic efficiency, not from the viewpoint of democracy. Models other than company-specific funds were not seriously discussed, probably because they were considered politically impossible.[153] The committee noted that the Swedish model of regional funds had been unpopular and had not really increased employee participation.[154]

The committee report proposed voluntary, company-specific 'personnel funds.' This resembled the center-right and employer models in other countries, such as the SAF's Waldenström report in Sweden. The funds were to be financed from profits and employees could acquire individual holdings, which were to be reimbursable after a waiting period. The funds were to make investments in the stock market and use their assets for collective purposes, such as education.[155] The reforms were believed to improve employees' motivation and promote their awareness of the company's interests, which were the key to successful structural change.[156] The funds' democratic aspect was that they would allow personnel to participate in decision-making and balance power and responsibility. They would enable altering ownership structures but not change the prevailing economic system.[157]

The wage-earner side was not pleased with the committee's proposals. The SAK found that they required thorough examination but did not dismiss them outright. It insisted that the framework was to be negotiated between the labor market organizations to avoid growing wage differences and inequality.[158] All wage-earner organizations stressed that new practices should not undermine collective wage agreements.[159] The Social Democrats were more receptive to the committee's ideas, even though they were considered a compromise far from the party's original objectives.[160] The SDP wanted to proceed with the matter in the newly formed coalition government with the NCP, which had become a strong advocate for personnel funds. The SDP had already got its way in the cabinet's other working life reforms, such as strengthening the protection against dismissal.[161] These are discussed further in Chap. 6. The result nevertheless exemplifies SDP's pragmatic attitude. It had become customary after less than satisfactory reforms to remind that the SDP could not reach its ambitious goals with any quick solutions. This was becoming common within European left-wing parties. As electoral support was turning more precarious, reforms had to be conducted within the limits acceptable to center-right parties.[162]

Employers and nonsocialist parties considered personnel funds suitable for topical challenges, especially because of their voluntary and company-specific nature that allowed for flexibility.[163] Unlike in the case of many other reforms, the STK now argued that the proposals of the committee were not to be negotiated further but carried through in parliament as everyone agreed on their objective.[164]

The law proposal on personnel funds was given to the parliament in April 1989. The NCP minister Ilkka Kanerva presented it by appealing to the demands of the current era, which required constructive cooperation. Kanerva anticipated a move toward more decentralized bargaining and local agreements. He thus presented a historic picture, which had been common to employers: flexibility and harmonious cooperation as the characteristic of progress in the labor market.[165] The idea of economic democracy thus gave way to flexible cooperation between employers and employees. Some Social Democratic MPs were pessimistic about the progressive nature of the personnel funds. Jukka Gustafsson argued that only time could tell the significance of the voluntary law. Gustafsson considered it important that part of the fund capital would be collective, as otherwise the system would merely represent people's capitalism.[166] The most critical stances were heard from Communist MPs who argued that personnel funds were a "smokescreen of democracy," which only introduced a form of profit-related pay and weakened the trade union movement.[167] However, some social democratic commentators were optimistic and believed that personnel funds promoted employee influence and could serve as the "first step toward economic democracy."[168] The same metaphor had been used already after the Cooperation Act over 10 years earlier.

The Act on Personnel Funds gave companies with at least 30 employees the possibility to establish a fund after negotiating with their personnel. The assets were to be collected from profits and invested in the stock market or the home company. It was possible to reserve some for collective purposes, such as training. Against the wish of the wage-earner organizations, however, this was not made mandatory.[169] Personal holdings could be withdrawn from the funds after 10 years. The trade union movement still believed that this risked the funds becoming only a means for bonus payments, which undermined the collective wage policy. This fear had also been expressed in the LO's initial proposal for wage-earner funds in Sweden. The Finnish fund model followed the German and Danish proposals the LO wanted to avoid, but its collective element was even weaker. In theory, personnel funds gave the possibility to raise collectively owned capital and increase wage-earner ownership in private companies, but practice was quite different, as the funds mostly invested in the stock market. Following the principle of people's capitalism, this affected the distribution of wealth and income but not so much economic power. As *Teollisuusviikko* wrote, for employers, the system was mainly a new means of employee remuneration.[170]

The committee chair Matti Pekkanen encouraged employers to establish personnel funds. He wondered why Finnish companies were so cautious, as for him, economic participation would be "the most important event in our working life since the adoption of the collective bargaining system."[171] Despite Pekkanen's visions, employees never experienced the funds as a significant participation system, and interest was also modest on the employer side. In 1991, there were 40 personnel funds with 100,000 affiliated employees. They paid out profit bonuses amounting to half a week's salary on average, and part of the profits were invested for longer periods. However, as the Finnish economy soon faced a severe crisis, profit-sharing mostly stopped for a few years; for the next two decades, the number of personnel funds remained on the level of the early 1990s. Employers began to favor individual performance bonuses, and in 1994, as many as one-fifth of industrial employees had received them.[172]

People's Capitalism Instead of Collective Ownership

In the Swedish legislation for wage-earner funds, national economic interest occupied the top of the conceptual hierarchy, or at least it figured as the final and decisive step toward the prestigious goal of national welfare. The Social Democrats had since the first LO proposals geared their rhetoric from economic democracy toward economic necessity, which could not accommodate radical transfer of ownership. It was rather the employers and Moderates who framed the issue as an ideological battle between two economic and societal systems, socialism and the market economy—albeit with their own conception of economic necessity. The Social Democrats challenged this constellation with their third-way rhetoric, which in the end was based on depoliticizing beliefs about tackling the economic crisis. As always, however, this kind of rhetoric is also highly political in its pursuit to define the agenda and promote specific, decontested ideational constellations.

The Finnish personnel fund reform was even more moderate than the wage-earner funds realized in Sweden. It was acceptable to Finnish business due to its voluntary nature. The reform was in line with what business and employer representatives had already proposed for decades under labels like owner democracy and people's capitalism. The concept of economic democracy did not figure strongly in the final debates concerning personnel funds, even though they realized practical applications of the concept that had been discussed for over ten years. This shows that increasing employee influence or collective ownership had become politically difficult in other than consultative and voluntary forms. The trend was similar in other countries: In Denmark, even the last Social Democratic proposals for voluntary profit-sharing through funds were declined by the conservatives and liberals.[173]

The old debate on the limits of reformism is actual when assessing the wage-earner fund debates. Social Democrats sought to conduct reforms within the bounds of capitalism and to retain their political power, and ended up strengthening capitalism rather than transforming it.[174] Their ideational constellation was increasingly occupied by new beliefs on economic necessities. They were looking at the changing dynamics and regulatory environment of the global economy, which seemed to call for less state-led steering and more room for private enterprise.[175] Actors make their choices based on their various beliefs and attitudes, but stress different kinds of beliefs in different situations. Besides assessing the economic consequences of reforms, they can view some solutions as ideologically undesirable. For many leading Social Democrats, 'functional socialism' was not just a pragmatic way to carry out economically necessary reforms, but a more desirable societal vision than collective ownership, which carried the imprints of unfree Eastern state socialism.

Besides ideological and economic beliefs, also strategic considerations contributed to the outcome of the wage-earner fund question in Sweden. The center-right parties and white-collar organizations in particular moved to the right on the question, because they believed it would help them retain their voters or their internal unity.[176] Many scholars have emphasized the labor movement's disunity and lack of clear strategies on wage-earner funds.[177] Jonas Pontusson has suggested that these were partly caused by the strong opposition and structural constraints. In his words, "Labor lacks strategic capacity because business is able to exclude it."[178] In contrast, Ilja Viktorov also gives credit to the Social Democratic strategy. He argues that SAP succeeded in 'de-radicalizing' the question. Olof

Palme and the party leadership were mostly supporters of functional socialism, and they had to balance between the more radical wings of their party and LO, as well as the harsh opposition and unfavorable public opinion. Viktorov sees that the SAP leaders managed to channel a reform they did not necessarily believe in into a form that corresponded with their ideology. The party leaders won the struggle against both the fund opposition and their own members' discontent—at least for the time being.[179]

It is notable how severely the Swedish tradition of political compromise broke down in the case of wage-earner funds. Swedish employers seemed to believe that confrontation was a better way to pursue their interests. Pontusson has argued that the wage-earner fund proposal challenged the 'systemic interests' of business without providing any material incentives for cooperation, whereas codetermination had at least employee motivation and compliance to offer.[180] Instead, the fund debate provided a theme that could unify business and right-wing forces and promote their ideational constellations. They may have reasoned that without a compromise on wage-earner funds, they could gain even stronger public support for their beliefs in the virtues of market economy, lower taxes and a smaller public sector. As the fund opposition had become a true mass movement, it would have been quite an anticlimax to settle for a bland compromise.

Whether Swedish business and the political right succeeded in their battle over ideas is discussed more closely in the following chapters. However, some remarks on the relation of the wage-earner fund debate and broader political and ideational change are still in order. It has been quite common to treat the fund debate as a tipping point in Swedish politics, even as a central reason for the breakdown of the 'Swedish model' of cooperation, class compromise and Social Democratic rule.[181] However, less dramatic interpretations seem more plausible. The majority of citizens wanted to maintain the welfare state, and the Social Democrats did return to power in 1982, albeit their policies and ideational constellations had changed substantially.[182] A similar shift toward market-oriented policies and liberalization of labor markets was witnessed in most Western countries.[183]

What makes the Swedish case stand out is the emergence of a major political struggle that was about both the economy and ideology and had system-changing potential. In other countries, rightward political and ideational changes took place at approximately the same time without such conflict. In Finland, the Social Democrats modified their economic policy to the same direction due to the economic crisis. But they did so even before their Swedish counterparts and in cooperation with business organizations. Finnish postwar political culture and its tradition of coalition governments can in general be viewed less ideological and polarized than the Swedish one, especially since the inclusion of the Communists and the beginning of incomes policy in the 1960s. The context and process of political change were different in Finland and Sweden for many reasons, but the ideological and political results were similar: democratic steering of the economy was relaxed, and the expansion of the public sector halted.

In this light, it seems that the conflict over wage-earner funds was not a necessary factor in the Swedish case either, even though it gave the development distinct features. As Bo Stråth has put it, the wage-earner fund debate was not a cause for the deep changes in society, but rather a "symbol and a catalyst."[184] It was part of the process of defining new identities and interests, like the ATP question had been 20 years earlier. The debate started as a channel for the left-wing critique of the 1960s but ended up strengthening the right-wing critique that followed. The debate's impact, especially on the identity of Swedish business and the political right, seems important. After having felt themselves the underdogs in the time of Social Democratic rule, they now had a strong alternative ideology that was credible in the eyes of the public. They could gain resonance for their beliefs and attitudes on democracy, the economy and the relation between individuals and collectives. In this sense, it is not surprising that many contemporaries viewed the fund debate as a turning point.[185] For Finnish Social Democrats, trade unions and employers, the wage-earner funds were rather a symbol that served as a cautionary tale of political conflict. For its part, this example improved the prospects of cooperation and consensus in economic and labor market policy along the market-oriented lines adopted throughout the developed world.

To a certain degree, the wage-earner fund resolution was a victory for the 'functional socialist' interpretation of economic democracy. It associated the concept with employee influence in the workplace, still occasionally called enterprise democracy, as well as public regulation of the economy at large. However, even the functional socialist components were going through major changes, as the room for state intervention in the economy became constantly smaller, and as the extension of enterprise democracy did not cross the boundaries of mostly formal codetermination. The reasons for this conceptual and practical standstill of economic democratization are examined more closely in Chap. 5.

Notes

1. For example, Rudolf Meidner, *Spelet om löntagarfonder* (Stockholm: Atlas, 2005), 13–14. For the Danish debate see Niels Dalgaard, *Ved demokratiets grænse: Demokratisering af arbejdslivet i Danmark 1919–1994* (Copenhagen: Selskabet til Forskning i Arbejderbevægelsens Historie, 1995), 188–238.
2. Lars Ekdahl, *Mot en tredje väg: En biografi över Rudolf Meidner. II. Facklig expert och demokratisk socialist.* (Lund: Arkiv, 2005), 101–104.
3. See especially Bo Stråth, *Mellan två fonder: LO och den svenska modellen* (Stockholm: Atlas, 1998); Stefan Sjöberg, *Löntagarfondsfrågan – En hegemonisk vändpunkt: En marxistisk analys* (Uppsala: Universitetstryckeriet, 2003); Ekdahl, *Mot en tredje väg II.*
4. See especially Ilja Viktorov, *Fordismens kris och löntagarfonder i Sverige* (Stockholm: Stockholm University, 2006); Erik Åsard, *Kampen om löntagarfonderna: Fondutredningen från samtal till sammanbrott* (Stockholm: Norstedt, 1985); Ekdahl, *Mot en tredje väg II*; Sjöberg, *Löntagarfondsfrågan.*
5. Viktorov, *Fordismens kris*, 115–117.
6. Viktorov, *Fordismens kris*, 73–82; Ekdahl, *Mot en tredje väg II*, 45–46; Meidner, *Spelet om löntagarfonder*, 17–21.
7. Ernst Wigforss, *Kan dödläget brytas? Dagspolitik och utopi* (Stockholm: Tidens förlag, 1959); Ekdahl, *Mot en tredje väg II*, 101–104; Viktorov, *Fordismens kris*, 76–80, 165–170.
8. Lars Ekdahl, *Mot en tredje väg: En biografi över Rudolf Meidner. I. Tysk flyktning och svensk modell* (Lund: Arkiv, 2001), 12–13; Ekdahl, *Mot en tredje väg II*, 13–18, 40–43, 236–240.
9. Anders L. Johansson and Lars Magnusson, *LO – 1900-talet och ett nytt millennium* (Stockholm: Atlas, 2012), 104–116; Erik Åsard, *LO och löntagarfondsfrågan: En studie i facklig politik och strategi* (Stockholm: Rabén & Sjögren, 1978), 78–84; Ekdahl, *Mot en tredje väg II*, 109–116.
10. Johansson and Magnusson, *LO*, 113–116.
11. Ekdahl, *Mot en tredje väg II*, 158–160, 230–235; Viktorov, *Fordismens kris*, 65–71.
12. For a summary of the proposal see Viktorov, *Fordismens kris*, 96–99; Sjöberg, *Löntagarfondsfrågan*, 110–114; Åsard, *LO och löntagarfondsfrågan*, 138–144.
13. Rudolf Meidner, Anna Hedborg and Gunnar Fond, *Löntagarfonder* (Stockholm: Landsorganisation LO, 1975), 72–77.
14. Ibid., 72.
15. Ibid., 108–109; Ekdahl, *Mot en tredje väg II*, 262–263.
16. Meidner, Hedborg and Fond, *Löntagarfonder*, 59–60, 80–88.

17. Ibid., 62–66, 121–127; Meidner, *Spelet om löntagarfonder*, 49–53.
18. Meidner, Hedborg and Fond, *Löntagarfonder*, 78–79.
19. Meidner, *Spelet om löntagarfonder*, 138–140.
20. Meidner, Hedborg and Fond, *Löntagarfonder*, 18–20; Ekdahl, *Mot en tredje väg II*, 256–258; Sjöberg, *Löntagarfondsfrågan*, 129–131.
21. Meidner, Hedborg and Fond, *Löntagarfonder*, 17–18.
22. Ibid., 21, 28.
23. *Fackföreningsrörelsen* 19/1975, 1, 11–25.
24. *Fackföreningsrörelsen* 19/1975, 17; Åsard, *LO och löntagarfondsfrågan*, 147–148.
25. Meidner, Hedborg and Fond, *Löntagarfonder*, 21, 24–26.
26. Åsard, *LO och löntagarfondsfrågan*, 153–154.
27. Ekdahl, *Mot en tredje väg II*, 259–261, 266–267, 282–284; Viktorov, *Fordismens kris*, 158–164.
28. Lars Tobisson, *Löntagarfonder: Så nära men ändå inte* (Stockholm: Dialogos, 2016), 25–26; Åsard, *Kampen om löntagarfonderna*, 32, 39.
29. SAP congress protocol 1975, 115–117, 131–133; SAP congress motions 1975, 415–416, 550; Viktorov, *Fordismens kris*, 170–175; Åsard, *LO och löntagarfondsfrågan*, 151.
30. Ekdahl, *Mot en tredje väg II*, 266–269.
31. SAP congress protocol 1975, 97–106; Sten O. Karlsson, *Det intelligenta samhället: En omtolkning av socialdemokratins idéhistoria* (Stockholm: Carlssons, 2001), 651–653; Åsard, *Kampen om löntagarfonderna*, 38.
32. Kjell Östberg, *När vinden vände: Olof Palme 1969–1986* (Stockholm: Leopard, 2009), 251–252; Viktorov, *Fordismens kris*, 175–177; Ekdahl, *Mot en tredje väg II*, 266–269.
33. *LO-tidningen* 7/1976, 1, 12, 16.
34. "Massivt medlems-ja till löntagarfonderna," *LO-tidningen* 2/1976, 9; Viktorov, *Fordismens kris*, 113–115.
35. Ekdahl, *Mot en tredje väg II*, 272–274; Åsard, *LO och löntagarfondsfrågan*, 166–168.
36. LO, *Kollektiv kapitalbildning genom löntagarfonder* (1976), 16.
37. Sjöberg, *Löntagarfondsfrågan*, 117–118.
38. LO congress protocol 1976, 688–733; *LO-tidningen* 19/1976, 2; Åsard, *LO och löntagarfondsfrågan*, 169–173.
39. LO congress protocol 1976, 710, 731.
40. Åsard, *Kampen om löntagarfonderna*, 41–44.
41. Tobisson, *Löntagarfonder*, 48–49; Torbjörn Nilsson, *Hundra år av svensk politik* (Malmö: Gleerups, 2009), 120–122; Mikael Gilljam, *Svenska folket och löntagarfonderna: En studie i politisk åsiktsbildning* (Lund: Studentlitteratur, 1988), 221–227.

42. LO and SAP, *Löntagarfonder och kapitalbildning. Förslag från LO–SAPs arbetsgrupp* (1978), 18–23; Ekdahl, *Mot en tredje väg II*, 277–280; Viktorov, *Fordismens kris*, 101, 177–178; Åsard, *Kampen om löntagarfonderna*, 48–49.
43. LO and SAP, *Löntagarfonder och kapitalbildning*, 4–6; Viktorov, *Fordismens kris*, 102; Sjöberg, *Löntagarfondsfrågan*, 118, 132–133.
44. Viktorov, *Fordismens kris*, 101–103; Åsard, *Kampen om löntagarfonderna*, 47–48.
45. LO and SAP, *Löntagarfonder och kapitalbildning*, 30–36, 49–51.
46. Ibid., 36–41.
47. SAP and LO, *Arbetarrörelsen och löntagarfonderna* (1981), 18.
48. Kjell-Olof Feldt, "Löntagarägande och demokrati," *Tiden* 7/1980, 411–413; Stråth, *Mellan två fonder*, 190–192.
49. SAP and LO, *Arbetarrörelsen och löntagarfonderna*, 31–33, 64–78.
50. Ibid., 9–12, 82–102.
51. Cf. Sjöberg, *Löntagarfondsfrågan*, 124–125; J. Magnus Ryner, *Capitalist Restructuring, Globalisation and the Third Way: Lessons from the Swedish Model* (London and New York: Routledge, 2002), 166–168.
52. Ekdahl, *Mot en tredje väg II*, 285–287; Sjöberg, *Löntagarfondsfrågan*, 121–122.
53. Michael Freeden, *Ideologies and Political Theory: A Conceptual Approach* (Oxford: Oxford University Press, 1996), 459–461; Åsard, *LO och löntagarfondsfrågan*, 14–19. For the history of liberal profit-sharing ideas see Howell John Harris, "Industrial Democracy and Liberal Capitalism, 1890–1925," in *Industrial Democracy in America: The Ambiguous Promise*, eds. Nelson Lichtenstein and Howell John Harris (New York: Woodrow Wilson Center Press, 1993); Daniel T. Rodgers, *Work Ethic in Industrial America 1850–1920* (Chicago and London: University of Chicago Press, 1978), 45–50.
54. August Torngren Wartin, "Att kartlägga terrängen: Medarbetarägandets olika skepnader," in *Tillsammans: En fungerande ekonomisk demokrati*, ed. Bo Rothstein (Stockholm: SNS förlag, 2012), 47–67; John Logue, "Democratic Theory and Atheoretical Democracy: Reflections on Building Democratic Enterprises in the American Economy," in *Managing Modern Capitalism: Industrial Renewal and Workplace Democracy in the United States and Western Europe*, eds. M. Donald Hancock, John Logue and Bernt Schiller (New York: Praeger, 1991), 313–336.
55. Christer Lundh, *Den svenska debatten om industriell demokrati 1919–1924: 1. Debatten i Sverige* (Lund: Studentlitteratur, 1987), 48, 52–54; Åsard, *LO och löntagarfondsfrågan*, 14–19.

56. Stråth, *Mellan två fonder*, 148–152; Åsard, *LO och löntagarfondsfrågan*, 20–30, 40–41.
57. Viktorov, *Fordismens kris*, 212–214; Stråth, *Mellan två fonder*, 153–157.
58. SOU 1979: 8, *Löntagarna och kapitaltillväxten 1*, Stockholm 1979, 3–4; Stråth, *Mellan två fonder*, 158–162; Åsard, *Kampen om löntagarfonderna*, 16–23.
59. Viktorov, *Fordismens kris*, 215–217; Stråth, *Mellan två fonder*, 162–166.
60. For a summary of Waldenström group's report see Viktorov, *Fordismens kris*, 217–219; Sjöberg, *Löntagarfondsfrågan*, 143–146; Åsard, *Kampen om löntagarfonderna*, 57–58.
61. Sveriges Industriförbund and Svenska Arbetsgivareföreningen, *Företagsvinster, kapitalförsörjning, löntagarfonder. Rapport från en arbetsgrupp inom näringslivet (1976)*, 25–45.
62. Åsard, *Kampen om löntagarfonderna*, 103–104.
63. For example, Nils Henrik Schager, "Regeringen och facket avvaktande till förslagen om löntagarfonder," *Arbetsgivaren* 26/1975; Erland Waldenström, "Vad ont har småspararna gjort?" *Fackföreningsrörelsen* 27/1975, 10–11.
64. See also Stråth, *Mellan två fonder*, 164–166.
65. Åsard, *LO och löntagarfondsfrågan*, 165.
66. Sjöberg, *Löntagarfondsfrågan*, 146–148, 230–235; Olof Ehrenkrona, *Nicolin: En svensk historia* (Stockholm: Timbro, 1991), 295–296.
67. SAF, *SAF-kongressen sammanfattad* (1978), 108–110, 131.
68. For example, *Arbetsgivaren* 26/1977, 6; *Arbetsgivaren* 33/1977, 2.
69. Mark Blyth, *Great Transformations: Economic Ideas and Institutional Change in the Twentieth Century* (Cambridge: Cambridge University Press, 2002); Maiju Wuokko, *Markkinatalouden etujoukot: Elinkeinoelämän valtuuskunta, Teollisuuden keskusliitto ja liike-elämän poliittinen toiminta 1970–1980-lukujen Suomessa* (Helsinki: University of Helsinki, 2016); Maiju Wuokko, "Business in the Battle of Ideas, 1945–1991: Conclusions from the Finnish Case," *Scandinavian Economic History* Review 65, 3 (2017): 279–293.
70. Rikard Westerberg, *Socialists at the Gate: Swedish Business and the Defense of Free Enterprise, 1940–1985* (Stockholm: Stockholm School of Economics, 2020), 247–258.
71. Sveriges Industriförbund and Svenska Arbetsgivareföreningen, *Företagsvinster, kapitalförsörjning, löntagarfonder*, 107–110, 120–122; Waldenström, "Vad ont har småspararna gjort?".
72. Sveriges Industriförbund and Svenska Arbetsgivareföreningen, *Företagsvinster, kapitalförsörjning, löntagarfonder*, 122–129.
73. Cited in Stråth, *Mellan två fonder*, 236.

74. Robert Alderin, "Varför Meidnerfond över huvud taget?" *Arbetsgivaren* 10/1978.
75. For example, "LO:s fondsocialism," *Arbetsgivaren* 6 October 1977, 2; "Socialismens kris," *Arbetsgivaren* 22/1978, 2.
76. Christian Bratt, "Tre skilda nivåer på medbestämmande," *Arbetsgivaren* 20 October 1977.
77. Sveriges Industriförbund and Svenska Arbetsgivareföreningen, *Företagsvinster, kapitalförsörjning, löntagarfonder*, 22–24, 130–132.
78. Viktorov, *Fordismens kris*, 219.
79. Danne Nordling, "Meidners löntagarfonder ny väg till socialismen," *Arbetsgivaren* 30/1975, 6.
80. Danne Nordling, *Fritt näringsliv eller fondsocialism* (Stockholm: SAF, 1977); Tobisson, *Löntagarfonder*, 66–67.
81. Meidner, *Spelet om löntagarfonder*, 118–120; Tobisson, *Löntagarfonder*, 30–34.
82. Torbjörn Nilsson, *Mellan arv och utopi: Moderata vägval under hundra år, 1904–2004* (Stockholm: Santérus, 2004), 243; Sjöberg, *Löntagarfondsfrågan*, 148–150; Ehrenkrona, *Nicolin*, 293; "Vårt parti bästa värnet för friheten i Sverige," *Dagens Nyheter* 9 October 1975.
83. Sjöberg, *Löntagarfondsfrågan*, 153–154; Tobisson, *Löntagarfonder*, 47–48.
84. Tobisson, *Löntagarfonder*, 48; "Så här tycker borgarna om kongressen," *LO-tidningen* 19/1976, 24.
85. Meidner, *Spelet om löntagarfonder*, 127–131.
86. Henrik Berggren, *Underbara dagar framför oss: En biografi över Olof Palme* (Stockholm: Norstedts, 2010), 570–573; Nilsson, *Hundra år av svensk politik*, 179.
87. Åsard, *Kampen om löntagarfonderna*, 74–101.
88. Åsard, *Kampen om löntagarfonderna*, 123–125, 135–140; Tobisson, *Löntagarfonder*, 108–112.
89. Viktorov, *Fordismens kris*, 250–261.
90. Viktorov, *Fordismens kris*, 237–244; Blyth, *Great Transformations*, 209–211.
91. Tobisson, *Löntagarfonder*, 118–119.
92. Kalle Karlsson, "Fonderna slår hårdast mot de minsta företagen," *SAF-tidningen* 28/1982, 3.
93. Berggren, *Underbara dagar framför oss*, 604–607, 615–617; Nilsson, *Hundra år av svensk politik*, 179; Viktorov, *Fordismens kris*, 197–199; Stråth, *Mellan två fonder*, 199–203.
94. Viktorov, *Fordismens kris*, 199–201; Ekdahl, *Mot en tredje väg II*, 287–289.

95. Westerberg, *Socialists at the Gate*, 273–280; Tobisson, *Löntagarfonder*, 134–140.
96. Meidner, *Spelet om löntagarfonder*, 87.
97. Åsard, *Kampen om löntagarfonderna*, 9–11; Tobisson, *Löntagarfonder*, 151–156.
98. Per-Olof Edin, Klas Eklund and Hans-Eric Holmqvist, *Detta är Steget! Förslag till löntagarfonder i ATP-systemet* (Stockholm: SAP, 1983); Viktorov, *Fordismens kris*, 108–109; Sjöberg, *Löntagarfondsfrågan*, 125–127; Jonas Pontusson and Sarosh Kuruvilla, "Swedish Wage-earner Funds: An Experiment in Economic Democracy," *Industrial and Labor Relations Review* 45, 4 (1992): 783–785.
99. Philip Whyman, "An Analysis of Wage-Earner Funds in Sweden: Distinguishing Myth from Reality," *Economic and Industrial Democracy* 25, 3 (2004): 411–414; Jonas Pontusson, *The Limits of Social Democracy: Investment Politics in Sweden* (Ithaca: Cornell University Press, 1992), 201–216.
100. Lars-Olof Pettersson and Robert Björkenwall, "Löntagarfonder – och sedan?" *Tiden* 5–6/1984, 336–341.
101. Villy Bergström and Lennart Låftman, "Misstag i fonddebatten," *Dagens Nyheter* 3 March 1987, 5.
102. Moderata samlingspartiet, *Valmanifest 1985. Framtid i frihet.* Stockholm 1985. http://snd.gu.se/sv/vivill/party/m/v/1985; Moderata samlingspartiet, *Valmanifest 1988. Framtidens idéer – 20 punkter för ett bättre Sverige.* http://snd.gu.se/sv/vivill/party/m/v/1988; Folkpartiet, *Ny kurs för Sverige. Valmanifest inför valet 1985 antaget av Folkpartiets partistyrelse den l juni 1985.* http://snd.gu.se/sv/vivill/party/fp/v/1985.
103. "Motstånd är nödvändigt," *Svenska Dagbladet* 19 February 1987, 2.
104. "Folkstyre i hemlighet," *Svenska Dagbladet* 15 April 1987, 2.
105. "Meidners misslyckande," *Dagens Nyheter* 11 January 1987, 2; "De galna fonderna," *Svenska Dagbladet* 27 February 1987, 2.
106. "Meidners misslyckande," *Dagens Nyheter* 11 January 1987, 2; "Oförskämt mot löntagarna," *Dagens Nyheter* 8 September 1987, 2.
107. Hagman, Lennart, "Årtiondet då vi gick med +++++," *Aftonbladet* 9 December 1989, 16–17.
108. Whyman, "An Analysis of Wage-Earner Funds in Sweden," 429–430, 439–440; Pontusson, *Limits of Social Democracy*, 216–219; Pontusson and Kuruvilla "Swedish Wage-earner Funds," 786–791.
109. The remainder of this chapter is mostly reproduced, with the publisher's kind permission, from Ilkka Kärrylä, "A Cautionary Tale: Reception of the Swedish Wage-Earner Fund Debate in Finland," *Työväentutkimus* 34 (2020): 21–37.

110. Jenny Andersson, *Between Growth and Security: Swedish Social Democracy from a Strong Society to a Third Way* (Manchester: Manchester University Press, 2006); Sami Outinen, *Sosiaalidemokraattien tie talouden ohjailusta markkinareaktioiden ennakointiin: Työllisyys sosiaalidemokraattien politiikassa Suomessa 1975–1998* (Helsinki: Into, 2015).
111. SDP, *Sosialidemokratian suunta. SDP:n tienviitat 1980-luvulle.* Hyväksytty SDP:n 31. puoluekokouksessa v. 1978 Espoossa. https://www.fsd.uta.fi/pohtiva/ohjelmalistat/SDP/462.
112. Tapio Bergholm, *Laatua ja vapaa-aikaa. Tulopolitiikan aika II. Suomen ammattiliittojen keskusjärjestö vuodesta 1977.* (Helsinki: Suomalaisen kirjallisuuden seura, 2018), 166–178.
113. SDP Congress 1981, Motions, 67–70.
114. SDP Congress 1981, Motions, 74–75; Bergholm, *Laatua ja vapaa-aikaa*, 179–181.
115. For example, *Palkkatyöläinen* 18 April 1982, 13–14; *Palkkatyöläinen* 13 September 1982, 8; *Palkkatyöläinen* 27 September 1982; *Palkkatyöläinen* 1 August 1983, 2.
116. Outinen, *Sosiaalidemokraattien tie*, 81–90.
117. Markku Mansner, *Suomalaista yhteiskuntaa rakentamassa. Suomen työnantajain keskusliitto 1980–1992.* (Helsinki: Elinkeinoelämän keskusliitto EK, 2005), 322–336, 344–345.
118. Prime Minister Kalevi Sorsa: National economic, business economic and agreement policy starting points for Cooperation funds. EVA autumn meeting 19 December 1983, 4, Meeting minutes 1983–1986, EVA Archive, The National Archives of Finland, Helsinki (KA).
119. SAK congress protocol 1981, 96–98; Bergholm, *Laatua ja vapaa-aikaa*, 181.
120. Bergholm, *Laatua ja vapaa-aikaa*, 182–183; *Palkkatyöläinen* 21 January 1985, 6; *Palkkatyöläinen* 4 February 1985, 7.
121. SAK, *Taloudellinen demokratia ja palkansaajarahastot* (1985), 3.
122. SAK board meeting minutes, 4 Feb 1985, 19, SAK Archive, The Labour Archives, Helsinki (TA).
123. SAK, *Taloudellinen demokratia ja palkansaajarahastot*, 1, 11, 13.
124. Ibid., 3, 6, 30.
125. Ibid., 2.
126. Ibid., 5–7, 20–21.
127. Ibid., 23, 80–82.
128. SAK board meeting minutes, 4 March 1985, 41, SAK Archive, TA.
129. SAK congress protocol 1986, 183–184.
130. Ibid., 198–199.
131. Ibid., 286.

132. Bergholm, *Laatua ja vapaa-aikaa*, 447–448; Mansner, *Suomen työnantajain keskusliitto 1980–1992*, 213–216.
133. STTK Congress Statement 1981, Cb:5, STTK congress protocol 1981, STTK archive, The Archives of Salaried Employees, Helsinki.
134. TVK, *Palkansaajarahastoista puheenollen!* (1984).
135. For example, *Palkkatyöläinen* 1 June 1981, 12.
136. STK board meeting, 10 September 1981, appendix 4, 1969, Board meeting minutes 1981–1983, STK Archive, Central Archives for Finnish Business Records, Mikkeli (ELKA).
137. *Teollisuus* 9/1978, 12–13.
138. "Palkansaajarahastot Ruotsissa mahdollisia aikaisintaan 1982," *Suomen Sosialidemokraatti* 3 March 1981.
139. Tapani Saukkonen: The work of the working group investigating economic democracy. Meeting of the Central Committee of Finnish Industry, 20 Dec 1984, 16, Meeting minutes 1981–1985, Archive of the Central Committee of Finnish Industry, ELKA.
140. *Yritystalous* 11/1982, 3.
141. For example, *Teollisuus* 7–8/1979, 7; *Teollisuusviikko* 22 October 1981, 9; *Teollisuusviikko* 25 March 1982, 8; *Teollisuusviikko* 3 June 1982, 8.
142. "Palkansaajarahastot ja "Ruosin tauti,"" *Teollisuusviikko* 24 September 1981.
143. *Teollisuusviikko* 8 September1982, 10; *Teollisuusviikko* 22 September 1982, 16.
144. National Coalition Party, *Työ- ja ammattiyhdistyspoliittinen ohjelma 1984.* https://www.fsd.uta.fi/pohtiva/ohjelmalistat/KOK/92.
145. Center Party of Finland, *Keskustapuolueen tavoitteet 1980-luvun alkupuoliskolle.* (1980). https://www.fsd.uta.fi/pohtiva/ohjelmalistat/KESKP/234.
146. Committee report 1987: 40, *Tuottava osallistuminen uudistuvassa työelämässä.* (Helsinki, 1987), 1–2; Ville Yliaska, *Tehokkuuden toiveuni. Uuden julkisjohtamisen historia Suomessa 1970-luvulta 1990-luvulle.* (Helsinki: Into, 2014), 223.
147. Committee report, *Tuottava osallistuminen uudistuvassa työelämässä*, 2; Mansner, *Suomen työnantajain keskusliitto 1980–1992*, 329–331.
148. STK board meetings, 28 August and 1 October 1985, 1970, Board meeting minutes 1984–1986, STK Archive, ELKA.
149. STK board meeting, 15 October 1987, 1971, Board meeting minutes 1987–1988. STK Archive, ELKA.
150. Appointment of a committee to investigate the prospects of new forms of cooperation to promote economic democracy and competitive production, I.1, Participation Systems Committee's Archive, KA.
151. Heikki Oksanen: Wage-earner participation in decision-making within enterprises, 24 Jan 1987, I.3, Sent letters, Participation Systems Committee's Archive, KA.

152. Committee report, *Tuottava osallistuminen uudistuvassa työelämässä*, I.
153. Appendices from committee meetings, 2 and 19 Dec 1986 and 5 Jan 1987, I.2, Participation Systems Committee's Archive, KA, Helsinki.
154. Committee report, *Tuottava osallistuminen uudistuvassa työelämässä*, 9–11.
155. Ibid., 18–22, 40, 90–101; Yliaska, *Tehokkuuden toiveuni*, 225–226; Mansner, *Suomen työnantajain keskusliitto 1980–1992*, 331–332.
156. Committee report, *Tuottava osallistuminen uudistuvassa työelämässä*, 40.
157. Ibid., 88.
158. SAK's statement on the report of the Participation Systems Committee. STK managing group meeting, 9 February 1988, appendix 3, STK Archive, ELKA.
159. Mansner, *Suomen työnantajain keskusliitto 1980–1992*, 333–334.
160. *Suomen Sosialidemokraatti* 4 December 1987; *Palkkatyöläinen* 16 January 1989; Heikki Oksanen, "Mietintö taloudellisesta demokratiasta ja tuottavasta osallistumisesta," *Sosialistinen aikakauslehti* 4/1987, 30–35.
161. Outinen, *Sosiaalidemokraattien tie*, 218–220.
162. Donald Sassoon, *One Hundred Years of Socialism: The West European Left in the Twentieth Century* (London: Fontana Press, 1996), 731–742.
163. STK board meeting, 10 December 1987, 1972, Board meeting minutes 1987–1988, STK Archive, ELKA.
164. STK managing group meeting, 8 Dec 1987, Managing group minutes, STK Archive, ELKA; "Suuntaa osallistumiselle," *Teollisuusviikko* 4 February 1988.
165. Records of the Finnish parliament 1989, 1067–1068.
166. Ibid., 1069–1070.
167. Social committee statement (SoVM) 15/1989. Finnish parliamentary documents 1989, 8–11.
168. Aimo Kairamo, *Tärkeintä on liike: Demokraattisen sosialismin edellytykset ja sosialidemokratian uudet tehtävät* (Helsinki: Tammi, 1989), 107–108.
169. Act on Personnel Funds. Säädös 814/1989, *Henkilöstörahastolaki*. http://finlex.fi/fi/laki/alkup/1989/19890814?search%5Btype%5D=pika&search%5Bpika%5D=henkil%C3%B6st%C3%B6rahastolaki.
170. *Teollisuusviikko* 23 November 1989, 9.
171. *Teollisuusviikko* 7 September 1989, 4.
172. Mansner, *Suomen työnantajain keskusliitto 1980–1992*, 335–336; Matti Vartiainen and Christina Sweins, *Henkilöstörahastot Suomessa: Toimivuus ja kannustevaikutukset* (Helsinki: Työministeriö, 2002), 12–17, 48–51, 63–65; Liisa Kauppinen, "Yrityksissä yleistyy nyt vanha palkitsemistapa, joka tekee työntekijöistä sijoittajia," *Helsingin Sanomat* 1 July 2019. https://www.hs.fi/talous/art-2000006159032.html.
173. Dalgaard, *Ved demokratiets grænse*, 247–252.
174. Ekdahl, *Mot en tredje väg II*, 304–306, 313–314.

175. Henrik Malm Lindberg and Stig-Björn Ljunggren, *Från jämlikhet till effektivitet: Om lärande socialdemokrati under 1980-talet* (Stockholm: Hjalmarson & Högberg, 2014), 97–100, 183–185; Johannes Lindvall, *The Politics of Purpose: Swedish Macroeconomic Policy after the Golden Age* (Göteborg: Göteborg University, 2004), 74–77; Andersson, *Between Growth and Security*, 105–108.
176. Åsard, *Kampen om löntagarfonderna*, 142–145.
177. Ekdahl, *Mot en tredje väg II*, 299–302; Sjöberg, *Löntagarfondsfrågan*, 162–165, 173–175; Ryner, *Capitalist Restructuring*, 171–174.
178. Pontusson, *Limits of Social Democracy*, 232–235.
179. Viktorov, *Fordismens kris*, 201–203.
180. Pontusson, *Limits of Social Democracy*, 228–232.
181. Sjöberg, *Löntagarfondsfrågan*, 185–189, 212–215; Lindvall, *The Politics of Purpose*, 46–50; Blyth, *Great Transformations*, 207–209; Pontusson, *Limits of Social Democracy*, 138–142.
182. Andersson, *Between Growth and Security*, 112–113; Blyth, *Great Transformations*, 219–222, 244–247.
183. For example, Sassoon, *One Hundred Years of Socialism*, 445–449, 458–461.
184. Stråth, *Mellan två fonder*, 207–209. The Finnish policy change of the late 1970s and consensus between the Social Democrats and business interests has a similar symbol, the conference of Korpilampi in 1977, which is discussed in Chap. 5.
185. Stråth, *Mellan två fonder*, 207–209; Blyth, *Great Transformations*, 266–270.

CHAPTER 5

New Economic Paradigm Narrows the Horizon of Democratization

From the 'Golden Age' to the 'New Spirit' of Capitalism

The post–World War II period in Western countries was characterized by 'democratic capitalism' and 'mixed economies,' which meant constraining private capitalism and markets with regulation and taxation, while states took responsibility for redistribution, social security and services.[1] During the 1970s, however, the economic situation in the West took a turn for the worse, and the prospects of reformist policy eroded along with the growth formula of the 'golden age' of capitalism. Multiple problems emerged around the same time. Profit rates had already fallen since the 1960s, and demand for unskilled labor decreased due to increasing competition especially from East Asia. Global economic regulation and efficient taxation became more difficult due to the internationalization of trade and gray finance markets. The Bretton Woods currency regime was broken down as the United States needed to fix its balance of payments deficit that had deepened due to the Vietnam War. The first oil crisis of 1973 and more volatile currency markets kept inflation high even during economic stagnation, and the resulting phenomenon of 'stagflation' was alien to mainstream economic theory. All these changes were widely perceived as elements of an economic crisis and made new economic policies a credible option.[2]

I. Kärrylä, *Democracy and the Economy in Finland and Sweden since 1960*, Palgrave Studies in Political History,
https://doi.org/10.1007/978-3-030-80631-6_5

New growth formulas had to be sought from trends that were already visible. Western economies went increasingly global, and industrial mass production began to give way to services and the 'information society.' In economic history this has been called the 'third industrial revolution' or the transition from 'Fordism' to 'post-Fordism.' This meant demands and changes toward more flexible production and labor markets, which made the lives of Western wage-earners more uncertain. It became easier for firms to outsource and move to other parts of the world, which increased the risk of unemployment and urged employees to constantly develop themselves and gain new competences that have value for employers.[3]

A shift toward anti-inflationary and market-oriented policies began in most Western countries in the second half of the 1970s. Maintaining Keynesian demand stimulation in the context of high inflation, rising public debt and balance of payments deficits became increasingly difficult. Socialist and Keynesian ideas were gradually discredited, and politicians turned to conservative and liberal economic beliefs as well as neoclassical and monetarist economics. The latter seemed more credible in solving actual economic problems, and they were backed by political forces that were growing stronger, which formed a self-strengthening cycle. The new economic paradigm looked at the macroeconomy through microeconomic models that were based on utility-maximizing, rational individuals. It advocated free markets to take over resource allocation instead of the allegedly inefficient public sector. The main task of the public authorities was controlling the money supply and inflation.[4]

Experiences of failed expansive policies during the crisis served as warnings to other countries. International organizations, especially the IMF and the OECD, began to advocate new economic doctrines and demand austere policies. For example, the British Labour government had to turn to anti-inflationary and budget-balancing policy in 1976 to secure a loan from the IMF. After this, Prime Minister James Callaghan declared that the principles of Keynesianism no longer worked.[5] In the United States, Jimmy Carter's administration turned toward monetarist anti-inflationary economic policy and carried out substantial deregulations in public transport, telecommunications and finance.[6] In some countries the neoliberal paradigm change was more abrupt and ideological, while in others it was piecemeal and driven by economists and other technocrats.[7] Below I will show that the Nordic countries fall into the latter category.

Politically, the turn to global capitalism and more uncertain and competitive labor markets has been interpreted as signifying the break of the 'postwar compromise' between capital and labor in Western countries. During the golden years of economic growth, labor gained a growing share of welfare. But when growth declined, capital had to ensure its profits by means that had become available, such as moving production to developing countries. This left labor in a weaker position, while states increasingly had to issue public debt to finance public services and social benefits. At the same time, the finance sector increased its importance and became the paragon of flexible capitalism. Several scholars have argued that this development has since the 1970s accentuated the contradiction of capitalism and democracy. Capital can move freely to different locations, and transnational investors exercise increasing influence on the politics of indebted countries. The priority of governments is to offer lucrative business environments by decreasing regulation and taxation of capital. At the same time, citizens' interest toward democratic participation has declined.[8]

Sociologists Luc Boltanski and Ève Chiapello have argued that an important change since the 1970s was the waning critique of capitalism and the birth of a "new spirit of capitalism," which derived its legitimation especially from the concepts of flexibility and personal autonomy that had been heralded also by the New Left. The new spirit managed to legitimate changes in capitalism despite growing unemployment and uncertainty brought by economic crises and the flexibilization of working life.[9] Boltanski and Chiapello stress that capitalism has always been able to absorb parts of critique to repair its own contradictions and transform into more morally and economically viable forms. The postwar compromise was one phase of capitalism where demands for more stability, security and democracy were embedded in the system. However, capitalism has always sought more efficient means of accumulation, which has eventually transformed ideas and practices, undermined stability, and provoked new waves of critique.[10] This interpretation comes close to Karl Polanyi's classic argument of 'double movement' between market expansion and social protection.[11]

In a world of new economic ideas and dynamics, political actors perceived the possibilities of democratic control over the economy as more dubious. The aim of this chapter is to examine how economic beliefs changed in Finland and Sweden in the late 1970s and early 1980s, and how this can explain the changing meanings and usages of concepts like economic and enterprise democracy, which were witnessed already in Chaps. 3 and 4.

The Political Mobilization of Business

Along with the economic crisis, another key phenomenon that affected economic policy and the ideational landscape around economic democracy from the 1970s onward was the increasing political activity of private business. In Europe and the United States, business began to act as a more coherent group, pursue its interests politically and influence public opinion. From the late 1960s onward, companies had faced sinking profits while public opinion turned more critical of private business. Leftist movements spurred demands for the protection of workers, consumers and the environment, and regulation of these areas was increased during the 1960s and 1970s. As a response, employer unions and chambers of commerce became politically active and several business think tanks were established.[12] The offensive strategy of business succeeded in promoting new beliefs on viable economic policy, especially in the context of the global economic crisis. The idea of think tanks that would disseminate arguments and policies supporting the free market economy came from Friedrich Hayek and the Mont Pèlerin society, who initially called themselves 'neoliberals.' Largely thanks to the Society, think tanks became a transnational phenomenon. Hayek himself was still active in public debate during the 1970s, and in 1974 received the unofficial Nobel Prize in economics, awarded by the Bank of Sweden. As early as in the 1940s, he had explicitly declared a 'battle of ideas' for the market economy, against socialism and state intervention, but it was only in the 1970s that this battle seemed to be truly beginning.[13]

Development in Finland and Sweden during the 1970s resembled that in other Western and Nordic countries.[14] Employer and business representatives felt themselves underdogs compared to trade unions and socialist parties. Business wanted to influence the public atmosphere, which was perceived as very critical of capitalism and market economy.[15] However, the timing of actions was slightly different in Finland and Sweden. Finnish business began to raise its profile and PR work by establishing the think tank EVA (Finnish Business and Policy Forum) in 1974. It was founded and funded by Finland's largest industry and employer organizations to promote business- and market-friendly attitudes. Like SAF and Swedish think tanks, EVA became an outspoken critic of a large public sector, high taxation and state intervention in the economy, while also advocating a wide consensus between political and social groups. The organization sought to portray itself as a neutral forum of cooperation and information dissemination. In practice, EVA channeled financial support to center-right parties and organizations in order to prevent the looming left-wing hegemony. Cooperation between the Communists and Social Democrats was considered especially dangerous for a free society.[16]

EVA recognized the Social Democratic Party as the most significant political group in Finland and therefore sought to establish good contacts with it. SDP leaders were open to this pursuit and began regular meetings with the think tank as well as other business representatives, gradually forming a mutual understanding of priorities in economic policy. These included securing the competitiveness of the export industry, preventing inflation and reaching moderate wage agreements, which became key elements of the new Social Democratic policy in the late 1970s.[17] This kind of cooperation between SDP, business and right-wing groups was not a novel phenomenon, but it had roots in the anticommunist endeavors of the 1940s and 1950s. However, the cooperation had mostly been on hiatus during the terms of Paasio and Sorsa as SDP's leaders since the mid-1960s.[18]

As described in Chap. 4, Swedish business also increased its political activity considerably in the latter half of the 1970s. This was a break from the cooperative policy of the 1950s and 1960s. There were certain continuities with the campaign against the planned economy in the 1940s, during which the first business-funded think tanks and foundations had been established in Sweden. The campaign had utilized Hayek's arguments and the translation of his *Road to Serfdom* was funded by the Swedish Free Enterprise Fund (*Näringslivets Fond*).[19] In the 1970s, similar development took place as the employer confederation SAF broadened its role from labor market issues to economic policy in general and launched an extensive PR campaign to promote a positive image of the market economy. As in many other countries, Swedish business found itself politically and ideologically cornered. Member companies expressed their frustration with SAF during the economic crisis. Market shares were declining and especially in the technology sector there was pressure for more decentralized wage bargaining due to the transnational movement toward more flexible production.[20] At SAF's general meeting in May 1976, CEO Curt-Steffan Giesecke stated that as the labor market was increasingly regulated politically, employers also had to strengthen their political contacts.[21]

SAF's new chair Curt Nicolin became a central architect of the organization's new and more active role.[22] SAF's PR campaign was partly a counter-move to the LO campaign for wage-earner funds, but SAF went beyond that single question and launched a general campaign for the market economy. Employers wanted to challenge the leftist ideological debate, which had especially attracted young people. Besides its own members, SAF wanted to influence schools, universities and the media.[23] SAF spent millions on campaigning and propagating its beliefs. The main theme at first was stopping the growth of the public sector, for which SAF offered a positive alternative with its main slogan, "free entrepreneurship." As part of its PR efforts, SAF began to arrange congresses, like political parties and wage-earner organizations had done for decades, to discuss and gain publicity for the themes of free market economy and entrepreneurship.[24]

In Sweden, free market ideas were also promoted by think tanks such as the newly established Timbro. They did not portray themselves as political actors but claimed to tell the truth about the Swedish economy. New economic ideas started to gain growing support in the economic downturn of the late 1970s. Beliefs in the public sector hindering economic development also began to be expressed in the media.[25] Bo Stråth has emphasized that SAF's new line was not a radical renewal but marked the reemergence of ideas that had been latent for a couple of decades. Stråth finds that the ideas of business had connections to Anglo-American neoliberalism but also distinctly Swedish traits. There were continuities with the planned economy and pension fund debates, but political dynamics changed considerably when SAF and LO moved from partners to adversaries.[26]

Mark Blyth has argued that the political mobilization of Swedish business in the 1970s was a counter-move to the mobilization of labor, which had brought about working life reforms through legislation instead of agreements.[27] This was certainly one reason for mobilization, although Stråth has argued that SAF did not see labor legislation as a large threat, but partly a necessary concession to tone down the leftist critique. Only the wage-earner fund proposal raised stronger concerns.[28] According to Peter Swenson, the main thrust for mobilization against the centralized labor market model came from the extremely solidaristic wage policy LO was pushing in the 1970s. This made especially the engineering industries question the 'Swedish model.'[29] Many scholars have argued that the internationalization of the Swedish export sector was a key factor behind the increasing political activity and influence of business. Export companies prioritized low inflation and flexible wages that increased international competitiveness instead of maintaining demand in the domestic market with full employment.[30] Sweden's centralized bargaining model began to break down in the early 1980s. SAF tried to confront LO with a shutdown in 1980, but found the employee side too strong. The breakthrough of sectoral bargaining came in 1983, when Metalworkers' Union made a separate agreement with *Verkstadsförening* (VF), which represented major export industries in the engineering sector.[31]

However, the public statements of Swedish employers make it attractive to lean on Blyth's interpretation. Even if the main reasons for decentralization of wage bargaining were changes in production methods and global economic dynamics, the mobilization in general may well have been a counter-move to the political activity of trade unions. Swedish employers often expressed beliefs about the trade union movement becoming too strong a player in politics, threatening the market economy.[32] The employers commonly portrayed their activity as a response to this politicization. In 1980, Curt Nicolin argued in an interview with *Tiden* that the Social Democrats had previously been more pragmatic and willing to cooperate. Ernst Wigforss, for example, had realized that generous corporate taxation would create resources to build the welfare state. Now the attitude was different, Nicolin argued. Corporate profits had to be increased and investments made profitable to get Sweden out of economic crisis, but this had proven to be an unpopular strategy.[33]

The strategy of Finnish business differed greatly from the Swedish line of confrontation. From early on, EVA and its CEO, former diplomat Max Jakobson, began to pursue a politics of cooperation between interest groups. The practice of centralized incomes policy agreements was portrayed as an example of fruitful cooperation. EVA's strategy differed from the general right-wing critique, which portrayed interest organizations as obstructions to democracy, but there was a clear logic behind it. In the atmosphere of the 1970s, Finnish business conceived that left-wing forces were hegemonic, and the state already restricted the power of business considerably. Corporatist practices could thus be viewed as a viable way to make the voice of business better heard. Jakobson began to talk about the 'social contract,' the classic concept in political philosophy, to denote a regime where economic and labor market policy would be determined through negotiation and mutual understanding.[34]

Belief in the importance of corporatist practices was shared by most Social Democrat and trade union leaders, who often considered them a vital part of Finnish democracy. The counter-belief of corporatism undermining parliamentary democracy was voiced often but supported by minorities mostly on the farther edges of the political left and right. During its first years EVA sometimes portrayed trade unions as centralized and undemocratic organizations, but it later raised cooperation between interest groups and the state almost as the highest form of democracy. This ideal of cooperation and consensus soon manifested in the new economic policy of the Social Democratic government, which is discussed below.[35] Swedish employers sometimes viewed Finland as a model country of sorts, where Social Democrats and even some Communists had realized the importance of free enterprise and market economy.[36] Perhaps the best explanation to this difference between Finland and Sweden was the position of the Social Democrats. Finnish left-wing and trade union radicalism was at least as strong as the Swedish, but the Social Democrats did not have the means and perhaps not even the will to channel this radicalism into political decisions as effectively. They had to make compromises with the center-right parties, and the constitution formed more severe boundaries to policymaking. It is noteworthy that at the turn of the 1970s and 1980s, political relations in Sweden were characterized by confrontation and in Finland by cooperation, but similar political and ideational developments toward the emphasis of free markets took place in both countries.

It is not unproblematic to label the mobilization of business in the Nordic countries as rise of 'neoliberalism,' even though the ideas they promoted corresponded well with those of neoliberal thinkers. However, it is noteworthy that when the concept of neoliberalism made its breakthrough in Sweden, it was for a short period used for positive self-identification. The Swedish newspaper database reveals that the use of words with the root 'neoliberal' (*nyliberal*) shot up from fewer than 10 hits per year to over 20 in 1980 and over 200 in 1981. This was thanks to the translation of the international bestseller *Tomorrow, Capitalism* (in Swedish *I morgon* kapitalism, original title *Demain le capitalisme*) by the French journalist and member of the Mont Pèlerin Society, Henri Lepage. The book was a popularized account of new economic theories, such as monetarism, human capital and public choice theories, whose conceivers the author called 'neoliberal economists.'[37]

The conservative newspaper *Svenska Dagbladet* in particular treated neoliberalism as a positive phenomenon.[38] It was sometimes equated with 'neoconservatism' (*nykonservatism*), perhaps because the liberal-conservative hybrid ideas and policies of Margaret Thatcher and Ronald Reagan caused some conceptual confusion.[39] However, quite soon the connotation of neoliberalism became predominantly negative, as had already happened in the English-speaking world.[40] Swedish Social

Democrats used the concept in their 1981 crisis program to signify the right-wing ideas they opposed, while business representatives and center-right parties continued to advocate the concept of the free market economy rather than a distinct ideology like 'neoliberalism.'[41] In Finland, the breakthrough of neoliberalism (*uusliberalismi*) as a term is more difficult to trace, but the database of the largest newspaper, *Helsingin Sanomat*, implies that its use became more common only in 1985.[42]

Cooperation and Participation Instead of Democracy

Finnish and Swedish center-right and employer ideas on economic democratization retained its general character in the political mobilization of the late 1970s and early 1980s. Employer and business representatives stressed economic efficiency as the key concept to which democracy was to be adapted. The thought and rhetoric of employers and center-right parties became fixed in the sense that the concept of economic democracy—if it was used at all—would refer exclusively to the workplace level. The ideas of collective ownership or public steering of the economy were not taken up in any positive sense. The concepts of 'owner democracy' and 'people's capitalism' were rarely expressed, even though their key element of dispersed private ownership was retained. However, its relation to democracy became more ambiguous.[43] In general, the underlying belief in democracy's unsuitability to the economic sphere seems to have strengthened in employer and center-right ideational constellations.

Democracy at the workplace level was conceptualized as before: Employee decision-making, control over corporate management and significant redistribution of power and ownership were not considered necessary criteria for democracy. Instead, employers and center-right parties emphasized employees' rights to be informed and consulted on corporate matters. As seen in Chap. 3, this had been the most common usage of the concept of enterprise democracy in employer rhetoric in the 1960s and even in earlier debates.[44] The concepts of participation, cooperation and communication played key roles in defining the borders of desirable democratization, which was adapted to 'economic facts,' efficiency and competitiveness. In this ideational constellation, individual employee participation was considered a source of productivity, but collective employee influence and ownership continued to be portrayed as bureaucratic and inflexible, therefore jeopardizing economic efficiency.

In Finland, the think tank EVA put the issues of economic and enterprise democracy on its agenda soon after its creation.[45] The CEO Max Jakobson in particular took up the concepts frequently. Jakobson's previous post as Finland's ambassador in Sweden had acquainted him with the debate on economic democracy. When Jakobson stated provocatively that Finland had a dangerous neighbor, he did not refer to the Soviet Union but to Sweden, whose social reforms and growing public sector also put pressure on Finland.[46] EVA tried to channel reform demands in a direction that would not put too much strain on private business. In 1975, Jakobson gave a speech where he expressed the widely held belief that extending democracy in the economic sphere was a crucial developmental feature of contemporary societies. It was not to be taken as a "necessary evil," as fulfilling employee needs provided a potential solution to problems like alienation in working life and the scarcity of workforce. Jakobson conflated economic democracy and enterprise democracy, leaving macro-level economic planning and steering outside their scope. He gave economic democracy a meaning that was in line with the views that emphasized individual participation and questioned the conflict between capital and labor.[47]

Jakobson found that increasing demands for employee participation in capital formation would make it a necessary element of economic democracy, but like most business representatives, he advocated individual instead of collective solutions. Jakobson referred to the 1976 electoral campaigns in Sweden and believed the debate was bound to migrate to Finland and Finnish business should actively develop systems that would widen the ownership base.[48] By giving positive comments on economic democracy, EVA tried to appear a reformist and conciliatory organization while simultaneously guarding the interests of business and preventing the most undesirable versions of reforms. It was an explicit aim for EVA to avoid the "harmful course" the wage-earner fund debate had taken in Sweden, as the think tank's chair, banker Mika Tiivola stated in 1976.[49] EVA warned that if the left and the trade union movement took the initiative, the debate was in danger of being locked into Swedish-type "socialization plans."[50] Economic democracy was a top theme to EVA for a few years, but in the early 1980s it increasingly concentrated on the need to slow down the growth of the public sector.[51] The think tank noticed that the societal atmosphere had turned rightward in Finland, and the Communists in particular were rapidly losing support. Instead of socialism, the main opponents to the market economy were growth criticism and environmental values.[52]

Major organizations of Finnish business and industry followed EVA's advice and began proactively formulating a new stance on economic democracy and wage-earner funds, the debate on which was landing in Finland from Sweden. In 1978, STK chair Stig H. Hästö made the familiar point that economic democracy was desirable on the condition that it was defined properly—so that it promoted Finland's economic success. For him, there was only a shade of difference between redistribution of economic power and outright socialism.[53]

In 1978, a working group between STK and the Central Association of Finnish Industry (*Teollisuuden keskusliitto*, TKL) determined eight criteria to be taken into account when developing economic democracy. This meant a detailed delimitation of the desirable scope of the concept. The first criterion was the one that had been central all along: Economic democracy should have a positive effect on motivation for work and productivity. As was common, the employers believed that material incentives had the biggest impact on motivation, although they were only one of many management methods that should be used. The second criterion was that economic democracy should secure capital formation in the whole national economy. STK and TKL believed this required making the system mandatory or so lucrative that most companies would participate voluntarily. In addition, economic democracy was to support the functioning of the market mechanism and be based on private ownership and the personal input of participants. These criteria were considered necessary for motivation and productivity, and they denied the chance of collective ownership and restrictions on the strategic decisions of companies. Economic democracy was also to be voluntary and company-specific, which effectively ruled out the earlier mentioned possibility of a nationwide system. Fund accumulation was to be based primarily on payroll taxes instead of profit-sharing, and the system was to receive public support, for example in the form of tax exemptions. STK and TKL believed that a simple model of stock-saving might be the most viable solution, but they suspected that it would not be considered satisfactory from the perspective of the distribution of power in enterprises.[54] The above criteria summed up the business and employer constellation of economic and enterprise democracy that had already been visible for decades: Efficient decision-making and private ownership were to be secured, and only models of economic democracy supporting these principles could be accepted.

Even though some business representatives continued to treat the concepts of economic and enterprise democracy as something potentially desirable, their use became rare in employer and right-wing rhetoric in the early 1980s. This was an intentional rhetorical move in both Finland and Sweden. We have already seen that SAF was very suspicious of the concept of economic democracy, as it was considered too strongly linked to collective ownership. Soon after their 1978 working group memo, the Finnish STK and TKL chose a strategy similar to their Swedish counterparts' and decided not to stimulate the debate by bringing forward their own model of wage-earner funds.[55] The debate around economic democracy and wage-earner funds was then relatively calm until 1981 and SDP's proposal on cooperation funds. This prompted the employer side to again prepare arguments to counter attempts to limit managerial power.[56] The next spring, however, STK decided that the public debate on economic democracy should not be stimulated at all. The employers therefore did not want to follow their Swedish counterparts, who used a lot of money and workforce for propaganda against economic democracy.[57] This choice was understandable, as Finnish wage-earner organizations and social democrats were rather silent on the issue, which made counter-campaigning potentially counterproductive.

In the early 1980s, Finnish employer and center-right rhetoric on economic democratization hence turned from proactive to reactive. Economic and enterprise democracy had been difficult concepts for the employers all along due to their strong links to the ideas of redistributing power and making leaders accountable to their subjects. This can be seen in the arguments claiming that democracy, especially representative democracy, was unsuitable for economic life and should remain a political practice.[58] Letting go of the concept of democracy as applied to economic and working life—regardless of its force as a legitimation concept—supports my interpretation that the employer side's strategy regarding economic and enterprise democracy was mostly reactive to begin with. They had previously adopted and sought to redefine the concepts of economic and enterprise democracy because the trade unions and left-wing parties advocated them so strongly and thereby condemned the prevailing practices of the economy and working life as undemocratic. This was a serious attempt to delegitimize prevailing economic relations. However, as the employers' position strengthened from the late 1970s onward, they did not find the concepts of democratization necessary, but could more freely promote the belief of politics and the economy being separate spheres operating on different logics and rules. For example, STK's anniversary conference of 1982 did not include any explicit discussion on economic or enterprise democracy, but demands were made for industrial peace and more flexible collective agreements.[59]

Even though they were no longer explicitly connected to democracy, the concepts and beliefs used by the employers in their earlier redefinitions retained their rhetorical and practical importance. During the 1980s, terms such as cooperation and employee participation were increasingly used in employer rhetoric and management theory in order to promote the ideals of human-centered leadership and affirm the beliefs of working life as harmonious activity contributing to the common good. These terms and concepts were earlier grouped under the category of enterprise democracy, but at this point 'working life reform' and 'new work organizations' became more common future-oriented umbrella concepts. In employer thought, the ideas of cooperation and participation thus continued to provide a horizon of possibilities for improving efficiency and competitiveness. As before, employers believed that increasing employee influence could have them perceive the interests of the enterprise and accept necessary changes. One could interpret that the remaining terms continued to embody a certain conception of democracy, but it seems clear that by discarding economic and enterprise democracy as explicit terms, the employer side sought to shrug off some of their undesirable historical meanings and references.

As discussed previously, participation and cooperation had become key concepts in organization and management theories during the 1960s and 1970s and continued to increase in importance. A common belief, which made participation demands more pressing in the late 1970s and early 1980s, was that 'soft' measures were in fact the only significant way left for increasing productivity in a postindustrial world.[60] The participation discourse was therefore connected to concepts such as structural change and industrial renewal, which signified the erosion of the old 'Fordist' economic order. A new key concept in the 1970s was 'flexibility,' which pointed to the need to invent new practices that would help enterprises to adapt quickly to the internationalized information society.[61] The concepts of corporate and organizational culture also became prominent around this time as means of improving competitiveness and coping with constant change. Viewing employees as a resource and allowing their participation in planning and executing new practices was central to these approaches as well.[62] These developments are good examples of the 'artistic critique' of capitalism becoming part of management practices, even though they were perhaps not primarily conceived as measures to increase the legitimacy of capitalism.

The employer desire for local and flexible participation was objectivized and given a scientific form in management guidebooks and articles in the 1970s and 1980s. It was included in most new management approaches, such as management by objectives and management by results. These were commonly based on distributing operational power while strategic power—and determination of the aspired results—remained in the hands of senior management.[63] Some researchers have argued that the approaches of the human relations school were adopted slowly in Finland, and were rather combined with technical rationalization than replacing it.[64] This seems accurate when looking at the management discourse of the 1980s. Even though the topics of cooperation, participation and organizational culture were popular, much was also written about 'traditional' management issues such as rationalization, technology and productivity, with little reference to human relations.

The effort to combine human and technical aspects was interestingly visible in an article titled "Modern Rationalization is Cooperation," published in the business magazine *Tehokas yritys* (Efficient enterprise). It emphasized that all employees should consider rationalization as part of their job description and the development of the whole company. Practical cooperation could begin only after this.[65] In Sweden, too, many beliefs were expressed that implied the hybridization of old hierarchical and new participatory management and organization models. One could simultaneously say that strong leaders were needed, but they had to give employees influence and responsibility, and aim at meaningful work instead of mere efficiency.[66] In fact, these beliefs in rationalization through cooperation and participation had quite old elements that had already figured in the tasks of works councils from the 1940s onward.

Even though occasional use continued, it is notable that the concepts of economic and enterprise democracy faded from employer rhetoric in the 1980s. New practices of shop floor participation and employee autonomy, such as quality circles adopted from Japan, were introduced constantly. They were close to the earlier ideas of self-managing groups and aimed at increasing efficiency and work satisfaction by sharing operational power. In quality circles, employees cooperated semi-autonomously to find ways to improve productivity and product quality. However, these practices were rarely connected to the concept of democracy in books and articles.[67]

The Market Economy and Free Enterprise as Guardians of the Common Good

As we have seen before, employers were not sacrificing all other values at the altar of economic efficiency, even though efficiency and productivity usually occupied the top of their conceptual hierarchy. If we look at employer rhetoric more broadly, their hierarchy was firmly aimed toward the common good, national interest, welfare and at times freedom as the ultimate legitimation concepts. However, the content of the common good was not portrayed as open or negotiable but as an objective fact with a very economic nature. As many scholars have argued, the objectivity of the common good has been a common belief in Finnish political and especially employer thought and rhetoric.[68] The national interest included the growth of the national economy, living standards and welfare. Efficiency and competitiveness were necessary for securing the national interest, not ends in themselves.

This kind of hierarchy was a fundamental part of employer rhetoric in Finland and Sweden. STK consciously built its self-image around the story of the Finnish welfare state and emphasized its role in promoting social reforms.[69] In 1982, this idea was brought into the title of STK's 75th anniversary conference: "Profitable Enterprise—Welfare of Society." According to the organization's historical interpretation, "with the help of profitable companies we have been able to lift Finland from the underdeveloped country it was in the turn of the century among the world's welfare states."[70] The welfare state was hence conceived as a crucial component of the common good and an important legitimation concept in Finland. Employer thought and rhetoric often placed employee participation and motivation in a hierarchical relation to serve the national mission of growing the national economy and increasing welfare.[71]

At SAF's congress of 1977, the agenda of Swedish business was expressed clearly. Its main components were the same as their Finnish counterparts'. Expansion of the public sector and selective support to declining industries were criticized, increased mobility in the labor market demanded and the connection of work motivation and more flexible wage systems emphasized.[72] Like STK, SAF sought legitimation to private business by appealing to the common good and benefits to society—especially employment. According to Chair Curt Nicolin, the task of enterprises was "to plan their operations in the service of society with resourcefulness and foresight." But this did not mean that employment could be secured everywhere. According to Nicolin, these kinds of pursuits would only have harmed companies, employees and society.[73]

Nicolin argued that critique against private business was exaggerated and backed up his argument by showing statistics on the improvement of living standards and working conditions in the postwar era. Real wages had risen significantly, while working hours and the number of accidents had decreased.[74] Nicolin hoped that the Swedish trade unions would retain their positive attitude toward rationalization to increase productivity. Unfortunately, in recent years wage increases had exceeded productivity, which had damaged the competitiveness of Swedish companies. Nicolin found it hard to see how balance could be restored in the economy without decreasing living standards. Among the most important policy measures, according to Nicolin, were general decreases in employer fees and marginal taxes.[75] According to the congress statement, Sweden's economic problems could be solved only from the foundations of a market economy. SAF argued that this required tackling inflation and restoring the profitability of business.[76]

Like their Finnish counterparts, Swedish employers were constantly worried about the state of the market economy, which had a certain connection to democracy, at least as a precondition. At SAF's congress of 1977, employer representatives leaned on the traditional combination of market economy and political democracy, which at least implicitly made a distinction between the concepts political and economic, democracy and market. They were separate but mutually supportive domains. Carl-Johan Westholm from SAF's PR department was worried that the space for commercial activity was constantly narrowing, while the economy was increasingly regulated by political decisions. Westholm argued that demands for economic democracy would always lead to majority rule, whereas a market economy was based on the free interplay of large or small groups of producers and consumers. In Westholm's view, the principle of freedom of contract was not a system of privileges, but the majority principle would lead to one: namely, to control of enterprises by politicians and eventually the destruction of the market economy, which "in a historically unique way combines freedom and the rule of the people into something practically achievable."[77] Westholm thus implied that the market economy had democratic qualities in and of itself, even though he did not identify market transactions with voting. Nevertheless, he expressed liberal beliefs where the markets figured as a realm of free individuals making contracts with each other on a level playing field without coercion by any majority or collective. The possibility of market freedom being based on unequally accumulated resources rather than intrinsic rights was seldom reflected in employer rhetoric.

In the rhetoric of the Swedish Moderate party, individual freedom figured in the same fashion almost as a synonym for democracy. It was argued that if the right of personal ownership was discarded, "freedom would vanish and democracy lose its content."[78] The relation of freedom and democracy was interestingly reflected in Moderate study circle material written by the journalist Bo Ekegren for the election of 1979. According to Ekegren, freedom was not the same thing as democracy but something more. Democracy was a method of making decisions on common matters, and as such even a restriction to freedom—at least if it was constantly extended to new areas as socialists wanted. Ekegren wrote: "But the more is handled and decided commonly in society, the smaller becomes the space for the individual's freedom. Increased politicization means that individuals gain more chances to decide how others can shape their lives, but less chances to shape those of their own."[79] This shows that at least some Moderates found freedom more important than democracy. Ekegren did not conflate the two concepts but perceived a tension between them.[80] If these kinds of beliefs were widely held, they testify to the prevalence of the belief that democracy was an unsuitable principle and practice for the economic sphere. The free market economy was a sphere of individual freedom, not democracy. Politics and the economy were hence conceived as separate domains, even though economic freedom was often viewed as a prerequisite for democracy.

Ekegren argued clearly for the qualitative distinction of the two spheres: "The individual will steer economic life as a consumer and political life as a citizen." According to him, one had to assume that consumers had true power and were not easily manipulated, because if the opposite view was applied to political democracy, one could not rely on their making rational choices at the ballot box, either.[81] This view evokes the analogy between markets and democracy, which was seldom expressed in official party programs. However, as we have seen, the Moderates were not as confident of people's competence to make decisions in their third role, as employees, and were not willing to grant them more than consultative power in the management of enterprises. Moreover, it seems that while the market gave freedom to consumers, it dictated necessities to states and enterprises. Therefore, the preferred mode of governance in these collectives was expertise, based on ample knowledge of economic necessities.

According to Torbjörn Nilsson, debate on neoliberal ideas had started slowly among the Moderates, but the party's youth and student organizations propagated them actively. Traditional conservatives found the party's 1978 idea program too market liberal, but in effect it was a quite balanced combination of the two ideological strands. Nilsson prefers to use the notion 'liberal renaissance' instead of neoliberalism to highlight the continuities in the Moderates' ideology.[82] The Moderates adopted new market-oriented policies in the early 1980s, toward the end of their second term in government. This happened as professional economists let go of Keynesianism, which the Moderates had accepted as the basis of sound economic policy. Again in opposition from 1982 onward, the party adopted a more liberal position and demanded, for example, the abolishment of currency regulation.[83] Soon the Moderates began to talk about a full-fledged "systemic change," which meant decreasing the state's role, lowering taxes and privatizing and marketizing public services. The Moderates thus adopted neoliberal ideas earlier than the Finnish National Coalition Party but slightly later than the Danish liberal party *Venstre*, which began its reorientation in the early 1970s.[84] However, Nilsson points out that the Moderates retained many elements of conservative communitarianism despite increasing economic liberalism.[85]

Demands for free markets and entrepreneurship strengthened in the 1980s. The theme of SAF's congress of 1980 was "Creative or Guarding Sweden?" which referred to the choice of either letting creative entrepreneurs restart economic growth or keep guarding the bloated public sector. SAF's CEO Olof Ljunggren argued that Sweden was not experiencing a crisis of capitalism but of state power. Never before had there been such a powerful public sector, and so little room for the free market, he stated.[86] Curt Nicolin again showed telling charts, which illustrated how returns on capital had dropped below bank account interest, and how labor costs were around 25 times higher than profit after tax, even though many citizens believed differently.[87] SAF also started to criticize centralized wage bargaining more openly, and could portray it as a counter-concept to democratization. Nicolin stated that detailed central agreements did not rhyme with dispersion of power, market economy or optimization of freedom.[88] This time he concluded his speech with an uplifting note, reaffirming the belief in the great mission of private enterprises, their contribution to the common good and the constraints on their operations.

> it is the mission of entrepreneurs to fight for the people's interest. It is our duty to utilize our competences and the resources we have been placed to administer for the benefit of everyone. (...) We will not let ourselves be disturbed if the noble pursuits are placed under suspicion. We will fearlessly fight against ignorance, bureaucracy, indecisiveness and cowardice.[89]

This kind of rhetoric exemplifies how legitimizing power can be added to concepts related to private business and the market economy. Employers often talked in general terms about the tasks, interests and hardships of the 'entrepreneur,' even if they were referring to large corporations. The terms for 'enterprise'—*yritys* in Finnish and *företag* in Swedish—have the same root as the term 'entrepreneur' (*yrittäjä—företagare*). This easily leads to an intuitive identification of all companies, regardless of their size and branch, with the idea of an individual entrepreneur—a highly moral character who through their own sacrifices and risk-taking participates in creating common welfare. This has been a central principle of legitimation for capitalism and neoliberalism in general.[90] Finnish and Swedish employers also gained a powerful rhetorical tool in the term 'entrepreneur,' whose inherently positive connotation could be extended to large, even multinational, companies.

Finnish employers drew on the same beliefs and rhetorical figures that connected entrepreneurial spirit to the national interest and placed small businesses and large corporations under the 'entrepreneurial' bannèr . The official statement of STK's 1987 congress declared that entrepreneurial activity had created the foundation of Finland's welfare. New resources were to be released also in the future by fostering entrepreneurial spirit.[91] The concepts of employee and entrepreneur were brought closer to each other by conceptual innovations that developed the ideas of participation and employee responsibility in new directions. STK promoted the concept of 'inner entrepreneurship,' which meant that all employees should adopt an entrepreneurial attitude in their work and become more accountable in order to serve competitiveness.[92] As Pauli Kettunen has shown, demanding employees to think and act like entrepreneurs was no novel idea.[93] Entrepreneurs, who express the virtues of initiative, responsibility and risk-taking and do not depend on others, have always been model subjects in capitalist societies. At this point in history, the constellations behind the demand seem to have approached neoliberal ideas of 'entrepreneurship of the self' first analyzed by Michel Foucault.[94]

Social Democrats Choose the 'Third Way'

Like most other political groups, Social Democratic parties also turned to a new economic policy paradigm during the late 1970s and early 1980s. This happened at different times in different countries. The Finnish Social Democrats began to move toward anti-inflationary and budget-balancing economic policy as early as in 1975 when the economic crisis reached Finland. However, this was not a major break from the country's traditional prudent economic policy orientation. Finland prepared to apply for an IMF loan due to depleting currency reserves, which restricted economic policy even though the loan was eventually not needed.[95] SDP made a determined modification of its economic policy a couple of years later. The party went into opposition in September 1976, after the 'emergency government' with the Center Party and the People's Democrats resigned. Prime Minister Martti Miettunen continued with a centrist minority government.[96]

After only eight months, in May 1977, a new a coalition government including SDP, People's Democrats and the Center Party was formed by SDP's leader Kalevi Sorsa. SDP's leadership had a few months earlier held a meeting where they decided on an economic policy that would concentrate on stimulating private business and investment by subsidies and tax cuts, as well as preventing inflation through wage restraint. This line was motivated by perceived economic necessity, but also competition for middle-class voters. The party leadership feared they were being alienated by too leftist and socialist programs. The party also wanted to avoid an offensive opposition policy that could have increased the prospects of a bourgeois coalition between the Center and Conservative Parties.[97]

Within SDP, there was still support for state intervention and expansive policy, but the austere and business-friendly line prevailed. SDP's new policy, which shared many components with the emerging neoliberal thought, was manifested in the program of Sorsa's new government.[98] The government referred to its subsidies and tax cuts to private business with the concept of 'stimulation,' but as a whole it practiced austere fiscal policy, even though the economy was still stagnating. Historian Ville Yliaska has argued that this was a creative redefinition of 'stimulation,' which had not really belonged to the vocabulary of Finnish economic policy.[99] The Finnish word for economic stimulation—*elvytys*—literally means resuscitation. It is a rather dramatic medical metaphor, which may strengthen the image of the national economy as a matter of life and death and of objective expert knowledge.

According to Yliaska, however, Sorsa's government was not neoliberal in a Thatcherite sense, but rather Blairites 20 years before Tony Blair. Social Democratic policy in Finland now leaned on a thriving private sector but emphasized active employment policy and supporting research and development. Prime Minister Sorsa already talked about the information society as the goal of the next structural change and wanted to increase research and development expenditures.[100] In the late 1970s, the ideas of promoting research and innovation in the private sector to boost national competitiveness and hasten the development of a post-Fordist 'knowledge economy' became advocated by OECD economists. It is not surprising that the Social Democrats also adopted a 'Schumpeterian' view on competition and even creative destruction.[101] Blair was rather a latecomer, as it took 20 years for Labour to be able to implement this kind of policy.

The new economic policy consensus which the Social Democrats had negotiated with business organizations gained a visible public manifestation in autumn 1977 at a seminar held at the Korpilampi conference hotel. The event was organized to gain support for the policy that had already been formulated, but it became an important symbol and gave birth to the notion of 'the spirit of Korpilampi.' This was coined at the conference by Prime Minister Sorsa and referred to a qualitatively new mutual understanding between different social groups.[102] Many historians and contemporaries have considered the Korpilampi conference a milestone in Finnish consensus-building. It strengthened shared conceptions of national interest, which had already been present in incomes policy thinking: the necessities of securing international competitiveness and containing inflation. At this point, the Finnish Social Democrats had assumed the position of a 'state manager' cooperating more closely with business. In the process, economists and business think tanks assumed more power in defining policy content.[103]

The social scientist Juho Saari has argued that Korpilampi was significant in the sense of cultural redefinition and power of ideas: It contributed to defining the common interests of the nation.[104] According to Saari, the voice of business was the loudest at Korpilampi, which accentuated its dominant role in Finnish society.[105] Historian Antti Kujala has argued that Korpilampi was the single most important endpoint of left-wing radicalism in Finland. Following the trend of other European countries, it signified the waning influence of leftist thinking.[106] Historian Tapio Bergholm has provided a less dramatic view, according to which economic policy in the late 1970s represented a return to a stabilization policy traditionally practiced in Finland in economically difficult times. Concern for the competitiveness of the Finnish export industry was by no means new to the Social Democrats. Bergholm has also questioned the existence of consensus due to substantial disagreements between SDP and the Center Party, as well as between labor market organizations. There was perhaps consensus on the importance of competitiveness, but not on the means of promoting it.[107]

Whether a major turning point or not, perceived political and economic necessities played a significant role in facilitating the 'spirit of Korpilampi,' as they would a few years later in the crisis policy of the Swedish Social Democrats. These perceived necessities are a key explanation for the breakthrough of neoliberal thinking and fading rhetorical power of economic democracy during the following decade. As Pauli Kettunen has put it, in the late 1970s, state intervention in the economy began to turn into the economy's intervention in the state, and politics was giving way to neutral administration.[108] In Finland, economic necessity had traditionally played a major role in policymaking, but soon Sweden also turned away from the idea that the economy can be steered by active policymaking. In this sense, the political cultures of the two countries were moving closer to each other.

Beliefs on economic constraints and necessities were very much present in the speeches held at the Korpilampi conference. They exemplify Finland's traditional self-image in foreign and economic policy. Prime Minister Kalevi Sorsa stated that Finland was a small country, whose economy was strongly hit by tides from the external world. Finland could not dictate rules to others, but the country had to "compete with the stronger on their terms."[109] Sorsa argued that Finland could not "jump out of the world" and stay behind trade barriers, but social and economic development required "hard work and competition in an integrating world."[110] This did not mean concentrating exclusively on cost competitiveness, but Sorsa also emphasized the Schumpeterian components in SDP's thinking. Finland had to invest in technological development, product quality and marketing. As a policy priority, Sorsa mentioned aiming at full employment, but the task was difficult, and its target was set to the early 1980s. More immediate goals were lowering inflation and increasing the competitiveness of Finnish production.[111]

Prime Minister Sorsa emphasized economic policy as a national mission. Achieving its goals required open and confidential cooperation between the government and economic interest groups. Sorsa said that there were of course contradicting interests, but "(a)s a nation, we have so many common interests that we have all the reasons to make efforts for getting more planning, common sense and mutual responsibility into economic policy."[112] In the rhetoric of consensus-seeking, a recurring belief was the need to somehow get beyond politics and find out what was objectively good for the country. In his closing speech, Sorsa added that an important step was to find an agreement on "basic facts" that were independent from political and economic interests. However, he also emphasized democratization of working life as an important goal and said that it was not necessarily in contradiction with the stimulation of private business. Adaptation to the new economic situation required "flexibility and a spirit of conciliation" ranging from enterprises to the national level.[113] This view of enterprise democracy approached the employer side's version, where mutual interests would be perceived and seeming contradictions evaporate.

The Social Democratic turn from economic steering to market adaptation continued in the early 1980s. The party retained their anti-inflationary and restrictive fiscal policy and prioritized structural renewal of the economy over maintaining full employment. There were grounds for austerity, as the Finnish economy was already growing steadily, although employment had not reached pre-crisis levels. SDP's leadership portrayed its policy as an alternative to Thatcherism and Reaganism, but it also had its internal critics who argued that policy was conducted too much on the terms of business. The party continued to pay attention to the growing number of white-collar employees, who had overtaken blue-collars as the largest employee group in 1977. The government also started the privatization and restructuring of state-owned enterprises and made profitability a norm for all of them. This was influenced by bad experiences: A new public venture, the teletube manufacturer Valco, had proven an outright disaster in the late 1970s and was closed after only four years of operation.[114] However, most major state-owned companies, such as the oil refiner Neste and steel manufacturers Outokumpu and Rautaruukki, had always operated under professional management and pursued strong profitability.

The Swedish Social Democrats perceived the same changes in the global economy in their 1975 congress, even though major policy change took some years. The Finance Minister Gunnar Sträng stressed the importance of the current account balance, which had become a problem for many countries due to the economic crisis. Sträng explained that Sweden's exports should grow in order to maintain foreign exchange reserves and avoid taking more debt.[115] According to Sträng's belief, the economic environment had changed drastically and become more unpredictable, which meant that economic policy had to be flexible. Old solutions did not seem to hold any longer: Previously it had been down to stimulating demand by increased public spending, but now all countries had to be wary of inflation, which had remained high despite economic stagnation. Sträng explained that economic policy was more complicated as "we have moved to an international economy of unprecedented scale and breadth."[116]

Sträng's speech exemplifies the crisis of Keynesian economic policy, which occurred after the oil crisis brought about an almost unprecedented phenomenon: Stagflation. Demand stimulation through public spending lost its viability as an option, as it was feared to increase inflation and balance of payments problems. In addition, the disbanding of the Bretton Woods system had made the international currency markets more volatile, which increased the role of current accounts and currency reserves. In the ideational constellations of contemporaries, economic necessities thus had a clear and quantifiable foundation: They were based on indicators like inflation, exchange rates, reserves and current account balances. In an increasingly interconnected world, the possibilities of national economic policy were perceived as more limited.[117] This also limited the prospects of economic democracy—especially its common component in Social Democratic constellations, state control over the economy.

In Sweden, political power relations shifted in September 1976, when the Social Democrats' 44-year term in government ended. Even though SAP retained its position as the clearly largest party with over 42% of the vote, the bourgeois parties gained a slight majority in parliament. The Center Party gained notable support with its antinuclear campaign. It became the largest bourgeois party, with 24% of the vote and its chair Thorbjörn Fälldin the new prime minister.[118] The alternative to Social Democratic rule had thus finally been actualized. This also paved the way for policy changes, as the radical development of enterprise democracy practically stopped during the center-right rule.[119] However, at first the bourgeois parties implemented expansive economic policy in the steepening economic downturn. They wanted to stick to the objective of full employment, which enjoyed overwhelming support among citizens. A majority of Swedish economists continued to vouch for Keynesianism. The government subsidized declining industries and devalued the currency instead of letting unemployment rise. This did not stimulate investments, jobs and growth sufficiently, as Swedish companies increasingly invested abroad, and growing demand was directed to imports. Instead, inflation remained high and the current account deficit became a growing problem for the Swedish economy.[120]

The Social Democrats interpreted the economic situation as the worst crisis in capitalism since the Great Depression. They criticized the government's policy and called for larger public investments to stimulate the economy, but perceived inflation, public debt and current account deficit as growing constraints to economic policy.[121] SAP's 1978 congress was penetrated by concerns regarding the economic crisis. The main motivation behind statements and policy proposals was restoring economic growth and securing full employment in Sweden by increasing capital formation and investing in industrial development.[122] As discussed in Chap. 4, wage-earner funds were now perceived as an important instrument for these tasks.[123] However, traditional ideas of the planned economy and employee codetermination were also voiced. The Social Democrats found that the crisis proved how capitalism fell short of securing employment and investments.[124] The dominant solution was still increased democratic control over investments and the state's active role, not its retreat, which was already being advocated and practiced in many other European countries.[125]

Despite expressing conviction on democratic steering and control of the economy, the Social Democrats' awareness of economic constraints for reforms had become more explicit. The increasing trend of Swedish firms investing abroad was found especially worrisome. SAP's Executive Committee agreed that regulation of direct foreign investments and international currency flows should be stricter, but the bourgeois government was blamed for being too passive on the issue. International cooperation was considered necessary for retaining economic sovereignty.[126] The Social Democrats were balancing between state-led steering, wage-earner influence and market orientation. A more market-oriented approach was visible in a new industrial strategy, which emphasized support for research and development in the private sector. This resembled the Schumpeterian information society ideas of Kalevi Sorsa and the Finnish Social Democrats. According to SAP's MP Thage G. Peterson, the state had to support the industry's forward-looking actions and adapt to international changes in socially acceptable forms.[127]

The main themes of Sweden's 1979 parliamentary election were again nuclear power and the general economic situation. SAP's election manifesto stated that state finance had to be reorganized, but otherwise relied on traditional themes: jobs for everyone, active industrial policy, and democratization of the economy. The party stated that aggressive right-wing forces, which had gained ground in other countries, had to be confronted.[128] Although victory had seemed almost certain, SAP failed to return to power. The result of the 1979 election was extremely slim, and the bourgeois bloc won by only one mandate. The Moderates became the largest bourgeois party with 20.3% of the vote, but it was politically impossible to make their leader Gösta Bohman prime minister, so the Center's Thorbjörn Fälldin returned to the post after one year's absence.[129]

SAP took the second electoral defeat seriously. They had not been able to benefit from the bourgeois government's instability and failure in remedying the economy. The party began to reevaluate its economic policy more seriously.[130] Many party members were reluctant but found that they had to address issues that had become important in the rightward-moving political climate.[131] The bourgeois government had also begun to perceive the limits of expansive fiscal policy as inflation, current account deficit and budget deficit continued to increase. In spring 1981, the government stated that expansive fiscal policy was no longer an option, but cuts in state spending had to be made and the export industry's competitiveness increased. New economic ideas were now making their breakthrough in Sweden, a few years later than in many other European countries. In addition to the Finnish SDP, for example, the Norwegian Social Democrats had taken a market-oriented turn in 1977.[132]

After the election of 1979, a working group of Social Democratic economists began to formulate a new economic policy for the party. One of the reasons for the electoral loss was believed to be the failure of promoting an alternative to right-wing policies. It seemed that the traditional Social Democratic policy did not function in the internationalized and more volatile economy. SAP's economic experts, like Klas Eklund, Kjell-Olof Feldt and Erik Åsbrink, took seriously the new monetarist economic ideas and investigated which parts of the right-wing or neoliberal—as it was already called—agenda could be appropriated to serve their goals. It became clear for the economists that the welfare state and the public sector had to be reformed in order to preserve them. This important process of how Swedish Social Democrats appropriated transnational economic ideas has been analyzed quite thoroughly in previous research. For example, Jenny Andersson has argued that it meant moving away from the concept of 'social efficiency' toward more easily quantifiable cost efficiency, while 'security' became perceived rather as a cost than a potential contributor to growth.[133] In both Sweden and Finland, the economic paradigm change was quite technocratic and expert-driven, justified as a necessity rather than a political choice.

In the early 1980s, SAP's economic reorientation was expressed in public statements by economists and the party leadership. MP Kjell-Olof Feldt assumed the role of SAP's primary economic expert. He wrote about the need for the Social Democrats to balance the economy and invest in industrial development. Feldt pointed out that the party had governed mostly in times of economic growth, but now the task was to restore growth in order to secure resources for future reforms. This required directing resources to productive investments instead of speculation, but also increasing savings, abstention from consumption, and acceptance of increasing profits and stagnant real wages. Feldt argued that the party had to orientate for a society of scarce resources instead of an affluent society.[134] The economist Klas Eklund, in turn, wrote that Keynes was not 'dead,' but his macroeconomic theories were complemented and revised with supply-side measures and neoclassical microeconomics, which were experiencing a renaissance. What had been buried, according to Eklund's historical interpretation, was 'vulgar Keynesianism,' which had maintained that general demand stimulation could always solve economic crises.[135] Prudent and anti-inflationary policy had not been alien to the Rehn-Meidner model, either, but now the Social Democrats saw less room for social reforms, economic redistribution and public control of private business.

In addition to the economist group, SAP formed a 'crisis group' to prepare a program for tackling the economic crisis in Sweden. The program *Framtid för Sverige* (Future for Sweden), presented at SAP's congress of 1981, was largely based on the suggestions made by the economist group instead of the traditional views of trade union economists.[136] Beliefs concerning the new economic situation and its constraints were dominant. Internationalization of the economy had been perceived as a political challenge for many years, but now its dynamics had prompted the party to make a clear policy change. The introduction stated that the program differed from previous labor movement programs of the postwar era, which had been able to lean on a strong economy. New measures were needed to return balance to the economy.[137] Production and investments had to be stimulated and the budget and current account deficits fixed simultaneously. The program argued that the choice between "working" and "saving" was not actual, but one had to do both.[138]

The Future Program admitted that cuts in public spending would be inevitable, wage restraint was needed, and social reforms had to be postponed until the economy was stronger.[139] However, the writers emphasized that these necessary policy adjustments did not mean letting go of the traditional goals of social democracy, such as everyone's right to work, social security, and people's right to democratic influence. Adjustments were in fact necessary preconditions for reaching these goals in new circumstances.[140] The program portrayed neoliberal and neoconservative policy as direct opposites to the Social Democratic project, as they would increase inequality. They were also claimed to be inefficient ways to fight against economic crises.[141] As usual, the Future Program portrayed welfare as the highest national achievement at the top of the conceptual hierarchy, and the economic situation only dictated the necessary steps toward its preservation.[142]

SAP's Future Program has often been considered neoliberal,[143] even though its architects portrayed it as a counter-movement to neoliberalism. These interpretations can be questioned in the light of the program's positive rhetoric on the public sector. However, the Social Democrats undeniably took policy elements from neoliberal thought and made a rightward shift in their economic policy resembling that of their Finnish counterparts a few years earlier. SAP emphasized anti-inflationary policies, wanted to increase the role of private business and advocated wage restraint as well as stopping the growth of the public sector and the tax rate—at least for the time being.[144] This could justify calling the Future program a contribution to neoliberalization, to borrow Jamie Peck's notion. The new social democratic policy of the 1980s, which later became called the 'Third Way,' was more strongly adapted to the perceived constraints of capitalism and market economy. As Lars Ekdahl has argued, it was situated between neoliberalism and the earlier ideas of Keynesianism and the planned economy, not between capitalism and state socialism like earlier notions of the third way.[145] According to Ekdahl's interpretation, SAP's new policy meant adaptation to markets and abandoning even the old 'functional socialist' strategy of regulating capitalism.[146]

The Social Democrats returned to power in the election of 1982. SAP and the Communists achieved a parliamentary majority with 186 seats against 163 for the bourgeois bloc. SAP now had a clear mandate to execute its crisis program. Its campaign had concentrated on the economy and rising unemployment. Wage-earner funds were a secondary theme despite the vigorous bourgeois campaign against them. SAP portrayed the funds as a partial but not a central solution to the economic crisis. After their victory, SAP concentrated on the competitiveness of Swedish industry and stimulating investments. Taxes could not be increased, and the public sector was not to expand.[147] A major economic policy move was the devaluation of the Swedish krona by 16%. SAP had been silent about this plan before the election in order to avoid market speculation. Devaluation was considered a better way to boost Swedish competitiveness than a deflationary policy that could have increased unemployment.[148]

Decentralization and Local Democracy as Guiding Stars

Despite the new course in economic policy, extending democracy into the economy and working life was in the late 1970s and early 1980s still an important political objective in Social Democratic rhetoric. Economic and enterprise democracy continued to play key roles in the programs and rhetoric of SDP as future-oriented concepts. At the time, SDP was the most powerful political group in Finland, although not hegemonic. It was the largest party in parliament and had the seats of the prime minister and, from 1982 onward, the president. In President Mauno Koivisto's term, it became a norm that governments would stay in office for the entire four-year term and the president would abstain from interfering with domestic politics. These steps toward stronger parliamentarism stabilized Finnish politics. Between 1977 and 1987, the government was always led by SDP, with the Center Party as its main coalition partner. In its programs, SDP continued to define itself as a labor party promoting democratic socialism and public steering of the economy. Some scholars have considered that the programmatic statements were a rhetorical concession to the party's left wing, while actual policy from the second half of the 1970s onward was aimed at increasing competitiveness and curbing inflation.[149]

The Finnish debate on economic democracy drew much inspiration from Sweden and its new working life legislation that had been passed in the 1970s, including codetermination and employee representation in corporate governance. The SDP connected economic and enterprise democracy to similar criteria and reference as earlier: Public control over major economic institutions, increased employee decision-making, and in the more distant future transition to some form of socialism, which could mean collective ownership or merely 'functional socialist' economic regulation. The roles of economic democracy and socialism, as well as planning and socialization, went through some changes in the Social Democratic programs of the late 1970s.

In 1978, SDP published a "Roadmap" for the 1980s, which stated the traditional objective of bringing democracy to new walks of life: "Extending democratic principles to economic life—to production and to work communities—is a precondition for the development of a socialist society."[150] The program talked about "replacing the capitalist ownership and control of means of production," and "the necessity of a planned economy," but SDP emphasized gradual and democratic implementation of reforms. Under the section "Toward Economic Democracy," the program listed objectives such as public steering of investments, stricter public control of financial institutions, establishing wage-earner funds, and promoting worker and consumer cooperatives. Diffusion of economic power was justified by appealing to the values of equality and social justice.[151]

Even though SDP's 1978 program drew on traditional socialist rhetoric and advocated radical reforms such as the wage-earner funds, it left the extent of the desired redistribution somewhat unclear. SDP phrased their objectives in a way that could not be interpreted as demanding the complete nationalization of financial institutions: Public control meant, for example, appointing political representatives to the supervisory boards of commercial banks, as had been done in Sweden and Norway.[152] In addition, the idea of economic planning was giving way to the market mechanism as a principle of allocating resources. By the end of the 1970s, many Finnish social democrats considered democratic socialism to be a model of a mixed economy between a free market economy and centralized planning. This dichotomy was becoming more important than the one between planning and socialization. For example, the influential party official Paavo Lipponen stated that social democracy was based on the prevailing mixed economy. According to him, private business was an important force of motion, and markets were needed to unveil people's "true needs." However, markets needed "socialism" as a counterweight, especially a larger role for society and employees in the economy. Lipponen argued that it was better to talk about socialist reform policy than transition to socialism.[153]

As before, the distinction between 'macro' and 'micro'—national and workplace—levels of economic democratization was common in Social Democratic thinking, as was maintaining that the two levels should be viewed as a whole. In March 1979 party leader Kalevi Sorsa expressed this distinction, which was identical to the one advocated by Olof Palme in Sweden. Sorsa stated that there were two main lines of action to be pursued regarding economic democracy: Extending the authority of the government and parliament in steering economic life and increasing the direct influence of wage-earners.[154] The problematic relation of central steering and local participation was always present in Social Democratic constellations, but in Finland less explicitly than in Sweden. In a sense, the connecting factor between the two levels of democratization was the trade union movement. The Social Democrats emphasized that working life democratization also meant stronger rights of collective representation. According to the Roadmap program, the rights of individual employees should always be complemented with forms of representation, such as voluntary employee organizations, shop stewards and safety delegates.[155]

Concentration of power continued to figure as a counter-concept to economic democracy and democracy in general. It was an overwhelmingly negative and highly contested concept. All groups sought to modify its ranges of reference to portray their opponents as promoting concentration. In the left's rhetoric, concentration figured especially as a synonym for economic oligarchy. As seen, the employers and the right also often used terms such as 'bureaucratic,' 'centralized,' 'inflexible' and 'group interests' as closely bundled and even interchangeable to delegitimize leftist models of economic democracy. Hence, while claiming to be against concentration, the left had to show that their own models did not represent concentration.[156] SDP had pains especially with the term 'bureaucracy,' because opponents used it to condemn societal steering and collective practices, thereby calling for less regulation and more individualism. The Roadmap program acknowledged this by stating that developing society by socialist methods could not lead to such centralization and bureaucracy, which would harm democracy and civil rights. The party secretary Ulf Sundqivst wrote that the Social Democrats had been too defensive against the attack from "anti-bureaucrats." According to Sundqvist, bureaucracy had also positive content, which was related to traditional social democratic demands, such as equal public handling of common matters.[157]

Criticism toward bureaucracy and representative modes of democracy had brought about a growing interest in participation at grassroots level, which was a notable transnational development in the 1960s and 1970s.[158] It took some time until these ideas became established in the rhetoric of the Finnish Social Democrats, but in the late 1970s they were already widespread. The use of concepts like 'self-governance' (*autogestion*), which had been appropriated from the French socialists, also increased notably.[159] In 1979, the Social Democratic MP Seppo Tikka wrote a book on the new direction of his party, entitled *Toward Soft Politics* (*Pehmeään politiikkaan*). The notion was invented by party leader Kalevi Sorsa and referred to politics that would be closer to ordinary people, listening to their concerns. Tikka took up a whole array of problems perceived by SDP, such as individualization, movement to the political right, alienation from politics, and critique of bureaucracy.[160]

The book included a long interview with Sorsa, who said that he believed the time of large organizations to be over. He suspected that people now wanted to concentrate on the issues of their local environments and determine them for themselves. According to Sorsa, the party had to find new meanings for democratic socialism, where a core element would be decentralizing power to citizens.[161] Sorsa also declared that the state's influence in the economy had increased in recent years, but he was hesitant to call this socialism. However, Sorsa wanted democratic socialism to develop in the future from the basis of wage-earners' influence on their immediate environment. This meant self-governance and an enterprise democracy instead of centralized and bureaucratic structures, which came too close to communism.[162] Sorsa also found the division between the political left and right was too strict. He would rather have sought a broad alliance between reformist socialists and bourgeois parties. The left alone had rarely gained a majority in Finland, and because of the constitution, even a simple majority was not enough to pass the most ambitious reforms.[163] This belief on the limits of reformism in Finnish politics was experienced strongly by the Social Democrats—at least judging by the frequency of its expression.

Democratic influence over the economy also remained among the key objectives of the Swedish Social Democrats. The Future program reminded that the party's 1975 platform had defined economic democracy as the main objective of the future, and it had become even more actual at the beginning of the new decade. The crisis had undermined confidence in the democratic system, but the writers of the report believed it could be restored by giving people the chance to participate more directly, for example, through municipal and enterprise democracy.[164] The program utilized traditional rhetoric, for example, by stating that citizens must be able to demand democratic control over capital formation to oversee that capital is used for truly productive investments.[165] However, the concrete meaning of economic democracy and democratic control had narrowed. The program, of course, had no room for detailed action plans, but as discussed in Chap. 4, the 1981 proposal on wage-earner funds, for example, entailed smaller possibilities to control capital formation and investments than the previous versions. Statements on developing employee codetermination were also quite vague. Concrete statements concentrated on influence in work environments, introducing new technology, and "solidaristic personnel policy" that would help to include as many people in working life as possible.[166]

'Third Way' as Ideational Change

Much has been written about the changing economic thought and policy of the 1970s and 1980s in general, and about the Swedish Social Democrats in particular. In order to understand this change and its impacts on the relation of democracy and the economy better, I will assess more closely some previous interpretations on ideational change. A common narrative is the one I have already suggested: The Social Democrats adopted and applied new economic ideas and policy because they believed that old ideas and practices did not work in what they perceived as a drastically changing economic environment. In Mark Bevir's words, they faced dilemmas, which made them modify their webs of belief. As in the case of wage-earner funds, the Social Democrats also faced a 'dilemma of reformism' in their general economic policy. They sought to conduct reforms within the bounds of internationalizing capitalism, as they could not count on solving the crisis or winning elections with more expansive or 'socialist' policies. Therefore, they chose a strategy that in fact strengthened global capitalism by loosening political steering of capital, even if it was not their main intention.

There was a strong element of perceived necessity and inevitability that facilitated SAP's ideational change. As Lars Ekdahl has argued, the Social Democratic leaders perhaps could not envision reformism or democratic socialism that would have been anticapitalistic.[167] Or as Jenny Andersson has noted, their ideational constellations were increasingly occupied by new beliefs in economic necessities. They were looking at the changing dynamics and regulatory environment of the global economy, which seemed to call for less state intervention and more room for private enterprise.[168] Bo Stråth has summarized this by saying that the "frame of interpretation" was questioned. Neoliberal ideas seemed to fit better in a world where work increasingly took place outside factories and global capital could not be regulated as efficiently as before.[169] Henrik Malm Lindberg and Stig-Björn Ljunggren argue that the Social Democrats "learned" from their own mistakes and those of others, especially from the expansive Keynesian policy that was practiced in Sweden in the latter half of the 1970s but did not manage to improve the economic situation. Alternatives were still voiced in the public debate: SSU talked about self-governance in workplaces, and many LO and party members supported a stronger take on demand stimulation and economic democratization. However, the party leadership chose a different line of thought and action.[170]

Of the interpretations that view this policy change as result of reflected change in economic beliefs, Jenny Andersson's is among the most plausible. She emphasizes the continuities between SAP's new and old economic ideas. As discussed before, she argues that the economic model of Swedish Social Democracy has always been economistic and growth-oriented. After a few years of strong equality rhetoric, during the 1970s the Social Democrats turned again to emphasize economic growth as an ideological priority and a prerequisite for security. At this point, the traditional view of security as supporting growth, 'productive social policy,' made way for a conception of security and social policy as costs and the private sector as productive. However, new ideational elements were also introduced. Andersson emphasizes the role of Social Democratic economists in formulating new policy, which could respond to the new economic reality of slow growth, rising inflation and unemployment. She argues that the Social Democrats adopted a new language and began to view the economy not as something that could be steered with policy, but to which policy had to be adapted. Expansive economic policy, which was practiced up until the end of the 1970s, was no longer an option and cuts in the public sector had to be accepted to secure the most important goals of security and solidarity. New economic ideas faced opposition within SAP and especially within the trade union movement, but by the end of the 1980s they became a hegemonic ideology and discourse within the Swedish left.

According to Andersson, ideas such as economic democracy could no longer be incorporated into this kind of neoliberal language.[171] This interpretation of ideational change is convincing, but what need more careful analysis are the actual ideational and conceptual features that made economic democracy incompatible with 'neoliberal' language. It was perhaps unnecessary to legitimize the economic order with democracy, as the ideational constellation where free markets were a precondition for democracy was becoming dominant.

Besides the above interpretations that are compatible with Mark Bevir's view on ideational change, more elaborate views have also been offered. Political economist Magnus Ryner has explained the shift in the economic policy of the Swedish Social Democrats by utilizing Michel Foucault's concept of *episteme*. Ryner argues that Social Democratic thinking shifted from Marxist-Keynesian regulation of capitalism first to Popperian piecemeal social engineering and later to utilitarian managerialism, as SAP assumed the position of state manager in Sweden during its long stay in power. In this context, the Social Democrats continued to implement policies of full employment and universalistic welfare state but for different reasons than they originally did in the 1930s. According to Ryner, policy change occurred only when the economic crises and stagflation of the 1970s could be interpreted as a "Popperian falsification" of expansive economic policy. This resulted in Social Democrats adopting neoliberal ideas to adapt to the changing global economy. Ryner argues that the wage-earner funds could have provided an alternative strategy to guard the Swedish model of full employment and economic coordination. They were watered down partly because many of the party executives were engaged in a social policy discourse, which made the function of the funds hard to understand and they regarded them as a secondary objective compared to social policy.[172] In general, Ryner's conclusions are compatible with those of Andersson and Stråth who emphasize the role of Social Democratic economists in formulating new ideas, but Ryner goes one step further.

Like many discourse analysts, Ryner argues that epistemic change does not concern the content of policy, but rather its "form."[173] This resembles Johannes Lindvall's attempt to explain Swedish economic policy change with 'extra-rational' factors, such as norms.[174] Both Lindvall and Ryner seem to mystify the process of human thought—perhaps too far. I do not mean to deny the existence of extra-rational factors or ideational 'structures' that hold beliefs and attitudes together. As I have argued, it is possible to analyze human thought as ideational constellations where concepts and beliefs can assume different roles and positions. However, scholars who use ideational structures as explanatory categories do not usually offer good ways to operationalize them besides looking at concepts and beliefs. The changes they analyze can be explained by changing beliefs, which are often quite reflected and rational, but sometimes unreflected or even unconscious. I will return to this argument and Lindvall's interpretation of the Swedish abandonment of full employment in Chap. 7.

In the case of Ryner, it is hard to see what epistemic 'forms' could concretely mean, while it is easy to point out many beliefs that changed—perhaps in part unconsciously. Practical changes included new beliefs such as "internationalization of the economy restricts national economic policy more than before," and, "expansive economic policy no longer works, as it only aggravates inflation and budget deficit." Based on these, a conclusion was drawn: "We must prioritize battle against inflation instead of social reforms and full employment."[175] These new beliefs, most of which are noted by Ryner, may have contributed to changes in more fundamental beliefs at the core of the Social Democratic ideology, such as weakening the belief that "capitalism can and should be transformed." New beliefs already explain the economic policy shift a great deal. Moreover, I find that the earlier shift from Marxism to Popperian social engineering is also more about changing beliefs, that is, the propositional content of thought, than about some underlying 'forms.' It makes perfect sense to say that Marxism and Popperianism are different ways of thinking and doing politics, but it is primarily because of different background beliefs, such as "We should transform capitalism into a socialist society" versus "Let's try some piecemeal reforms and see what works without any clear vision of an ideal society." Perhaps the lack of a clear end-state vision constitutes a different ideational or narrative 'form,' but the transition between these two structures is hard to conceive without some reflected change in beliefs. For example, the Marxist belief "history is on our side" should change to the Popperian "history has no predetermined course and the future is essentially unknown."[176]

The penetration of neoliberal ideas and the changing meaning of democracy in Swedish public debate have also been noted by the political scientist Kristina Boréus. She has argued that by the end of the 1980s, the concept of democracy was being used mainly as a general label for Western parliamentary political systems, while ideas of increased citizen participation and public control over the economy had virtually vanished. According to

Boréus, this represents a 'neoliberal' conception of democracy, where democracy is not something to be gradually increased or extended, but a binary category where democracy either exists or does not. In this conception, democracy means formal rights such as universal suffrage and freedom of speech, whereas socialist and social liberal conceptions emphasize democratic participation and consider that there are different degrees of democracy. In their neoliberal rhetoric, employer organizations and the Moderate Party began to equate economic democracy with socialization.[177]

According to Boréus, these groups had used and accepted the term economic democracy in the 1970s, but in light of the debates examined in the previous chapters, this view does not hold. Equation with socialism had for the employers and conservatives always been a potential strategy against the leftist visions of economic democracy. Sometimes the argument was more subordinate, but in the 1970s it became very dominant, especially in the wage-earner fund debate. The attitude toward economic democracy was always uneasy, even though there were efforts to redefine the concept. Boréus argues that the attitude toward economic democracy became more negative, because the concept had the potential to criticize neoliberalism by demanding people's power over the economy.[178] This reasoning goes one step further than Andersson's, but relies on a simplified view of neoliberal conceptions of democracy and leaves one question open: Why was neoliberalism in contradiction with people's power over the economy? Some explanations have already been provided, such as the key role Nordic variants of neoliberal thought gave to expertise as opposed to democracy in economic governance. The question is examined further in subsequent chapters.

Boréus does not offer as clear explanations for the neoliberal wave and ideational change as do Ryner and Andersson. She does express a circular argument, according to which the increasing strength of private business gave power to its ideas, and the legitimacy of these ideas increased the strength of business. This illustrates the complexity and multicausality of ideational change. Ultimately Boréus suggests that economic circumstances affected the change considerably.[179] Boréus probably does not mean that there is a direct causal link from the economy to ideas, but I would nevertheless emphasize that economic circumstances in themselves do not cause ideational, conceptual or policy change. What matters is how people perceive and interpret these circumstances. As Mark Bevir might say, perceptions of new circumstances create dilemmas—new beliefs that challenge parts of the existing webs of beliefs.[180]

The Role of Ideas in Political Change

During the late 1970s and early 1980s, political and economic ideas changed significantly in Sweden, Finland and the entire Western world. Perceptions of new economic circumstances created 'dilemmas' for political actors and prompted them to modify their beliefs. Beliefs that the economy can be steered rationally and democratically were questioned by the experience of economic downturn and simultaneous inflation, which could not be corrected using mainstream policy tools. The end of the Bretton Woods currency regime had made exchange rates more volatile, which forced politicians to consider public debt and current account deficits more seriously. Social democrats in most countries turned from their traditional emphases on economic steering and a growing public sector to adopt new economic ideas, which can be viewed at least partly as neoliberal. They focused on inflation and competitiveness more than employment and stressed the market mechanism and private profits as motors of economic growth and welfare. This happened at different times in different countries—in Finland in the late 1970s and in Sweden in the early 1980s. It was a largely intentional and reflexive adaptation to changing circumstances and appropriation of new doctrines. However, it also faced a lot of resistance within Social Democratic parties.

For business and employer organizations as well as center-right parties, the economic crisis provided an opportunity to promote their traditional ideas of decreased state intervention, lower taxation and a smaller public sector. The political mobilization of business had already begun in many countries before the most severe phases of the crisis, but the difficulties of Keynesian policy fueled the ideational change they were pursuing. During the 1970s, business and nonsocialist groups gained the agenda-setting power the left had held in the previous decade. This was most clearly manifested in the rise of prominent right-wing leaders, such as Margaret Thatcher and Ronald Reagan, but also in the willingness of left-wing parties in Finland, Sweden, France, Britain and many other countries to modify their beliefs and policies in a business- and market-friendly direction. The first signs of these changes were visible already in the mid-1970s during the economic crisis.

The ideational change undermined especially one traditional element of economic democracy: State-led democratic steering of the economy. Even though social democrats continued to talk about this at least as a long-term objective, they also stressed the role of private enterprise and profits and in effect let go of most concrete pursuits toward a more democratically controlled economy. Economic democracy's range of reference was narrowing, and it began to refer more clearly to collective ownership and wage-earner funds, which were also losing credibility due to the political conflict in Sweden. The concept of enterprise democracy, in contrast, retained its place in leftist thought and rhetoric, but its reference was narrowing to encompass only modest developments in established practices of codetermination and cooperation.

In center-right and business rhetoric, the role of economic democracy changed more thoroughly. It gained negative connotations due to the association with socialism in the wage-earner fund debate, and in the early 1980s its use became much rarer. Proponents of the free market economy and liberation of capital did not find it necessary to continue their reactive struggle of appropriating and redefining left-wing concepts. They used the concepts of free markets, decentralization, cooperation and participation instead of the concept of democracy, which had been found to be dubious when applied to the economic sphere. Even though explicit redefinitions of economic and enterprise democracy were occasionally made, center-right and business representatives preferred to portray the economy as a domain of individual freedom and harmonious cooperation, instead of power and conflict implied by the concept of democracy.

To state a cliché: In the epochal change of the 1970s, concepts and beliefs mattered.[181] Changing ideas, practices and political agendas were not determined by impersonal economic forces but were shaped gradually through intentional and reflexive action. Even though unreflected elements were also at play, political actors assessed carefully the changing circumstances and power relations. They modified their concepts and beliefs to form ideational constellations that would help them to navigate and pursue their goals in a reality they believed to be changing rapidly. This was inspired by neoliberal thought and the new consensus in neoclassical economics, and the process continued far into the 1980s.

Notes

1. Sheri Berman, *The Primacy of Politics: Social Democracy and the Making of Europe's Twentieth Century* (Cambridge: Cambridge University Press, 2006), 5–8, 177–187; Tony Judt, *Postwar: A History of Europe since 1945* (London: Penguin, 2005), 67–77; Eric Hobsbawm, *Age of Extremes: The*

Short Twentieth Century 1914–1991 (London: Abacus, 1995), 267–275; Lars Magnusson, *Sveriges ekonomiska historia* (Stockholm: Norstedts, 2010), 374–378, 418–422.

2. Robert Brenner, *The Economics of Global Turbulence* (London and New York: Verso, 2006), 27–40;

   Andrew Glyn, *Capitalism Unleashed: Finance Globalisation and Welfare* (Oxford: Oxford University Press, 2006), 1–15; Andrew Glyn, "Aspirations, Constraints, and Outcomes." In *Social Democracy in Neoliberal Times*, ed. Andrew Glyn (Oxford: Oxford University Press, 2002), 8–13; Judt, *Postwar*, 453–462; Hobsbawm, *Age of Extremes*, 403–418.
3. Luc Boltanski and Ève Chiapello, *The New Spirit of Capitalism* (London and New York: Verso, 2005), xxxv–xl, 217–229, 429–433; Brenner, *The Economics of Global Turbulence*, 27–40, 97–142; Glyn, *Capitalism Unleashed*, 1–15.
4. Stephanie L. Mudge, *Leftism Reinvented: Western Parties from Socialism to Neoliberalism* (Cambridge, MA: Harvard University Press, 2018), 250–253; Daniel Stedman Jones, *Masters of the Universe: Hayek, Friedman, and the Birth of Neoliberal Politics* (Princeton: Princeton University Press, 2012), 232–240; Daniel T. Rodgers, *Age of Fracture* (Cambridge, MA & London: Belknap Press of Harvard University Press, 2011), 44–50, 63–68; Ville Yliaska, *Tehokkuuden toiveuni. Uuden julkisjohtamisen historia Suomessa 1970-luvulta 1990-luvulle.* (Helsinki: Into, 2014), 72–83; Johannes Lindvall, *The Politics of Purpose: Swedish Macroeconomic Policy after the Golden Age* (Göteborg: Göteborg University, 2004), 85–90, 94–100.
5. Mudge, *Leftism Reinvented*, 337–339; Stedman Jones, *Masters of the Universe*, 241–247; Donald Sassoon, *One Hundred Years of Socialism: The West European Left in the Twentieth Century* (London: Fontana Press, 1996), 499–506.
6. Stedman Jones, *Masters of the Universe*, 247–254; Rodgers, *Age of Fracture*, 59–63.
7. Marion Fourcade-Gourinchas and Sarah L. Babb, "The Rebirth of the Liberal Creed: Paths to Neoliberalism in Four Countries," *The American Journal of Sociology*, 108, 3 (2002): 533–579.
8. Wolfgang Streeck, *Buying Time: The Delayed Crisis of Democratic Capitalism* (London and New York: Verso, 2014); Colin Crouch, *Post-Democracy* (Cambridge: Polity Press, 2004); Glyn, *Capitalism Unleashed*, 24–76; Philip G. Cerny, "International Finance and the Erosion of Capitalist Diversity," in *Political Economy of Modern Capitalism*, eds. Colin Crouch and Wolfgang Streeck (London: Sage, 1997), 173–181; Boltanski and Chiapello, *The New Spirit of Capitalism*, xl–xliii.

9. Boltanski and Chiapello, *The New Spirit of Capitalism*, xxxvi–xxxviii, xliii, 3–4, 167–168, 499–506.
10. Boltanski and Chiapello, *The New Spirit of Capitalism*, xxiv–xxvii, 28–30, 40–42, 199–202, 514–519.
11. Karl Polanyi, *The Great Transformation: The Political and Economic Origins of Our Time* (Boston: Beacon Press, 1971 [1944]), 130–135.
12. Mark Blyth, *Great Transformations: Economic Ideas and Institutional Change in the Twentieth Century* (Cambridge: Cambridge University Press, 2002), 152–160; Maiju Wuokko, *Markkinatalouden etujoukot: Elinkeinoelämän valtuuskunta, Teollisuuden keskusliitto ja liike-elämän poliittinen toiminta 1970–1980-lukujen Suomessa* (Helsinki: University of Helsinki, 2016), 36–37; David Harvey, *A Brief History of Neoliberalism* (Oxford and New York: Oxford University Press, 2005), 43–53.
13. Philip Mirowski, *Never Let a Serious Crisis Go to Waste: How Neoliberalism Survived the Financial Meltdown* (London and New York: Verso, 2013), 43–49; Dieter Plehwe, "Introduction," in *The Road from Mont Pèlerin: The Making of the Neoliberal Thought Collective*, eds. Dieter Plehwe and Philip Mirowski (Cambridge, MA and London: Harvard University Press, 2009), 10–26; Stedman Jones, *Masters of the Universe*, 134–138, 152–173.
14. On business mobilization in Denmark and Norway, respectively, see Niklas Olsen, "A Second-Hand Dealer in Ideas: Christian Gandil and Scandinavian Configurations of European Neoliberalism, 1945–1970," in *Re-inventing Western Civilisation: Transnational Reconstructions of Liberalism in Europe in the Twentieth Century*, eds. Hagen Schulz-Forberg and Niklas Olsen (Newcastle upon Tyne: Cambridge Scholars Publishing, 2014); Francis Sejersted, *The Age of Social Democracy: Norway and Sweden in the Twentieth Century* (Princeton: Princeton University Press, 2011), 309–313.
15. Maiju Wuokko, "Business in the Battle of Ideas, 1945–1991: Conclusions from the Finnish Case," *Scandinavian Economic History Review* 65, 3 (2017): 279–293; Wuokko, *Markkinatalouden etujoukot*, 70–72, 83–86, 291–292; Johannes Koroma, *Suomalaisten hyvinvointia rakentamassa: Teollisuuden keskusliiton historia* (Helsinki: Suomalaisen kirjallisuuden seura, 2015), 13–19.
16. Wuokko, *Markkinatalouden etujoukot*, 74–80, 292–294; Jukka Tarkka, *Uhan alta unioniin: Asennemurros ja sen unilukkari Eva* (Helsinki: Otava, 2002), 86–98.
17. Wuokko, *Markkinatalouden etujoukot*, 125–135; Tarkka, *Uhan alta unioniin*, 106–107; Paavo Lipponen, *Muistelmat 1* (Helsinki: WSOY, 2009), 455–458.

18. Ritva Savtschenko, *Kompuroiden korporatismissa: Eheytyneen SAK:n ristipaineet suomalaisessa korporatismissa 1968–1978* (Doctoral dissertation, University of Helsinki, 2015), 94–98.
19. Rikard Westerberg, "The Alternative: How Nordic Business Interest Associations Attempted to Formulate an Ideological Programme, 1945–1975," *Scandinavian Journal of History* 2018, https://doi.org/10.1080/03468755.2018.1532316; Niklas Stenlås, *Den inre kretsen: Den svenska ekonomiska elitens inflytande över partipolitik och opinionsbildning 1940–1949* (Lund: Arkiv, 1998).
20. Joakim Johansson, *SAF och den svenska modellen: En studie av uppbrottet från förvaltningskorporatismen 1982–91* (Doctoral dissertation, Uppsala University 2000), 62–66; Christer Lundh, *Spelets regler: Institutioner och lönebildning på den svenska arbetsmarknaden 1850–2000* (Stockholm: SNS förlag, 2002), 237–238, 248–255.
21. "Vi måste öka kontakten med politiken," *Arbetsgivaren* 26 May 1976, 5.
22. Olof Ehrenkrona, *Nicolin: En svensk historia* (Stockholm: Timbro, 1991), 295–296.
23. Bo Stråth, *Mellan två fonder: LO och den svenska modellen* (Stockholm: Atlas, 1998), 213–216.
24. SAF, *SAF-kongressen sammanfattad* (1978).
25. J. Magnus Ryner, *Capitalist Restructuring, Globalisation and the Third Way: Lessons from the Swedish Model* (London and New York: Routledge, 2002), 169–170; Blyth, *Great Transformations*, 213–219; Stråth, *Mellan två fonder*, 173, 233–235.
26. Stråth, *Mellan två fonder*, 239–242.
27. Blyth, *Great Transformations*, 202–204.
28. Stråth, *Mellan två fonder*, 250–253.
29. Peter A. Swenson, *Capitalists against Markets: The Making of Labor Markets and Welfare States in the United States and Sweden* (Oxford: Oxford University Press, 2002), 314–316; Jonas Pontusson, and Peter Swenson. "Labor Markets, Production Strategies, and Wage Bargaining Institutions: The Swedish Employer Offensive in Comparative Perspective," *Comparative Political Studies*, 29, 2 (1996): 223–250.
30. Gregg M. Olsen, *The Struggle for Economic Democracy in Sweden* (Aldershot and Brookfield: Avebury, 1992), 66–67, 85; Ryner, *Capitalist Restructuring*, 144–147.
31. Blyth, *Great Transformations*, 211–213; Lundh, *Spelets regler*, 256–260.
32. "Fackorganisationerna får inte bli en sorts politiska överinstanser," *Arbetsgivaren* 2 June 1977, 3; SAF, *SAF-kongressen sammanfattad*, 145–146.
33. Bengt Lindroth, "Vad felas Sverige?" *Tiden* 8/1980, 495–499.

34. "Some viewpoints on EVA's tasks." 31 CEO's manuscripts 1975–1980, EVA archive, The National Archives of Finland, Helsinki (KA).
35. Wuokko, *Markkinatalouden etujoukot*, 137–139.
36. "Brödrafolkens val," *SAF-tidningen* 30/1980, 2; "Samförstånd – väg till framgång," *SAF-tidningen* 30/1980, 11.
37. Henri Lepage, *I morgon kapitalism* (Stockholm: Ratio, 1980); Bertil Östergren, "En intellektuell revolution," *Svenska Dagbladet* 4 November 1980, 2; Henrik Malm Lindberg and Stig-Björn Ljunggren, *Från jämlikhet till effektivitet: Om lärande socialdemokrati under 1980-talet* (Stockholm: Hjalmarson & Högberg, 2014), 48–56.
38. Nina Ersman, "Kulmen på kampanjen för nyliberalismen," *Svenska Dagbladet* 17 November 1980, part 2, 1.
39. Bo Södersten, "Klarar sällan granskning," *Svenska Dagbladet* 30 November 1980, 3. On the fusion of liberalism and conservatism see Stig-Björn Ljunggren, *Folkhemskapitalismen: Högerns programutveckling under efterkrigstiden*. (Stockholm: Tidens förlag, 1992), 406–417.
40. Taylor C. Boas and Jordan Gans-Morse, "Neoliberalism: from New Liberal Philosophy to Anti-Liberal Slogan," *Studies in Comparative International Development* 44, 2 (2009): 145–152.
41. Lindberg and Ljunggren, *Från jämlikhet till effektivitet*, 48–50.
42. Searches with terms "uusliberalismi," "uusliberaali," "uusliberalistinen." Helsingin sanomat Aikakone. https://www.hs.fi/aikakone/.
43. Moderata samlingspartiet, *Ägandespridning – som vi ser det* (1978).
44. Christer Lundh, *Den svenska debatten om industriell demokrati 1919–1924: 1. Debatten i Sverige* (Lund: Studentlitteratur, 1987), 479–484.
45. Tarkka, *Uhan alta unioniin*, 122–124.
46. Wuokko, *Markkinatalouden etujoukot*, 87–88.
47. Enterprise and society. Speech at "idea days," 30 October 1975. 31 CEO's manuscripts 1975–1980, EVA Archive, KA.
48. Business and political decision-making. Speech at Finnovaatio days in Lahti 24 Aug 1976; In the midst of change. 31 CEO's manuscripts 1975–1980, EVA Archive, KA.
49. EVA spring meeting 10 June 1976, Appendix A1, Mika Tiivola's account. 1 Meeting minutes 1974–1976. EVA Archive, KA.
50. Meeting of EVA's executive committee 11 January 1977. Appendix B3. "Economic democracy and extension of ownership base." 2 Meeting minutes 1977–1978, EVA Archive, KA.
51. For example, EVA, *Minne menet hyvinvointiyhteiskunta?* (1981); EVA spring meeting 22 May 1981. Appendix A1. Opening speech by Mika Tiivola. 3 Meeting minutes 1979–1982, EVA Archive, KA.
52. EVA spring meeting 22 May 1981. Appendix A5: Max Jakobson's account on current issues. 3 Meeting minutes 1979–1982, EVA Archive, KA; Yliaska, *Tehokkuuden toiveuni*, 141–142.

53. *Teollisuus* 6/1978, 30.
54. Important general principles for the industry in developing economic democracy. Memo 25 May 1979. Tapani Saukkonen, STK. File II.1 Background material, Participation Systems Committee's Archive, KA.
55. For example, STK board meeting 14 December 1978. 1968 Board meeting minutes 1978–1980. STK Archive, Central Archives for Finnish Business Records, Mikkeli (ELKA).
56. Meeting of STK's managing group 10 September 1981. 1993 Managing group minutes 1981–1983. STK Archive, ELKA.
57. Meeting of STK's managing group 25 February 1982. 1993 Managing group minutes 1981–1983. STK Archive, ELKA.
58. *Teollisuus* 3/1980, 37–38; Johan Myhrman, "Hur demokratibegreppet missbrukas," *Svenska Dagbladet* 19 May 1983, 2.
59. Markku Mansner, *Suomalaista yhteiskuntaa rakentamassa: Suomen työnantajain keskusliitto 1980–1992* (Helsinki: Elinkeinoelämän keskusliitto EK, 2005), 121–123.
60. Raija Julkunen, *Työprosessi ja pitkät aallot* (Tampere: Vastapaino, 1987), 11–16; 377–396; Kari Lilja, *Työntekijöiden osallistuminen hallintoon teollisuusyrityksissä: Tutkimus työnantajapuolen toiminnan kehityksestä* (Helsinki: Helsingin kauppakorkeakoulun julkaisuja B-22, 1977), 15–28.
61. Rodgers, *Age of Fracture*, 108–109.
62. Anneli Nikula, "Kilpailukykyä henkilöstöstrategialla," *Teollisuusviikko* 25 August 1983; *Teollisuusviikko* 26 September 1985, 9; *Teollisuusviikko* 3 October 1985, 7; *Yritystalous* 11/1984, 3.
63. Yliaska, *Tehokkuuden toiveuni*, 220–228; Timo Santalainen, Eero Voutilainen, Pertti Porenne and Hannes Nissinen, *Tulosjohtaminen* (Helsinki: Weilin + Göös, 1980); Arvo Saarikko and Eero Voutilainen, *Johtaminen, yhteistoiminta ja yritysdemokratia* (Helsinki: Weilin + Göös, 1977).
64. Anna Kuokkanen, *Johtamisen ihmissuhdekoulukunta Suomessa: Työntekijäkeskeiset johtamisopit suomalaisen työelämän muutoksessa* (Helsinki: Työterveyslaitos, 2015), 87–89; Pauli Kettunen, *Suojelu, suoritus, subjekti: Työsuojelu teollistuvan Suomen yhteiskunnallisissa ajattelu- ja toimintatavoissa* (Helsinki: Suomen historiallinen seura, 1994), 361–369.
65. *Tehokas yritys* 1/1980, 40–43.
66. For example, "Morgondagens arbetsorganisation kräver starka och bra chefer," *Arbetsgivaren* 32/1979, 3.
67. STK, *Laatupiirit Yhdysvalloissa* (1983); *Yritystalous* 3/1981, 17–27; *Yritystalous* 4/1981, 14–16; *Teollisuusviikko* 18 March 1982, 4; *Teollisuusviikko* 6 October 1983, 6; Yliaska, *Tehokkuuden toiveuni*, 433–436.

68. Risto Alapuro, "Ulkoinen ja sisäinen: Suomen poliittisen kulttuurin pitkä linja," *Yhteiskuntapolitiikka* 75, 5 (2010): 534–536; Pauli Kettunen, *Globalisaatio ja kansallinen me: Kansallisen katseen historiallinen kritiikki* (Tampere: Vastapaino, 2008), 88–89.
69. *Teollisuusviikko* 5 March 1987, 5.
70. "Työnantaja suomalaisessa yhteiskunnassa," *Teollisuusviikko* 25 February 1982.
71. For example, *Teollisuusviikko* 25 February 1982, 3.
72. SAF, *SAF-kongressen sammanfattad*, 15–18, 21.
73. Ibid., 40.
74. Ibid., 41–42.
75. Ibid., 43–47.
76. Ibid., 124.
77. Ibid., 11–12; ""Ekonomisk demokrati" hot mot friheten," *SAF tidningen* 35/1982, 3.
78. Moderata samlingspartiet, *Moderata Samlingspartiets idéprogram antogs vid 1978 årspartistämma*. http://snd.gu.se/sv/vivill/party/m/p/1984.
79. Bo Ekegren, *Frihet eller socialism?* (Uppsala: Medborgarskolan, 1979), 3–4.
80. For similar dissociations of freedom and democracy among members of the Mont Pèlerin Society see Lars Cornelissen, "'How can the People be Restricted?': The Mont Pèlerin Society and the Problem of Democracy, 1947–1998," *History of European Ideas* 43, 5 (2017): 511–512.
81. Ekegren, *Frihet eller socialism?*, 8.
82. Torbjörn Nilsson, *Mellan arv och utopi: Moderata vägval under hundra år, 1904–2004* (Stockholm: Santérus, 2004), 248–251.
83. Nilsson, *Mellan arv och utopi*, 253–254.
84. Niklas Olsen, *The Sovereign Consumer: A New Intellectual History of Neoliberalism* (Cham: Palgrave Macmillan, 2019), 200–218.
85. Nilsson, *Mellan arv och utopi*, 265–267, 272–273; Ljunggren, *Folkhemskapitalismen*, 411–412.
86. Olof Ljunggren, *SAFs uppgift. Speech at SAF congress 1980* (Stockholm: SAF, 1981), 29.
87. Curt Nicolin, *Företagandets uppgift. Speech at SAF congress 1980* (Stockholm: SAF, 1981), 3–5.
88. Ibid., 11.
89. Ibid., 20.
90. Andrew Sayer, *Why We Can't Afford the Rich* (Bristol: Policy Press, 2015), 122–125; David Schweickart, *After Capitalism* (Lanham: Rowman & Littlefield, 2002), 31–33.
91. *Teollisuusviikko* 5 March 1987, 3.
92. Ibid.

93. Pauli Kettunen, *Työjärjestys: Tutkielmia työn ja tiedon poliittisesta historiasta* (Helsinki: Tutkijaliitto, 1997), 103–105, 123–124.
94. Mirowski, *Never Let a Serious Crisis Go to Waste*, 92–102; Jenny Andersson, *När framtiden redan hänt: Socialdemokratin och folkhemsnostalgin* (Stockholm: Ordfront, 2009), 27–30.
95. Sami Outinen, *Sosiaalidemokraattien tie talouden ohjailusta markkinareaktioiden ennakointiin: Työllisyys sosiaalidemokraattien politiikassa Suomessa 1975–1998* (Helsinki: Into, 2015), 43–48, 56–60; Jarkko Vesikansa, *Laman taittaja: Raimo Sailas ja kolme talouskriisiä* (Helsinki: Otava, 2016), 147–154.
96. Outinen, *Sosiaalidemokraattien tie*, 68–72.
97. Ibid., 72–80.
98. Ibid., 81–84; Vesikansa, *Laman taittaja*, 196–206; Program of Kalevi Sorsa's II government (1977). http://valtioneuvosto.fi/hallitusohjelmat/-/asset_publisher/60-paaministerin-kalevi-sorsan-ii-hallituksen-ohjelma.
99. Yliaska, *Tehokkuuden toiveuni*, 142–145.
100. Yliaska, *Tehokkuuden toiveuni*, 142–145; Outinen, *Sosiaalidemokraattien tie*, 97–103.
101. Anu Kantola, "Unholy Alliances: Competitiveness as a Domestic Strategy," in *National Policy-Making: Domestication of Global Trends*, eds. Pertti Alasuutari and Ali Qadir (London and New York: Routledge, 2014), 47–48; Jenny Andersson, *The Library and the Workshop: Social Democracy and Capitalism in the Knowledge Age* (Stanford: Stanford University Press, 2010), 28–30, 79–87; Bob Jessop, "Post-Fordism and the State," in *Post-Fordism: A Reader*, ed. Amin Ash (Oxford: Blackwell, 1994), 251–279.
102. Outinen, *Sosiaalidemokraattien tie*, 85–90; Wuokko, *Markkinatalouden etujoukot*, 136–138; Yliaska, *Tehokkuuden toiveuni*, 135–141.
103. Juho Saari, "Suomalainen konsensus: Korpilammen konferenssi (-77) käännekohtana," *Yhteiskuntapolitiikka* 75, 5 (2010): 472–474; Heikkinen and Tiihonen, *Hyvinvoinnin turvaaja*, 147–151.
104. Saari, "Suomalainen konsensus," 469–471.
105. Ibid., 483.
106. Antti Kujala, *Paperiliiton historia 1906–2005: Paperiteollisuuden työmarkkinasuhteet ja suomalainen yhteiskunta* (Helsinki: Paperiliitto Ry, 2006), 353–355; Sassoon, *One Hundred Years of Socialism*, 445–468.
107. Tapio Bergholm, *Laatua ja vapaa-aikaa. Tulopolitiikan aika II: Suomen ammattiliittojen keskusjärjestö vuodesta 1977* (Helsinki: Suomalaisen kirjallisuuden seura, 2018), 52–53, 74–78, 95.
108. Pauli Kettunen, *Historia petollisena liittolaisena: Näkökulmia työväen, työelämän ja hyvinvointivaltion historiaan* (Helsinki: Työväen historian ja perinteen tutkimuksen seura, 2015), 180–181.

109. *Elvytyksen linjat. Talouspoliittinen konferenssi 5.–6.9.1977* (Helsinki: Valtion painatuskeskus, 1977), 10.
110. Ibid., 11.
111. Ibid., 11–15.
112. Ibid., 16.
113. Ibid., 301–302, 305–306.
114. Outinen, *Sosiaalidemokraattien tie*, 113–119, 128–129, 135–137, 146–148.
115. SAP congress protocol 1975, 450–458.
116. Ibid., 460.
117. Glyn, *Capitalism Unleashed*, 1–15; Sassoon, *One Hundred Years of Socialism*, 445–449, 458–461; Judt, *Postwar*, 453–462; Hobsbawm, *Age of Extremes*, 403–418.
118. Kjell Östberg, *När vinden vände: Olof Palme 1969–1986* (Stockholm: Leopard, 2009), 179–193; Henrik Berggren, *Underbara dagar framför oss: En biografi över Olof Palme* (Stockholm: Norstedts, 2010), 532–534; Torbjörn Nilsson, *Hundra år av svensk politik* (Malmö: Gleerups, 2009), 120–122.
119. Birger Simonson, *Arbetarmakt och näringspolitik: LO och inflytandefrågorna 1961–1982* (Stockholm: Arbetsmiljöfonden, 1988), 197–199; Bernt Schiller, *"Det förödande 70-talet": SAF och medbestämmandet 1965–1982* (Stockholm: Arbetsmiljöfonden, 1988), 225–227.
120. Jonas Pontusson, *The Limits of Social Democracy: Investment Politics in Sweden* (Ithaca: Cornell University Press, 1992), 138–142; Lindvall, *The Politics of Purpose*, 46–63; Stråth, *Mellan två fonder*, 291–295.
121. For example, Villy Bergström, "Stabiliseringspolitiken," *Tiden* 3/1977, 176–180; Carl Johan Åberg, "Att hamna fel," *Tiden* 3/1977, 182–185.
122. SAP congress protocol 1978, 22, 116–118.
123. SAP congress motions 1978, 1322–1369.
124. SAP congress protocol 1978, 139, 171, 270–272.
125. SAP congress motions 1978, 322.
126. SAP congress motions 1978, 1393–1395.
127. SAP congress protocol 1978, 121–123.
128. SAP, *Valmanifest 1979*. http://snd.gu.se/sv/vivill/party/s/v/1979.
129. Östberg, *När vinden vände*, 202–212; Berggren, *Underbara dagar framför oss*, 560–563, 570–573; Nilsson, *Hundra år av svensk politik*, 179.
130. Andersson, *Between Growth and Security*, 105–107; Kjell-Olof Feldt, *Alla dessa dagar – i regeringen 1982–1990* (Stockholm: Norstedt, 1991), 13–14; Ingvar Carlsson, *Så tänkte jag: Politik & dramatik* (Stockholm: Hjalmarson & Högberg, 2003), 173–174.
131. For example, "Den svenska modellen," *Tiden* 5/1980, 266–267; Östberg, *När vinden vände*, 280–283.

132. Lindvall, *The Politics of Purpose*, 68–73; Lindberg and Ljunggren, *Från jämlikhet till effektivitet*, 62–63.
133. Andersson, *Between Growth and Security*, 107–109; Mudge, *Leftism Reinvented*, 317–321; Lindberg and Ljunggren, *Från jämlikhet till effektivitet*, 63–66.
134. Kjell-Olof Feldt, "Arbete, sparsamhet och hushållning," *Tiden* 4/1980, 223–229.
135. Klas Eklund, "Är Keynes verkligen död?" *Tiden* 8–9/1981, 503–513.
136. Andersson, *Between Growth and Security*, 112–113; Lindvall, *The Politics of Purpose*, 76–77.
137. SAP, *Framtid för Sverige* (1981), 6.
138. Ibid., 23–24.
139. Ibid., 42–47, 63–66.
140. Ibid., 124.
141. Ibid., 25–27.
142. Ibid., 125–126.
143. Ryner, *Capitalist Restructuring*, 148–153; Andersson, *Between Growth and Security*, 112–115.
144. Lindberg and Ljunggren, *Från jämlikhet till effektivitet*, 66–68; Lindvall, *The Politics of Purpose*, 76–77. On the problem of labeling Social Democrats neoliberals, see Mudge, *Leftism Reinvented*, 15–17.
145. Ekdahl, *Mot en tredje väg II*, 287–289, 295–297, 304–306; Ryner, *Capitalist Restructuring*, 123–124.
146. Lars Ekdahl, "Den fackliga rörelsen mellan två modeller," in *Det långa 1990-talet: När Sverige förändrades*, eds. Anders Ivarsson Westerberg, Ylva Waldemarson and Kjell Östberg (Umeå: Boréa, 2014), 232–234.
147. Östberg, *När vinden vände*, 287–291; Berggren, *Underbara dagar framför oss*, 604–607, 615–617; Nilsson, *Hundra år av svensk politik*, 179.
148. Lindberg and Ljunggren, *Från jämlikhet till effektivitet*, 83–86, 97–100; Lindvall, *The Politics of Purpose*, 74–75; Östberg, *När vinden vände*, 299–301.
149. Outinen, *Sosiaalidemokraattien tie*, 106–109; Vesikansa, *Laman taittaja*, 155–156.
150. SDP, *Sosialidemokratian suunta: SDP:n tienviitat 1980-luvulle.* Hyväksytty SDP:n 31. puoluekokouksessa v. 1978 Espoossa. https://www.fsd.uta.fi/pohtiva/ohjelmalistat/SDP/462.
151. Ibid.
152. Outinen, *Sosiaalidemokraattien tie*, 106–107.
153. Lipponen, *Muistelmat 1*, 500–509, 524–529; Outinen, *Sosiaalidemokraattien tie*, 110–112.
154. *Palkkatyöläinen* 9/1979, 4.

155. SDP, *Sosialidemokratian suunta*; Savtschenko, *Kompuroiden korporatismissa*, 118–121.
156. On the critique of centralization and the debate on public administration see Yliaska, *Tehokkuuden toiveuni*, 160–183.
157. Ulf Sundqvist, "Byrokratia, herra vai renki," *Sosialistinen aikakauslehti* 1/1979, 3–4.
158. Ingrid Gilcher-Holtey, "Political Participation and Democratization in the 1960s: The Concept of Participatory Democracy and its Repercussions," in *Democracy in Modern Europe: A Conceptual History*, eds. Jussi Kurunmäki, Jeppe Nevers and Henk te Velde (New York: Berghahn, 2018), 257–273; Yliaska, *Tehokkuuden toiveuni*, 163–164.
159. Rauli Mickelsson, *Samanlaiset ja erilaiset puolueet: Retoriikka- ja diskurssianalyyttinen tutkimus kokoomuslaisten ja sosiaalidemokraattien jäsenlehdissä ilmaisemista käsityksistä omista puolueistaan vuosina 1965–1995* (Turku: University of Turku, 1999), 131–133. On *autogestion* see Frank Georgi, *L'autogestion en chantier: Les gauches françaises et le « modèle » yougoslave (1948–1981)* (Nancy: Arbre bleu, 2018); Gilcher-Holtey, "Political Participation and Democratization," 262–263; Boltanski and Chiapello, *The New Spirit of Capitalism*, 195–198; Sassoon, *One Hundred Years of Socialism*, 561–564.
160. Seppo Tikka, *Pehmeään politiikkaan* (Helsinki: Kirjayhtymä, 1979), 7–9, 50–52.
161. Ibid., 55–56.
162. Ibid., 73–74.
163. Ibid., 94–95.
164. SAP, *Framtid för Sverige*, 124, 126.
165. Ibid., 37
166. Ibid., 111–114.
167. Ekdahl, *Mot en tredje väg II*, 304–306, 313–314.
168. Andersson, *Between Growth and Security*, 105–108; Lindberg and Ljunggren, *Från jämlikhet till effektivitet*, 97–100, 183–185; Lindvall, *The Politics of Purpose*, 74–77.
169. Stråth, *Mellan två fonder*, 243–245, 299–311.
170. Lindberg and Ljunggren, *Från jämlikhet till effektivitet*, 41–44, 183–190.
171. Andersson, *Between Growth and Security*, 14–21, 105–114.
172. Ryner, *Capitalist Restructuring*, 171–187. For similar transnational developments see Mudge, *Leftism Reinvented*, 38–40, 365–375, passim.
173. Ryner, *Capitalist Restructuring*, 179–182.
174. Lindvall, *The Politics of Purpose*, 12–14.
175. Lindvall has stressed SAP's adherence to full employment at this point, but other scholars have deemed this a rhetorical trick, while the actual

priority was fighting inflation. Lindvall, *The Politics of Purpose*, 146–149; Östberg, *När vinden vände*, 302–303.

176. Karl Popper, *The Open Society and its Enemies* (London: Routledge, 2002 [1945]), 1–3, passim.
177. Kristina Boréus, *Högervåg: Nyliberalism och kampen om språket i svensk offentlig debatt 1969–1989* (Stockholm: Tiden, 1994), 275, 278–283.
178. Boréus, *Högervåg*, 321–324.
179. Ibid., 340–341.
180. Blyth, *Great Transformations*, 9–10, 270–275.
181. Ibid., vii–ix, 251.

CHAPTER 6

Last Struggles for Economic Democracy

Contradictions of Democratization and Liberalized Capitalism

Market-oriented ideas had quickly gained currency in Finland and Sweden in the early 1980s, as the economic crises and stagflation of the previous decade had undermined trust in expansive economic policy and a growing public sector. In some countries, like Britain, economic growth was restored albeit at a lower level than before the crisis. Therefore, the ruling Conservative Party could retain majority support despite growing inequality. In other countries, like France, socialist attempts at expansive policies were trumped by market reactions, which forced everyone to follow the policy of anti-inflation, stable currency, budget balance and market liberalization.[1] The advancing European integration, in which Sweden and Finland wanted to participate, also pushed countries in this direction. The political atmosphere was changing in a more business- and market-friendly direction in most Western countries. Alternatives became less credible, as they were associated with concepts like bureaucracy and inefficiency. Even the Soviet Union was taking steps toward a more market-oriented and open society under Mikhail Gorbachev's leadership from 1985 onward. All this helped legitimize globalization and economic liberalization. The support of the far left stagnated in most countries, and parties increasingly moved toward the political center and competed for middle-class voters.[2]

I. Kärrylä, *Democracy and the Economy in Finland and Sweden since 1960*, Palgrave Studies in Political History,
https://doi.org/10.1007/978-3-030-80631-6_6

New intellectual strands in Western academic and public debate included 'postmodernism,' which declared the death of grand narratives and emphasized relativism and uncertainty. In many countries, the political field became more fragmented as new single-issue movements and protest parties emerged. They could be viewed as manifestations of the new individualized culture whose horizon of expectation was becoming increasingly fuzzy. The rise of environmental thought in Finland and Sweden, too, provided a new political issue to mobilize people who did not find the traditional left–right division meaningful. Traditional parties began to adopt environmental rhetoric to speak to new and broader audiences.[3] Moreover, social sciences increasingly let go of social class as an analytical concept and concentrated on the diversity of identities and political movements.[4]

The above developments are relevant, because historical actors perceived them very strongly, which affected their beliefs and attitudes. Like other European countries, Finland and Sweden had experienced the growth of the middle-class white-collar population, which made left-wing parties inclined to broaden their electorate and adopt policies closer to the new mainstream. Center-right parties, in turn, had to take into account the strong support for the welfare state among the middle class, which included many public sector employees. Many politicians interpreted the 1980s as an era of rising individualism. Grand visions for the future made way for more reactive and pragmatic politics, and parties' base in popular movements began to erode.[5] In Finland, many contemporaries perceived the social and political shift. They looked back at the 1960s and 1970s as very radical and politicized decades in contrast to the political consensus that had begun to develop.[6] Business think tank EVA's CEO Max Jakobson made this kind of historical interpretation before his retirement in 1984. He reminisced that when EVA was founded 10 years earlier, "entrepreneurs" had felt themselves cornered.

> Within the economic life, a certain mentality of defeat prevailed: It was feared that our country would inevitably slide into some sort of socialism. (…) Now afterward we can see that the phenomena of the 1970s represented rather the end of an era than the beginning of a new one. We have moved into a new societal situation which is characterized by individualism and market orientation. Radical demands for change have silenced and we live in an era of consensus.[7]

For Jakobson, consensus was a highly positive concept and its definition followed traditional employer thinking. Consensus meant recognizing the good of the nation, which in Jakobson's rhetoric gained a very objective character, rising above group interests and political struggles. Jakobson considered the era of consensus an improvement compared to more polarized times.[8] Jakobson's successor Kauko Sipponen expressed a familiar interpretation of the situation as adapting to external circumstances. After Finland's structural change of opening toward Europe and adopting free trade in the 1970s, the current change meant "adapting to competition that encompasses the entire world." This posed companies the demand for ever bigger resources, capability to bear risk, innovations, and human-centered leadership. Sipponen argued that in this situation, politicians should stick to managing political life and the public economy, not "intervening with the operations of private enterprises through detailed regulation."[9] The rhetorical figure of dissociating public and private spheres had become even more viable than at the time EVA was established.

Parties of the left were concerned about the political initiative moving to the bourgeois side, and their declining electoral support. In the Finnish parliamentary election of 1983, the Social Democrats and People's Democrats together received 40.2% of the vote. This was mostly due to the decline of the People's Democrats, but it was the worst result for the left since 1936 when the Communist Party had been illegal. The Social Democrats continued as the main party in government, maintaining their pro-business economic policy and believing that structural unemployment had become permanent.[10] Scholars also noted people's movement to the middle regarding both politics and class. People's alienation from politics, parties and voting was already a significant concern in the mid-1980s. Parties seemed to move toward the center and let go of their programmatic goals.[11] There were predictions that trade union solidarity could be undermined as especially white-collar employees stayed out and rather negotiated their wages and terms of employment independently. Old institutions did not seem to correspond to the new working life brought about by technological development.[12]

With over 3% annual growth, Finland's economy was faring better than that of Sweden and most European countries. The country could balance its economy with small devaluations instead of austerity, and the public sector was still growing.[13] However, the perception of changed economic preconditions was strong, leading to avoidance of budget deficit and public debt. The Social Democrats governed in Finland and Sweden, but they had to conduct policies to the benefit of private capital. The process of reforming the public sector toward more market-like practices in the spirit of 'New Public Management' was also beginning.[14] In Sweden, all this created contradictions within SAP and between the party and LO, which was dubbed the 'war of the roses' in the Swedish press.[15] *Tiden* criticized capital-friendly policy in a 1984 editorial. It argued that the Social Democrats had let go of the most important aspect of their postwar policy: extending democratic influence over investments and capital markets. Instead, the political and economic power of finance capital had grown, while state finance remained in bad shape.[16]

Swedish employers and the Moderate Party continued their radical rhetoric. Before the election of 1985, the Moderates occasionally used the concept 'systemic change' (*systemskifte*). It meant basically their traditional objectives of more economic freedom, lower taxation and a smaller public sector. The Social Democrats clung onto the concept and launched a strong counter-campaign.[17] SAP portrayed systemic change as a transition from a solidaristic welfare society to a class society where the strongest would prevail. SAP could also lean on its economic policy, which had managed to restore economic growth, hold back inflation, and maintain the lowest unemployment in Europe, even though full employment had not been reached.[18] The defense of the Swedish model worked, and SAP stayed in power. Its support dropped only from 45.6 to 44.7%, but it meant the loss of seven mandates and stronger dependence on the Communists. The Moderate and Center Parties lost a few seats, while the biggest winners were the Liberals with their new leader Bengt Westerberg. They became the second-biggest bourgeois party with 14.2% support. This marked an increase of 8 percentage points from the previous election.[19]

Social Democratic rhetoric continued its move from democratic steering of the economy toward emphasizing the welfare state and correcting markets through social redistribution. This constellation was portrayed as a sharp alternative to right-wing ideas. After the election, Prime Minister Olof Palme declared the result as a defeat for "neoliberalism." According to him, the election had not been about single policy questions but about the image of society behind policy. "The people's home's view of society, which is based on everyone's equal value and rights, or neoliberalism with its song of praise to egoism, and the right of the strongest?"[20] Palme was glad that SAP had been able to defeat the 'neoliberals' with fact-based arguments and a credible alternative, which was "not only morally more attractive, but also economically more efficient."[21] Sociologist Göran Therborn argued that the right-wing current was nevertheless a serious phenomenon, based on postindustrial technological and financial changes. The Social Democrats had been saved by moderate conservatives who did not believe in all neoliberal ambitions, but to maintain their support SAP needed new goals, such as the right to creative work, developing work environments, and de-bureaucratizing the public sector.[22] Therborn's suggestions were thus closer to the ideas of near democracy and 'artistic critique' of capitalism than the substantial redistribution of economic power which he had advocated 20 years earlier.

Before the election, the architects of SAP's new economic policy, Kjell-Olof Feldt and Klas Eklund, explained the successes of the policy now called 'Third Way.' According to Eklund, this third way was situated between an austerity policy that created unemployment and economic expansion that increased deficits. The government had succeeded in its partly contradictory goals of 'working and saving,' as most of the increase in industrial production had been channeled into exports and investments. The government had taken redistributive measures, while the bourgeois alternative would have been more substantial public cuts and lower taxation.[23] According to Finance Minister Feldt, the third way was a countermovement to neoliberalism. It did not mark a retreat from fundamental Social Democratic demands for solidarity and social justice, even though it could be viewed as a break in ideological tradition. Feldt argued that the Social Democrats took collective responsibility for full employment and welfare, but also created preconditions for growth and efficient markets. Feldt predicted that the ability to guard the welfare society while securing growth and stability could become as important achievements for SAP as their breakthrough in the 1930s.[24] Thus also for Feldt, the 'welfare society' was a stronger concept than economic democracy for describing the present and future society.

In Social Democratic rhetoric, neoliberalism had assumed a similar role to the one communism and socialism played for nonsocialists. It was most of all a scare word, a caricature of all that was wrong in right-wing politics. The actual content of neoliberalism was not very clear. Deeper analyses usually associated it with the thought of Hayek and Friedman,[25] but analyses of their relation to the policy of the Swedish center-right were scarce. Even though SAP argued that its economic policy was an alternative to neoliberalism, measures that could be interpreted as neoliberalization were constantly taken. One of the most significant economic reforms of the 1980s in European countries was the liberalization of finance markets. As scholars often point out, deregulation is not the best term to describe these changes. Free markets also require regulation by the state, only in a different form. The reforms of the 1980s included much *reregulation*, for example competition and equity market legislation.[26]

Regardless of terminology, it is indisputable that in the 1980s the international movement of capital became much freer than in the first postwar decades, which had been characterized by protected domestic markets. Currency and credit regulations were lifted, and capital could roam freely to find the most profitable objects of investment. Steps toward this had already been taken in the 1960s and 1970s as gray finance markets grew and tax havens were established in offshore locations. Decision-makers in countries like Sweden and Finland believed they had no choice but to follow the global liberalization in order to retain the market shares of their export industries and attract new foreign capital. The Swedish and Finnish Central Banks liberated the finance markets partially from the 1970s onward. The most significant reforms of deregulating interest rates as well as foreign credit and investments were made in the mid-1980s. The reforms increased the independence of central banks and the power of private commercial banks, who could now issue credit more freely. However, they also made independent monetary policy difficult by forcing countries to adapt to international capital movements. The priority of maintaining stable currencies restricted the use of other policy tools.[27]

In Finland, finance market liberalization has often been portrayed as structural and inevitable due to economic globalization and technological change. The main ideational factor considered is the desire to participate in European integration.[28] This echoes the views of contemporaries. Finnish liberalization was carried through as administrative measures by the Central Bank with little public debate. They were mostly reactions to changes in the market, but there was also international pressure through the OECD and IMF. The most notable reforms were abolishing interest regulation in 1986 and liberalizing foreign investments in 1987. Few politicians criticized the decisions.[29] According to the legal historian Markus Kari, the reforms may have been as necessary for Finnish industry and national economy as contemporaries believed, but their implementation was not very well-planned or controlled. Policy measures to hinder credit expansion were almost nonexistent.[30] The Finnish Social Democrats acknowledged that liberalization narrowed the prospects of independent economic policy, but it was considered necessary to retain a strong currency and avoid devaluations. In a liberalized global economy, the main goal and constraint of economic policy was keeping real rates of interest positive and currencies stable to attract capital. Prime Minister Kalevi Sorsa said that he was not entirely familiar with the reasons that made the reforms necessary, but now Finland just had to struggle in the new reality.[31]

In Sweden, the process of liberalizing the finance markets was very similar. Credit and interest rate regulations were lifted in 1985, while currency flows, such as purchases of foreign stock and other assets, were gradually liberalized between 1986 and 1989. Like in Finland, liberalization was carried out mostly as a technical administrative procedure. It was portrayed as ideologically neutral and necessary due to budget deficit, international pressures on the currency and growing gray capital markets. The main actors responsible were the Bank of Sweden and the Ministry of Finance. Minister Kjell-Olof Feldt was active and well-informed of the reforms, but other politicians supervising the Central Bank approved the decisions without much discussion.[32] Even Prime Minister Palme was quite unaware of the details. According to Feldt's memoirs, when he in 1985 mentioned lifting the last remaining credit regulations, Palme uttered: "Do what you want. I don't understand any of that anyway."[33] This is a telling example of the new reality perceived by the Social Democrats. Feldt himself considered deregulation an ideological retreat that was nevertheless economically necessary.[34]

The point is that Social Democrats adopted neoliberal policy and liberated finance capitalism *but* also looked for alternatives. In the early 1980s, they made efforts to forge international cooperation on Keynesian full employment policy. Finland's Prime Minister Sorsa suggested coordination of Keynesian policy to European social democratic leaders in spring 1983. SAP's representatives actively promoted similar goals in the OECD at the time and had earlier been strong supporters of the United Nations 'New International Economic Order' initiative. However, these efforts were hampered by the fact that right-wing governments ruled the major economies of the United States, Britain and West Germany. Global Keynesianism was further undermined after President Mitterrand's socialist administration in France took a political U-turn from demand management and nationalizations toward neoliberalization.[35]

Local Bargaining and Flexible Wages: Increased Democracy?

Along with finance market liberalization, the pressure to liberalize and decentralize the labor markets became strong in the second half of the 1980s throughout Europe.[36] In both Finland and Sweden, the concepts of cooperation and employee participation were increasingly connected to a debate on local bargaining on the terms and conditions of employment. This became topical especially due to the belief in the need for new sources of competitiveness due to international competition and structural change toward post-Fordism and the information society. Employers wanted to move toward local and sectoral bargaining as production had also turned more flexible in many fields.[37] In Sweden, SAF already spoke for more decentralized wage bargaining in the late 1970s, especially due to the demands of the engineering sector.[38] This marked a change in the employer and employee sides' mutual emphasis on centralized collective bargaining of the 1960s and 1970s. The Cooperation and Codetermination Acts were also built on the distinction between central-level terms of employment and local-level cooperation issues, such as organizational and technological changes. These sets of issues were considered separate but mutually complementing. Through enterprise democracy, the trade union movement had sought to extend the scope of enterprise-level issues which were collectively negotiated or decided, whereas employers were reluctant to increase their obligations to negotiate. By contrast, on the issues already negotiated collectively on the central level, such as wages, working hours and regulations on dismissals and work safety, employers now wanted to bring negotiations back to the enterprise level, which would have allowed more flexibility for individual enterprises and the possibility to deviate from centralized agreements.

In the 1980s, employers maintained more strongly that increased employee participation would also entail flexibility on centrally agreed issues such as wages and working hours. This was commonly portrayed as a positive increase in the participation and influence of individual employees. In Finland, STK's CEO Pentti Somerto stated that the emphasis was moving from detailed regulation of labor relations toward increased cooperation, negotiation and decision-making at the company level.[39] This change was believed to emanate especially from the demands of employees themselves, who wanted more autonomy on their working hours.[40] The talk about local bargaining became pronounced in Finland especially after the difficult bargaining round of 1986. STK Chair Krister Ahlström pondered what could be the new practice after centralized incomes policy. He suggested relaxing collective agreements and giving employees better possibilities to negotiate their wages directly with their employers.[41] In the economic upswing of the late 1980s, centralized agreements became more difficult and the appeal of sectoral ones also increased among Finnish trade unions because of wage pressure. However, central incomes policy agreements were made despite difficulties, in 1986, 1988 and 1990.[42]

Employers sometimes legitimized their claims by appealing to the same concepts the trade union movement used in their arguments for economic democracy. One of these was "employee rights." In February 1987 *Teollisuusviikko* commented on Kalevi Sorsa's speech, in which the Prime Minister had expressed the common belief of Finland lagging behind other Western countries in employee rights. The editorial argued that Finnish employees were certainly not drudging without rights under employer authority, but certain rights should be increased: "their rights to make agreements with their employer at their own workplace."[43] The official statement of the STK's 1987 conference said that regulations should allow adapting working hours to "the needs of both the company and its personnel."[44] Employers' use of individual rights and freedom as legitimation concepts points to an implicit claim that individualism was more beneficial to the common good, even more democratic than collectivism. This belief gained currency in employer rhetoric during the 1980s.

As already seen, individualism had long been an emerging theme in left-wing, especially social democratic, thought and rhetoric. However, local agreements were a difficult subject, as they were normally believed to contradict the collectivism of the trade union movement. In Sweden, LO was constantly critical of decentralized bargaining and wage-setting, which were believed to undermine solidaristic wage policy.[45] SAK's stance on local agreements and flexibility had also traditionally been negative, as they believed they weakened the position of employees and increased wage differences compared to collective agreements. After all, the system of collective bargaining had been created to strengthen the position of individual employees vis-à-vis their employers. This principle remained central in the 1986 collective bargaining round in Finland, which included a major disagreement on locally agreed flexible working hours and led to an extensive two-day joint strike. SAK opposed STK's proposition on working hours fiercely, as they found that flexibility would be increased on employer terms.[46]

After the difficult bargaining round, SAK Secretary Lauri Ihalainen gave a critical May Day speech, stating that the employer side had clearly raised its ideological profile following the international example of "the new right." They now had a strong will toward decentralized bargaining, and Ihalainen suspected that this was to undermine the power of the trade unions and Social Democrats. As an opposing objective to decentralization, Ihalainen proclaimed the extension of democracy in economic and working life, especially through employee representation and wage-earner funds.[47] In this way Ihalainen implied that decentralized bargaining was in fact undemocratic or at least against the interests of employees. However, by the end of the year SAK had already become more receptive to increasing local bargaining. Ihalainen stated that branch-specific flexibility could be increased, and some issues could be decided in workplaces, provided that equality between employees and employers increased and firms would move in the direction of participatory and direct democracy.[48] SAK representatives began to acknowledge that structural change required a new combination of central, union-level and local agreements, which would also include employee participation in planning and execution of work. However, full decentralization was believed to lead to unfair competition in people's working and living conditions.[49]

Through local bargaining, the employer side wanted to make wage-setting more flexible to match new practices of production. One instrument for this was bonus payments for employees, especially performance-related bonuses. They substituted, for example, piecework and gave employers more power in wage-setting.[50] Bonuses had been an important part of the management theories of the 1960s and 1970s as a means of motivating employees, but they had not been adopted to a significant extent in Finland or Sweden due to the tradition of centralized wage bargaining. During the 1980s, however, the call for different bonuses intensified from the employer side. The demand for competent workforce grew and there was pressure to compete with wages.[51] In 1986, STK stated that developing performance-related pay was important and a "positive form of wage drift."[52] Eero Voutilainen, STK's former HR expert, wrote that according to studies, over 80% of employees would appreciate performance-related bonuses, which could strengthen the experience of having a personal impact on the company's success. Voutilainen linked bonus payments to the concepts of cooperation and participation and argued that they would increase the quality and efficiency of work.[53]

The trade union movement was not as enthusiastic about bonus payments. They pointed out their problems, especially regarding solidaristic wage policy, as bonuses increased wage differences. The SAK insisted that new wage-setting methods had to be always agreed in the collective bargaining rounds.[54] The readiness of Finnish trade unions to adopt local or sectoral flexibilizations in wages and working hours increased toward the end of the 1980s, but they always stressed the need for a framework for collective and preferably centralized bargaining. Potential benefits to employees were acknowledged, but trade union representatives usually called for an equal standing between employers and employees in order to reach these benefits.

Many Swedish intellectuals close to the labor movement commented on changes in the economy and the labor market. The gravity of change was sometimes conceptualized as a journey *Toward a New Swedish Model*, which was the title of a 1988 book edited by a group of economists and sociologists. The articles talked about the tradition of labor market cooperation and the 'stabilization problem' of combining full employment with low inflation as key traits of the Swedish model. This included the trade union movement's "social responsibility" for wage development. In his contribution to the book, the Director of the Labor Market Board Allan Larsson argued that a key question of the Swedish model had always been balancing citizens' and employees' need for security, with enterprises' need for flexibility. He found that the labor market model and social reforms had succeeded quite well in this task.[55] Larsson continued that a key challenge for the 1990s was combining wage demands and competitiveness. Trade union confederations had to show that they were "not only guardians of interests but also builders of society."[56] However, according to Larsson, employers also had to carry their responsibility instead of convincing employees that they would get better contracts without centralized bargaining. Larsson continued to warn about inflation and expressed the belief that with 2.5–3% unemployment Sweden had already reached the balance point of non-accelerating inflation.[57]

Social Democrats and Trade Unions Hold on to the Rhetoric of Economic Democracy

In the second half of the 1980s, traditional ideals of economic and enterprise democracy remained actual in the thought and rhetoric of the Social Democrats and trade unions, even though their content and perceived possibilities had changed quite drastically. In Finland, the 1986 SAK congress expressed the belief that employee influence was still weak in workplaces and society. Therefore, many reforms, such as strengthening the Cooperation Act, enabling employee representation in corporate governance, and establishing wage-earner funds were in order. As before, the overarching objective was democratic control of economic life, which was viewed as a remedy against unequal and unjust concentration of power and ownership.[58]

SAK's statement legitimized democratization by the security of the employees. It highlighted the belief in rationalization being a constant threat for wage-earners and their employment, which made it a crucial issue to be influenced.[59] The belief in democratization as beneficial to efficiency and competitiveness retained its central role in trade union rhetoric. An important reason for expressing it seems to have been to find common ground with the employer side. In this kind of rhetoric, the content of enterprise democracy was close to the concept of cooperation. In November 1986, SAK Chair Pertti Viinanen stated that competitiveness and cooperation between employees and employers were not mutually exclusive. Instead, employee participation in planning and developing products and services was among the most important labor market questions around the world.[60] SAK of course retained its own criteria for cooperation and democratization, but by emphasizing economic values the trade union movement partly adapted to the conceptual hierarchy of the employers, which maintained that democracy had to be subordinate to economic efficiency in the name of the national interest.

However, the Finnish trade union movement was ready for a new offensive for enterprise democracy. In January 1987, the SAK newspaper *Palkkatyöläinen* wrote in its editorial that bringing democracy into Finnish working life had been arduous, and therefore the theme had been taken up on SAK's 80th anniversary. The paper used the common dissociation between 'true democracy' and cooperation, the latter of which did not fulfill democratic criteria.[61] The paper also reported Prime Minister Sorsa's speech at a shop steward seminar, where he stated once again that Finland was significantly lagging behind in the development of labor rights and economic democracy. Sorsa referred to international reports, which had even argued that this weakened Finland's competitiveness. The Prime Minister put some blame on the Finnish manufacturing and service industries, which were still relatively young and had not developed a management culture which could utilize cooperation for the benefit of the whole.[62]

In Sorsa's rhetoric, economic democracy referred rather to "more efficient cooperation," which the trade union newspaper criticized. His comment exemplifies the rhetoric of democratization, which fluctuated between two arguments or value hierarchies, often also seeking to combine them. In this rhetoric, democracy was portrayed as, on the one hand, an indispensable human right and, on the other hand, a road to the common good in a capitalist or mixed economy, via economic efficiency and growth. While Sorsa on this occasion used competitiveness as a legitimation concept, the other pole of left-wing thought was voiced by SAK Secretary, Communist Pekka Ahmavaara. He referred to SAK's enterprise democracy program from 1969 and said that preconditions for democracy were to be established first, but alone they would merely bring about "a softer form of capitalism." According to Ahmavaara, "true enterprise democracy" was achieved only in socialism.[63]

The concept of economic democracy was strongly present in the renewed platform of the Finnish Social Democratic Party in 1987, although its rhetoric had been taken in a more moderate direction from the earlier programs. Acceptance of the market mechanism had become more explicit than before, but the Social Democrats continued to advocate a mixed economy with appropriate shares of private and public activities. The platform argued that democratic steering and planning were necessary alongside market-based allocation of resources. The control of financial institutions was no longer an objective, but the party aimed at their "societal supervision."[64] Sami Outinen has considered the new platform a move away from the ideal of a planned economy to a more moderate steering of capitalism, where markets played a key role as an information mechanism. Socialist long-term objectives became more distant, even though many Social Democrats continued to advocate a more radical approach. Outinen interprets that the platform exemplifies SDP's weakening reliance in the power of its traditional objectives, for example due to increasing individualization and the decreasing importance of class as the basis of political identity. The party no longer claimed to represent the interests of the working class but all social groups, even though wage labor retained its importance in the Social Democratic view of society. According to Outinen, SDP's strategy turned increasingly toward defending the welfare state instead of transforming capitalism.[65]

Interpretations of the history of the labor movement and societal development did figure strongly in the 1987 platform. Its rhetoric emphasized defending the welfare state as an historical achievement, which had already become an important theme in the late 1970s. Pauli Kettunen has considered the shift toward this kind of retrospective rhetoric a notable change in social democratic thought. It was no longer clear that history was on the side of the labor movement.[66] However, the forward-looking and reformist elements of labor movement's ideational constellations were also present in SDP's new platform. Mirroring the Swedish SAP, it still expressed belief in economic democracy being the next historical phase in the democratization process for which the labor movement had struggled during its entire existence.[67]

Outinen's interpretations of SDP's increased market orientation and waning class identity downplay some of the more radical and future-oriented content of the platform, such as claims for redistribution of power and wealth, which had retained their place from earlier programs. As before, SDP's platform of 1987 put forward slogans implying redistribution of power and new forms of democracy, such as "From the power of capital to the power of labor," "Work grants the right for self-governance" and "Toward participatory democracy." The document expressed the belief that uneven distribution of productive means and the resulting societal power of capital remained the most significant obstacles to personal autonomy, freedom and democracy. The party continued to call a system based on these ideals "democratic socialism" and used "economic oligarchy" as its counter-concept.[68]

In this kind of rhetoric, the Social Democrats continued to put forward an alternative conception of the common good against those voiced by the employers and the center-right, whose version was based on individual freedom and private ownership. However, socialist long-term objectives had been pushed into a more distant future. The platform of 1987 advocated extending democracy in working life and local government alike. It put forward the common notion of different spheres of democracy and connected them with corresponding civil rights: social, economic and cultural. In working life, rights were to be secured by familiar means: granting employees new rights of decision-making in companies, self-governance in their own work, and the possibility to control personnel funds.[69]

What was new in the platform was the growing emphasis on self-governance, which derived from the critique of bureaucracy originating from the 1960s. This was an attempt to tap into the general tendency of advocating individual participation and condemning centralization. It also affected statements regarding economic and enterprise democracy. The leader of the platform working group, Pentti Puoskari, wrote in *Socialist Periodical* that the old platform was already considered too "state socialist." Instead, party members wanted a reform strategy "from below" in order to bring about economic democracy. This included accepting markets as a natural system as long as there was also planning aimed toward the common interest.[70] In his commentary on the platform, another party intellectual, Aimo Kairamo, expressed the objective by saying that social democracy wanted to tame capitalism and its market forces "without destroying the productive and economic capabilities of the system or the already established democracy."[71] He argued that capitalism had already been tamed, but it had proven its life force and escaped national borders. Transnational capitalism did not care much about workers or the environment. Social democracy had to continue transforming capitalism to meet their needs and interests.[72]

However, Kairamo did not offer concrete ways for restricting the power of transnational capital. He acknowledged that this was difficult, as politics and the labor movement remained mostly national. The dualism of accepting the positive aspects of markets and restricting their negative ones dominated the rhetoric. Kairamo suggested that in some cases competition had to be created through regulation if it was not born otherwise. On the other hand, socialization was also to be kept in the policy toolbox. Referring to Keynes, Kairamo argued that socialization or strong regulation of capital formation could still be necessary for maintaining full employment.[73] Kairamo's general view on democracy originated largely from Bernstein, whose idea of democracy being both a means and an end for socialism Kairamo cited. Democracy was a 'form of life' and therefore to be implemented in all political activity. Even a deficient political democracy based on the principle of one person, one vote was more equal than economic power based on one mark, one vote, Kairamo argued. Therefore, the struggle to limit economic power in favor of democracy was always actual.[74]

SDP's platform and action programs also lacked concrete ways of restricting transnational capitalism, or even promoting the new key concept of self-governance. The platform turned economic democracy into an umbrella concept for all social reforms, such as improved security of employment and basic social security. Issues of working life democracy, such as personnel funds and employee representation in corporate governance, were also mentioned. As already noted, while the Social Democrats emphasized democratization of workplaces and local governance, the traditional idea of macro-level economic democracy became less pronounced. The means of achieving the ambitious goals of economic democracy had become more modest in step with growing acceptance of the market economy. The Social Democrats continued to emphasize their traditional values, but economic necessities formed ever stronger constraints to their pursuit.[75]

The rapidly changing society seemed to constrain political possibilities of the Social Democrats. In his later book, Pentti Puoskari acknowledged the nostalgia for the years of full employment and the 'historical compromise' between capitalism and democracy. He admitted that Social Democratic policy had been dependent on economic growth, but in the new financialized phase of growth, a similar compromise had not been created. One factor was the weakened reliance on progress and grand societal visions. The world had become more uncertain and faced, for example, environmental constraints. Puoskari also found the erosion of class identities and turn to 'post-material' values contemporary challenges.[76] Some answers to these challenges were appealing to 'wage-earners' instead of 'workers,' emphasizing environmental values, and finding new roles for markets and self-governance, which would avoid the problems of centralization and bureaucratization.[77] One of the key questions for Puoskari was determining boundaries for individualism. He found that extreme individualism only undermined its own foundations. Society and its democratic institutions were needed in order to develop individualism toward solidarity and sense of responsibility.[78] Puoskari considered the prospects of the European left as better than they had been a few years earlier. They were able to continue traditional reformism, restrain right-wing politics and defend the welfare state. However, economic austerity had come to stay, and Keynesianism had become outdated due to economic internationalization.[79] All in all, Puoskari did not put forward a very proactive leftist vision for the 1990s.

Adapting Economic Democracy to Individualism and the Market Economy

In Sweden, debate on economic democracy toned down during SAP's term in government 1982–1985. Besides moderate discussions on developing codetermination and wage-earner funds, the party did not put forward new visions of democratization. Both the Swedish and Finnish Social Democrats perceived similar problems. They believed that economic leeway became more restricted due to global interdependencies, and the growth of the middle-class undermined the traditional electoral base. Already in the early 1980s, talk about an ideological crisis of the Social Democrats began in Sweden. The journalist Anders Isaksson wrote in 1983 that SAP had earlier been "in step with time" but now lacked clear goals for the future and concentrated on defending previous achievements. Even talk about the third step of democratization, wage-earner funds and codetermination seemed to represent only redistribution policy to fine-tune the system.[80] The historian Arne Helldén called for a return to the successful reformism of previous decades, when SAP had united different groups and upheld a "positive tension" between retaining the existing social system and making socialist reforms. According to Helldén's interpretation, the "neoconservative" counter-movement had become so strong because the radicalism of 1960s and 1970s had gone overboard.[81]

One theme that was perceived as a potential solution to the ideological crisis and a new vision for the future was the same as in Finland: Democracy that would be closer to the common people. The ideas of participatory democracy, 'near democracy' and self-governance, which had been prominent since the 1960s, became even more actual due to the 'individualization' of society. Old concepts gained new parallel concepts and potential applications. Terms like 'citizen influence' and 'user influence' were coined to signify the reform of public administration and local governance, which were to serve as counter-strategies to the bourgeois aims of privatizing and marketizing the public sector. Concrete proposals included neighborhood councils and cooperatives to take on public services.[82] Even though the discussion was active throughout the 1980s, very little was manifested in concrete reforms. Familiar problems of local democracy were perceived, such as the threats of egoism and losing a wider societal perspective.[83]

After the electoral victory of 1985, debate on the need for new Social Democratic goals continued. Market-oriented beliefs were now truly making inroads, while the concept of democratization was situated increasingly in the workplace level, local communities and the hands of consumers instead of the national economy as a whole. SAP's strategy against what they called 'neoliberalism' was to become proactive reformers of the welfare state for their own right. Ingvar Carlsson argued that it was not enough to propose new roads toward old goals. For example, environmental policy had to be taken onto the agenda more strongly. The public sector had to be reformed toward "freedom of choice" between different school and welfare providers and decisions had to be taken closer to consumers. For Carlsson, this seems to have been a way to promote the ideals of local democracy and participation. This did not necessarily mean privatization, but the Social Democratic minister had appropriated some neoliberal ideas, which viewed citizens as customers and consumers of public services. According to Carlsson, the public and private sectors could support each other in service production. He also advocated reforming working life by introducing "true influence on all levels" and giving people chances to take the initiative and learn new things. Increasing the overall education level had become a key goal for the Social Democrats in the context of structural change and the emerging information society.[84] Instead of offering a polar opposite to neoliberalism, SAP attempted to counter it with 'middle-of-the-road' solutions: Appropriating some neoliberal elements of marketization and individualism while seeking to safeguard a larger degree of social justice by maintaining the welfare state.

Like SAP, LO also conducted debates on the need for new goals and organizational renewal. The trade union movement was facing a new situation as employers increasingly advocated decentralized bargaining and flexible wage-setting. The 1983 wage agreement between the engineering sector employers and the Metalworkers' Union was a significant break from the centralized 'Swedish model.'[85] Bo Stråth has described how LO in 1984 began to investigate means of strengthening its position as an opinion leader. LO concluded that its concrete power resources had not changed very much, but new attitudes posed a challenge. Individualism and market orientation had made a breakthrough among younger people. Other challenges were the growing distance from white-collar organizations and employer-driven individualizing reforms in working life, such as quality circles and bonus schemes. These were perceived as deliberate strategies to weaken the trade union movement, but LO found its prospects to fight back better than those of trade unions in many other countries. LO did not modify its traditional goals, such as everyone's right to work, equitable distribution and economic democracy, but they needed to find more concrete content and a new overarching symbol to replace the wage-earner funds.[86]

The tone of debate in Swedish politics changed drastically in February 1986, when Prime Minister Olof Palme was assassinated. The emerging conflict between SAP and more radical left-wing and trade union groups dissolved. Ingvar Carlsson took Palme's place as prime minister and profiled as a reformer of the Swedish welfare state and social democracy.[87] At the beginning of 1987, Carlsson elaborated the themes of collectivism, individualism and democracy in a long interview. He reflected on the reasons why in the 1960s and 1970s there had been debate about extending collective democratic influence, but now it was about restricting it. Carlsson believed this was partly based on disappointment in economic interest groups and in the reality of communist countries. He admitted that democracy required critical examination, but it was unfortunate if confidence in it was undermined. According to Carlsson, conceptions of the scope of democracy continued to differentiate Social Democracy and bourgeois thought. Expressing traditional Social Democratic beliefs, he argued that the retreat of the state would not mean increased power for individuals, but for different power groups. Carlsson argued that restricting the power of political bodies also meant restricting universal suffrage. Of course, bureaucracy and detailed regulation could become excessive, but this could be fixed by the democratic process itself.[88]

Regarding the economy, the tension between democracy and efficiency figured strongly in Carlsson's rhetoric. It was important to give citizens influence on the use of new technology, but profitability against competing countries had to be maintained. Carlsson argued that SAP was not a party of the past: For example, environmental problems remained unsolved, and capitalism was unable to tackle them with its short-sighted profit interests. The article ended on a note that illustrates SAP's attempt to again become a party of compromises that could unite workers, middle classes, and everyone who believed in the virtuous circle of economic efficiency and social justice. According to Carlsson, it was necessary to stress both the collective and the individual, freedom and solidarity.[89] At this point, however, it seems that the Social Democrats were moving toward more emphasis on the individual and freedom, less on the collective and solidarity.

In 1987, explicit debate on economic democracy intensified in Sweden once more. The LO Chair Stig Malm criticized the government's economic policy and called for new, broader debate on economic democracy and "issues of power." It was to touch not only wage-earner funds, but democratization of workplaces and different forms of democratic ownership.[90] Economic democracy was also discussed in a series of editorials in *Aftonbladet.* The newspaper criticized the reliance on individual saving and institutional ownership, which only cared for profitability. It argued that capitalism would be questioned only when citizens and wage-earners gave capital and production other tasks than maximizing profit. These could include welfare in working life and solidaristic wages. This kind of reorientation required distributing not only profits but also authority over enterprises.[91]

Similar problems were pointed out in the political statement by SAP's Executive Committee for the 1987 congress, but concrete proposals remained vague. Using traditional rhetoric, the statement called for extending and deepening democracy. Democracy was called a comprehensive "lifestyle," and one of its greatest obstacles was unequal distribution of economic resources and competences. Declining citizen participation was found worrisome, and economic democracy continued to figure as an important avenue of reform. The statement called for employee influence in their own work, a debate on renewing labor legislation, and more education to foster new competences. Concentration of ownership and economic power was perceived as a problem, but SAP did not propose much more than discussion on these issues. Wage-earner funds were viewed as an important but limited step, and cooperatives were taken up as a potential form of ownership.[92] The range of reference of economic democracy had narrowed, as industrial policy was no longer explicitly connected to it. Instead of democratic control over the economy, the main goals of industrial policy were increasing the competitiveness and competence of Swedish enterprises, for example by investing in research and development and promoting "creative environments."[93] This kind of conception of a 'Schumpeterian' competition state had been emerging since the late 1970s, but it gained a constantly larger role in Social Democratic thought and rhetoric.

At SAP's 1987 congress, Stig Malm again demanded economic democracy based on the right of work. Important economic decisions were not to be made exclusively in bank palaces and by "young finance lions." However, debate on the subject as well as the number of motions related to it was diminishing from congress to congress. Nationalization and control of banks, industry and natural resources were taken up in a few motions. The Executive Committee's response was familiar: Society already regulated the economy sufficiently and controlled directly or indirectly about one-third of production. New regulation was to be implemented as finance markets were opening, and further development employee influence was to be investigated. The Executive Committee welcomed debate on economic democracy but admitted that the large budget deficit decreased possibilities of steering the economy.[94]

Even though LO and many Social Democrats continued to advocate traditional conceptions of economic democracy, ideas of decentralization and self-governance as well as questions of adapting to freer markets made their way into the debate more strongly than before. This development was not very well-noticed by right-wing critics, who accused SAP of remaining on the path of socialism and collectivism.[95] SAP emphasized the need for a strong economy, low inflation, and international competitiveness. 'Third-way' economic policy had to be continued to restore full employment and increase equality.[96] A new emphasis, which had already been visible in Social Democratic rhetoric, was considering consumers as central actors that exercised authority in the economy. SAP stressed the local influence of citizens and reform of public services to allow more 'user influence.' However, commercialization and privatization of the public sector were opposed, because they did not necessarily fulfill consumer needs.[97] In this kind of rhetoric, the consumer was rising to be an even more central subject of democracy and freedom than the worker.

The need to find new content for economic democracy became voiced more often in public. This problem and the concept of the consumer were discussed in LO's 1988 book entitled *Mitt i steget* (In the Middle of the Step), which is a good showcase of the labor movement's changing beliefs and strategies.[98] Also in this case, the content of reform proposals moved toward stronger acceptance of market logic, and decentralization of authority to employees and consumers instead of public authorities. The book's title referred to the 'third step' of democratization, which was not yet complete. In her article, *Tiden*'s editor-in-chief Anne-Marie Lindgren defined economic democracy as "a summarizing term for demands that influence over production should be exercised by citizens/wage-earners instead of big capital owners."[99] In this light, there were many potential practices of economic democracy, such as associations of workers or producers that had been promoted by syndicalism, guild socialism, and the cooperative movement. Lindgren argued that the Swedish Social Democrats had often been close to guild socialists in their emphasis on the trade union movement. However, they had also learned that power and ownership were not intrinsically connected and developed their own approach that could be called 'functional socialism.' Lindgren pointed out that private business was strongly regulated in the spirit of functional socialism. Even though finance markets had been liberalized, new environmental regulation, for example, restricted the power of capital. Lindgren argued that it was possible to democratize the power of enterprises, but not the power of consumers. This was the key to the Social Democrats' view on markets. Lindgren explained that the party was keen on market forces that can be translated as 'consumer rule,' but against 'commercial profit interests'."[100]

Like SAP's platform, Lindgren's article drew on people's different roles as citizens, workers and consumers. She argued that the interests of workers, consumers and the state often contradicted, and "traditional socialism" had paid too much attention to production. Interests had to be prioritized, and different issues were appropriate to be decided on different levels. The state was usually not an appropriate owner, but it could decide on major investments and macroeconomic steering, while producers could decide on the terms and organization of employment, and consumers on the supply of commodities. Lindgren criticized the Social Democratic tendency of delegating most decisions to 'citizens' instead of those who were most closely affected.[101] She acknowledged that ownership did bring power, and her solution to distributing it was promoting different forms of ownership, such as cooperatives. Instead of employee influence, Lindgren talked most ardently about consumer influence, and the conflict of interest between consumers and employees, which in her view had often been neglected in visions of economic democracy. She argued that in an 'affluent society' markets were the only solution to resource allocation, because people's consumption preferences were so different.[102] Lindgren concluded that no model was perfect: All economies had to cope with conflicting interests, and that was what democracy was about. When different interests had equal possibilities to come forth, feasible compromises became possible.[103]

Lindgren's article is a good example of how ideational constellations were changing in the 1980s. In a liberalized economy, possibilities to control markets were constantly small. The main problem in economic democracy became finding a viable combination of democracy and markets instead of subordinating the latter to the former. Lindgren attempted to turn the connotation of markets more positive by evoking the old aim of consumer influence and portraying it as an aspect of economic democracy. But whereas consumer influence had earlier meant consumer education and increasing their power against enterprises and advertisers, who were potentially distorting preferences or selling deficient products, Lindgren now expressed quite neoliberal beliefs that consumers could pursue their interests in a free market if the interests of employees and the state did not distort them. This corresponds to Niklas Olsen's interpretation of the Danish Social Democrats adopting the figure of the 'sovereign consumer' in the 1980s.[104] The potentially democratic nature of markets meant in these cases mostly the principle of 'one dollar, one vote,' but Lindgren did not problematize its relation to democracy in the public sphere that was based on 'one person, one vote.' In contrast, the sociologist Bengt Furåker took up this problem and argued that markets and democracy should not be identified with each other. Even though markets had 'democratized' people's consumption chances, the inequality of purchase power remained, Furåker pointed out.[105]

Tiden also took up the centrality of economic democracy in its editorial and made interpretations of history that were common for Social Democrats: Every time SAP had mobilized for economic democracy, the bourgeois had responded with a strong counter-attack. This had happened in the 'Cossack election' of 1928, the planned economy debate of the 1940s, and most recently in the wage-earner fund debate. However, the editorial found it important to continue the debate on how to alter power and ownership relations. According to its optimistic belief, the third step of democratization had already begun. Wage-earners were no longer puppets in the hands of managers, and enlightened consumers were able to influence what was produced for the market. In a traditional social democratic manner, the editorial argued that authority was to be placed in the hands of the entire people, but on different levels of society and in ways that would be compatible with free markets.[106]

To conclude, the editorial took up the widely shared belief of increasing need for competence in working life. The trend was considered positive for wage-earners, as competence could become even more important than capital. But it concerned only certain sectors of the economy, and employees in stagnating sectors risked losing their power to negotiate. Hence, it was important to maintain full employment and increase general skills and 'citizen competences' such as the ability to take responsibility.[107] In the book *Mitt i steget*, the political scientist Jörgen Hermansson also stressed the need for increased competence. He hoped that polarization into high- and low-skill occupations could be avoided, and the Social Democrats were to promote the growth of general "citizen competences" to make sure that everyone could take part in professionalization.[108] The book's conclusion predicted optimistically that differences between blue- and white-collar employees would diminish along with growing influence and codetermination.[109]

These beliefs point to 'human capital' and the 'knowledge society,' which became key concepts in third-way Social Democracy. Knowledge and competence were viewed as means to endogenous economic growth in a postindustrial society. In a sense, the Social Democrats were moving from socializing capital to "capitalizing the social," as Jenny Andersson has put it. This included a new emphasis on people's responsibility to become productive members of society, instead of stressing their right to do so.[110] In the rhetoric of competence and human capital, there was a strong element of adaptation to economic necessities. In a way, this was a return to the ideational constellations of the 1960s, which emphasized 'security within change,' but in an even more fatalistic tone. Employees were given an active and self-developmental role, but the task of politics was not making them agents that could steer economic production or the pace and direction of structural change. Instead, they could and should be active in becoming competent and useful in whatever ways the forces of markets and technological development required. This was to secure the economic growth on which reformist Social Democracy had always rested. At the same time, beliefs in the waning significance of class were becoming more common.

However, Social Democratic rhetoric continued to acknowledge the importance of 'traditional' capital. Control of capital and investment was perceived as crucial for a fair and democratic economy, but the prospects for it had been narrowed. In the upswing of the late 1980s, boosted by financial liberalization, it became a problem that growing profits and 'over-liquidity' were channeled into speculation instead of productive investments and employment.[111] According to an editorial in *Tiden*, it was necessary to have a broader influence over the use of profits in order to decrease wealth differences, stabilize the economy, and invest in ecological technology. However, this did not mean a continuation of wage-earner funds but finding a way out of the dead end the debate had created. The basic principle had to be enterprises and employees deciding on the use of funds together, and that enterprises needed a certain profit that motivated saving. Society could give general guidelines as to which sectors money could be channeled into, but not choose individual projects.[112] LO even suggested making wage-earner funds more individualized due to political realities, but its focus turned to the changing labor market dynamics, as SAF was retreating from all centralized arrangements.[113]

Like their Finnish counterparts, the Swedish Social Democrats and LO therefore continued to find public steering of investments desirable, but they perceived its new limits and emphasized the need for consent and cooperation from private capital. In other words, they were looking for a new type of class compromise in a globalized economy. They tried to find new decentralized and market-oriented models for economic and enterprise democracy, but their reflections did not reach very concrete levels. Even though the roles of markets and consumers had become more prominent, it was believed that employees needed more influence and that traditional divisions of labor and authority needed to be considered anew. Developing collective funds and employee stock ownership were still considered viable means to reach stronger influence.[114] However, ideas on how influence could concretely be increased and how much power and ownership in the economy could realistically be distributed to wage-earners remained fuzzy. Socialization and nationalization were already quite firmly excluded as conceptual components of economic democracy. Collective ownership and economic steering were gliding in the same direction.

In the ideational constellations of the late 1980s, the main objectives of employee influence and ownership were not steering investments democratically to increase security and employment or transforming capitalism into a more stable and equitable system. The goal of ownership through different funds was instead generating assets and profits for wage-earners to support their adaptation to rapid economic and social changes, for example by enhancing their education. This constellation resembled earlier ideas of adapting to societal changes but included new beliefs related to education and human capital.[115] Moreover, consumers and users of public services had now emerged more strongly beside and even past workers as democratic agents in the economy. They were conceptualized as more autonomous and powerful than previously, even 'sovereign,' which stands out as a notable change in ideational constellations.

Center-Right Critique of Collectivism Persists

In the second half of the 1980s, Swedish employers and center-right parties had mostly abandoned economic and enterprise democracy as positive concepts. Economic democracy in effect gained negative connotations, as it was associated exclusively with wage-earner funds and collective ownership. For the Moderates and employers these practices represented socialism and destruction of private ownership, which had proven their deficiency in practice.[116] The 4 October manifestations continued as an annual tradition and provided a visible platform for critique. SAP and LO were criticized for clinging onto ideas of collective ownership when they took up the ideas of stronger control over pension funds in 1987. As before, it was argued that they were in fact trying to increase the power of trade unions, not wage-earners.[117] The center-right parties continued to call for the abolishment of wage-earner funds. Their main counter-concept and alternative was again diffused private ownership, especially stock-saving, but it was not referred to with the terms of economic democracy or owner democracy. Along with diffused ownership, employee influence remained an objective, especially in Liberal programs, but it had become more peripheral. The term enterprise democracy was entirely absent from programs and statements.[118]

After retiring from Asea and SAF, Curt Nicolin continued as a board professional and public commentator on economic issues. In his statements published in major newspapers, Nicolin utilized the familiar beliefs and tropes of economic democracy's proximity to socialism and the necessity of private ownership as a precondition for a truly free and democratic society. Nicolin argued that the concept of economic democracy was merely a means of seeking legitimacy for collective ownership, and its advocates had not been able to clarify how it differed from socialization. He expressed the belief in collective ownership not giving power to individual wage-earners. Instead, he advocated stimulation of private saving and co-ownership of enterprises. Nicolin made a rhetorical move used by many populist politicians: He criticized elites but referred exclusively to political elites. According to him, they had too much power, as it was possible to make decisions against the will of the people's majority. Wage-earner funds had been a case in point. According to surveys, Swedes wanted instead more referenda, local democracy and personal ownership.[119] Unlike traditional conservatives, Nicolin thus called for less restriction on the popular will, as he believed the majority would be on his side.

The new Moderate leader Carl Bildt expressed similar beliefs, drawing on the negative connotation of socialism. He argued that SAP was a socialist party no matter how much it tried to dissociate itself from socialist failures in other countries. Bildt reminded that the Social Democrats had always lost elections after expressing socialization demands. Had they succeeded in their pursuits, Sweden would have ended up with less welfare, he argued.[120]

Center-right politicians and business representatives were constantly worried that economic growth was slowing down, especially due to the remaining rigidities of the public sector and labor market. The Moderates' election manifesto of 1988 stated that economic growth and "tomorrow's welfare" had to be stimulated through "tax cuts, deregulation, privatization and European cooperation."[121] The party had been an ardent advocate of European integration since the early 1970s. The Center and Liberals were slightly more reserved due to Sweden's policy of neutrality.[122] The role of the free market economy increased in the rhetoric of all center-right parties. The Liberals' 1985 manifesto connected the market economy to concepts of private ownership and personal freedom in a familiar way. It was threatened especially by "stealth socialization" (*smyg-socialisering*), which was advancing through wage-earner funds but also hard taxation of "work and economic success."[123] Strong critique of socialism and advocation of market economy and deregulation did not help the bourgeois parties back to power in the elections of 1985 and 1988. The Moderates lost mandates in both elections, and the Liberals went slightly back in 1988 after having doubled their support in the previous election. As SAP lost only a few mandates each time, they were able to retain power. In 1988, the biggest winner was the Environment Party (*Miljöpartiet*), which managed to get past the 4% threshold and gain 20 mandates.[124]

Working Life Reform of the Finnish 'Blue and Red' Government

In the Finnish parliamentary election of 1987, working life reform, employee representation and wage-earner funds became key themes that were frequently taken up in the media. Unlike in Sweden, the debate was not very polarized, and all parties put forward positive alternatives for promoting these issues.[125] Economic democracy more broadly conceived was a central election theme for the Social Democrats. Their campaign utilized rhetoric familiar from the new platform, and their electoral declaration was titled "From the Power of Capital to the Power of Labor."[126] Therefore, 1987 marked the last major rhetorical offensive for economic democracy in both Finland and Sweden.

Finland's 1987 election ended the National Coalition Party's over-20-year period in opposition. The party was the biggest winner and gained 9 seats, totaling 53 MPs. The Social Democrats remained the biggest party in parliament with 56 MPs even though they lost 100,000 votes. Government formation was dramatic: President Mauno Koivisto prevented the formation of a secretly agreed bourgeois alliance between the National Coalition and Center Parties, which was supported by influential businesspeople. Instead of NCP leader Ilkka Suominen, the prime minister's post was given to Harri Holkeri, director of the Bank of Finland and former NCP leader, who was willing to form an alliance with the Social Democrats. SDP retained a strong position and manned the ministries of finance, foreign affairs, justice and labor.[127] The perspectives of two parties from different ends of the political spectrum were fused in the unorthodox 'blue-red' coalition. Its program included significant working life reforms, such as employee representation in corporate governance, increasing security of employment as well as personnel funds, which were discussed in Chap. 4. The government program stated that "(t)he possibility of wage-earners to influence changes in production, use of new technology, training, and working hours will be improved by renewing participation systems."[128] At this point, the use of the terms economic or enterprise democracy had become very scarce in official rhetoric. Besides the language of the government, state committees and their reports also spoke mostly about "reform," "participation" and "cooperation."

Scholars have debated whether the program of Holkeri's government can be considered neoliberal or not. Antti Kujala has argued that the objectives pointing to enterprise democracy were far from neoliberalism, but Sami Outinen has made a different interpretation and emphasizes that the government was committed to a stable currency, liberalizing the finance market and increasing the competitiveness and flexibility of economic life.[129] Ville Yliaska has pointed out the government's transfer of resources from social services to subsidizing private business, especially in research and development. Reforming public administration according to the principles of New Public Management was also on the agenda.[130] However, as has been common in Finnish politics, the program was a compromise between two coalition partners, both of whom had to adopt potentially undesirable objectives. The Social Democrats and SAK pushed working life reform onto the agenda, while NCP spoke for public sector reforms. The employers, however, opposed the government's working life reforms, which caused tension with their most natural political partner, NCP.[131]

As the labor market parties did not reach agreement on working life reforms, the government made its own proposals on the matter. The reform package of Holkeri's government included a revision of the Cooperation Act, especially regarding security of employment. The government's proposal included a three-month minimum duration for negotiations on lay-offs, and restricted lay-offs until options for relocation and training were examined in the cooperation procedure. Employers argued that this would make it impossible for companies to adapt to structural change.[132] The proposal was not changed significantly in parliament even though the first discussion lasted for eight hours and the social committee heard 72 experts while discussing the matter. Opposition parties were concerned about decreasing the flexibility and competitiveness of enterprises, while the Social Democrats appealed to employee security in structural change.[133]

The renewed Cooperation Act was passed in June 1988 alongside the modifications to the Work Safety and Employment Contract Acts. Paradoxically, the reform can be interpreted as a drift away from the concept of enterprise democracy: It strengthened the security of employees, but through binding general regulations to the employers, not by increasing employee influence in workplaces. Even though negotiations on collective lay-offs now lasted longer, the employer could make the final decision as before. The employee side, however, got one reform they had been striving for a long time: The right to interrupt dangerous work. This reform expanded the influence of work safety delegates, not regular employees.[134]

Holkeri's government also had to tackle the question of employee representation in corporate governance, which had been investigated in a committee since 1984.[135] It had spent much time debating on the appropriate sites of employee representation, because the roles of supervisory boards and boards of directors differed from company to company, and the majority of companies did not even have a supervisory board.[136] STK continued to find many problems in representation, but it discussed how long Finland could remain the only Western European country where employees had no representation in corporate governance. STK concluded that minority representation on supervisory boards would be acceptable if legislation could not be avoided.[137] The committee did not reach a unanimous proposal. Employers wanted only voluntary representation, while the employee side wanted a mandatory model that could be extended to boards of directors and managing groups.[138]

In the end, however, employee representation was settled without great governmental intervention. Perhaps due to the experience of the security of employment laws, the labor market parties were given time to negotiate between themselves. They came to an agreement in autumn 1989, and the law was passed close to the end of the Holkeri government's term in 1990.[139] It concerned companies with 150 employees or more but was not entirely mandatory, which pleased the employers. The primary way to establish representation was through a local agreement. If this was not reached and the majority of employees demanded representation, the company had to realize it according to the legislated model. Representation could take place in the supervisory board, board of directors or managing group. In the case of disagreement, the company had the right to choose the site of representation. Employee representatives had otherwise full mandates but were not allowed to participate in decisions concerning conditions of work, strikes and appointment of managers.[140] After the law's implementation, the employee side did not feel that influence had significantly increased. Most companies agreed on the form of representation voluntarily, but especially smaller ones realized it according to the law or the personnel did not demand it at all. The most common site of representation was the managing group. This may have been because operational decisions were considered more suitable for employee representatives than strategic ones, and with minority representation they were unable to determine the outcomes.[141]

All in all, the Finnish working life reforms of the late 1980s were quite moderate. Apart from stronger protection against dismissal, they were carried out in forms that were acceptable to Finnish business. Employee representation in corporate governance was established years after other Nordic countries, as the employers had been reluctant to accept even minority representation. The reforms were adapted to the demands of the market economy and global competition, which were at the time shaping labor market practices more than any legislation.

The concepts of economic and enterprise democracy no longer figured strongly in the debates concerning these reforms. Actors across the political spectrum were adopting an ideational constellation where apolitical enterprises would be governed by competent managers, while employees could be given operational power in their own work and possibly a share of the economic results without accompanying power or influence. Asymmetric power relations were not perceived as a problem. Instead, the constellation was based on belief in converging interests of capital, labor and the nation in the context of a globalizing economy and structural renewal, where only the most efficient and profitable industries, employees and nations would prevail.

Notes

1. Tony Judt, *Postwar: A History of Europe since 1945* (London: Penguin, 2005), 484–496, 535–558; Donald Sassoon, *One Hundred Years of Socialism: The West European Left in the Twentieth Century* (London: Fontana Press, 1996), 454–461.
2. Philip G. Cerny, *The Changing Architecture of Politics: Structure, Agency, and the Future of the State* (London: Sage, 1990), 242–246; Jenny Andersson, *När framtiden redan hänt: Socialdemokratin och folkhemsnostalgin* (Stockholm: Ordfront, 2009), 17–24; Judt, *Postwar*, 594–604; Sassoon, *One Hundred Years of Socialism*, 733–742.
3. Daniel T. Rodgers, *Age of Fracture* (Cambridge, MA & London: Belknap Press of Harvard University Press, 2011), 1–10; Jan-Werner Müller, *Contesting Democracy: Political Ideas in Twentieth Century Europe* (New Haven and London: Yale University Press, 2011), 237–242; Luc Boltanski and Ève Chiapello, *The New Spirit of Capitalism* (London and New York: Verso, 2005), 346–353; Francis Sejersted, *The Age of Social Democracy: Norway and Sweden in the Twentieth Century* (Princeton: Princeton University Press, 2011), 434–438, 466–467.
4. Boltanski and Chiapello, *The New Spirit of Capitalism*, 296–305, 324–327, 349–353; Rodgers, *Age of Fracture*, 39–40.
5. Kjell Östberg, "När ingen längre kokar kaffe – eller vad har hänt folkrörelsepartierna?" in *Demokratins drivkrafter: Kontext och särdrag i Finlands och Sveriges demokratier 1890–2020*, eds. Henrik Meinander, Petri Karonen and Kjell Östberg (Helsinki: Svenska litteratursällskapet i Finland, 2018), 409–414; Kjell Östberg, "Politikens förändrade villkor," in *Det långa 1990-talet: När Sverige förändrades*, eds. Anders Ivarsson Westerberg, Ylva Waldemarson and Kjell Östberg (Umeå: Boréa, 2014), 149–152, 164–172; Sami Outinen, *Sosiaalidemokraattien tie talouden ohjailusta markkinareaktioiden ennakointiin: Työllisyys sosiaalidemokraattien politiikassa Suomessa 1975–1998* (Helsinki: Into, 2015), 72–75, 128–129; Rauli Mickelsson, *Samanlaiset ja erilaiset puolueet: Retoriikka-*

ja diskurssianalyyttinen tutkimus kokoomuslaisten ja sosiaalidemokraattien jäsenlehdissä ilmaisemista käsityksistä omista puolueistaan vuosina 1965–1995 (Turku: University of Turku, 1999), 167–168, 184–186, 210–212, 223–225.

6. Jukka Tarkka, *Uhan alta unioniin: Asennemurros ja sen unilukkari Eva* (Helsinki: Otava, 2002), 292–305.
7. "Change and continuity in social development". Speech at EVA day 24 Oct 1984. CEO's manuscripts 1981–1985. EVA Archive, The National Archives of Finland, Helsinki (KA).
8. Ibid.
9. Kauko Sipponen's speech at the general meeting of Osuuspankkien keskuspankki Oy 17 April 1986. 36 CEO's manuscripts 1986. F7/34 EVA archive, KA.
10. Outinen, *Sosiaalidemokraattien tie*, 148–152; "Vasemmisto – ennen ja nyt," *Sosialistinen aikakauslehti* 1/1984, 25–27.
11. For example, Aulis Aarnio, "SDP:n periaateohjelma ja yhteiskunnan haasteet," *Sosialistinen aikakauslehti* 3/1984, 43–48.
12. For example, Nils Elvander, "Håller den fackliga solidariteten?" *Tiden* 9/1984, 536–544.
13. Sakari Heikkinen and Seppo Tiihonen, *Hyvinvoinnin turvaaja: Valtiovarainministeriön historia 3* (Helsinki: Edita, 2010), 122–123, 154–157.
14. Ville Yliaska, *Tehokkuuden toiveuni. Uuden julkisjohtamisen historia Suomessa 1970-luvulta 1990-luvulle.* (Helsinki: Into, 2014), 97–129; Ville Yliaska, "New Public Management as a Response to the Crisis of the 1970s: The Case of Finland, 1970–1990," *Contemporary European History* 24, 3 (2015): 435–459.
15. Lars Ekdahl, "Den fackliga rörelsen mellan två modeller," in *Det långa 1990-talet: När Sverige förändrades*, eds. Anders Ivarsson Westerberg, Ylva Waldemarson and Kjell Östberg (Umeå: Boréa, 2014), 226–232; Kjell Östberg, *När vinden vände: Olof Palme 1969–1986* (Stockholm: Leopard, 2009), 303–311.
16. "Gå inte som katten kring het gröt!" *Tiden* 4/1984, 198.
17. Östberg, *När vinden vände*, 366–367; Henrik Berggren, *Underbara dagar framför oss: En biografi över Olof Palme* (Stockholm: Norstedts, 2010), 643–647. In their election manifesto, Moderates did not use the term systemic change, but their rhetoric revolved around the key concept of freedom. Moderata samlingspartiet, *Valmanifest 1985. Framtid i frihet.* Stockholm 1985. http://snd.gu.se/sv/vivill/party/m/v/1985.
18. SAP, *Valmanifest.* Antaget av socialdemokratiska partistyrelsen den 9 augusti 1985 http://snd.gu.se/sv/vivill/party/s/v/1985; "Kampanjen

som brutit samman," *Tiden* 7/1985, 354–359; Gudmund Larsson, "Systemskifte – nu framträder modellen," *Tiden* 7/1985, 390–408.

19. Östberg, *När vinden vände*, 370; Torbjörn Nilsson, *Hundra år av svensk politik* (Malmö: Gleerups, 2009), 132–133, 177–79.
20. Olof Palme, "Ett rejält nederlag för nyliberalismen," *Tiden* 8/1985, 429.
21. Ibid., 436.
22. Göran Therborn, "Från konservatism till nya djärva mål," *Tiden* 8/1985, 456–460. See also Carl Tham, "Idéer från vänster motar nyliberalism," *Tiden* 8/1985, 451–455.
23. Klas Eklund, "Den tredje vägen – och alternativet," *Tiden* 3/1985, 143–149.
24. Kjell-Olof Feldt, "S-politiken offensiv mot nyliberalismen," *Tiden* 3/1985, 137–142.
25. For example, Mats Lundström, "Bisamhällets politiska filosofi," *Tiden* 7/1985, 409–413.
26. Philip Mirowski, *Never Let a Serious Crisis Go to Waste: How Neoliberalism Survived the Financial Meltdown* (London and New York: Verso, 2013), 50–57; Jamie Peck, *Constructions of Neoliberal Reason* (Oxford: Oxford University Press, 2010), 7 8, 24–26; Markus Kari, *Suomen rahoitusmarkkinoiden murros 1980-luvulla: Oikeushistoriallinen tutkimus* (Helsinki: Into, 2016), 51–54.
27. Torsten Svensson, *Marknadsanpassningens politik: Den svenska modellens förändring 1980–2000* (Uppsala: Statsvetenskapliga föreningen, 2001), 79–88, 237–239; Kustaa Hulkko and Jorma Pöysä, *Vakaa markka: Teot ja tarinat* (Jyväskylä: Atena, 1998), 129–136.
28. Tapani Paavonen, "Talouden kehitys ja talouspolitiikka hyvinvointivaltion kaudella," in *Eduskunta hyvinvointivaltion rakentajana. Suomen eduskunta 100 vuotta*, eds. Tapani Paavonen and Olli Kangas (Helsinki: Edita, 2006), 80–82; Jaakko Kiander and Pentti Vartia, *Suuri lama: Suomen 1990-luvun kriisi ja talouspoliittinen keskustelu* (Helsinki: Taloustieto, 1998), 55–57.
29. Hulkko and Pöysä, *Vakaa markka*, 138–154; Kiander and Vartia, *Suuri lama*, 279–287.
30. Kari, *Suomen rahoitusmarkkinoiden murros*, 207–215, 343–346, 472–476.
31. Sami Outinen, "From Steering Capitalism to Seeking Market Acceptance: Social Democrats and Employment in Finland, 1975–1998," *Scandinavian Journal of History* 42, 4 (2017): 399; Outinen, *Sosiaalidemokraattien tie*, 164–171.
32. Mark Blyth, *Great Transformations: Economic Ideas and Institutional Change in the Twentieth Century* (Cambridge: Cambridge University Press, 2002), 223–225; J. Magnus Ryner, *Capitalist Restructuring,*

Globalisation and the Third Way: Lessons from the Swedish Model (London and New York: Routledge, 2002), 161–162; Svensson, *Marknadsanpassningens politik*, 79–88, 169–176.
33. Kjell-Olof Feldt, *Alla dessa dagar – i regeringen 1982–1990* (Stockholm: Norstedt, 1991), 260; Östberg, *När vinden vände*, 313–314; Ryner, *Capitalist Restructuring*, 161.
34. Feldt, *Alla dessa dagar*, 260.
35. Outinen, *Sosiaalidemokraattien tie*, 146–148; Outinen, "From Steering Capitalism to Seeking Market Acceptance," 401. On NIEO see B. Vivekanadan, *Global Visions of Olof Palme, Bruno Kreisky and Willy Brandt: International Peace and Security, Co-operation and Development* (Basingstoke: Palgrave Macmillan, 2016), 15–32; Jennifer Bair, "Taking Aim at the New International Economic Order," in *The Road from Mont Pèlerin. The Making of the Neoliberal Thought Collective*, eds. Philip Mirowski and Dieter Plehwe (Cambridge (MA): Harvard University Press, 2009), 347–385.
36. Gerassimos Moschonas, *In the Name of Social Democracy: The Great Transformation: 1945 to Present* (London and New York: Verso, 2002), 182–188.
37. Outinen, *Sosiaalidemokraattien tie*, 221–223; Christer Lundh, *Spelets regler: Institutioner och lönebildning på den svenska arbetsmarknaden 1850–2000* (Stockholm: SNS förlag, 2002), 237–245.
38. SAF, *SAF kongressen 1980 sammanfattad* (1981), 136; Lundh, *Spelets regler*, 256–260, 266–270; Peter A. Swenson, *Capitalists against Markets: The Making of Labor Markets and Welfare States in the United States and Sweden* (Oxford: Oxford University Press, 2002), 312–316.
39. *Sosialistinen aikakauslehti* 1/1985, 4–8.
40. Finland 2010 Forum seminar 10 Mar 1986: How will Finns live in the near future? 36 CEO's manuscripts 1986, EVA Archive, KA, Helsinki.
41. Krister Ahlström's speech at the spring meeting of STK representative assembly 12 May 1986. File II.5, Participation Systems Committee's Archive, KA, Helsinki.
42. Tapio Bergholm, *Laatua ja vapaa-aikaa. Tulopolitiikan aika II: Suomen ammattiliittojen keskusjärjestö vuodesta 1977* (Helsinki: Suomalaisen kirjallisuuden seura, 2018), 491–495.
43. "Työelämän takapajulassa?" *Teollisuusviikko* 5 February 1987.
44. *Teollisuusviikko* 26 February 1987, 20–21; *Teollisuusviikko* 5 March 1987, 3.
45. "Vinstdelning hotar facket," *Dagens Nyheter* 7 September 1987, 12; Bo Stråth, *Mellan två fonder: LO och den svenska modellen* (Stockholm: Atlas, 1998), 255–257.

46. SAK also demanded a 35-hour working week, which was unacceptable to employers. Eventually the parties agreed on 37.5 hours. Bergholm, *Laatua ja vapaa-aikaa*, 443–465; Markku Mansner, *Suomalaista yhteiskuntaa rakentamassa: Suomen työnantajain keskusliitto 1980–1992* (Helsinki: Elinkeinoelämän keskusliitto EK, 2005), 213–222, 233–244.
47. SAK secretary Lauri Ihalainen in APJ May Day event in Saarijärvi, Viitasaari and Karstula 1 May 1986. Employee representation committee's archive, KA, Helsinki.
48. *Kauppalehti* 3 December 1986.
49. *Teollisuusviikko* 22 January 1987, 2; *Teollisuusviikko* 26 February 1987, 3; *Teollisuusviikko* 9 April 1987, 5.
50. Lundh, *Spelets regler*, 237–245; Sakari Timonen, *Paikallisen sopimisen käänne* (Helsinki: Työsuojelurahasto, 2000), 36–39.
51. Torben Iversen, "The Choices for Scandinavian Social Democracy in Comparative Perspective," in *Social Democracy in Neoliberal Times*, ed. Andrew Glyn (Oxford: Oxford University Press, 2002), 257–263; Lundh, *Spelets regler*, 266–270.
52. Meeting of STK's managing group 9 April 1986. Managing group minutes. STK Archive, Central Archives for Finnish Business Records, Mikkeli (ELKA).
53. Eero Voutilainen, "Tulospalkkiot olisivat yhteinen etu," *Helsingin Sanomat* 1 December 1987.
54. Statement of SAK's council 4–5 Dec 1987. File II.5, Participation Systems Committee's Archive, KA.
55. Allan Larsson, "Mot en ny svensk modell?" in *Mot en ny svensk modell*, eds. Per Olof Edin, Olle Hammarström, Bengt KÅ Johansson, Allan Larsson and Björn Rosengren (Stockholm: Tidens debatt, 1988), 12–14.
56. Ibid., 17.
57. Ibid., 21–22.
58. SAK congress protocol 1986, 397; *Palkkatyöläinen* 19 May 1986, 6–7.
59. SAK congress protocol 1986, 368.
60. *Helsingin Sanomat* 29 November 1986.
61. "Kansanvaltaa työelämään," *Palkkatyöläinen* 26 January 1987.
62. *Palkkatyöläinen* 26 January 1987, 8.
63. Ibid., 9.
64. SDP, *Periaateohjelma hyväksytty SDP:n 34. puoluekokouksessa Helsingissä 4.–7.6.1987.* https://www.fsd.uta.fi/pohtiva/ohjelmalistat/SDP/450; Outinen, *Sosiaalidemokraattien tie*, 181–184.
65. Outinen, *Sosiaalidemokraattien tie*, 181–193.
66. Pauli Kettunen, *Historia petollisena liittolaisena: Näkökulmia työväen, työelämän ja hyvinvointivaltion historiaan* (Helsinki: Työväen historian ja

perinteen tutkimuksen seura, 2015), 38–44. On a similar turn to 'people's home nostalgia' in Sweden see Andersson, *När framtiden redan hänt.*

67. SDP, *Periaateohjelma hyväksytty SDP:n 34. puoluekokouksessa Helsingissä 4.–7.6.1987.* https://www.fsd.uta.fi/pohtiva/ohjelmalistat/SDP/450.
68. Ibid.
69. Ibid.
70. Pentti Puoskari, "Haastavampi ohjelma – turvallisuusriski?" *Sosialistinen aikakauslehti* 2/1987, 22–25; Outinen, *Sosiaalidemokraattien tie*, 188–189.
71. Aimo Kairamo, *Tärkeintä on liike: Demokraattisen sosialismin edellytykset ja sosialidemokratian uudet tehtävät* (Helsinki: Tammi, 1989), 38.
72. Ibid., 47.
73. Ibid., 84–89, 92–95.
74. Ibid., 111–113.
75. Outinen, *Sosiaalidemokraattien tie*, 190–193.
76. Pentti Puoskari, *Liike ja linja* (Helsinki: Työväen sivistysliitto, 1989), 7–12, 18–20, 35–36.
77. Ibid., 48–49, 53–55, 58–65.
78. Ibid., 91–94.
79. Ibid., 111–113.
80. Anders Isaksson, "SAP inför 80-talet: Ett parti utan inre kompass," *Tiden* 4/1983, 207–210.
81. Arne Helldén, "Återfinn den "lyckade" reformismen," *Tiden* 6/1983, 339–342.
82. For example, Berndt Lindholm, "Den långsamma revolutionen." *Tiden* 7/1984, 394–400; Barry Holmström, "I Norge förs den – demokratidebatten!" *Tiden* 2/1985, 98–102; Stig Larsson, "Deltagande demokrati," *Tiden* 4/1987, 232–238.
83. Jan O. Karlsson, "Lärdomar från oppositionsåren," *Tiden* 6/1982, 407.
84. Ingvar Carlsson, "Ett nytt uppdrag för socialdemokratin!" *Tiden* 9/1985, 486–490. On freedom of choice in public services see Agneta Hugemark, *Den fängslande marknaden: Ekonomiska experter om välfärdsstaten* (Lund: Arkiv, 1994), 126–137; Östberg, *När vinden vände*, 312–313; Sejersted, *The Age of Social Democracy*, 391–392. In this case, the Danish Social Democrats seem to have followed their Swedish counterparts, although Denmark's center-right government of 1982–1993 also paved the way for neoliberally oriented public sector reforms. Niklas Olsen, *The Sovereign Consumer: A New Intellectual History of Neoliberalism* (Cham: Palgrave Macmillan, 2019), 213–240.
85. Blyth, *Great Transformations*, 211–213; Lundh, *Spelets regler*, 256–260.
86. Stråth, *Mellan två fonder*, 253–260.

87. Östberg, *När vinden vände*, 382–389; Nilsson, *Hundra år av svensk politik*, 133.
88. Anne-Marie Lindgren, "Vem skall bestämma?" *Tiden* 1/1987, 34–49.
89. Ibid.
90. *Dagens Nyheter* 5 June 1987, 12; *Svenska Dagbladet* 5 June 1987, 8.
91. "Det tredje steget," *Aftonbladet* 23 August 1987, 2.
92. SAP, *Ett rättvisare Sverige* (1987), 147–148, 163–165; *Dagens Nyheter* 10 July 1987, 12.
93. SAP, *Ett rättvisare Sverige*, 29–33.
94. SAP congress 1987, Partistyrelsens förslag 1, 43–45; Partistyrelsens förslag 9, 67–74.
95. For example, Curt Nicolin, "Mindre makt till herrarna," *Svenska Dagbladet* 11 September 1987, 3; *Svenska Dagbladet* 5 October 1987, 29.
96. SAP, *Ett rättvisare Sverige* (1987), 3–5, 13–17.
97. Ibid., 150–151, 155–157.
98. For an analysis of the book see also Stråth, *Mellan två fonder*, 275–279.
99. Anne-Marie Lindgren, "På många plan och i flera former," in *Mitt i steget – Om ägande och inflytande inför 90-talet* (Stockholm: Tidens förlag, 1988), 26.
100. Ibid., 27–33.
101. Ibid., 34–38.
102. Ibid., 39–43.
103. Ibid., 44–45.
104. Olsen, *The Sovereign Consumer*, 218–240.
105. Bengt Furåker, "Staten som chef," in *Mitt i steget – Om ägande och inflytande inför 90-talet* (Stockholm: Tidens förlag, 1988), 75–77.
106. "Inför nästa decennium, och nästa…" *Tiden* 9/1987, 456–457.
107. Ibid., 457–458.
108. Jörgen Hermansson, "Steget som kom bort: Om politisk framgång och misslyckande," in *Mitt i steget – Om ägande och inflytande inför 90-talet* (Stockholm: Tidens förlag, 1988), 56–61.
109. "Efterord," in *Mitt i steget – Om ägande och inflytande inför 90-talet* (Stockholm: Tidens förlag, 1988), 162–163.
110. Jenny Andersson, *The Library and the Workshop: Social Democracy and Capitalism in the Knowledge Age* (Stanford: Stanford University Press, 2010), 12–13, 24–31; Andersson, *När framtiden redan hänt*, 107–120, 130–142.
111. SAP congress protocol 1987, 179–182.
112. "Penningkarusellen," *Tiden* 10/1987, 518–521.
113. *Aftonbladet* 2 September 1987, 10; *Aftonbladet* 3 September 1987, 11; Stråth, *Mellan två fonder*, 260–262.

114. "Efterord," in *Mitt i steget – Om ägande och inflytande inför 90-talet* (Stockholm: Tidens förlag, 1988), 164–165.
115. On the change of the welfare state toward promoting people's competences and productivity instead of their security see Andersson, *När framtiden redan hänt*, 98–104, 121–122.
116. For example, "Klivet," *Svenska Dagbladet* 24 August 1987, 2.
117. Leif Widén, "Det geniala sättet att överta makten," *Svenska Dagbladet* 1 October 1987; *Aftonbladet* 5 October 1987, 12.
118. Moderata samlingspartiet, *Valmanifest 1985. Framtid i frihet.* Stockholm 1985. http://snd.gu.se/sv/vivill/party/m/v/1985; Moderata samlingspartiet, *Valmanifest 1988. Framtidens idéer – 20 punkter för ett bättre Sverige.* Moderata samlingspartiet. http://snd.gu.se/sv/vivill/party/m/v/1988; Folkpartiet, *Ny kurs för Sverige. Valmanifest inför valet 1985 antaget av Folkpartiets partistyrelse den l juni 1985.* http://snd.gu.se/sv/vivill/party/fp/v/1985.
119. Nicolin, "Mindre makt till herrarna"; Curt Nicolin, "Företagen förtvinar," *Dagens Nyheter* 22 January 1990, 5.
120. Carl Bildt, "Åldringens försvar för sitt verk," *Svenska Dagbladet* 22 April 1989, 3.
121. Moderata samlingspartiet, *Valmanifest 1988.*
122. Folkpartiet, *Valmanifest 88.* Stockholm 1988. https://snd.gu.se/sv/vivill/party/fp/v/1988.
123. Folkpartiet, *Ny kurs för Sverige.*
124. Nilsson, *Hundra år av svensk politik*, 134, 177–179.
125. *Helsingin Sanomat* 9–18 February 1987. File I.8 Press clips. Participation Systems Committee's Archive. KA, Helsinki.
126. SDP's election declaration 1987. HDA 112 Parliamentary election 1987. Parliamentary elections. SDP Archive, Finnish Labour Archives, Helsinki (TA).
127. Vesa Vares, *Korpivaellukselta vallankahvaan: Kansallisen kokoomuspuolueen historia 1966–1987* (Jyväskylä: Docendo, 2017), 402–416; Jouko Marttila, *Hillitty markkinatalous: Kokoomuksen ja SDP:n talouspoliittinen lähentyminen ja hallitusyhteistyö 1980-luvulla* (Jyväskylä: Docendo, 2016), 180–190; Mansner, *Suomen työnantajain keskusliitto 1980–1992*, 295–302.
128. Program of Harri Holkeri's government 30 April 1987 https://valtioneuvosto.fi/hallitusohjelmat/-/asset_publisher/64-paaministeri-harri-holkerin-hallituksen-ohjelma; Mansner, *Suomen työnantajain keskusliitto 1980–1992*, 337–342.
129. Outinen, *Sosiaalidemokraattien tie*, 194–198.
130. Yliaska, *Tehokkuuden toiveuni*, 230–238.

131. Marttila, *Hillitty markkinatalous*, 191–198; Mansner, *Suomen työnantajain keskusliitto 1980–1992*, 304–310, 337–342.
132. "Tyrmistyttäviä suunnitelmia," *Teollisuusviikko* 14 January 1988; "Asiat asioina," *Teollisuusviikko* 21 January 1988.
133. Marttila, *Hillitty markkinatalous*, 216–221; Finnish parliamentary proceedings 1988, 587–668.
134. Act on Renewing the Act on Cooperation within Undertakings. Säädös 724/1988, *Laki yhteistoiminnasta yrityksissä annetun lain muuttamisesta*. http://finlex.fi/fi/laki/alkup/1988/19880724?search%5Btype%5D=pika&search%5Bpika%5D=724%2F1988; Mansner, *Suomen työnantajain keskusliitto 1980–1992*, 343–345.
135. Mansner, *Suomen työnantajain keskusliitto 1980–1992*, 323–326.
136. Committee meeting minutes 12 March 1985. Employee Representation Committee's Archive, T018:1, KA, Helsinki.
137. STK board meeting 10 September 1986. Board meeting minutes 1984–1986. STK Archive, ELKA.
138. STK board meeting 19 March 1987. Board meeting minutes 1987–1988. STK Archive, ELKA.
139. STK board meeting 7 September 1989, Appendix 3. Board meeting minutes 1987–1988. STK Archive, ELKA; Marttila, *Hillitty markkinatalous*, 223–224.
140. Government proposal for Act on personnel's representation in corporate governance. HE 247/1989vp Laiksi henkilöstön edustuksesta yritysten hallinnossa. Finnish parliamentary documents 1990.
141. Mansner, *Suomen työnantajain keskusliitto 1980–1992*, 327.

CHAPTER 7

From Democratization to Liberalization

The Fall of Communism and the Transformation of Social Democracy

In the last years of the 1980s, democracy gradually lost its force as a future-oriented concept with regard to the economy and working life. It was substituted with more general terms, such as 'working life reform' and 'participation systems.' The change took place first in employer and center-right rhetoric and then moved to the official language of the state. In Finland, it was exemplified in the Holkeri government's program for working life reform. The employers had long been keen to talk about reforms or renewal instead of democratization, most likely for the same reasons why they preferred cooperation over enterprise democracy. The former term had weaker links to the ideas of redistributing power and democratic control over leaders. Cooperation meant especially communication and consultation and allowed sharing operational power while guarding strategic power and managerial hierarchies. Another major change took place in the object of reforms and economic democratization: The focus shifted from macro to micro. Reforming working life by increasing employee participation retained its place as a political objective, but the economy as a whole lost its role as an object of democratization and public control—instead it was liberalized and privatized to make room for the market mechanism.

I. Kärrylä, *Democracy and the Economy in Finland and Sweden since 1960*, Palgrave Studies in Political History,
https://doi.org/10.1007/978-3-030-80631-6_7

The significant change of the ideational constellation around economic and enterprise democracy was influenced by transformations in political thought and practice. They have been given many names such as neoliberalization, the new spirit of capitalism and the birth of the competition state.[1] The global trends of financial liberalization and extension of the market mechanism were antitheses to the idea of public control and planning of the economy, which had been key components for the concept of economic democracy in the leftist visions of the 1960s and 1970s. In the liberalization and marketization boom of the 1980s, a new generation of economists gained a strong position in policy formulation. This gave neoliberalization in Sweden and Finland a predominantly technocratic character. Ideational and rhetorical constellations were imported from business to politics and public services, and the vocabulary of competition and efficiency spread. The concept of competitiveness extended its frame of reference to new areas, such as science, education and taxation. Metaphors of markets and customers were increasingly applied to public services, which were reformed to function like private business.[2] Often these changes were not portrayed as political choices but natural and inevitable reforms on the road toward a more developed society—just like democratization of different societal spheres had been portrayed 20 years earlier. In the new ideational constellations, democratic steering of the economy through the state was deemed a harmful and even unnatural practice that restricted efficiency and freedom.

Political consensus on supporting private business and its profitability did not result in such a strong increase in investment that would have restored full employment during the 1980s. Hence, the bargaining power of labor was weakened, trade union membership declined and a shift occurred toward more decentralized bargaining in the labor market.[3] These developments also contributed to the decreasing support of left-wing parties in Finland and Sweden, even though their union density remained the highest in the world and more significant decline took place only in the 1990s.[4] 'Material' power relations are often ambiguous, but one of them is bargaining power based on scarcity or abundance of workforce. When there is oversupply of workforce, employers have less pressure to yield to the demands of employees. This dynamic affected demands for economic democracy, also because contemporaries believed it to be true.

A significant change at the turn of the 1980s and 1990s was the collapse of the Soviet bloc and most 'real and existing' socialism with it. The fall of the Berlin Wall in November 1989 and the mostly peaceful revolutions in Eastern European people's democracies were already perceived as a major turning point. The dissolution of the Soviet Union in the end of 1991 finalized the epochal change, which very few had been able to foresee a few years earlier despite the empire's economic decline and Gorbachev's reformist policy. The fall of the alternative social and economic order gave strength to neoliberalization and prompted the famous debate on 'the end of history,' inspired by the foreign policy consultant Francis Fukuyama. He predicted that capitalism and liberal democracy would remain the only ideologies and social orders capable of achieving wide support.[5] At least former communist states, with the help of Western economic advisers, began rapid and often socially destructive transitions to capitalism and market economy by liberalizing and privatizing their previously centrally planned economies.[6] The renewal and eventual defeat of Soviet communism was accompanied by increasing prominence of the concepts of human rights and civil society. Liberal constellations around these concepts in a way replaced previous ideas of democratization. In a global perspective, the meaning of democracy was consolidated on increasing rights of freedom in countries where they were lacking. Social and economic rights, by contrast, gained less attention.[7] Another key liberal concept, civil society, became a prominent counter-concept for the state in the 1980s, although in the Nordic countries the traditional identification of state and society made this usage less viable. However, in new ideational constellations civil society and markets were becoming more important spheres of citizen participation than the state and 'politics,' which had been deemed inefficient, bureaucratic and restricting individual freedom.[8]

By the end of the 1980s, as marketization was becoming common sense and the socialist bloc began to dissolve, concepts and beliefs with links to socialism and planned economy were pushed aside in the ideational constellations of political actors from left to right. In this situation, neither the left nor the right chose to make radical redefinitions of the concepts that explicitly connected democracy and the economy, but more often discarded them altogether. Explicit reasons for this conceptual turn are hard to find in any source material, but potential explanations can be suggested. For the right, it did not seem necessary to argue for the democratic nature of free markets. This was either due to their assumed intrinsic relation to democracy—at least as a necessary precondition—or due to their *de facto* incompatibility with some historical elements of democracy, such as collective decision-making and leaders' accountability to the people. As we have seen, many representatives of the right and the employer side considered economic and enterprise democracy as dangerous concepts that had the potential to question prevailing economic institutions and power relations. The left, in turn, was struggling to modify its traditional ideational constellations to fit the new globalized world of free capital flows and collapsing real socialism. In Finland and Sweden, one of the left's main aims was guarding the welfare state in the new reality, and comprehensive visions of a good society beyond that were lost.[9] Borrowing their traditional metaphor, the left backed down to the 'second step' of democratization. In doing so, they often ended up being more advocates than critics of global capitalism.

Donald Sassoon has argued that the Western European left was in crisis throughout the 1980s. This interpretation can also be made from the policy and rhetoric of Finnish and Swedish Social Democrats and trade union movement examined in previous chapters. By the end of the decade, the center-right could be viewed as the definitive 'winner' in history, and capitalism as the only possible economic system, which existed in symbiosis with liberal democracy. When in power, left-wing parties felt the restrictions of the new economic situation very strongly. In a world of more precarious economic growth, state intervention was no longer considered a viable policy, taxes could not be increased, and inflation was the prime concern. Due to the liberalization of finance markets, it became increasingly important to make countries lucrative for investment. The state's new role, which many scholars call the 'competition state,' was being formed.[10]

Some researchers have also interpreted the situation as a result of rising standards of living for the employed, which led to a content majority being able to silence a growing underclass of poor and unemployed. The means of creating economic growth to reach full employment were outside the power of a single country. All this led to what Sassoon and Gerassimos Moschonas call 'new revisionism' within the European left. The Social Democrats increasingly considered market orientation a modern and realistic approach to economic policy, while state intervention and too-extensive welfare states were now viewed as potential threats to economic growth and competitiveness. In 1989, the Socialist International renounced many elements and symbols of socialism, such as economic planning and state ownership, as well as the objective of replacing capitalism. Even the names and logos of socialist parties started to change.[11] The use of the concept of socialism was going through major changes: Its connotation became more negative due to the association with Soviet communism,[12] and its range of reference was narrowing to encompass only an ideology and a value system instead of an actually or potentially existing social and economic system.[13] However, socialist value hierarchies and the meanings of key values were also changing. Despite constant appeals to equality and solidarity, Social Democracy moved from "moderate promotion of equality" to "moderate promotion of inequality in the face of forces that are even more inegalitarian," as Moschonas has polemically argued.[14]

Many scholars have assessed whether European socialists and social democrats were right or wrong in advocating market-oriented policy, and whether this could be interpreted as adoption of neoliberalism. Swedish historian Urban Lundberg has made an illustrative typology of different interpretations of social democratic change: Scholars who emphasize external constraints explain the change with lost power resources or adaptation to new (perceived) circumstances, whereas those who stress social democrats as active agents view it as intentional betrayal or renewal.[15] Lars Ekdahl and Magnus Ryner come close to the betrayal view in maintaining that the Swedish Social Democrats could have acted otherwise, for example by drawing on the huge public support of the welfare state and using it to legitimize a more radical version of the wage-earner funds.[16] Sassoon's view is closer to adaptation. He argues that the left's 'new revisionism' was not the result of right-wing coups within the parties or treachery by party elites but a response to electoral defeats and new historical conditions. Unlike scholars such as Ryner and Ashley Lavelle, Sassoon thinks that European socialists did not adopt neoliberal thought as such. Maintaining welfare states just became increasingly difficult due to anti-inflationary politics and rising unemployment. Sassoon has deemed this change of doctrine as confused, uncoordinated and driven by the contingency of day-to-day politics.[17]

Gerassimos Moschonas is also closest to the adaptation view and argues that the Social Democrats did not become entirely neoliberal. However, he puts some blame on them for undermining the working classes as collective political agents while seeking to attract middle-class support.[18] Moschonas has shown how the declining or fluctuating support of social democratic parties was not only due to the decreasing size of the working class but also by declining support among it. Among the middle classes, social democrats have always been able to attract salaried employees and civil servants rather than upper managers and the self-employed.[19] Recently, Stephanie Mudge has also questioned the interpretations of social democratic change being driven by changing preferences of electorates. She points out the well-documented trend that changes in social democratic policy orientation in major Western countries have more often been followed than preceded by drastically decreasing turnout rates and increasing support for both the far right and far left. This can be interpreted as a protest against traditional parties' 'race to the middle.'[20]

Urban Lundberg points out that all the four traditions of interpretation are possible from their respective viewpoints. His own analysis of the Swedish SAP points to aspects of both renewal and adaptation. Lundberg stresses the active stance of the Social Democrats in changing their political identity as they had done several times in history.[21] On the other hand, he points out how visions of the future changed from open and positive ones into a deterministic image of threat that was based on demographics and other scientific 'facts.' From this perspective, politicians faced the choice between reducing public spending and reforming the welfare state and an outright disaster.[22] As Pauli Kettunen has argued, the Social Democrats and the left in general lost confidence in history being on their side. Their horizon of expectations became murky, and priority was given to the existing space of experience occupied by the achievement of the welfare state.[23]

I am not going to delve deep into the counterfactual debate on whether European social democrats truly had a choice. However, I find it important to emphasize—as do most of the abovementioned scholars—that the perceived policy restrictions were not caused by impersonal and inevitable forces of technological progress and economic globalization. Instead, they were brought about by clear shifts in political thinking and power relations since the early 1970s, which led to intentional actions that changed capitalism and its regulation. Therefore, it might have been possible to counter the change with intentional and determined action—preferably on a global scale. However, this kind of coordinated action was weak or nonexistent, and the way in which beliefs and practices did change is among the most significant factors in explaining the changing meaning and importance of the concept of economic democracy.

A major change in the early 1990s was that the concepts of economic and enterprise democracy found themselves astray and rarely expressed in rapidly changing ideational constellations. They were disappearing from political thought and rhetoric as both terms *and* concepts: Besides many of their traditional references, like democratic steering and planning of the economy, wage-earner funds and democracy in workplaces, the main criterion of more equally distributed economic power also became rarely expressed. Paradoxically, democracy itself became an even stronger legitimation concept than before, but the idea of democratizing different spheres of society was losing its viability—apart from democratization of functions that already belonged to the public and political sphere, like public services and administration.

Democracy became an integrating concept, which could not accommodate any other epithets than 'Western' or 'liberal.' This conception of democracy labeled the entire society as democratic but retained the distinction between its political and economic spheres. In Finland and Sweden, instead of democracy or even economic freedom, the ultimate principle for legitimating power in the economic sphere was usually economic expertise, which was claimed to secure efficient use of resources as well as their fair distribution.[24] Neoliberal thinkers have often conceptualized the economy and the free market as democratic arenas by defining the sovereign consumer as a democratic subject, but this was seldom done in Finland and Sweden. Instead, in both countries, political groups increasingly portrayed the economy as rather a domain of necessities than liberties. This strategy was more in line with the countries' intellectual and institutional traditions, but it also brought their political cultures closer to each other at this point. In Finland, external necessities had always dictated the scope of policy, whereas in Social Democratic Sweden, politicians had traditionally seen more possibilities to steer the country's economic course and conduct ambitious reforms. Economic growth had been perceived as a necessity, but politics had not been merely about adapting to necessities but about will or determination, as Olof Palme famously stated.[25]

Economic Crisis Consolidates Depoliticization and Expert Rule

An event that further narrowed down perceived alternatives in economic policymaking was the economic crisis that hit Finland and Sweden at the beginning of the 1990s. The crisis resulted from the badly timed and uncoordinated liberalization of financial markets during the 1980s in countries that had until then practiced strict regulation of credit, interest rates and foreign capital. Deregulation led to credit expansion, inflow of foreign capital and rapidly increasing debt in the private sector. Current account deficits deepened due to increased imports. Real estate and other asset bubbles grew, and development was accelerated by low real rates of interest and the tax deductibility of interest payments. Governments did not curb the overheating economy sufficiently through fiscal policy or regulation of the finance sector. This was due to exclusive reliance on monetary policy as well as the lack of communication between central banks and governments. Eventually real interest rates rose, growth expectations diminished, the debt bubble burst and a banking crisis followed when the payment ability of debtors was compromised.[26] Despite falling into recession, Finland and Sweden held on to their policies of strong currency, which kept real rates of interest high and made debt payments increasingly difficult. This steepened the downward spiral of declining aggregate demand, decreasing asset values and debt deflation, leading to bankruptcies and soaring unemployment rates. In both countries the unemployment rate at least quadrupled, to 8% in Sweden and 18% in Finland. The Finnish situation was escalated by the decreasing Eastern trade due to the problems of the Soviet bloc.[27]

The economic crisis made it ever more credible to appeal to external necessities in economic policy. It became 'common sense' to call for cuts in government spending and a too-large public sector, which some viewed as a cause of the crisis even though its origins lay in the private-sector debt crisis.[28] For example, Sweden's new Conservative Prime Minister, Carl Bildt, described his government's policy with the concept of 'the only way.'[29] The Finnish Center Party returned to power in a landslide victory in the 1991 election and likewise portrayed it necessary to roll back the welfare state.[30] In the midst of the economic crisis, cuts in public spending were considered inevitable because of current account deficit and the climbing public debt rate created by rising unemployment and expensive bank bailouts. Stimulating investment and employment with government spending was portrayed as an irresponsible option that would only increase public debt. Expenditure cuts contributed to creating mass unemployment in Finland and most likely prolonged the recession.[31] In Sweden, cuts were scheduled after the economy had started to recover, which may have hindered the growth of unemployment.[32]

According to the economist Jaakko Kiander, Finnish economic policy of the 1990s was similar to the policy during the 1930s Depression: In both cases fiscal policy was kept tight, but currency devaluation eventually paved the way for export-led growth.[33] In the 1990s, in both Finland and

Sweden, the economy began to recover only after the countries devalued their currencies and ultimately let go of the pegged exchange rates that they had safeguarded in fear of inflation and market reactions.[34] The price of the crisis—especially in Finland—was persistent mass unemployment, a chronic need for public sector savings, and thousands of home owners and small entrepreneurs in permanent debt prison. The economic austerity policy of the depression continued the long Finnish tradition of frugality and balanced budgets, but it was also in line with many neoliberal fundaments such as trimming and marketizing the public sector as well as increasing flexibility in the labor market. In a Schumpeterian manner, many decision-makers found the crisis a necessary phase of 'creative destruction' that would restore the vitality and morality of the Finnish economy.[35]

Finnish decision-makers of the time and their biographers have argued that the primary factor in surviving the crisis was austerity policy, which restored market confidence and allowed the interest rate to be lowered. They believe that the floating and devaluing currency that restored export competitiveness would not have lifted Finland out of the crisis on its own.[36] Some scholars have also suggested that more severe austerity, especially an internal devaluation through wage cuts, which the trade unions prevented, would have decreased the damages of the crisis. At least it could have saved some of the firms and entrepreneurs with loans in foreign currencies, as a smaller external devaluation would have sufficed.[37] However, austerity's dismal historical track record in solving or alleviating crises raises some doubts regarding its efficiency in the Finnish case.[38] Even if austerity had some effect in restoring market confidence, the notable drop in interest rates began after the September 1992 decision to let the currency float. At that point depleting currency reserves had made it extremely difficult to protect the exchange rate. However, decision-makers' helplessness when facing perceived external constraints seems genuine. They believed that the prospects of sovereign economic policy had greatly decreased and could not see all the alternatives that present themselves in hindsight, such as floating the currency earlier.

As the debates on economic democracy since the 1960s have revealed, the tendency to lean on expertise instead of democracy to legitimize economic policy and power relations has been common in Finland. Critical scholars have examined the Finnish crisis rhetoric of the 1990s as yet another example of governance through de-politicizing the economy and narrowing the scope of democracy in the name of the national interest.[39]

According to Social Scientist Anu Kantola, political and economic elites were openly suspicious toward democracy and especially parliament as caretaker of the economy, and instead concentrated power in a small number of experts.[40] Historian Jarkko Vesikansa, in contrast, has defended this kind of practice in his biography of Raimo Sailas, the finance ministry's budget chief who took a notable public role during the crisis. Vesikansa argues that rather than a lack of democracy, Finland's problem was a lack of responsibility. Identifying Sailas with the wise 'guardians' of Plato's ideal society, Vesikansa maintains that national economies need people to "take ownership" and "consider economic realities" in difficult situations, when politicians are likely to avoid actions that could anger their voters. In other words, nations need brave people to reorganize the state budget, just as managers of private enterprises do when their company is in trouble.[41]

The analogy between enterprises and national economies that Vesikansa puts forward is of course problematic, but one can criticize his view while assuming the analogy to hold. Firstly, there is the fallacy of composition, which Keynes made famous: Even though it can be rational for a single state or enterprise to cut costs, if too many try to do it at the same time, it just decreases aggregate demand and necessitates even further cuts. However, even if cuts were restricted to one state or enterprise, their human costs could be significant.[42] Moreover, experts usually lack definitive knowledge of complex human practices like the economy. Usually there are alternatives to austerity, even if governing experts do not perceive them as realistic. Here we arrive at the recurring historical and theoretical disagreement between different conceptions of democracy: Should we give people the chance to influence decisions concerning their own lives and livelihoods—within states and enterprises alike—or should we leave the decision to 'guardians' who allegedly know better?

Changing Sites of Democratization: From the Economy to the Public Sector

As was the case all over Europe, the Finnish and Swedish left-wing parties in the late 1980s also began to discuss whether the concept of socialism should still be utilized in political discourse. At the same time, belief in the conflict between capital and labor was weakening within the trade union movement, and mobilizing employees was more difficult. It became increasingly difficult for the left-wing parties to portray themselves as representing a better future. Pauli Kettunen has pointed out that the narratives of the Finnish Social Democrats changed in the 1980s from projecting future reforms to emphasizing past achievements. The welfare state became a prized asset, while the concept of 'reform' changed its meaning in political discourse from developing and extending the welfare state to rationalizing and marketizing it. Center-right parties now gained the image of reformers, while the left sought to uphold previous achievements.[43]

As part of the radical changes in their beliefs and rhetoric after the fall of the Berlin Wall, left-wing parties and the trade union movement increasingly adopted the language of participation instead of democratization. Ideas of steering the economy democratically were marginalized. This new constellation had already been emerging during the 1980s in debates on market liberalization as well as public service and labor market reform. However, a clear rhetorical and conceptual break took place around the turn of the decade, and the use of the concepts of democracy became notably rarer.

In Finland, the SDP congress of 1990 hardly discussed economic and enterprise democracy, even though the traditional objective of "deepening democracy" was present in some statements.[44] More pressing themes were the changing international situation, ecological concerns, and the crisis of the welfare state and of social democracy itself.[45] In this context, discussion on the concept of 'socialism' and its implications for the concept of democracy are noteworthy. After all, SDP stated in its platform that it sought to establish democratic socialism, which became questioned in the rapid dissolution of 'real and existing' socialism. This led some party members to reflect that it might be better to start emphasizing democracy instead of socialism. However, many Social Democrats portrayed themselves as winners in the battle of ideologies. Communism had failed but Social Democracy would prevail.[46] Party Secretary Ulpu Iivari wrote that democratic socialism had always advocated equality, human rights, democracy and freedom against the authoritarian communist systems. She even suspected that the Finnish left could now be united under the banner of Social Democracy.[47]

Finnish Social Democrats expressed mixed views on the viability of socialism. MP Kimmo Kiljunen found it unfortunate that socialism was becoming a swearword. He believed that all Social Democrats would be labeled socialists even though they had opposed the authoritarian system of the socialist bloc. He argued that change in Social Democratic ideology was not needed, but the party should continue promoting equality, solidarity and a mixed economy, which was one of the greatest achievements of Social Democratic policy. Using a common metaphor, Kiljunen argued that the market was a good servant but a bad master, and the public sector was crucial in softening its impacts.[48] Historian Eino Ketola, by contrast, argued that 'democratic socialism' was an oxymoron. He suggested that instead of being socialists, Social Democrats should proudly be Social Democrats and acknowledge the intrinsic link between democracy, individual freedom and the market economy.[49]

Like their Swedish counterparts, the Finnish Social Democratic leaders believed that the party needed to change its thinking, especially on economic issues. The emerging economic crisis made these concerns more pressing. Before the parliamentary election of 1991, former Prime Minister Kalevi Sorsa acknowledged the growing constraints of international economy and compared the situation to the crisis of the 1970s. Sorsa reminisced about how Finland had suffered from budget and current account deficits, but SDP gradually modified its thinking and reached an agreement on "responsible" policy. However, growth had again ended in overheating. According to Sorsa, the operating environment had changed, and decision-making power moved elsewhere. One had to now "acknowledge the facts," which meant keeping inflation in check, increasing competition in the economy, and attracting foreign capital.[50]

SDP's statement on the objectives for the coming years, ratified in the congress of 1990, signified a shift in priorities toward environmental issues. The document took a stance on the fall of Communism: It saw the democratization of Eastern Europe as mainly positive as it decreased the threat of war and could act as a vehicle for the further integration of Europe. SDP took the market economy as the self-evident form of society but stressed limits to "blind market forces." The idea of democratic control was invoked, although in a rather general form: "Decisions which affect the lives of peoples and citizens must always be based on the mandate of the people and democratic supervision."[51]

SDP's objectives concerning the economy and working life included the traditional demand of restricting the power of banks and insurance companies. However, the means for achieving this had changed from public control to "increased competition." The section on work differed from previous programs. SDP was turning from redistributing power in workplaces to increasing employee safety through regulations. The same trend had been visible in the working life reforms of Holkeri's government. SDP continued to advocate more rights for wage-earners and the extension of enterprise democracy into multinationals. The main topics, however, were improving the work environment, work safety and individual flexibility of working hours. Democratic control and extended codetermination were nowhere to be seen, which exemplifies a transition from the rhetoric of democratization to that of flexibility and participation.[52]

For the Finnish Communists, the end of the 1980s was more tumultuous than for the Social Democrats. In 1990, the Finnish Communist Party and their election alliance 'Finnish People's Democratic League' (SKDL) ceased to exist, and a new Left Alliance was formed. The concept of the 'left' was now used to differentiate from real socialism and communism, as well as the old bureaucratic party structures. As noted, communist and socialist parties across Europe made similar revisions. In Finland, the perceptions of the growing middle-class population and emerging consumer lifestyle were significant factors behind the party reform. The Communists believed their traditional working-class constituency was quickly diminishing: SKDL's support had dropped to 13.5% in the 1987 parliamentary election, and the party was not attracting new young members. According to a common fatalistic belief, history worked against the old communist parties and the future belonged to new civic movements.[53]

In its first platform, the Left Alliance renounced socialism as well as its identity as a labor party. Instead, it tried to attract people from different ideological standings, such as greens and feminists.[54] Traditions were not completely abandoned, as the Left Alliance was "on the side of labor against the power of money." The platform also included some traditional components of enterprise democracy without using the term itself. It talked about increasing employees' right to decision-making on all levels. This meant a veto right on important issues concerning employees as well as an interpretation privilege in labor disputes.[55] The Left Alliance therefore maintained the traditional features of enterprise democracy more strongly than the Social Democrats, but the terms economic and enterprise democracy disappeared along with references to socialism.[56] It seems the Left Alliance was not entirely ready to adopt the new necessities of the free markets, even though it had moved in that direction. As with the Social Democrats, an element of critique remained, but not many true alternatives were presented.

In Sweden, the Social Democrats adopted a new platform at the 1990 congress, just after the fall of the Berlin Wall. This abrupt change could not affect the platform's rhetoric very much, and it was quite close to the previous platform of 1975 and the Finnish SDP's platform of 1987. It included many traditional beliefs and objectives, such as increased wage-earner influence and supervision of financial institutions. The classic first paragraphs demanding authority over production and its distribution for the people remained. The platform stated that economic and social differences gave citizens different possibilities to use their rights and freedoms. The historical narrative of social democracy and the development of the welfare state was mostly the same as before. However, now the old concept of a 'people's home' had been reappropriated to denote Social Democratic achievements.[57]

In the platform, SAP referred to new societal challenges that had already been discussed for several years. For example, the working class in its original meaning had diminished in size and fewer people identified themselves with it, but the great majority were still wage-earners. New features of the platform included a stronger consciousness of economic internationalization restricting possibilities to fulfill democratically decided goals. As before, capitalism was portrayed as an economic order that created inequality, inefficiency, environmental degradation and economic crises. Privatization of public services and new forms of speculation were argued to make profits at the expense of the majority without creating new value for society. The platform pointed out that communism had also failed in creating justice and security. It argued that capitalism and communism resembled each other in distributing economic resources unequally and outside the people's control. They both had caused severe environmental damage, which was one aspect of the platform's strong ecological rhetoric. Democracy was of course a key concept in SAP's 1990 platform, but it had gained more individualistic connotations. Civil society was given a bigger role as a democratic arena along with the state. SAP explicitly retained the objective of extending democracy into the realm of production as part of the "full realization" of a democratic society. Leveling social and economic differences was portrayed as necessary for individual freedom.[58]

The tension between centralized steering and local influence was taken up in SAP's platform of 1990. In a familiar way, it emphasized the power of individuals as employees in workplaces and through the market as consumers. SAP wanted to "make citizen right superior to ownership right, labor's right superior to capital's, and consumers' right superior to production." The means were economic-political steering, collective capital formation and more equal distribution of wealth.[59] Different forms of ownership—state, cooperative and private—were to "promote pluralism and competition." According to the platform, it was false to portray the planned economy and market economy as opposites—in reality, the goals of fair distribution and economic development could be achieved only by combining markets with planning. Thus, the rhetorical figure of the 'middle way' and the idea of the 'virtuous circle' continued to play key roles in Social Democratic rhetoric.

All in all, SAP remained attached to its traditional ideational constellations, but since the 1970s emphasis on the positive sides of markets had grown significantly. Not only the choice between private and public ownership, but also between markets and planning, was portrayed as a pragmatic consideration. It was pointed out that markets and the price mechanism could not cater to all social needs, such as healthcare, education and environmental protection. But bureaucracy was to be avoided and the public sector had to have a strong base in local democratic participation—the ideal of decentralization. The planned economy no longer figured as a means to control structural changes in society, like in the 1975 platform. Instead, changes in class and production structure were portrayed almost like forces of nature caused by new technology and mostly beyond political control. SAP's view of society and politics had thus turned from social engineering into a more fatalistic stance.[60]

At the 1990 congress, SAP also ratified a more concrete short-term program for the 1990s (*Nittiotalsprogram*). It represented a certain return to the 1950s line of social reforms in a capitalist market economy that was silent on questions of stronger democratic influence in the economy. In this sense, it resembles the Finnish SDP's objectives for the 1990s.[61] The program's tone was quite individualistic, as the starting point of politics was defined as "a person's wish to lead a good life." This also mirrors the transnational rise of human rights rhetoric. However, existing class divisions were named as a major obstacle toward this goal, and politics as the means to overcome it.[62] A belief in collective action as a guarantee of individual freedom was strongly present, but the balance of collectivism and individualism was highlighted: Individuals were to gain possibilities for development and growth—to "be their own boss." It was argued that Tage Erlander's vision of a strong society had reached its goals of material security, which gave the foundation for new individual demands for choice and flexibility.[63] SAP thus perceived the trend of individualization as so strong that it had to be given a large role in politics. SAP gave considerable attention to the emerging 'postmodern' uncertainty, but strong traits of modernist development theories remained in its conception of history. In this constellation, individualization replaced democratization as the dominant historical tendency. As before, society's task was to provide chances for a good life in the form of social services and redistribution, but an extension of democracy into the economic sphere or transformation of the economic system were no longer central in SAP's rhetoric.[64]

The program's section on developing working life was strongly connected to the individualist viewpoint, resembling SDP's new programs and the Finnish working life reform of "productive participation." SAP wanted to create a working life that allowed personal growth and active influence on one's own work. The concept of influence no longer meant participation in strategic management, but only in organizational development and the work environment. Concepts like codetermination and self-determination were absent from the program, which implies employee influence that would have been less binding to employers. A key slogan was "the good work" (*det goda arbetet*), which entailed that dangerous and monotonous jobs were to be reduced to a minimum. Distribution of 'good' and 'bad' jobs was portrayed as a tangible example of class divides.[65]

Rather than the economy and working life, SAP related the concept of democratization to renewing the public sector. Freedom of choice, "user influence" and "deepened democracy" figured as key goals, along with higher quality and efficiency of services.[66] The rhetoric of decentralization was strong throughout the program. It stated that the labor movement had to break down "passivizing large-scaledness and bureaucracy."[67] This kind of rhetoric had been heard for most of the 1980s. During this time, SAP seems to have truly adopted a fusion of neoliberal and New Left critiques of the state, while the latter's critique of capitalism had moved to the background. In a sense, the rhetoric had moved close to the liberal concept of 'near democracy,' even though that was seldom mentioned at this point. For SAP, the most urgent sphere of democratization in the 1990s was not private enterprise but state bureaucracy, which citizens experienced as "anonymous administration."[68] It was perhaps viewed as a sphere closer to the 'political' and one of the few that could still be influenced democratically.

The program's last section highlighted a core belief in SAP's constellations: The necessity of a strong market economy for the Social Democratic goals of full employment, rising material standards and social security. However, negative tendencies of the market economy, such as monopolization and environmental exploitation, had to be restricted politically.

SAP pointed to its crisis policy of the early 1980s, which had succeeded in strengthening the economy without increasing social divides.[69] The program noted that freer and more globalized markets had come to stay. SAP wanted to promote free trade and open Europe economically, because Sweden needed to have access to the common market on the same terms.[70] SAP greeted integration and the liberation of socialist countries with hope and enthusiasm. Prime Minister Ingvar Carlsson declared at SAP's 1990 congress that Olof Palme's and Willy Brandt's vision of a borderless Europe, where cooperation would replace confrontation, was becoming a reality.[71]

SAP's programs represented a major change in their conceptions of democracy and the economy, but some party members held onto old ideas. At the 1990 congress, many motions continued to call for stronger debate on economic democracy, planned economy, collective ownership and socialism.[72] However, the share of motions of this character was diminishing, and debate on these issues was short.[73] SAP's Executive Committee argued again for the unnecessity of nationalization. However, it considered important that the debate on employee and citizen influence in working life continued.[74] SAP therefore gave rhetorical backing to parts of their old ideational constellations around economic democracy, but most reform proposals followed the principles of flexibility and individualism.

Economic democracy in the form of collective capital formation continued to be discussed occasionally in Sweden, especially as the 1991 parliamentary election came closer and increasing wealth differences became topical.[75] But instead of new ideas on democratic control of investments, the main road for SAP and LO was now freer investment policy of the ATP pension funds. SAP proposed that the pension and wage-earner funds could be combined into five large funds that could make risk investments.[76] However, the idea that the funds should allocate investments differently than the prevailing market mechanism was no longer expressed. Securing good profits had become the main goal for different funds in the labor movement's thought and rhetoric.[77]

The center-right parties opposed even these proposals strongly, portraying them as socialization and extension of state power.[78] SAP minister Margot Wallström wanted to tone down these fears and stated that the proposal was merely about "extension of ownership" instead of "power."[79] Thus, she curiously reversed the traditional functional socialist principle of socializing power instead of ownership. Wallström implied that dispersed ownership would not change the prevailing system if it operated according to market logic without transferring power. With the emphasis on ownership instead of power, SAP's view moved closer to the concept of 'owner democracy,' even though the question of collective and individual ownership continued to divide the left and right. The Social Democrats had again faced economic constraints during their latest term in government. Sweden was falling into a recession, but inflation remained over 6%. The government's proposals for wage restraint and a two-year ban on strikes to curb inflation were turned down by trade unions, which caused the resignation of Finance Minister Kjell-Olof Feldt.[80] Around the same time, in autumn 1990, the SAP leadership stated that Sweden should apply for membership of the European Community. This was especially considered necessary for improving the economic situation.[81]

Trade Unions Searching for Their Place in Decentralizing Labor Markets

The Finnish and Swedish trade union movements stuck to the traditional ideational components of economic and enterprise democracy more strongly than the Social Democratic parties. However, in Finland the SAK's rhetoric changed clearly in the early 1990s. The content of demands remained largely the same, calling for more influence and an equal position for wage-earners, but the language was practically stripped of democracy terminology.

SAK's congress of 1991 assembled in a time of recession, and was preceded by the attempt of the newly formed center-right government of Esko Aho to reach a 'social contract' with the labor market organizations on lowering wages and making cuts in social security in order to balance the state budget and improve competitiveness. Employer organizations had also made their own demands on lowering wages, increasing working hours and cutting employer fees and unemployment benefits.[82] SAK Chair Lauri Ihalainen opened the congress by calling for the end of inequality in working life and a new system of participation and cooperation, where employers would treat wage-earners as equals.[83] Ihalainen took up many of the objectives that had been topical throughout the 1980s, such as improving the rights of trade unions at the workplace level and getting rid of employers' privilege of interpretation. Ihalainen also emphasized that

union agreements must remain generally binding and decentralizing all bargaining to the workplace level was not accepted.[84]

SAK's new platform did not mention economic democracy explicitly, but democracy in general as well as the influence of employees were important themes. The platform was built around rights in different walks of life. This kind of rhetoric had been used occasionally since the 1960s, but now it was possibly an attempt to draw on the rhetoric of human rights, which had strengthened since the 1980s.[85] Along with far-reaching reform propositions, SAK used language emphasizing shop-floor participation that was closer to employer thinking. SAK's target program acknowledged that it was necessary to carry out parts of bargaining activities closer to work and employees.[86] It was implicitly argued that this would also benefit the employer by enabling creativity and development. The need for local bargaining was also seen to derive from the employee side, who wanted more flexibility in adapting work to their own needs. SAK's stance on this matter had taken a notable turn in only five years.[87]

SAK had clearly reassessed the social and political circumstances, where employees themselves also demanded more flexibility. The program explained the need for flexibility by the internationalization of the economy and new production methods. However, SAK was careful not to allow any reforms that would undermine collective power. Minimum protection was to be determined at the central and union levels, and the program insisted that unions should have a right of veto on local agreements. In effect, SAK wanted extension of local agreement to mean extension of the cooperation procedure. Possible issues to be negotiated locally included the introduction of new technology, content and organization of work, education and replacement. However, SAK was also willing to negotiate locally on working hours, wages, personnel funds and bonus payments "without endangering laws and collective agreements."[88]

In the early 1990s, the Swedish labor market moved toward a decentralized model, as SAF withdrew from collective bargaining and tripartite bodies, such as the Labor Market Board. SAF wanted to move bargaining to the sectoral and local levels and adopt flexible practices such as performance-related pay. These became more common in sectoral agreements, but not as quickly as employers wanted.[89] The direction was the same as in Finland and other European countries, but in Sweden the end of centralized, tripartite practices was more abrupt. Bo Stråth has argued that a "new Saltsjöbaden spirit" was being formed. LO lost the counterpart, which had legitimized its role and actions, and the organization had to reform its identity.[90] LO's 1991 report on *The Developing Work* (*Det utvecklande arbetet*) paid attention to trends that had been going on for years, like economic globalization, the increase in the white-collar workforce and individualization especially among the youth. European integration had also become a major question for LO, and its stance toward EU membership was positive. According to Stråth, LO had trouble finding out how to mobilize people with new demands for equitable distribution. The solidarity and operational preconditions of the trade union movement had changed drastically as finance capitalism was replacing industrial capitalism and as the economic crisis turned the focus from demanding better wages, work environments and influence to defending employment and the welfare state.[91]

LO was not yet as ready to modify its ideational constellation as SAP leadership. LO Director Göran Färm criticized SAP's platform draft for adapting to "liberalism." He argued that the demand for "real power on all levels of the enterprise" had been changed into insight and codetermination.[92] In contrast to Färm's statement, LO Chair Stig Malm used mostly similar rhetoric to the SAP leadership. He defended "the good work," full employment, equality and the welfare state against alleged right-wing attacks, while stressing the necessity of environmental protection and renewal of the public sector, party and LO organizations. Malm briefly mentioned fair distribution of profit and wealth, calling for freer investment rules for pension funds. He also connected the themes of working life democracy and European integration by stating that democratization had to be pursued on the European level. Like Ingvar Carlsson, Malm thus perceived integration as a positive development that gave new possibilities for reaching old goals.[93]

LO continued to talk about pursuing stronger influence in working life, but just as in SAP's rhetoric, the constellation of concepts and beliefs around this demand was being reorganized. The 1991 report argued that the people's power and freedom had increased as citizens and consumers, but not so much as employees. A recent committee report on power (*Maktutredning*) had also shown this state of affairs.[94] But like SAP's, LO's rhetoric had taken a more individualistic orientation and concentrated on issues such as "increased freedom and responsibility," "personal growth" and "meaningful work" instead of collective and democratic influence over production or the whole economy.[95] It was stated that the report was about power in working life, although "not power over others but power over one's own life."[96]

Distribution of wealth was still discussed, and collective saving was considered more efficient than individual.[97] Demands for collective saving, however, had moved closer to liberal ideas of profit-sharing and 'owner democracy.' LO's main motivation for wage-earner ownership was now distributing wealth more equally. The report pointed out that ownership was neither a necessary nor a sufficient condition for positive working life development. It argued that worker cooperatives had not proven an internationally competitive form of enterprise, but they could be useful in providing social services. The only concrete reform suggested by LO was again freer investment policy of pension funds. Ownership through pension funds was called economic democracy, but its primary aim was securing profits rather than steering production and investment. Behind this emphasis was especially concern about the increasing strain on the system as baby boomers became pensioners.[98]

For the most part, LO's rhetoric and demands were restricted to the 'micro level' of work environment and organization, where the employer side had already for 20 years taken the initiative with new individualized forms of participation. Concrete demands mostly concerned working hours, more diverse career opportunities and breaking down the strict division of labor between manual and administrative employees.[99] As at the SAP congress, motions calling for stronger codetermination or wage-earner ownership were fewer. The LO leadership responded by pointing to the new report as the "alternative strategy to democratize working life"—thus confirming that the focus would be on work organizations and individual development opportunities.[100] This exemplifies the trend of adaptation to global capitalism instead of its transformation, following the lines of the old principle "security within change."

Anders Johansson and Lars Magnusson have interpreted that the era of progress in work environment policy ended along with the economic crisis and decentralized bargaining of the early 1990s, and soon this individualistic rhetoric was also toned down. Too-expensive work environment reforms, like self-managing groups, were pushed to the background.[101] A more significant change, however, was the decreased ambition to steer the entire economy democratically. The fact that unemployment rose to close to 10% in the economic crisis would earlier have been a strong motivation for controlling investments, but new constraints hindered LO's demands. The perception that the welfare state and future pensions had to be funded in the new reality where capital could abandon Sweden worked as an efficient barrier against radical demands. Productivity and competitiveness were again priorities for the trade union movement, which is visible especially in statements on industrial policy. As in SAP's rhetoric, the range of reference of industrial policy had changed almost completely: It did not mean steering production and investments but creating preconditions for private enterprise and making markets function more efficiently. Sweden was to be made an attractive environment because international enterprises were able to move production to other countries.[102] In a way, this is another example of returning to the ideas of the 1950s and early 1960s: The logic of capital and free markets was accepted, and the labor movement focused on adaptation and remedying their worst side effects. What made the situation drastically different, however, was economic internationalization, declining growth and rising unemployment.

According to Lars Ekdahl, the economic crisis made the trade union movement assume a more conciliatory approach toward private business and accept the basic tenets of SAP's third-way policy. This marked an end to the 'war of the roses' between LO and SAP, which had largely been about LO's continuing demands for stronger political control of capital and investment against SAP's policy of increasing private profits as the motor of economic growth. Göran Johansson, Chair of the Metalworkers' Union, stated in 1993 that a new Swedish model was needed, which would be based on cooperation between business and trade unions. Together they could demand effective industrial policy from the state. Ekdahl interprets that the trade union movement had accepted the new power configuration and decided to let go of demands for democratization that could hamper cooperation.[103] Similar beliefs were expressed by Stig Malm after he left his post as LO chair in 1993. Even though he continued to call for economic democracy and correction of markets by politics, his rhetoric was dominated by notions of adaptation. Malm admitted that LO had made some short-sighted decisions in the 1980s. He called for renewal of the trade union movement, wage restraint and aversion to conflicts. Trade unions and business had to take "mutual responsibility" for the shared goals of efficient production and economic growth.[104] When growth was weak, extending democracy to the economy had become an ever more distant dream for the trade union movement.

Center-Right Parties Take Power in the Midst of the Economic Crisis

While Social Democratic thought and rhetoric was constantly moving from macroeconomic steering and collectivism to emphasize markets, the individual and the local, center-right and employer rhetoric continued to criticize the Social Democrats for 'socialist' ideas. Proposals for renewal and extension of pension funds and other forms of collective ownership were attacked in Sweden by many politicians and employer representatives. They advocated instead more extensive marketization and traditional ideas of dispersed private ownership, using the failure of 'real and existing' socialism as justification.

The link between economic democracy, collective ownership and socialism persisted in the bourgeois rhetoric, stripping the former concept of most positive connotations. *Svenska Dagbladet*'s editorial called economic democracy an "embellished redescription of politician—and bureaucrat—steered enterprise," which was now being replaced with the market economy in Eastern Europe.[105] Tom Wachtmeister, the CEO of Atlas Copco, wrote that economic democracy was "merely another term for socialism that has been abandoned everywhere—except in Sweden."[106] However, Curt Nicolin now had a slightly more positive view of economic democracy, which he could still associate with private ownership in the fashion of 'owner democracy.' Nicolin argued that economic democracy had to mean giving more ownership and determination to individuals instead of the public sector.[107]

In his articles, Nicolin expressed many key beliefs of neoliberal ideational constellations. Private ownership and economic freedom were necessary conditions of democracy, while socialism was incompatible with these. Public ownership was inefficient. It was in fact healthy that governments now faced stronger competition for capital and production. All in all, increasing the roles of private ownership and the market economy created more "true welfare."[108] Welfare was thus again situated highest in the conceptual hierarchy. Nicolin's rhetoric points to the implicit separation of the political and economic spheres often seen in employer thought. Even though the spheres were mutually supportive, the economy had little room for collective decisions made in politics. The economy was a realm of individual freedom, but also affected by the necessities of competition.

Separation of the political and the economic was the most common way to conceptualize the relation of the two spheres in the bourgeois rhetoric, but distinct beliefs of democracy *within* the economic sphere can also be found. These entail a conception of democracy that differs from the majority principle or 'one person, one vote.' As the columnist 'Sander' argued in *Dagens Nyheter*, binding majority decisions could and should not be applied to production and consumption. "Economic democracy can be found only in an entirely free market economy: There the choices of consumers function as a constant referendum. And with that politicians have nothing to do."[109] This explicit analogy between markets and voting was quite rare in Swedish and Finnish debates. Beliefs in a 'one dollar, one vote' market democracy were expressed only occasionally by the most ardent advocates of market liberalism, even though this idea was also implicit in the concepts of owner democracy and people's capitalism.

As real and existing socialism was falling apart in the early 1990s, liberals, conservatives, and other advocates of capitalism and free market economy around the world believed they were on the right side of history. Francis Fukuyama's thesis on the 'end of history' also served as inspiration for the debate in Sweden and Finland.[110] Belief in being on the right side of history was evident in bourgeois election manifestos of 1991. The Swedish Moderates declared that "(t)he brisk winds of freedom sweep across Europe and the world." According to their manifesto, the 'third way' had failed and there was no middle way between socialism and freedom. Sweden's development had been hindered by high taxes, monopolies and regulations, but now the country was heading for the top of Europe. The Moderate recipe for future growth was lower taxes that would stimulate investment, increasing the freedom of citizens and decreasing the power of public officials. Important aspects of future success were also Sweden's membership of the European Community and the abolishment of 'fund socialism.'[111]

1991 was an election year in both Finland and Sweden and marked the victory of bourgeois parties. In Sweden, the Moderates remained the largest bourgeois party, gaining 14 mandates since the last election with 21.9% of the total vote. The Social Democrats dropped to 37.7% and lost 18 mandates. The election marked a protest and a shift to the right. Populist and anti-immigrant 'New Democracy' and conservative Christian Democrats entered parliament for the first time with 6.7% and 7.1% of the vote, respectively. The Environment Party, in turn, was left under the vote threshold with 3.4% and lost its 20 MPs. The Center and Liberal Parties lost a few percentage points and remained under 10% of the vote. The Moderate leader Carl Bildt became Prime Minister and formed a government with the Center, Liberals and Christian Democrats, whose total support was 46.7% against the socialist bloc's 42.2.%. The bourgeois bloc had presented a common program for the election and was more capable of cooperation than 10 years earlier. New Democracy was kept outside the political blocs, because it was considered too radical.[112]

Compared to previous bourgeois governments, Bildt's government was more confrontational toward the Social Democrats. It sought to tackle the economic crisis by promoting free competition and private ownership. This was done by carrying out reforms that the Moderates and employer organizations had demanded throughout the 1980s. The government lowered taxes on capital gains, abolished the wealth tax entirely, loosened public supervision of banks and began selling state ownership in several enterprises. Deregulations were made in housing, education and labor market policy. As promised, wage-earner funds were disbanded, and their assets directed to support research and development, higher education and small and medium-sized businesses. The government was forced to subsidize banks during the economic crisis, and unemployment rose to 8%, which was unheard of in postwar Sweden. Cuts were made in social benefits and public sector jobs, whose share dropped from 26% to 21% of the total workforce. Full employment was still an explicit objective due to its huge public support, but the government was more concerned about inflation, even though the country was closer to deflation.[113] Prime Minister Bildt's rhetoric of 'the only way' strengthened the image of economic necessity. He argued that cutting public debt with savings was the only way to gain market confidence and boost the economy. The alternative was increasing taxes, which would only slow down economic activity.[114] The Social Democrats criticized the government but accepted some of its measures and did not engage in major confrontations.

During the term of Bildt's government, a committee led by the economist Assar Lindbeck proposed several ways to reform Sweden. In addition to public sector cuts and marketization, it proposed more dynamic decision-making by concentrating power in the government. The budgetary power of parliament was to be restricted. Not all the reforms were carried out right away, but the budget process was centralized and the prime minister's office was given new tasks, while much operational power and responsibility for producing services was decentralized to municipalities.[115] According to Johannes Lindvall and Bo Rothstein, public administration in general assumed new "ideological" tasks of designing policies instead of just implementing them.[116] As Lindvall has put it, economic policy had been gradually decoupled from other policy areas, beginning from increasing the Central Bank's independence and liberalizing finance markets in the 1980s. Other policy sectors had to operate within the bounds of budget and price stability targets set by experts at the Central Bank and key ministries.[117] The development was very similar in Finland, where budgetary power was concentrated in the Ministry of Finance with the help of tools like budget frames introduced in 1991. At this time, municipalities were given more autonomy in deciding how to arrange their services, while their resources were reduced considerably.[118]

Building 'constitutional' constraints to economic policy was a transnational phenomenon. New rule-based restrictions, for example on budget deficits and public debt, were also formed by European integration.[119] In Sweden, the Moderates and SAF continued to campaign strongly for membership of the European Union. Europe represented modernization, whereas a welfare state with closed borders was argued to belong to the past. EU membership was applied for in autumn 1991 and approved by referendum in November 1994. Even though the Left and Center parties were very critical of membership, and the Social Democrats had significant internal opposition, key politicians reached a consensus on the need to participate in the integration.[120]

Right-wing ideational constellations of the time are illustrated in the Moderate action program from 1993. Besides praise for European integration, it argued that the welfare state was at "the end of the road." This did not mean complete dismantling but breaking the public monopolies, bringing services closer to regular people and easing their tax burden in order to increase freedom and efficiency.[121] The program leaned on the traditional values of individual and economic freedom, community and citizenship. It stated that Swedish democracy needed more citizen participation. The program spoke for a limited state and low taxation, and emphasized the independent communities of civil society, which were vital for an "all-sided society" (*allsidighetens samhälle*). The rhetoric of small-scaledness and connections to 'near democracy' were therefore prominent and exemplify the lasting communitarian tradition within the Moderate Party.[122] According to the program, Sweden was to be a "democratic legal state" (*demokratisk rättsstat*), where constitution and the rule of law protected individual liberties against the state and municipalities. The current constitution was criticized for sometimes subordinating citizen rights to parliamentary majority decisions. The Moderates wanted to get rid of regional democracy, which was responsible for healthcare for example, and reallocate its tasks to municipalities and civil society, where people could participate in decisions close to themselves.[123]

In the program's economic section, key concepts were again market economy and private ownership, which were to be secured by constitution. The program drew an implicit analogy between democracy and markets by utilizing the principle of affected interests: "In a market economy, economic decisions are made by those who are directly concerned. … A market economy gives consumers power to choose and power to unchoose."[124] It was argued that this also allowed the interests of smaller groups to be heard. The demand of a majority was not necessary for a product or service to be produced—profitability was the only criterion. Free markets were again contrasted with politically steered economies, where prices might be kept artificially low, which led to a waste of resources and technological stagnation. A market economy, in contrast, fostered innovation, progress and economic growth, which were hindered by regulation and taxation. As cornerstones of economic policy, the Moderates defined stable currency, low inflation, low taxation and balanced budget. The market economy was to be brought to regulated sectors like housing, and state-owned enterprises privatized as far as possible.[125]

In the Moderates' labor policy, flexibility remained a key concept, figuring as a counter-concept to the regulations of the 1970s. Like the Social Democrats, they also stressed knowledge and competence. There were many similarities in this rhetoric: Competence and education were viewed as ways to avoid unemployment and enhance national competitiveness. But the Moderates viewed lower taxes, flexible wages and working hours as ways to build and utilize competences. Traditional anti-collectivism was present in statements that called for the influence of individual employees instead of trade unions. According to the program, conflict between capital and labor was a Marxist idea that did not correspond to reality. The labor market was to be based on cooperation and freedom of contract.[126]

The Moderate program did not connect democracy explicitly to the economy or working life. Terms like owner democracy were absent, even though the ideas of dispersed ownership and employee influence in workplaces were still present. There were many continuities with the programs of the 1950s and 1960s: the conception of democracy as a combination of a pluralistic civil society and a limited state, the harmonious picture of economic relations as transactions between equals, and the goals of increasing individual freedom by lowering taxes and supporting private ownership. The greatest change in their ideational constellations throughout the decades had been in decreasing the role of the state and increasing the role of markets. Demands for privatizations, deregulations and labor market decentralization had increased significantly since the 1970s, but the basic view of society was largely the same. In a sense, the Moderates had only modified the settings of their core beliefs and concepts according to new economic ideas and the perceived reality of globalization. According to Prime Minister Bildt, a liberal systemic shift was taking place globally, which called for adaptation.[127] However, even if the rise of neoliberal thought influenced Moderate thought and rhetoric, the change was not a revolution but rather a renaissance, as Torbjörn Nilsson has argued. Demands for lower taxes and protection of private ownership had been on the agenda since the Right Party had been founded in 1905. Now the circumstances for them were just perceived as more beneficial.[128]

Most importantly, the Moderates had always wanted to restrict the state's role and distinguish between the political and private spheres—the economy belonging to the latter. Even though relations and analogies between the markets and civil society, on the one hand, and democratic politics, on the other hand, were drawn, an important difference remained. Civil society and the market were domains of voluntarism and individual freedom, whereas political democracy was about collective majority decisions. In the former, asymmetric power relations were not a major concern, but pluralism and freedom of contract ensured dispersion of power. In the latter, by contrast, majority decisions or the bureaucratic state apparatus could oppress individuals. Therefore, the civil society's scope was to be extended and the state's restricted. The concept of democracy could be related to both spheres, but its historical layers were more closely connected to the state, political democracy and collective decisions, which also brought unwelcome meanings and references. One could interpret this uneasy attitude as a layer of beliefs dating back to the critique of democracy and universal suffrage of previous centuries.

In the postwar era, there had been two possible strategies for qualifying conservative and liberal visions of society as democratic without extending the scope of collective decisions: Portraying market transactions and contracts between individuals as analogous to voting and hence democratic, or defining democratic society as the symbiosis of free markets and political democracy, where the former was a necessary condition for the latter. Both beliefs were at least implicit in the Moderate program of 1993. In the latter, the separation of economic and political spheres was retained, whereas in the former, democracy was defined as individual, not collective, decision-making. To use the common metaphor, this conception entailed the principle of 'one dollar, one vote' rather than 'one person, one vote.'

The Finnish parliamentary election of 1991 was also a protest against the incumbent government. The Center Party took a major victory after criticizing the blue-red government strongly in its campaign. It gained 15 mandates and conquered the position of the largest party, which Social Democrats had held since 1966. The Center Party took the bulk of its new votes from the National Coalition Party, which lost 14 mandates while SDP lost eight. The Center Party was hoping for a coalition of all three major parties to tackle the economic crisis. However, the Social Democrats announced right after the election that they would remain in opposition, which left little choice but to form a bourgeois government with NCP. The young Center leader Esko Aho became Prime Minister, and NCP's Iiro Viinanen Finance Minister.[129] Like Bildt's government in Sweden, they had to find solutions to the deepening crisis. Aho's government conducted similar reforms to correct the budget deficit and gain market confidence, such as lowering capital gains taxes and cutting social expenses, especially unemployment benefits, which had exploded due to the crisis. The constitution was modified to allow decisions on cuts to be made by a simple majority in parliament.[130]

Despite their similar policies, the crisis rhetoric of the Finnish center-right parties was more moderate than their Swedish counterparts'. Finnish employer organizations, which demanded cuts in wages and benefits as well as significant labor market flexibilizations, were at this point the country's most outspoken deregulators. In its 1991 election manifesto, the National Coalition Party did not mention privatizations or deregulations, and even lowering taxes played a relatively small role. Instead, the party focused on improving basic social security and investing in research and education.[131] NCP's Program of Principles from 1993, in turn, resembled the Moderates' program more in its communitarianism, not so much in economic liberalism. It stressed individual freedom and responsibility, as well as a pluralistic society, as the foundation of "genuine democracy." The objective of increasing people's influence on their local environments was again highlighted. Enterprise and workplace democracy were not mentioned, but the program stated that people's participation possibilities could be improved by "developing new forms of democracy such as user and customer democracy."[132] This exemplifies the tendency visible also in Social Democratic constellations: making consumers and service users rather than employees the central democratic agents in the economic sphere.

The term economic democracy was also absent, but NCP was willing to regulate the economy, especially on environmental terms. The party modified its old key concept by talking about an "eco-social market economy." This included making environmental costs visible and effective.[133] However, these ideas were mostly restricted to programs that were written by young and progressive party members.[134] NCP advocated also some liberalization measures, such as increasing freedom of choice in public services by introducing private providers. The public sector's share of the national economy and public debt were to be decreased in order to guarantee necessary services in the future. This was a common legitimation for savings and restructuring in both Finland and Sweden. The National Coalition Party sought to retain the "welfare society," for which it stated it had worked for over 70 years. Its main strategy for the Finnish economy resembled the Social Democrats': education, competence and innovation that would restore growth in the context of global competition.[135]

The Finnish Center Party was more critical of the market economy and global capitalism than NCP, but concepts like economic and enterprise democracy no longer figured in its programs. The Center's alternative to marketization and centralization was the traditional view of decentralization and near democracy, where people would gain more influence in local communities instead of being subject to bureaucrats. This mode of thought was based on a similar distinction between state and civil society expressed by the Moderates and NCP. Ecological concerns increased their weight in the Center Party's programs, but like NCP, the Center wanted to lower taxes and decrease the public sector's relative size. These measures were portrayed as necessary due to the economic crisis and exploded public debt.[136]

The economic reality was the primary legitimation for the Finnish center-right parties, while the Swedish Moderates often legitimized liberalization and privatization as ideologically desirable. Echoing the rhetoric heard all over Europe, Center politicians argued that the heavy public sector prevented dynamic economic development. The Center Party's young market liberal MP Olli Rehn argued that Finland had to be turned from a corporatist regulated economy into a European market economy that leaned on high competence. The prevailing model was viewed primarily as a Social Democratic creation. However, many Center Party supporters found the party's policy too right-wing. In the municipal election of autumn 1992, the Center Party already suffered a major loss, while Social Democrats were overwhelmingly the largest party.[137] It did not help that the government was taking Finland toward the EU, while especially in the countryside many people were highly suspicious of it.[138]

Many scholars have interpreted that center-right governments promoted 'neoliberalization' in Finland and Sweden with their austerity policy, marketization and privatization of the public sector.[139] However, opposite views also have been expressed. Regarding Finland, Jarkko Vesikansa, Markus Kari and Jouko Marttila have argued that reforms were driven by pragmatic consideration instead of neoliberal ideology. Furthermore, they point out that the reforms were far more moderate than in the English-speaking world: Finland represented a 'constrained market economy' where welfare policies, trade unions and cartels played a large role.[140] However, the existence of an explicitly neoliberal program is not a decisive feature in determining whether political and ideational change can be called neoliberalization. A change in political concepts and ideas is significant regardless of whether it results from ideological design or 'pragmatic' decision-making. Furthermore, I disagree with Marttila and Vesikansa on the level of reforms required to qualify the change as neoliberalization. It is beyond dispute that free markets and economic experts gained a stronger role in economic governance at the expense of democracy, even if the change was not as thorough as in some other countries. Financial liberalization, as well as marketization and privatization of the public sector, began in the 1980s, while the most significant cuts in welfare and tax exemptions for the well-off took place during the economic crisis of the 1990s. Steps toward labor market decentralization were also taken, following the example of Sweden.[141] Since the mid-1980s, Finnish economic policy met all three criteria for neoliberalization suggested by Political Economist Cornel Ban: achieving credibility with financial markets, ensuring trade and financial openness, and safeguarding internal and external competitiveness.[142] As in Sweden, this new ideational constellation offered less space for concepts like economic and enterprise democracy.

Regarding Sweden, Johannes Lindvall has pointed out the change of political norms in the early 1990s, as the shared objective of full employment was let go in favor of balancing state finance and preventing inflation. However, Lindvall's view of this change being 'extra-rational' does not seem credible. Lindvall utilizes a division into extra-rational 'norms' and rational 'ideas' that derives from rational choice theory.[143] But this distinction does not hold: People can adhere to different norms entirely rationally, at least if we understand norms as ethical beliefs on holding something desirable. Norms may of course be extra-rational in the sense of forming boundaries to policymaking that are not reflected on or questioned. However, this does not mean that the process of replacing the guiding norm of full employment with something else would have been extra-rational. As Lindvall acknowledges, new economic ideas may have paved the way for normative change, for example, by introducing new beliefs on the proper role and tasks of the state.[144] Therefore, Mark Bevir's more rationalistic and intentionalistic view on ideational change is more plausible: New beliefs had already been introduced to ideational constellations, and when political actors faced the ultimate 'dilemma' of economic crisis, they believed—or at least argued—that full employment had to be sacrificed for the sake of more important short-term normative goals, such as competitiveness and economic stability, which were argued to support the more important long-term goals of employment and national welfare. This process of norm-modification and legitimation may well have been largely rational, even if it included some unreflected and even unconscious elements.

Social Democrats Return to Office with Convergent Policy But Divergent Rhetoric

Despite the relative unpopularity of the bourgeois governments, the Social Democrats' capability of proposing alternative economic policies diminished further during the economic crisis. In Finland, SDP criticized the austere policy of Esko Aho's government, but shared the belief that it was crucial to gain market confidence. Most of the party leadership believed that economic stimulation would be counterproductive and raise interest rates. Restricted stimulation was to be accompanied with promises of austerity during the next economic upswing. SDP approved many of the government's cuts and the goal of labor market flexibilization. Prospects of monetary policy were also perceived as limited, as politicians believed that letting go of the strong currency would lead to negative market reactions. Instead, SDP supported the government's aim of an internal devaluation. Former Prime Minister Kalevi Sorsa helped prepare a 'social contract,' which would have included a 3% cut in wages and 4% transfer of pension payments from employers to employees. SAK was behind the proposal, but major trade unions turned it down, which eventually forced the government to devalue the currency.[145]

Following their Swedish counterparts, the Finnish Social Democrats turned to support EC/EU membership in 1991, even though a large opposition remained within the party. The decision was justified by belief in its necessity for Finnish competitiveness and employment. It was acknowledged that membership would restrict sovereign economic policy, but as a small open economy, Finland was dependent on the external world anyway. Leading Social Democrats believed that safeguarding the welfare state would be easier within the EU, which might even have worked as a counterforce to international capital. SDP hoped that the EU would take employment as a political priority. When SAK turned to support membership in 1994, it called for discussions on a European-wide stimulation program. Critics argued, however, that EU regulations on budget deficit would make economic stimulation impossible, and integration was conducted on the terms of big business.[146]

Long-standing party official and MP Paavo Lipponen was elected SDP's leader in 1993. He continued the party's market-adapting policy and declared that the welfare society was to be saved by making public sector cuts to end debt accumulation. Instead of public spending, the economy was to lean on private-sector growth and structural renewal, which would boost employment. When economic growth began, SDP did not consider stimulation necessary but wanted to secure market confidence for Finnish policy. This was exemplified by Lipponen's interview in the *Financial Times*, where he declared that the Finnish economy needed a "paradigm change" toward more competition and flexibility.[147]

After one term of bourgeois rule, the Social Democrats returned to power in Sweden and Finland with strong electoral support. SAP gained 8 percentage points in the 1994 election and with a total of 45% reached its highest support since 1982. The Moderates kept their position, but other bourgeois parties fell back.[148] The Finnish SDP's result in 1995 was relatively as good as that of SAP. It achieved 63 mandates with over 28% support. This was the party's best postwar result, but the Finnish left as a whole had lost ground over a longer period. However, the Left Alliance also gained three new mandates, totaling 22.[149] The Social Democratic victories did not mean that the relation of democracy and the economy would be re-problematized. This was partly due to more acute problems that had to be tackled, but it was also difficult to fit economic democracy into changing ideational constellations. SAP's election manifesto focused on the economic crisis, unemployment and budget deficit without calls for democratization.[150] Recovery from the economic crisis had begun in both countries, but the Social Democrats believed that in the context of globalized capitalism there was little choice but to keep budgets in balance, support private-sector competitiveness and flexibilize the labor market. The prospects of alternative policies and democratic choices in the economy were perceived as very limited. The Swedish and Finnish Social Democrats hence continued 'third-way' policies, which were in the 1990s also picked up by other center-left parties returning to power: Bill Clinton's Democrats in the United States, Tony Blair's 'New Labour' in the UK, and Gerhard Schröder's Social Democrats in Germany.[151]

In Finland, the new prime minister, Paavo Lipponen sought consensus on economic fundamentals and the requirements of Finland's EU membership by forming an exceptionally broad coalition government with the National Coalition Party, Swedish People's Party, Green Party and Left Alliance. Only the Center and the small Christian Party were left in opposition. Finland suffered from persistent mass unemployment, as economic growth did not produce enough job-creating investments. In 1995, 15% of the workforce remained unemployed. The government made further spending cuts and privatized state-owned companies in order to decrease public debt and gain market confidence. The measures were justified by securing the economic foundations of the welfare state. They were also necessary for fulfilling the membership criteria of the European Monetary Union, which Lipponen believed to strengthen the stability and growth of the Finnish economy. Finland hence restricted its economic policy by accepting the EU and EMU norms on acceptable levels of budget deficit and public debt.[152] Later, Lipponen defended his government's policy by stating that socialism in a single country would not have been possible due to external constraints.[153]

Sami Outinen has interpreted that with labor market flexibilization and activation policies for the unemployed, Lipponen's government turned to emphasize people's own responsibility for their employment. SDP's objective of decreasing unemployment by half during the government's term proved difficult, as the reliance on private-sector growth boosting employment did not pay off as expected. Finland's annual GDP growth was between 3% and 6% until the turn of the millennium, but companies used the bulk of their profits to invest abroad and pay off debt. By the next election in 1999, the unemployment rate was still over 10%, but Lipponen's coalition secured a second term and promised to continue the tight budget policy. The Social Democrats lost 12 mandates, but NCP gained 7, which guaranteed a healthy majority.[154]

Ingvar Carlsson's and from 1996 onward Göran Persson's Social Democratic governments in Sweden pursued similar policies as their Finnish counterparts but also rolled back some of the bourgeois government's labor market reforms and cuts to social benefits. However, on the macroeconomic level, preventing inflation and balancing the budget were prioritized over employment. Economists did not offer alternatives to neoliberally oriented measures. EU membership restricted the possibilities of economic policy, but, unlike Finland, Sweden stayed outside the European Monetary Union due to a negative result in its referendum.[155] The SAP government reformed the pension system to be more market-based and sensitive to economic development instead of securing a certain level of benefits. The process had begun during the term of Bildt's government and was based on an agreement between the Social Democrats and bourgeois parties.[156]

SAP also continued the privatization of state-owned companies, for example by selling off its share in the once entirely state-owned PK-banken. Before this it had merged with the private Nordbanken and Finnish Merita to form Scandinavia's largest commercial bank, Nordea. Bildt's government had already ended political representation in bank governance, and this move further decreased the regulation of the Swedish banking sector, which was dominated by an oligopoly of four major banks.[157] SAP's policy increased tensions between the party and LO, even though LO was now more committed to economic balance and wage restraint than in the 1980s.[158] In the labor market, local flexibility of collective agreements increased, but centralized coordination was not given up entirely. Framework agreements such as the Industry Agreement of 1997 were made in order to ensure that wages were tied to productivity growth.[159]

According to Lars Ekdahl's interpretation, SAP had now definitively abandoned functional socialism and chosen market adaptation as its strategy.[160] However, SAP still expressed strong commitment to the welfare state—in rhetoric but also in practice. Elements of functional socialism persisted, as SAP continued to envision ways of regulating capitalism. Admittedly, regulation was now strictly limited to measures like labor legislation, social security and services, which were going through restructuring and flexibilization. Reforms were constrained by the imperatives of competitiveness and budget balance, and issues like production, finance and investment decisions were left outside the scope of democratic decision-making. SAP's austerity policy contributed to a serious setback in the election of 1998. Persson's government was able to continue in office, even though SAP faced its worst result since 1921 with 36.4% of the vote. Support from the Environment and Left Parties secured the red–green bloc a majority. As a clear protest against SAP, the Left Party doubled its support to 12%. In 2002, however, SAP went back up to 39.9% and secured a third consecutive term. The Moderates dropped to 15.3%—their worst result since 1973.[161]

During the 1990s, concepts and beliefs in the programs of Finnish Social Democrats changed, mirroring their practical policy changes. If the party in the 1980s had held onto its traditional rhetoric of democratic socialism and economic democracy, language was now adapted to perceived new circumstances. Concepts like economic and enterprise democracy vanished entirely from SDP's programs, while the meanings and references of many other concepts changed. SDP's new platform from 1999 was much shorter than the platform of 1987. The concept of socialism remained in the program, but it did not refer to a social and economic order that would form an alternative to capitalism. Instead, it was portrayed as a system of values that guided social reforms.[162] These included human rights and people's common responsibility for each other and their community. SDP's ideal society—both coming and already existing—was called a welfare society, not state. It was described as "a community of liberties, responsibilities and equal opportunities, where a balance of rights and responsibility is realized."[163] This language did not differ markedly from the rhetoric of the center-right parties. The growing emphasis on responsibilities as conditions for social rights was common to third-way social democracy in most countries, and a certain step away from earlier welfare universalism.[164]

However, many traditional ideas remained in SDP's thought, even if in moderated forms. In the 1999 platform, SDP declared it was against inequality and oppression, globally, too. A global outlook was also present in describing democracy as multilayered: It was to be respected locally, nationally and internationally. Local democracy was emphasized strongly: Democracy would strengthen when people were able to have influence in their communities and as service users, employees and consumers. As before, the concepts of democracy, influence and equal distribution were connected to the economy, but with a view on the mutual support of democracy and markets that resembled conceptions of liberal democracy: The increase of citizens' material welfare and security depended on productivity, but the market economy had to be steered democratically by employees and consumers.[165]

The concept of capitalism was mentioned in the program only twice, but its critique was implied in sections on the "world economy." The program stated that without international cooperation on the regulation of capital flows and transnational enterprises, the world economy would undermine both democracy and the market economy. The importance of work as a means of social attachment was emphasized, as well as employees' right to gain their share of economic growth and welfare. Labor market policy was needed to improve worker rights, to even out income differences and to stabilize the economic development. Rhetoric on working life was familiar: Cooperation, influence and participation were to be increased in workplaces, but democracy was not mentioned. Necessities of competition were present, for example, in the emphasis on "learning organizations," which was a new way to phrase the old ideals of flexibility and adaptability.[166] SDP therefore continued to state its objective as steering and regulation of the market economy in order to create security, freedom and equality in a "welfare society." It did not pursue economic planning, collective ownership, a socialist society or even economic democracy.

Even if the practical policies of the Swedish and Finnish Social Democrats were close to each other in the 1990s, there were notable differences in their programmatic rhetoric. SAP's platform of 2001 utilized traditional concepts and beliefs much more thoroughly than the programs of its Finnish counterpart. Many elements from previous platforms were again retained, such as the ideal of democracy characterizing the whole society, and the goal of people's influence as citizens, wage-earners and consumers. As before, SAP used the concepts of democratic socialism and economic democracy, declared that it was an anticapitalistic party and wanted to erase class divisions.[167] The breakthrough of democracy in former dictatorships was noted, but the platform also stated that democracy was threatened by the strong interests of capital as well as nationalist and fundamentalist movements. Like its Finnish counterpart, SAP believed that internationalization of the economy posed new challenges to democracy, as power was concentrated in transnational enterprises, "outside democratic control." This called for the respective internationalization of politics and trade union activity.[168] Democracy and human values therefore continued to figure as counter-concepts to capitalism and its "hard profit interests." As before, a democratic society meant that people would have the authority to determine the direction of production and its distribution, as well as the terms of working life. It was argued that drawing boundaries between politics and markets was a task only democracy could carry out. Economic interests would never have the right to restrict democracy.[169]

However, many ideational changes were also apparent. As in SDP's program, SAP's vision of society was no longer called socialism, but the "democratic society," "welfare society" and "knowledge society." As an economic system, Sweden was firmly a "mixed economy." For both parties, socialism now figured as a system of ideas and values, not as an economic and social order. Mutations the relation of democracy and the economy had gone through in the past decades, such as stressing the local dimensions of democracy, were also strengthened. The platform restated the belief that economic democracy should not be based on concentrating power in a few instances, referring also to the state and trade unions.[170]

SAP's platform emphasized the need to combine democracy and efficiency, stressing the importance of a mixed economy in this task. It made the distinction between market economy and capitalism and pointed out the markets' positive feature as an efficient signal system. It even pointed out a fact well-known to neoliberal thinkers: Markets needed societal regulation and rules of play to be stable and functioning. However, it was emphasized that there were many social commodities that could not be distributed through markets.[171] In sections concerning working life, the term democracy did not figure at all. The standard goal of employee influence on their work again only concerned work environments, working hours and chances to develop one's competences. SAP's human-capital-centered strategy was emphasized by stressing the importance of R&D funding. The overarching goal was economic growth, and the concept of 'growth politics' (*tillväxtpolitik*) frequently used. In this Schumpeterian framework, a key component was the human capability to create and innovate. It also had the potential to empower and emancipate people. According to the platform, in a 'knowledge society,' knowledge had in principle been democratized by information technology, but working life tended to distribute knowledge and competence unevenly. This was to be corrected with education.[172]

The ideational constellation of competence, knowledge and innovation seems to have replaced the traditional concepts of industrial policy and economic planning, which were completely absent from SAP's 2001 platform. The rhetoric of economic democracy remained prominent but had become more isolated and lost its references to concrete policy measures and visions of the future. Like SDP in Finland, SAP acknowledged that only international cooperation could bring about significant change in global capitalism.[173] The platform did point to an idea that was raised regularly in Sweden after wage-earner funds failed: Pension funds could give wage-earners new possibilities to influence the use of capital and thus strengthen their position.[174] As Anders Johansson and Lars Magnusson have shown, discussion on wage-earner control through some type of funds continued within LO during the 1990s and early 2000s. This is taken as proof that demands for wage-earner influence in the economy did not end with the wage-earner funds, or even at the economic crisis. But it should be added that for LO, the range of reference of these concepts also clearly changed. LO congresses witnessed, for example, discussions on holding companies that could administer wage-earner shares in pension funds or use parts of their assets to form 'employment funds' for job creation. Social and ethical investment that would consider the environment or regional development was also proposed. However, these debates always boiled down to the inescapable goal of securing sufficient profits for future pensioners. Active ownership to promote economic democracy and social goals remained a distant vision.[175]

Differences between the ideational and rhetorical constellations of the Finnish and Swedish Social Democrats can be explained by the different historical roles of the concept of economic democracy in the two countries. In Sweden, the concept had been closer to SAP's ideological core throughout the twentieth century. Programs written by Ernst Wigforss and other canonical figures of the party were valued highly by following generations, and concepts like economic democracy and democratic socialism were modified rather than replaced. In Finland, economic democracy was adopted slightly later and became common only after World War II. Even though it could be viewed as a core concept in SDP's constellations from the 1960s until the late 1980s, it did not gain as established a position as an emblem of party history and identity. It was rather a variation of the root concept, democracy, which remained indispensable despite its changing meaning and reference. In Sweden, the gap between practical policy and programmatic rhetoric became wider than in Finland, where rhetoric changed along with policy in the 1990s. It can of course be interpreted that the Swedish Social Democrats just pushed long-term objectives like economic democracy into a more distant future, as they had done after the previous phases of intensive debate on democratization of the economy.

Vision of the Future Becomes a Relic of the Past

Some historical components of economic and enterprise democracy have lived on in rhetoric and practice since the 1990s. Research has generally reached the conclusion that people's influence on their immediate environments has increased since the 1970s. This was also the result of two major committee reports made in Sweden in 1989 and 1998. Especially, increased freedom of choice in public services was felt positively. In working life, possibilities to influence aspects of everyday work, such as working hours, have increased. On the other hand, influence on the management of enterprises has not increased and higher unemployment has meant that people have less choice in what kind of work they can do. Even though influence on a local level has increased in many respects, transnationalization of capital, privatizations, marketizations and the decline of corporatism have increased the political influence of business and capital.[176]

However, in Sweden and Finland not all sectors have been marketized as extensively as in the Anglo-American world. Finance has been significantly liberated from public steering compared to the 1970s, but public finance and ownership prevails in welfare services and infrastructure. Political scientist Torsten Svensson, among others, has taken this as proof that globalization did not lead to a 'race to the bottom' for welfare states. He argues that public sector cuts have been caused by budget deficits rather than free capital movements.[177] However, Svensson does not take into account that free capital movements have been a major cause of budget deficits: They have increased unemployment, made tax evasion easier and contributed to the Swedish and Finnish financial crises of the early 1990s. Along with the commonly agreed guidelines of the European Union, they have restricted national economic policy and hence also the prospects for economic democracy in many of its historical meanings. Even with their strong welfare states and corporatist institutions, Sweden and Finland have not been able to escape this development.

Historian Francis Sejersted has argued that the free flow of international capital and increasing flexibilization of working life have marked a retreat of the Social Democratic order in Nordic countries. It was based on regulating the economy in relatively closed environments, where the role of capital was limited, while jobs were relatively stable. However, Sejersted points out that in the rise of financial capitalism, public savings have also grown considerably in the form of pension funds and other state funds. He argues that this has meant democratization of capitalism in terms of spreading ownership but not in the sense of coordinating it through democratic decision-making. The funds are instead controlled by professional managers who seek to maximize profits for distant owners. Sejersted interprets this as the idea of shareholder value replacing the more Social Democratic idea of stakeholder value. He prefers a stronger political coordination of large funds—not only pension funds but also private equity funds, which have more aggressive investment strategies and create instability in the economy. However, Sejersted sees prospects in the fact that Nordic states have remained significant owners of enterprise, even though they have privatized parts of their assets and taken most of the remaining ones into the stock exchange. Continued state ownership has been justified by securing national interests, such as employment and security of supply. A new argument is that welfare states can be financed with capital income. Sejersted argues that the Social Democratic retreat was therefore not total, and there was ambiguity regarding the countries' democratic character and their political control of economic development.[178]

However, like pension funds, state ownership in its current form seems to primarily pursue as good a profit as possible. Using economic power and steering investments to reach other goals, such as full employment, is nowadays a marginal motive for state ownership. The Norwegian Oil Fund, which has gained much publicity with its ethical investment strategy, could perhaps be used as a counterexample, but it remains a relatively passive owner after distinguishing 'good' companies from 'bad' ones.[179] Furthermore, there has been a tendency to move state-owned assets from political control to professional managers,[180] which goes against certain historical elements of economic democracy. Social and environmental goals have also remained subordinate in private enterprise. The idea of considering the demands of all stakeholders, not just shareholders, has been widespread at least since Eric Rhenman's theories in the early 1960s. However, the prominent concepts of the last couple of decades, 'corporate social responsibility' and 'corporate citizenship,' have signified mostly voluntary self-regulation of business, whose positive social and environmental impacts have remained modest.[181]

In the 2000s, the concepts of economic and enterprise democracy have been largely excluded from everyday public and political debate and been confined to narrower academic and activist circles. Thus far, even the prominent debates on economic inequality and social movements like Occupy Wall Street have not been able to change this. Several movements and scholars nevertheless define their ideas as 'economic democracy' or at least imply that they would make the economy more democratic. For example, the International Movement for Monetary Reform seeks to 'democratize money' by making its creation the monopoly of states and their central banks. This would allow interest-free money, the use and quantity of which could be decided democratically.[182] Another version of a 'democratized' economy is found in the theory of 'participatory economics' by economist Robin Hahnel and philosopher Michael Albert. They suggest an economic system where production and investment plans and decisions would be made via participatory democracy in consumer and worker councils with coordination and iteration by central and local administrations. The model's most original feature is an equitable division of labor and possibility of self-fulfillment by having everyone divide their time between jobs of high and low desirability and empowerment.[183] These ideas, however, have gained very little public and political attention.

The support of Social Democratic parties, historically the most visible proponents of economic democracy, has been in steady decline in Finland and Sweden. At the time of writing, their performance in opinion polls is close to all-time lows in both countries. Despite this, they have been able to form governments: In Sweden until 2006 and again from 2014 onward, and in Finland as a junior coalition partner with the Center Party in 2003–2007 and with the National Coalition Party in 2011–2015. In 2019, SDP became the biggest party with an extremely slim margin and formed a center-left government. At the same time, the populist and nationalist right wing has increased in popularity. This has lifted immigration and security among the most discussed political issues. Despite the financial crisis of 2008 and lasting unemployment, the political mainstream continues to propose reforms along neoliberal lines in order to increase national competitiveness and ultimately secure the welfare state. This means further economic liberalization, labor market flexibilization and cuts to public services and social benefits. In Finland, the employer confederation EK (successor to STK) realized its long-standing goal of withdrawing from centralized bargaining in 2016—25 years after its Swedish counterpart. This happened despite a historically low strike rate and the fact that central agreements had been more successful in wage restraint than sectoral ones.[184] The impact of the financial crisis has been most notable in transnational efforts to increase regulation of the finance sector and prevent tax evasion, but these reforms are not usually referred to as economic democracy.

In the twenty-first century, 'democratization' is normally used in the same reference that became dominant in the 1980s. It means democratizing 'political' and 'public' but not 'economic' entities: Political parties, public administration and local communities should be made more open and participatory for citizens.[185] Concepts like 'democracy policy' have been invented in the 2000s to describe governmental measures for enhancing democratic and electoral participation. These views have been criticized for a depoliticized image of democracy, where conflicting interests are once again forgotten; democracy is restricted to the national space and subordinated to administration, which tries to impose 'participation' from above. Mirroring traditional constellations of the center-right parties, civil society is portrayed as the social base of democracy. Citizens are encouraged to participate actively on the terms of the prevailing system instead of transforming it.[186]

In Sweden, the concept of economic democracy is still taken up occasionally in public debate, where left-wing thinkers call for bringing questions of power and ownership back onto the agenda.[187] These openings usually do not present clear visions for the future but settle for calling for new debate on the issue. Often economic democracy figures as a relic of the past whose declined importance seems perplexing: "Why don't we talk about economic democracy anymore?" people may ask.[188] Alternatively, economic democracy—especially in the form of wage-earner funds—can be portrayed as a concept that has already been proven unviable and is better to be left in the dustbin of history. Wage-earner funds remain a common tool in the rhetoric of the Swedish center-right for criticizing proposals of economic regulation, such as restricting the profits of private welfare service providers.[189]

In Finnish public debate, by contrast, the concepts of economic and enterprise democracy are almost nonexistent. The conceptual elements that have remained from earlier debates are confined to 'people's capitalism' and cooperation and participation in working life. The image of Finland as a latecomer persists: Reforms that were made in other Nordic countries are periodically taken up in discussions of working life reform. Performance-related pay and stronger employee representation in corporate governance are still portrayed—by center-right parties and Social Democrats alike—as potential means to increase employee motivation, adherence to corporate goals and acceptance of 'necessary' working life flexibilization.[190] As in other Nordic countries, Finnish trade unions and employee protecting legislation remain strong in international comparison. However, they are under constant pressure, as Finland is considered to lag behind most other Western and Nordic countries in labor market flexibility. Juha Sipilä's center-right government, in office 2015–2019, aimed to increase local bargaining in workplaces and, as a concession to the employee side, promote participation in corporate governance.[191]

While working life reforms have been adapted to the imperatives of competitiveness and flexibility, legitimations drawing on the security, equality or power of employees have become even more marginalized than in earlier decades. Today, very few Finnish politicians argue that the economy and working life should be democratized or economic power be distributed differently, which is a striking difference from the political language of the 1960s and 1970s. However, research constantly provides new data on the growing economic inequalities in Finland, Sweden and the West in general since the neoliberal turn.[192] As the critique of this development and of finance capitalism has gradually increased since the financial crisis of 2008, it might sooner or later give new life to the concept of economic democracy.

Notes

1. Philip Mirowski, *Never Let a Serious Crisis Go to Waste: How Neoliberalism Survived the Financial Meltdown* (London and New York: Verso, 2013); Jamie Peck, *Constructions of Neoliberal Reason* (Oxford: Oxford University Press, 2010); Luc Boltanski and Ève Chiapello, *The New Spirit of Capitalism* (London and New York: Verso, 2005); Philip G. Cerny, *The Changing Architecture of Politics: Structure, Agency, and the Future of the State* (London: Sage, 1990).
2. Daniel T. Rodgers, *Age of Fracture* (Cambridge, MA & London: Belknap Press of Harvard University Press, 2011), 41–44; Anu Kantola and Johannes Kananen, "Seize the Moment: Financial Crisis and the Making of the Finnish Competition State," *New Political Economy* 18, 6 (2013): 814–815; Agneta Hugemark, *Den fängslande marknaden: Ekonomiska experter om välfärdsstaten* (Lund: Arkiv, 1994), 170–178.
3. Boltanski and Chiapello, *The New Spirit of Capitalism*, 273–296; Andrew Glyn, *Capitalism Unleashed: Finance Globalisation and Welfare* (Oxford: Oxford University Press, 2006), 104–128.
4. Göran Therborn, *Kapitalet, överheten och alla vi andra: Klassamhället i Sverige – Det rådande och det kommande* (Lund: Arkiv, 2018), 74–77.

5. Francis Fukuyama, "The End of History?" *National Interest*, Summer 1989, 3–18.
6. Rodgers, *Age of Fracture*, 242–254; Tony Judt, *Postwar: A History of Europe since 1945* (London: Penguin, 2005), 603–633, 645–659; Eric Hobsbawm, *Age of Extremes: The Short Twentieth Century 1914–1991* (London: Abacus, 1995), 476–499.
7. Jessica Whyte, *The Morals of the Market: Human Rights and the Rise of Neoliberalism* (London and New York: Verso, 2019); Samuel Moyn, *Not Enough: Human Rights in an Unequal World* (Cambridge, MA: Belknap Press of Harvard University Press, 2018), 172–211; Samuel Moyn, *The Last Utopia: Human Rights in History* (Cambridge, MA: Belknap Press of Harvard University Press, 2010), 216–227; Rodgers, *Age of Fracture*, 251–252.
8. Whyte, *The Morals of the Market*, 15–17, 24–25; Lars Trägårdh (ed.), *Civilt samhälle kontra offentlig sektor.* (Stockholm: SNS förlag, 1995); Kristina Boréus, *Högervåg: Nyliberalism och kampen om språket i svensk offentlig debatt 1969–1989* (Stockholm: Tiden, 1994), 269–275.
9. Pauli Kettunen, *Historia petollisena liittolaisena: Näkökulmia työväen, työelämän ja hyvinvointivaltion historiaan* (Helsinki: Työväen historian ja perinteen tutkimuksen seura, 2015), 38–44; Jenny Andersson, *The Library and the Workshop: Social Democracy and Capitalism in the Knowledge Age* (Stanford: Stanford University Press, 2010), 17–19, 150–158.
10. Donald Sassoon, *One Hundred Years of Socialism: The West European Left in the Twentieth Century* (London: Fontana Press, 1996), 731–742, 750–752; Pauli Kettunen, "The Tension between the Social and the Economic," in *The Road to Prosperity: An Economic History of Finland*, eds. Jari Eloranta, Jukka Jalava and Jari Ojala (Helsinki: Suomalaisen Kirjallisuuden Seura, 2006), 310–313; Cerny, *The Changing Architecture of Politics.*
11. Sassoon, *One Hundred Years of Socialism*, 733–735, 753–754; Gerassimos Moschonas, *In the Name of Social Democracy: The Great Transformation: 1945 to Present* (London and New York: Verso, 2002), 289–297.
12. Michael Freeden, *Ideologies and Political Theory: A Conceptual Approach* (Oxford: Oxford University Press, 1996), 480–482.
13. Mikko Majander, "SDP:n ensimmäinen periaate- ja puolueohjelma Forssan ohjelman merkitys Suomen kehittämisessä," in *Vasemmiston tulevaisuus*, eds. Pirjo Alijärvi, Hildur Boldt, Ismo Kainulainen and Katri Söder (Helsinki: Into, 2014), 42–43; Andersson, *The Library and the Workshop*, 10–12.
14. Moschonas, *In the Name of Social Democracy*, 293; Andersson, *The Library and the Workshop*, 12–13.

15. Urban Lundberg, *Juvelen i kronan: Socialdemokraterna och den allmänna pensionen* (Stockholm: Hjalmarson & Högberg, 2003), 25–26.
16. Lars Ekdahl, *Mot en tredje väg: En biografi över Rudolf Meidner. II. Facklig expert och demokratisk socialist* (Lund: Arkiv, 2005), 304–314; J. Magnus Ryner, *Capitalist Restructuring, Globalisation and the Third Way: Lessons from the Swedish Model* (London and New York: Routledge, 2002), 163–168, 185–186.
17. Sassoon, *One Hundred Years of Socialism*, 750–754.
18. Moschonas, *In the Name of Social Democracy*, 305–311, 316–324.
19. Ibid., 40–51, 84–116.
20. Stephanie L. Mudge, *Leftism Reinvented: Western Parties from Socialism to Neoliberalism* (Cambridge, MA: Harvard University Press, 2018), 306–311.
21. For interpretations stressing the Social Democrats' market-oriented tradition see Adam Przeworski, "How Many Ways Can Be Third?" in *Social Democracy in Neoliberal Times*, ed. Andrew Glyn (Oxford: Oxford University Press, 2002), 312–313, 322–324; Ashley Lavelle, *The Death of Social Democracy: Political Consequences in the 21st Century* (Farnham: Ashgate, 2008), 2–3, 19, 30–32; Jonas Hinnfors, *Reinterpreting Social Democracy: A History of Stability in the British Labour Party and Swedish Social Democratic Party* (Manchester University Press, Manchester 2006), 143–159.
22. Lundberg, *Juvelen i kronan*, 298–299.
23. Kettunen, *Historia petollisena liittolaisena*, 38–44; Jenny Andersson, *När framtiden redan hänt: Socialdemokratin och folkhemsnostalgin* (Stockholm: Ordfront, 2009).
24. Anu Kantola, *Markkinakuri ja managerivalta: Poliittinen hallinta Suomen 1990-luvun talouskriisissä* (Helsinki: Loki-kirjat, 2002), 248–265. On expert governance see also Nikolas Rose, *Powers of Freedom: Reframing Political Thought* (Cambridge: Cambridge University Press, 1999), 131–133, passim.
25. Olof Palme, *Politik är att vilja* (Stockholm: Prisma, 1968).
26. Lars Jonung, Jaakko Kiander and Pentti Vartia, "The Great Financial Crisis in Finland and Sweden: The Dynamics of Boom, Bust and Recovery, 1985–2000," in *The Great Financial Crisis in Finland and Sweden: The Nordic Experience of Financial Liberalization*, eds. Lars Jonung, Jaakko Kiander and Pentti Vartia (Cheltenham and Northampton: Edward Elgar, 2009), 19–27, 29–37; Peter Englund and Vesa Vihriälä, "Financial Crisis in Finland and Sweden: Similar but not Quite the Same," in *The Great Financial Crisis in Finland and Sweden: The Nordic Experience of Financial Liberalization*, eds. Lars Jonung, Jaakko Kiander and Pentti Vartia (Cheltenham and Northampton: Edward Elgar, 2009), 71–89;

Jaakko Kiander, *Laman opetukset: Suomen 1990-luvun kriisin syyt ja seuraukset* (Helsinki: Government Institute for Economic Research, 2001), 8–23, 37–39; Sakari Heikkinen and Seppo Tiihonen, *Hyvinvoinnin turvaaja: Valtiovarainministeriön historia 3* (Helsinki: Edita, 2010), 271–285; Mark Blyth, *Great Transformations: Economic Ideas and Institutional Change in the Twentieth Century* (Cambridge: Cambridge University Press, 2002), 223–227.

27. Jonung, Kiander and Vartia, "The Great Financial Crisis in Finland and Sweden," 37–45; Englund and Vihriälä, "Financial Crisis in Finland and Sweden," 119–122; Raija Julkunen, *Suunnanmuutos: 1990-luvun sosiaalipoliittinen reformi Suomessa* (Tampere: Vastapaino, 2001), 64–66; Kiander, *Laman opetukset*, 13–16, 23–30.
28. Kantola and Kananen, "Seize the Moment," 815–816; Kettunen, "The Tension between the Social and the Economic," 310; Kiander, *Laman opetukset*, 24–25, 56–58, 101–105.
29. Carl Bildt, *Den enda vägen* (Stockholm: Moderata samlingspartiet, 1994); Blyth, *Great Transformations*, 228–229.
30. Seppo Kääriäinen, *Sitä niittää, mitä kylvää: Keskustan strategiset valinnat 1964–2001* (Jyväskylä: Gummerus, 2002), 284, 294–297.
31. Jonung, Kiander and Vartia, "The Great Financial Crisis in Finland and Sweden," 38–39; Kiander, *Laman opetukset*, 28–35; Julkunen, *Suunnanmuutos*, 69–75.
32. Lars Magnusson, *Sveriges ekonomiska historia* (Stockholm: Norstedts, 2010), 434–438; Johannes Lindvall, *The Politics of Purpose: Swedish Macroeconomic Policy after the Golden Age* (Göteborg: Göteborg University, 2004), 125–128; Kiander, *Laman opetukset*, 98–99.
33. Jaakko Kiander, "1930-luvun pulakausi ja 1990-luvun talouskriisi: Talouspolitiikan ja taloudellisen ajattelun vertailua," in *Lamakirja: Näkökulmia 1990-luvun talouskriisiin ja sen historiallisiin konteksteihin*, eds. Helena Blomberg, Matti Hannikainen and Pauli Kettunen (Turku: Kirja-Aurora, 2002), 57–60.
34. Jonung, Kiander and Vartia, "The Great Financial Crisis in Finland and Sweden," 45–50; Englund and Vihriälä, "Financial Crisis in Finland and Sweden," 91–98.
35. Kantola, *Markkinakuri ja managerivalta*, 126–127. On creative destruction see also Mark Blyth, *Austerity: The History of a Dangerous Idea* (Oxford: Oxford University Press, 2013), 119–121.
36. Jarkko Vesikansa, *Laman taittaja: Raimo Sailas ja kolme talouskriisiä* (Helsinki: Otava, 2016), 371–372; Johannes Koroma, *Suomalaisten hyvinvointia rakentamassa: Teollisuuden keskusliiton historia* (Helsinki: Suomalaisen kirjallisuuden seura, 2015), 188–190.

37. Markku Mansner, *Suomalaista yhteiskuntaa rakentamassa: Suomen työnantajain keskusliitto 1980–1992* (Helsinki: Elinkeinoelämän keskusliitto EK, 2005), 469–472.
38. For a thorough discussion, see Blyth, *Austerity*, 178–226.
39. Kantola, *Markkinakuri ja managerivalta*, 290–306; Pauli Kettunen, *Globalisaatio ja kansallinen me: Kansallisen katseen historiallinen kritiikki* (Tampere: Vastapaino, 2008), 116–121.
40. Kantola, *Markkinakuri ja managerivalta*, 290–292.
41. Vesikansa, *Laman taittaja*, 369, 479–488.
42. For example, Blyth, *Austerity*, 10–15.
43. Kettunen, *Historia petollisena liittolaisena*, 41–44; Rauli Mickelsson, *Samanlaiset ja erilaiset puolueet: Retoriikka- ja diskurssianalyyttinen tutkimus kokoomuslaisten ja sosiaalidemokraattien jäsenlehdissä ilmaisemista käsityksistä omista puolueistaan vuosina 1965–1995* (Turku: University of Turku, 1999), 263–265, 267–268, 282–285.
44. For example, speech by Secretary General Ulpu Iivari. SDP congress protocol 1990, 40.
45. For example, speeches by Chair Pertti Paasio and Paavo Lipponen, Ibid., 30–35, 47.
46. Mickelsson, *Samanlaiset ja erilaiset puolueet*, 236–239.
47. Ulpu Iivari, "Sosialidemokratian asema vasemmiston murroksessa," *Sosialistinen aikakauslehti* 4/1990, 8–11.
48. SDP congress protocol 1990, 118; Outinen, *Sosiaalidemokraattien tie*, 227–230.
49. SDP congress protocol 1990, 71.
50. Kalevi Sorsa, "Luottavasti tulevaisuuteen – kunhan eväät uusitaan," *Sosialistinen aikakauslehti* 1/1991, 8–12.
51. SDP congress protocol 1990, 616.
52. SDP congress protocol 1990, 618–619; SDP, *SDP:n tavoitteita 1990-luvulle -asiakirja* (1990).
53. Sirpa Puhakka, *Vasemmistoliiton synty* (Helsinki: Into, 2015), 160–170, 176–182.
54. Ibid., 205–209, 225–227.
55. Left Alliance, *Ohjelma hyväksytty perustavassa kokouksessa Helsingissä 28.–29.4.1990.* https://www.fsd.uta.fi/pohtiva/ohjelmalistat/VAS/799.
56. Ibid.
57. SAP, *Socialdemokraternas partiprogram.* Antaget på socialdemokraternas 31:a kongress 1990. https://snd.gu.se/sv/vivill/party/s/p/1990.
58. Ibid.
59. Ibid.
60. Ibid.

61. SAP, *Riktlinjer för nittiotalet. Antagna på Socialdemokraternas 31:a kongress*, 9–10, 24–25.
62. Ibid., 11–13.
63. Ibid., 18, 34–35.
64. SAP congress protocol 1990, B105–B130. On the role of individualism and postmodernism in the 1990s program, see also Andersson, *The Library and the Workshop*, 50–52.
65. SAP, *Riktlinjer för nittiotalet*, 45–49.
66. Ibid., 51–57.
67. Ibid., 44.
68. Ibid., 54.
69. Ibid., 59–67.
70. Ibid., 21, 62.
71. SAP congress protocol 1990, A:21.
72. SAP congress 1990. Motions on democracy, 3–49; SAP congress 1990. Program motions, 3–4, 25–32, 107–109.
73. SAP congress protocol 1990, D127–D137, D140–D143.
74. SAP congress 1990. Executive committee's statements on motions on democracy, 3–8.
75. *Dagens Nyheter* 8 May 1990, 30; Rune Molin, "Ge AP-fonderna frihet att köpa aktier," *Svenska Dagbladet* 31 May 1990, 11.
76. *Dagens Nyheter* 28 August 1991, 14.
77. "Debattera fonderna!" *Aftonbladet* 7 May 1990, 2.
78. *Svenska Dagbladet* 5 September 1991, 8–9.
79. *Svenska Dagbladet* 6 September 1991, 6.
80. Torbjörn Nilsson, *Hundra år av svensk politik* (Malmö: Gleerups, 2009), 133–134; Sassoon, *One Hundred Years of Socialism*, 745.
81. Bo Stråth, *Folkhemmet mot Europa: Ett historiskt perspektiv på 90-talet* (Stockholm: Tiden, 1993), 23–27; Sassoon, *One Hundred Years of Socialism*, 742–743, 746–747.
82. Tapio Bergholm, *Laatua ja vapaa-aikaa. Tulopolitiikan aika II: Suomen ammattiliittojen keskusjärjestö vuodesta 1977* (Helsinki: Suomalaisen kirjallisuuden seura, 2018), 511–513; Outinen, *Sosiaalidemokraattien tie*, 245; Mansner, *Suomen työnantajain keskusliitto 1980–1992*, 443–453.
83. CA69 SAK congress protocol 1991, 4. Congresses. SAK Archive. Finnish Labour Archives, Helsinki (TA).
84. Ibid., 5–6.
85. SAK Congress 1991, Appendix 16b, 7. Congresses. SAK Archive. TA, Helsinki; Moyn, *Not Enough*; Moyn, *The Last Utopia*; Judt, *Postwar*, 564–566.
86. SAK Congress 1991, Appendix 45a. SAK's Target Program 1991–1996, 13–14. Congresses. SAK Archive. TA, 13.

87. Ibid., 14–15.
88. Ibid.
89. Hans De Geer, *Från svenska modellen till Svenskt Näringsliv: Om SAF och den svenska arbetsmarknadens organisering under 1990-talet* (Stockholm: Ratio, 2007), 57–60; Joakim Johansson, *SAF och den svenska modellen: En studie av uppbrottet från förvaltningskorporatismen 1982–91* (Doctoral dissertation, Uppsala University 2000); Blyth, *Great Transformations*, 228–229.
90. Bo Stråth, *Mellan två fonder: LO och den svenska modellen* (Stockholm: Atlas, 1998), 260–266; Christer Lundh, *Spelets regler: Institutioner och lönebildning på den svenska arbetsmarknaden 1850–2000* (Stockholm: SNS förlag, 2002), 274–280.
91. Stråth, *Mellan två fonder*, 284–288.
92. Göran Färm, "En anpassning till liberalismen," *Aftonbladet* 23 July 1989, 2.
93. SAP congress protocol 1990, B132–B141.
94. LO, *Det utvecklande arbetet* (1991), 22–25.
95. Ibid., 35–38, 42.
96. Ibid., 429.
97. Ibid., 340–341.
98. Ibid., 69–72, 97–98, 430, 436–437.
99. Ibid., 431–435.
100. LO congress protocol 1991, 760–767, 776–781, 859–876, 953–981.
101. Anders L. Johansson and Lars Magnusson, *LO – 1900-talet och ett nytt millennium* (Stockholm: Atlas, 2012), 372–374.
102. LO, *Det utvecklande arbetet*, 361–365, 436–437; LO congress protocol 1991, 1082–1083, 1091–1106.
103. Lars Ekdahl, "Den fackliga rörelsen mellan två modeller," in *Det långa 1990-talet: När Sverige förändrades*, eds. Anders Ivarsson Westerberg, Ylva Waldemarson and Kjell Östberg (Umeå: Boréa, 2014), 215–218, 238–245.
104. Stig Malm, "Visst begicks misstag," *Dagens Nyheter* 6 December 1993, 4.
105. "De sista entusiasterna," *Svenska Dagbladet* 23 May 1990, 2.
106. Tom Wachtmeister, "Endast Sverige satsar på ökat statligt företagande," *Svenska Dagbladet* 1 August 1990, B6.
107. Curt Nicolin, "Välfärdspolitiken har kommit till vägs ände," *Svenska Dagbladet* 31 August 1990, 3.
108. Curt Nicolin, "Marknadsekonomin måste utvecklas i Sverige," *Svenska Dagbladet* 3 August 1991, 3.
109. Sander, "Demokratiserad ekonomi," Dagens Nyheter 6 May 1990, 2.
110. Mickelsson, *Samanlaiset ja erilaiset puolueet*, 255–258; Mats Svegfors, "Den återupprättade idyllen," *Svenska Dagbladet* 4 August 1991, 2.

111. Moderata samlingspartiet, *Framtidens idéer – Det bästa för Sverige. Valmanifest 1991.* http://snd.gu.se/sv/vivill/party/m/v/1991; Torbjörn Nilsson, *Mellan arv och utopi: Moderata vägval under hundra år, 1904–2004* (Stockholm: Santérus, 2004), 284.
112. Nilsson, *Mellan arv och utopi*, 284–285; Nilsson, *Hundra år av svensk politik*, 134–135.
113. De Geer, *Från svenska modellen till Svenskt Näringsliv*, 62–66; Nilsson, *Mellan arv och utopi*, 285–288; Blyth, *Great Transformations*, 228–235; Svensson, *Marknadsanpassningens politik*, 89–90.
114. Bildt, *Den enda vägen*, 34–51.
115. SOU 1993: 16, *Nya villkor för ekonomi och politik*; Östberg, "Politikens förändrade villkor," 152–157; Lindvall, *The Politics of Purpose*, 131–134.
116. Johannes Lindvall and Bo Rothstein, "Sweden: The Fall of the Strong State," *Scandinavian Political Studies* 29, 1 (2006): 47–63.
117. Lindvall, *The Politics of Purpose*, 134–137.
118. Juri Mykkänen, "Kuka päättää hyvinvointimallin tulevaisuudesta?" in *Kilpailuvaltion kyydissä: Suomen hyvinvointimallin tulevaisuus*, ed. Johannes Kananen (Helsinki: Gaudeamus, 2017), 110–127; Ville Yliaska, *Tehokkuuden toiveuni: Uuden julkisjohtamisen historia Suomessa 1970-luvulta 1990-luvulle* (Helsinki: Into, 2014). *Tehokkuuden toiveuni*, 518–520, 526–527; Kantola and Kananen, "Seize the Moment," 816–818; Heikkinen and Tiihonen, *Hyvinvoinnin turvaaja*, 342–348.
119. Hagen Schulz-Forberg and Bo Stråth, *The Political History of European Integration: The Hypocrisy of Democracy-through-market* (Abingdon & New York: Routledge, 2010), 51–55; Wolfgang Streeck, *Buying Time: The Delayed Crisis of Democratic Capitalism* (London and New York: Verso, 2014), 58–62, 91–102; Antero Jyränki, "Kansanedustuslaitos ja valtiosääntö 1906–2005," in *Eduskunnan muuttuva asema: Suomen eduskunta 100 vuotta*, eds. Antero Jyränki and Jaakko Nousiainen (Helsinki: Edita, 2006), 125–150.
120. De Geer, *Från svenska modellen till Svenskt Näringsliv*, 69–78; Nilsson, *Mellan arv och utopi*, 289–292.
121. Moderata samlingspartiet, *Idé och handlingsprogram* (1993), 20–25, 48–52; Nilsson, *Mellan arv och utopi*, 286–287.
122. Moderata samlingspartiet, *Idé och handlingsprogram*, 15–19; Nilsson, *Mellan arv och utopi*, 265–267, 272–273.
123. Moderata samlingspartiet, *Idé och handlingsprogram*, 25–29.
124. Ibid., 31.
125. Ibid., 31–38.
126. Ibid., 39–43.
127. Bildt, *Den enda vägen*, 17–19.

128. Torbjörn Nilsson, "Nyliberalismens spöke och Moderaternas politik," in *Det långa 1990-talet: När Sverige förändrades*, eds.Anders Ivarsson Westerberg, Ylva Waldemarson and Kjell Östberg (Umeå: Boréa, 2014), 45–50.
129. Outinen, *Sosiaalidemokraattien tie*, 231; Kääriäinen, *Sitä niittää, mitä kylvää*, 258–259, 287.
130. Matti Tuomala, *Markkinat, valtio ja eriarvoisuus* (Tampere: Vastapaino, 2019), 194–198; Heikkinen and Tiihonen, *Hyvinvoinnin turvaaja*, 355–358; Jyränki, "Kansanedustuslaitos ja valtiosääntö," 102–105; Kääriäinen, *Sitä niittää, mitä kylvää*, 305–307; Julkunen, *Suunnanmuutos*, 112–115.
131. National Coalition Party, *Kansallisen kokoomuksen vaaliohjelma eduskuntakaudeksi 1991–1995.* http://www.fsd.uta.fi/pohtiva/ohjelmalistat/KOK/932.
132. National Coalition Party, *Programme of Principles. Approved by the Party Conference on 11–13 June 1993.* http://www.fsd.uta.fi/pohtiva/ohjelmalistat/KOK/1033.
133. Ibid.
134. Mickelsson, *Samanlaiset ja erilaiset puolueet*, 247–248.
135. National Coalition Party, *Kansallinen Kokoomus Tavoiteohjelma 1995–1999.* Hyväksytty ylimääräisessä puoluekokouksessa 27.–28.8.1994 Espoo. http://www.fsd.uta.fi/pohtiva/ohjelmalistat/KOK/83.
136. Center Party of Finland, *Kestävän kehityksen ja vapaan ihmisen vuosikymmen. Suomen keskustan ohjelma 1990-luvulle.* (1990). http://www.fsd.uta.fi/pohtiva/ohjelmalistat/KESK/215; Center Party of Finland, *Kestävän työllisyyden ja yrittäjyyden yhteiskunta.* Suomen Keskustan 65. puoluekokous, Jyväskylä 17.–19.6.1994. http://www.fsd.uta.fi/pohtiva/ohjelmalistat/KESK/246.
137. Kääriäinen, *Sitä niittää, mitä kylvää*, 294–299.
138. Ibid., 302, 310–317.
139. Outinen, *Sosiaalidemokraattien tie*; Ryner, *Capitalist Restructuring*; Kantola, *Markkinakuri ja managerivalta*; Julkunen, *Suunnanmuutos*.
140. Vesikansa, *Laman taittaja*, 486–487; Marttila, *Hillitty markkinatalous*, 307–308; Kari, *Suomen rahoitusmarkkinoiden murros*, 514–518.
141. Bergholm, *Laatua ja vapaa-aikaa*, 498–499, 513.
142. Cornel Ban, *Ruling Ideas: How Global Neoliberalism Goes Local* (Oxford and New York: Oxford University Press, 2016).
143. Lindvall, *The Politics of Purpose*, 12–14.
144. Ibid., 143–144, 149–151.
145. Outinen, *Sosiaalidemokraattien tie*, 232–240, 321–322.
146. Outinen, *Sosiaalidemokraattien tie*, 249–255, 325–326; Sassoon, *One Hundred Years of Socialism*, 742–743.

147. Outinen, *Sosiaalidemokraattien tie*, 256–264; Sassoon, *One Hundred Years of Socialism*, 742.
148. Nilsson, *Hundra år av svensk politik*, 179.
149. Outinen, *Sosiaalidemokraattien tie*, 264–265; Kääriäinen, *Sitä niittää, mitä kylvää*, 321–322.
150. SAP, *Valmanifest antaget av den socialdemokratiska partistyrelsen, 1994-08-19.* http://snd.gu.se/sv/vivill/party/s/v/1994.
151. Niklas Olsen, *The Sovereign Consumer: A New Intellectual History of Neoliberalism* (Cham: Palgrave Macmillan, 2019), 240–250; Mudge, *Leftism Reinvented*, 55–58; Judt, *Postwar*, 792–796.
152. Outinen, *Sosiaalidemokraattien tie*, 265–273, 322–323; Heikkinen and Tiihonen, *Hyvinvoinnin turvaaja*, 303–304, 307–310, 324–329; Program of Paavo Lipponen's first government, 1995. https://valtioneuvosto.fi/hallitusohjelmat/-/asset_publisher/66-paaministeri-paavo-lipposen-hallituksen-ohjelma.
153. Paavo Lipponen, *Järki voittaa: Suomalainen identiteetti globalisaation aikakaudella* (Helsinki: Otava, 2008), 53–57.
154. Outinen, *Sosiaalidemokraattien tie*, 322–323; Kantola and Kananen, "Seize the Moment," 818–820.
155. Blyth, *Great Transformations*, 235–238; Moschonas, *In the Name of Social Democracy*, 191.
156. Claes Belfrage, and Magnus Ryner, "Renegotiating the Swedish Social Democratic Settlement: From Pension Fund Socialism to Neoliberalization," *Politics & Society* 37, 2 (2009): 257–287; Lundberg, *Juvelen i kronan*, 305–311.
157. Svensson, *Marknadsanpassningens politik*, 92–94.
158. Johansson and Magnusson, *LO*, 351–354.
159. De Geer, *Från svenska modellen till Svenskt Näringsliv*, 142–148; Svensson, *Marknadsanpassningens politik*, 132–137.
160. Ekdahl, "Den fackliga rörelsen mellan två modeller," 232–242.
161. Nilsson, *Hundra år av svensk politik*, 142–143.
162. SDP, *Sosialidemokratian periaatteet.* Hyväksytty XXXVIII puoluekokouksessa Turussa 29.5.1999. http://www.fsd.uta.fi/pohtiva/ohjelmalistat/SDP/451; Majander, "SDP:n ensimmäinen periaate- ja puolueohjelma," 42–43.
163. SDP, *Sosialidemokratian periaatteet.*
164. Andersson, *När framtiden redan hänt*, 107–120.
165. SDP, *Sosialidemokratian periaatteet.*
166. SDP, *SDP:n työelämän uudistamisohjelma.* Hyväksytty puoluehallituksessa 11.6.1998. https://www.fsd.uta.fi/pohtiva/ohjelmalistat/SDP/478.

167. On Persson-era SAP's utilization of traditional rhetoric see also Andersson, *The Library and the Workshop*, 58–60.
168. SAP, *Partiprogram för Socialdemokraterna. Antaget vid partikongressen 2001.* https://snd.gu.se/sv/vivill/party/s/p/2001.
169. Ibid., 16, 18–19.
170. Ibid., 12.
171. Ibid., 19–20.
172. Ibid., 26–28, 30. On Social Democratic growth strategies in a knowledge economy see also Andersson, *The Library and the Workshop*, 32–35.
173. SAP, *Partiprogram för Socialdemokraterna.*
174. Ibid., 7.
175. Johansson and Magnusson, *LO*, 374–378; LO, *Ägaransvar och ägarmakt* (2006).
176. Francis Sejersted, *The Age of Social Democracy: Norway and Sweden in the Twentieth Century* (Princeton: Princeton University Press, 2011), 380–381; Svensson, *Marknadsanpassningens politik*, 270–275; SOU 1990: 44. *Demokrati och makt i Sverige* (Stockholm: Statsrådsberedningen,1990).
177. Svensson, *Marknadsanpassningens politik*, 280–285.
178. Sejersted, *The Age of Social Democracy*, 381–387.
179. Thore Johnsen and Ole Gjølberg, "Management of the Norwegian Oil Fund: The Challenges and Costs of Being Ethical," *Beta* 01 (2009): 1–26; Damian Carrington, "'Historic Breakthrough': Norway's Giant Oil Fund Dives into Renewables." *The Guardian* 5 April 2019. https://www.theguardian.com/environment/2019/apr/05/historic-breakthrough-norways-giant-oil-fund-dives-into-renewables.
180. Pasi Nevalainen and Ville Yliaska, "From State-owned Smokestacks to Post-industrial Dreams: The Finnish Government in Business, 1970–2010," *Business History* 62 (2020). https://doi.org/10.1080/00076791.2020.1842874; Markku Kuisma, *Valtion yhtiöt: Nousu ja tuho* (Helsinki: Siltala, 2016), 297–298.
181. Teivo Teivainen, *Yritysvastuun umpikuja* (Helsinki: Kalevi Sorsa -säätiö, 2013); Kettunen, *Globalisaatio ja kansallinen me*, 183–208.
182. International Movement for Monetary Reform. https://internationalmoneyreform.org/. The movement's Finnish branch has explicitly named itself 'Economic democracy.' Talousdemokratia ry. http://talousdemokratia.fi/.
183. Robin Hahnel, *Economic Justice and Democracy: From Competition to Cooperation* (New York: Routledge, 2005); Michael Albert and Robin Hahnel, *The Political Economy of Participatory Economics* (Princeton: Princeton University Press, 1991).
184. Bergholm, *Laatua ja vapaa-aikaa*, 516–520.

185. For example, Lindvall and Rothstein, "Sweden: The Fall of the Strong State," 48, 60–61; SOU 2000: 1 *En uthållig demokrati*, 240–52.
186. Kari Palonen, "Demokratiapolitiikka – demokratian epäpolitisointia. Reunahuomautuksia oikeusministeriön keskusteluasiakirjaan "Demokratiapolitiikan suuntaviivat"," *Politiikka* 51, 2 (2009): 146–150; Kettunen, *Globalisaatio ja kansallinen me*, 67–69, 93–97. For original documents see Regeringens proposition 2001/02:80, *Demokrati för det nya seklet*. https://www.riksdagen.se/sv/dokument-lagar/dokument/proposition/demokrati-for-det-nya-seklet-prop-20010280_GP0380; Oikeusministeriö, *Kansalaisvaikuttamisen politiikkaohjelman loppuraportti* (2007); Oikeusministeriö, *Demokratiapolitiikan suuntaviivat: Demokratiapoliittinen keskusteluasiakirja* (2009).
187. For example, Roland Paulsen, "Drömmen om utopin," *Dagens Nyheter* 2 April 2017, 53–55; Daniel Suhonen, "Vi ser en renässans för den demokratiska socialismen," *Dagens Nyheter* 26 March 2016, 6; Göran Greider, "Nystarta debatten om ekonomisk demokrati!" *Dalademokraten* 5 October 2016, 2.
188. Bo Rothstein, "Ekonomisk demokrati? Reflexioner kring en borttappad diskussion," in *Tillsammans: En fungerande ekonomisk demokrati*, ed. Bo Rothstein (Stockholm: SNS förlag, 2012); Ann Towns, "Demokrati i arbetslivet är en glömd fråga," *Bohusläningen* 15 March 2014, 2.
189. For example, Lars Tobisson, "Vinsttak steg mot socialism," *Svenska Dagbladet* 22 October 2017, 6; Tove Lifvendahl, "Socialismen var nära," *Svenska Dagbladet* 9 October 2016, 4; Karl Sigfrid, "Har läkarna "överlöner"?" *Svenska Dagbladet* 2 September 2016, 4; Maria Ludvigsson, "Vinstfrågan är vår tids löntagarfondsstrid," *Svenska Dagbladet* 20 September 2012, 4; Ekdahl, *Mot en tredje väg II*, 9–10.
190. Teija Sutinen, "Sdp:n Antti Lindtman vaatii radikaalia uudelleenajattelua työmarkkinoille: lisää tulospalkkausta, joka voisi joustaa myös alaspäin," *Helsingin Sanomat* 1 September 2018. https://www.hs.fi/politiikka/art-2000005811708.html; Petri Sajari, "Rehn: Liittojen palkkasopimukset kallis virhe," *Helsingin Sanomat* 13 June 2015. https://www.hs.fi/kotimaa/art-2000002831575.html.
191. Harri Hietala, *Paikallista sopimista koskeva selvitys* (Helsinki: Työ- ja elinkeinoministeriö, 2015); Program of Juha Sipilä's first government. *Ratkaisujen Suomi. Pääministeri Juha Sipilän hallituksen strateginen ohjelma*. Hallituksen julkaisusarja 10/2015. https://valtioneuvosto.fi/hallitusohjelmat/-/asset_publisher/73-stubb-24-6-2014-29-5-2015-.
192. For example, Thomas Piketty, *Capital in the Twenty-First Century* (Cambridge, MA: Belknap Press of Harvard University Press, 2014); Therborn, *Kapitalet, överheten och alla vi andra*; Tuomala, *Markkinat, valtio ja eriarvoisuus*.

CHAPTER 8

Conclusion

The Rise and Decline of Economic Democracy

This book has examined the history of concepts that explicitly relate democracy and the economy—'economic democracy,' 'industrial democracy' and 'enterprise democracy'—in Finland and Sweden. Changing meanings of these concepts give new perspectives to broader political and ideational changes in the post–World War II and post–Cold War era. Methods of conceptual and intellectual history have shed light on the relationship between democracy and the economy by examining the contested meanings, references and valuations of concepts, their roles in the ideational constellations of different actors, and the mechanisms of conceptual change. The study shows that by combining a diachronic analysis of theoretical writings and political programs with a synchronic analysis of day-to-day political debates, the history and change of political thought, rhetoric and concepts can be both understood and explained. Mark Bevir's view of explaining ideational change with new beliefs that question existing ones is especially fruitful. It also provides explanations for the declining role of economic democracy. In addition, the comparative perspective on Finland and Sweden shows how different historical contexts and traditions lead to different uses and trajectories of concepts even in neighboring countries that are culturally close to each other.

I. Kärrylä, *Democracy and the Economy in Finland and Sweden since 1960*, Palgrave Studies in Political History, https://doi.org/10.1007/978-3-030-80631-6_8

From the 1960s, there was a wide consensus on a basic criterion of economic democracy in Sweden and Finland: It meant distributing economic power more evenly to citizens and/or workers. This was justified by appealing to the principle of affected interests: People should be able to influence matters that concerned their own lives. Economic democracy was a future-oriented concept and intrinsically connected to the ideas of modernization and progress. However, how this ideal would be concretely realized—the concept's range of reference—was explicitly contested. Many Social Democrats and trade union representatives argued that economic democracy would be realized by increasing democratic steering and planning of the economy and even by socializing means of production. Another realization, which was called industrial or enterprise democracy, was giving employees more power within enterprises and workplaces. These objectives were interpreted and weighted differently among the left. The tension between participatory and representative democracy was a recurring problem between and within left-wing parties.

Center-right parties and employer representatives were reluctant to increase centralized coordination and the state's role in the economy, even though they had accepted a certain degree of steering and planning in the postwar democratic capitalism. They emphasized democracy through civil society and against the state, while the left's visions of democracy were often realized through the state and against 'economic oligarchy.' Center-right parties advocated a decentralized model, where ownership would be dispersed among citizens and their local influence increased. Conservatives named their models with concepts of Anglo-American origin, such as 'owner democracy' and 'people's capitalism.' They attempted to occupy the semantic field of economic democratization, but unlike their Finnish counterparts, Swedish conservatives rarely used the concept of economic democracy. Democratization of enterprises was accepted as part of the decentralized vision of democracy, but mostly in the form of cooperative consultation already practiced in works councils, as well as participation in everyday work.

In both Sweden and Finland, proposed democratic reforms were legitimized predominantly by appealing to economic efficiency and competitiveness, which were key components of national interest and welfare. Struggle over the value of economic democracy concerned especially its ability to promote these more important values. However, the emergence of democratization as a central topic of debate included a challenge to these traditional value hierarchies. Especially in Sweden, New Left and trade union activists argued for the primacy of democracy, equality and security instead of economic values. The strength of this alternative constellation prompted traditional power-holders to rethink their ideas and strategies. The most notable difference between Sweden and Finland was that in the former, the primacy of economic values and the restrictions they created to democratic politics were questioned more strongly. In a sense, Swedish debates were more 'ideological,' as center-right parties also more often appealed to individual freedom instead of 'objective' national interest. This difference may be explained by the countries' different experiences of external constraints, such as wars and pressure from great powers. However, decontested views of national interest were never forgotten, and economic realities also determined the political leeway for Swedish Social Democrat and trade union leaders. In this sense, the basic orientation of Swedish and Finnish politics was largely similar.

During the 1970s and 1980s, the range of reference of economic democracy began to change. This was closely connected to changing perceptions of economic realities. Mark Bevir's notion of 'dilemmas' well explains this ideational change. The prospects of understanding economic democracy as state-led steering and planning of the economy deteriorated as economic crises and internationalization were believed to narrow the leeway of national economic policy. Social Democratic beliefs and rhetoric turned from democratic planning and steering to supporting private business and its profits as main sources of investment and employment. This had of course been the main policy line for the entire postwar period, especially in Sweden, where the state-owned sector was not nearly as significant as in Finland. The traditionally technocratic view of the economy made it easier to adopt beliefs and practices that a new generation of economists was advocating. However, now democratic steering of the economy also became weaker as a vision of the future. Many existing means of regulation were weakened or abandoned. Capital flows, credit and interest were liberalized in the 1980s, which shifted the locus of economic governance increasingly from states and politicians to markets and managers. Belief in the market mechanism as the desirable principle of resource allocation strengthened, partly as free markets were perceived necessary for international competition and national interest, but partly as they were believed to promote individual autonomy and responsibility, which had become stronger legitimation concepts than equality or democracy—increasingly also for the Social Democrats. In the context of economic liberalization, economic democracy as a macroeconomic concept lost much of its viability and traditional content.

In addition, Social Democratic leaders in Sweden and Finland were uncomfortable with treating collective ownership as a form of economic democracy. In the wage-earner fund debate of the 1970s and early 1980s, the Swedish SAP took it onto its agenda mostly due to pressure from the trade union confederation LO and the left-wing factions of the party. In both Sweden and Finland, it was argued that some forms of collective ownership would be desirable, for example cooperatives and pension funds, but large-scale transfer of ownership to trade unions or other collectives was not advocated. When established, wage-earner funds' possibilities to increase employee power in the economy remained very limited. They were instead legitimized as means of capital formation for the benefit of the national economy. During Olof Palme's leadership, SAP took clear steps toward emphasizing the 'micro level' of economic democracy: Employee influence in workplaces. In Finland the tendency was similar, and SDP's stance on wage-earner funds became even more careful, as they wanted to avoid a similar conflict to that which had broken out in Sweden. Eventually, Finland legislated on individualized and voluntary 'personnel funds,' which resembled center-right and employers' ideas of people's capitalism.

Center-right parties' and employer organizations' concrete ideas on economic democracy did not change as much as Social Democratic ones. For decades, they had advocated decentralizing ownership on the condition that it remained in individual instead of collective hands. They also accepted employee influence at the 'micro level' of economic activity, if it meant participation in the work environment and organization instead of influence on strategic management. The Liberal and Center Parties especially connected enterprise democracy to the idea of local or 'near' democracy, which meant participation in local communities as opposed to centralized bureaucracy. The reforms in working life democratization that were carried out in the 1970s and 1980s mostly followed center-right lines: Employees gained more consultation rights, and new management methods allowed them more autonomy in their immediate work environment. Economic and enterprise democracy never began to refer to these established practices. They had been future-oriented concepts and remained so. In this sense, they differ from 'political democracy,' which was consolidated at the beginning of the twentieth century to denote universal suffrage and parliamentary representation. In a sense, 'owner democracy' and 'near democracy' were at least partially realized, but the use of these terms also became rare. However, despite new forms of employee and citizen participation, strategic power in enterprises and public administration has been concentrated in senior managers and experts.

One notable change did take place among center-right parties and employer representatives: By the early 1990s, they had ceased using the concept of democracy in economic contexts. They no longer created explicit conceptual relations between democracy and the economy otherwise than through 'political' institutions and the regulation they practiced. Left-wing parties mostly followed this trend, although especially the Swedish Social Democrats kept economic and enterprise democracy in their programs due to their historical position as the party's key concepts. However, their reference had been hollowed out and they were scarcely capable of pointing to a new social and economic order or even to significant reforms. This conceptual and ideational change was closely connected to the modification of socialist thought and language after the fall of the Soviet bloc, when socialism itself began to denote a value system rather than an economic system. However, it seems that declining use of the concepts of economic and enterprise democracy by the left was partly an unreflected-on by-product of broader changes, which made old concepts and beliefs less compatible with new ideational constellations. It is difficult to find explicit discussions on the concepts' fate, and especially decisions on abandoning them.

Certain concepts and beliefs became dominant, even hegemonic, in the changing constellations of all political groups in both Sweden and Finland. On the macro level, free markets became the main principle of economic activity while the idea of democratic steering of the economy weakened. The latter was labeled bureaucratic and artificial as opposed to the 'natural state' of markets. However, at the same time economic governance that was necessary for securing the functioning of markets was concentrated in experts in central banks and ministries of finance. Bureaucracy was thus strengthened or reformed instead of doing away with it. Economic crises and the free global movement of capital increased public debt and the imperative of attracting capital by subsidies and lower taxes. This restricted the prospects for steering and regulating the economy via state budget and fiscal policy. In addition, the founding treaties of the European Union introduced constraints on national economic policy and contributed to the move from 'popular' to 'constitutional' democracy.

The development could be interpreted as democracy and economy flipping their former roles: In the 1960s and 1970s there was an attempt to extend democratic decision-making over the economy, whereas from the late 1970s onward the economy and its necessities began increasingly interfering with democratic politics. To be sure, postwar democratic capitalism was already a rather economistic regime, although it was at least claimed to be politically controlled. It was more strongly anchored to democracy rhetorically and institutionally, but in a way the change since the 1970s concerned the nature of economistic governance rather than an outright move from politics to economics. In the new constellations, economic expertise was not used to steer production and investment for optimal use and allocation of resources, but to create an environment where free markets would reach the same goal.

On the level of enterprises, the concept of democracy vanished, but those of cooperation and employee participation remained. This happened mostly in forms advocated by employers and center-right parties: Participation did not mean making leaders accountable to workers or redistribution of strategic power, but influence on the content, environment and organization of one's own work. The emphasis turned from collective interest representation to individual participation. Operational power was shared but strategic power concentrated—a trend also visible in public administration. Instead of democracy, the modes of governance in working life were legitimized with efficiency, flexibility and competence that would contribute to the common goods of competitiveness and economic growth. In this ideational constellation, which employer representatives in particular had advocated throughout the twentieth century, working life appears as an apolitical sphere, where exertion of power and conflicts of interest are not relevant phenomena. Working life is rather viewed as a harmonious activity where people take care of their functional tasks according to their competence to reach the common good—in other words, they pursue high efficiency to survive in global competition. This entails weakening belief in conflict between capital and labor more generally. The economy is portrayed as a domain of free individuals and their voluntary associations. These collectives face external constraints, but their members are always on the same boat. In this constellation, there are no asymmetric power relations in the economy, and hence no need for democratization.

Material circumstances affected the changes described above, but I want to emphasize the ideational element of perceiving these circumstances. Most political actors, especially leaders and ministers in major parties, adopted new beliefs and practices, because they believed them to be necessary for securing the national interest, welfare and other prestigious values in the globalizing economy. The change was not as much about certain political groups and their ideas gaining an upper hand, but about economic experts adopting new beliefs and convincing politicians. Soon politicians also began to believe that liberalized, marketized and individualized ideas and practices were something voters increasingly desired. For some actors, especially for center-right parties, these principles were also ideologically desirable as opposed to 'regulation,' 'collectivism' and 'socialism,' which were believed to belong to the past. To summarize the analysis of ideational change in the relationship of democracy and the economy, the role of democracy in changing ideational constellations still requires closer examination.

Democracy and the Economy in Neoliberal Capitalism

The mode of thought and governance that has gradually become commonplace in Finland, Sweden and most Western countries since the 1970s corresponds to interpretations of 'neoliberalization.' It can also be conceptualized as the rise of a 'new spirit of capitalism' and a Schumpeterian 'competition state.' As the other side of the coin, the development can be called the decline or crisis of 'democratic capitalism.' Democracy's role in the current neoliberal phase of capitalism is ambiguous but crucial for explaining the weakened explicit connection between democracy and the economy. Some have argued that economic democracy was incompatible with neoliberalism,[1] but to justify this assertion we need to lay out in detail the ideational and conceptual features that cause this incompatibility. Neoliberal capitalism is of course not a monolithic regime, but an analytic generalization of ideas and practices shared widely across countries and political groups. Regardless of whether the beliefs have been adopted as necessities or as desirable values, they have restricted the potential scope of democracy and pushed alternative conceptions to the margins of political thought and practice. This can be viewed as exertion of power: Dominant ideational constellations in the era of neoliberal capitalism promote certain decontested ideas of reality. Sketching out these ideal typical features helps to clarify common beliefs that make it difficult to imagine 'economic democracy' today. These beliefs are often left unexpressed, but they seem to form a rather unquestioned constellation that has conditioned political thought and language in the post–Cold War era.

Interpretations of neoliberal thought as both pro-democratic and anti-democratic have merit, but they refer to different types of legitimation. Neoliberals do often promote free markets as necessary preconditions to democracy or even as democratic in themselves. However, they also advocate hierarchical managerialism and concentrating power in experts to create markets in the first place. Neoliberal and capitalist conceptions of democracy entail applying democracy to the economy neither in the form of strong political regulation nor representation and collective decision-making within economic institutions. The social order can be called a 'democracy,' but this entails the separation of political and economic spheres. Liberal or capitalist democracy usually restricts democracy to the political sphere. It can be realized in issues that are 'public' as opposed to 'private' or concern 'values' as opposed to 'facts.' Therefore, democracy does not have a similar role of legitimating power in the economic sphere as in the political sphere. The economy is considered a private sphere of free individuals, whose regulation—if needed at all—is based on objective knowledge. Portraying economic freedom and free markets as preconditions for political democracy retains the distinction between spheres and renders freedom a more fundamental value than democracy.

However, neoliberal conceptions of society also need democratic legitimation. There are two main strategies for seeking it: (1) regulation by political, democratically elected entities; and (2) identifying economic freedom and free markets as democratic. The latter is done especially by defining the free consumer as a democratic subject and portraying buying as analogous to voting. This constellation associates the concept of democracy with the economic realm but not according to 'one person, one vote.' Instead, market democracy is based on the less egalitarian principle of 'one dollar, one vote.' However, references to this kind of democracy have not been commonly used to define and legitimize free markets in Sweden or Finland. Free markets have been identified more closely with individual freedom, which is not synonymous with democracy despite their conceptual proximity. This conception entails that the economy is a private domain of autonomous individuals, which should not be interfered with democratic politics and collective decisions. Political regulation of the economy may give democratic legitimacy but today comes close to technocratic administration. It is restricted to making markets function better and minimizing harm, for example, by environmental legislation. The ideal is that politics does not intervene with investment and production decisions but only their general terms and conditions based on 'objective' definitions of common good. New modes of economic governance have also assumed the task of creating new markets for previously public goods, such as education, healthcare, and infrastructure. This is a key element that distinguishes neoliberalism from many earlier varieties of liberalism.

The separation of the political and economic spheres and depoliticization of the economy has often been naturalized as the true essence of society. In neoliberal ideational constellations it has had two main legitimations that are more important than democracy: (1) a rationalistic one appealing to objective knowledge and economic necessities, and (2) an openly normative one appealing to individual freedom, whose scope should be extended as far as possible. The former has been more natural for Social Democrats to adopt. However, these legitimations have often supported each other, and the normative one also has rational justifications. Individual freedom is often portrayed as necessary for efficiency, welfare and national interest, whereas more egalitarian images of society are portrayed as unrealistic, leading to decreasing living standards and even totalitarianism. At first sight, normative and rationalistic legitimations thus seem to form a distinct hierarchy, as individual freedom can be legitimized with economic necessities. In many empirical cases, especially in Finland but since the 1970s increasingly also in Sweden, the rationalistic legitimation has indeed been more common. In this conception, the economy figures rather as a domain of necessities and restraints than liberties. The logical conclusion is the need to govern it by 'objective' knowledge and expertise instead of political opinions. This imperative applies to national economies as well as enterprises and makes democracy seem a dubious form of economic governance. Actors advocating governance based on 'economic necessities' may of course follow Hayek and pursue a perfect market where the need for expert rule would be negligible, but this utopia lies in the distant future.

The role of enterprises and their employees in the tension of freedom and necessity is the most ambiguous one. According to a strong narrative that has been used to question too far-reaching forms of enterprise democracy, market competition forces enterprises to find the most efficient practices based on objective knowledge. Hence, employees are also forced to adapt to competition and develop their competences according to fluctuating market demand. This increases their insecurity and restricts their influence on their work. However, according to a more positive neoliberal narrative, enterprises can use their creativity, innovate and find markets for new commodities. Employees, in turn, have nearly unlimited freedom in developing their competences and moving to work for different employers and sectors.[2] But even in this case, enterprises, employees and ultimately capital face the imperatives of developing competences and producing goods that satisfy consumer preferences more efficiently than their competitors do. Therefore, in a neoliberal conception of society, the only truly free agents in the economic sphere are consumers. As Niklas Olsen has suggested, they surpass entrepreneurs as the key subjects of neoliberal thought and its legitimation.[3] The restricted freedom of individuals as employees and entrepreneurs is conceived as being compensated by their freedom as consumers, but this dualism of roles and their conflicting interests also creates major problems. Highly flexible labor markets may be beneficial for consumers but are often harmful for employees, who are one and the same person.

Despite seeming contradictions, freedom and necessity may become compatible in neoliberal conceptions of society. Freedom is the normative starting point and a necessity for reaching individual and common good, but freedom of individuals as consumers is also a source of necessities for collective actors in the economy. It can be interpreted that the free market and its economic power relations are legitimized by economic freedom—and democracy, to a certain extent—in the relations and transactions *between* individuals and organizations in the market. However, in macroeconomic governance that upholds the market as well as in relations *within* organizations that operate and compete in the market, such as enterprises and public offices, the legitimation is based on economic expertise and hierarchy. It is another question as to whether this neoliberal conception represents a realistic interpretation of society. It is clear, however, that the dualism of freedom and necessity leaves little room for rule by the people or collective decisions in the economic sphere.

Neoliberal principles of freedom and necessity lead to critique of collective democratic decisions that restrict markets. Both the normative and rationalistic legitimations are difficult to reconcile with democracy as a historically layered concept, whose key components include the principles of 'rule by the people,' 'one person, one vote,' and leaders' accountability to the people. I argue that these persistent layers of meaning have been among the main reasons for center-right, employer and business representatives abandoning concepts like 'economic democracy' that build an explicit link between democracy and the economy. Even though these groups have used the concepts and at times even succeeded in redefining them, they have expressed strong reservations against their use. The Swedish Conservatives did not use 'economic democracy' but devised their own concept of 'owner democracy,' which referred to distribution of individual ownership rather than collective economic power. The Swedish Employer Confederation SAF stated that enterprises were not an appropriate environment for democracy, which was to remain a political practice. Finnish actors were more willing to use the concepts of democracy but gave them similar content to their Swedish counterparts. The economy was portrayed as a realm of individual choices and objective knowledge, not one of collective decisions or political opinions.

All this suggests that center-right, employer and business representatives had problems with conceptual elements that are nearly inescapable when we talk about democracy. These include especially *power* and *decision-making*. If democracy is applied to economic institutions and understood as 'rule by the people' (as in the Finnish and Swedish translations *kansanvalta* and *folkstyre*) or 'collective decision-making,' it faces the risk of conflicting with historical key components of capitalism: private ownership and accumulation of capital. Collective decision-making has also been difficult to reconcile with the principle of individual freedom, which legitimates capitalist institutions. These contradictions can partly explain why center-right and employer representatives have especially since the 1980s rather been silent about democracy in the economy and working life than sought to define it according to their preferences. Even if they succeeded in conflating democracy with individual freedom, consumer choice and freedom of contract, or with cooperation and participation in workplaces, there is always the risk that the layers of meaning pointing to power, conflict and collective decision-making could be actualized in calls for new reforms. When applied to the economic realm, the concept of democracy always carries the potential of immanent critique and analogy to political democracy.

Furthermore, the fact that economic democracy has always figured as a future-oriented concept instead of describing established states of affairs exemplifies its potential for political mobilization. In the prevailing conception of liberal or capitalist democracy, it is thus safer to seek democratic legitimacy for the social order without extending democracy into all spheres of life. Instead, democracy can be defined according to the formula of 'political democracy + free markets.' It might be possible to include ideas of more evenly distributed private ownership in this constellation, but it has not been as appealing an objective for center-right parties as it was until the early 1990s. Perhaps they do not want to point out downsides in the prevailing capitalist order by admitting the concentration of ownership. Explicit connections between democracy and the economy even in the form of 'owner democracy' are rather avoided. It is also possible that this redescription of democracy was not widely adopted just because it did not include the conventional meanings of power and collective decisions.

Can the Economy be Re-Politicized?

Today's widespread conceptions of democracy often call for pluralism of alternatives,[4] which makes it even more striking that during the last 40–50 years alternatives to the meaning, application and scope of democracy itself have narrowed. It does not seem, however, that the economy is such a neutral or unproblematic domain of knowledge and action that it should be depoliticized and detached from democratic principles and practices. Even if we accept the definition of democracy in a strictly procedural sense and restricted to 'politics,' it is clear that modes of thought and action conceived as 'economic' narrow its scope. Transnational economic elites have great power over democratic politics, and money buys votes even in liberal democracies.[5] Therefore, if we are concerned about the current state of democracy, it is worth reflecting on the potential meanings and realizations of economic democracy in the contemporary world of globalization, digitalization, economic inequality and precarious working life. These reflections could also help to reintroduce the concept in everyday political discourse. This book thus has normative implications, but the aim is not to advocate or condemn any specific historical conceptions of economic democracy. My critique is aimed only at tendencies of removing the concept entirely from the political agenda and permanently delimiting the scope of democracy. Instead, debate on the boundaries of democracy should be a continuous process.

In hindsight, the 1960s and 1970s represent a historical juncture, during which conceptions of the economy being 'political' and legitimations based on concepts like democracy and equality challenged the principles of economic efficiency and freedom as well as the technocratic view of economy. However, in the following decades, a conception of the economy as an apolitical or private sphere strengthened. It entailed governance mainly through markets, with economic experts stepping in when needed. After the early 1990s, it became rare to connect democracy explicitly to the economy and working life in Finland and Sweden. Similar changes had taken place after previous debates on democratizing the economy in the 1920s and 1940s. In these cases, too, the center-right and employers turned down radical reforms, and the left reoriented toward political cooperation. Social democrats turned their attention to 'functional socialism' in the form of social reforms and labor market regulation. However, after the latest phase of debate, the concept of economic democracy has been undermined more profoundly. Previously it was rather pushed into a more distant future as a long-term goal of socialism. In Finland, the concept rarely figures in political language, whereas in Sweden it continues to appear in Social Democratic programs, but as a vague ideal and relic of the past rather than a future-oriented movement concept. In public debate, economic democracy represents demands that were once made but are now forgotten. Depending on the speaker, this is considered a welcome or an unfortunate development.

A significant factor behind the decline in the use of 'economic democracy' is its historical proximity to the concept of socialism—both in the positive images of the left and the negative ones of the right. The decreased legitimacy of socialism since the 1980s also shattered the horizon of expectation and the vision of an alternative social and economic order that were associated with the concept. Socialism was reduced to a system of values, and the concept of economic democracy also suffered from losing its future orientation. It had always referred to a coming social order rather than an existing one, but today it is difficult to imagine what economic democracy could mean in practice. The future has become more contingent, but regarding economic systems, only one alternative seems to remain. Demands for democratic steering, or even for enterprise democracy, seem outdated in a globalized world, where capital can always move to the most profitable locations. Perceived economic necessities created by this dynamic are not absolute or irreversible, but today economic democracy would need to be global in order to have strong impact. However, there has been no political power or will to pursue this goal. International institutions mostly uphold the prevailing regime, although the OECD and IMF have since the financial crisis of 2008 become more critical of neoliberal policies and economic inequalities.[6] The liberal global economy has brought some people unprecedented possibilities for consumption and individual choices, which they want to hold on to. Others, however, must deal with unemployment, poverty, wars, diseases and consequences of climate change.

Since the 1990s, the left has not had the capacity to take up old demands for economic democracy in any Western country. Reform proposals that would have true democratic and decommodifying potential in the global economy are scarce. Parties of the left have largely renounced the concept of socialism and the goal of transforming the economic system and directed their attention to other issues. Their most far-reaching ideas for democratic reforms are related to the ideas of participatory democracy that became prominent in the 1960s. These include practices like participatory budgeting and the traditional idea of employee-owned enterprises. Otherwise the left is more preoccupied with climate change and identity politics. In Finland and Sweden, it also seeks to reform welfare states and ensure their finance by investing in education and innovation policies, fighting tax evasion, and even introducing some version of basic income. These are compatible with individualized politics that are based on identities and single-issue movements rather than collectivism and encompassing societal visions.

The most promising debates for re-politicizing the prevailing economic order and its relation to democracy are those on economic inequality and climate change. The interest of economists and social scientists in the former has produced proposals for stronger regulation of global capitalism. Promising initiatives and reforms for regulating the finance sector and preventing tax evasion have already been made. On the other hand, tackling climate change properly would require such massive global cooperation and re-allocation of economic resources that it has prospects to produce new forms of economic governance in the process.[7] These might become more democratic than the current regime ruled by experts and markets. If substantial reforms are not made globally, it seems entirely possible that populist and nationalist groups will continue to gain power and re-politicize the economy on their own terms, which differ greatly from liberal and leftist ones. Currently, they want to restrict the movement of people and goods, but not of finance capital. If globalization is rolled back and international cooperation weakened as nationalists demand, we might end up with increasing and eventually armed competition over decreasing resources. One might ask the point of talking about economic democracy when even liberal political democracy seems to be in jeopardy. However, it does not seem that liberal democracy can take us very far in remedying the grievances it has contributed to causing.

Abandoning the concept of economic democracy has been a logical but not necessary part of the ideational changes that have taken place in recent decades. It is not impossible to re-politicize the economy and challenge the prevailing conception of democracy by other than populist and nationalist ideas. If economic and enterprise democracy could make their way back to mainstream public and political discourse from their current use in academic and activist circles, what would they look like today? Have all possible principles and institutions already been presented in different historical and theoretical models? Traditional features of the concept already provide many different configurations that could be tried today, but they easily bring us back to the systemic conflict between capitalism and socialism. One possibility would of course be moving again closer to 'socialism'—or at least postwar 'democratic capitalism' with stronger democratic regulation of capital, investment and employment. However, especially if we want to retain a relatively free international trade, this would require global cooperation and perhaps even a global democracy of some kind. Currently, we are drifting further away from these, as the frustration of the 'losers' of globalization and identity-political struggles is channeled into nationalism and protectionism. Moreover, postwar democratic capitalism was based on record-high economic growth and exploitation of natural resources, which renders it a less viable solution in a situation where we should cut down consumption and find ways of living reasonably in a low-growth context. Perhaps a more viable 'democratic capitalism' could be forged by introducing new elements of regulation, such as efficient taxation of socially and environmentally harmful activities, support for people in precarious labor market positions, control of capital and investments, and even radical reforms such as a public monopoly on money creation. But all this would not necessarily entail stronger citizen participation in economic decisions.

Alternatively, if 'economic democracy' is adapted to the prevailing frame of global capitalism and market economy, it seems that possibilities are limited to developing the practices established previously: Moderate regulation of worst inequalities, cooperation and participation in workplaces, small-scale profit-sharing and wealth distribution, and perhaps employee-owned enterprises. To be acceptable to capitalists, these would have to remain in forms that do not create strong collective power centers. But would they be significant democratic reforms? What are the prospects of democratic enterprises adopting other goals than profit, if the logic of transnational capital remains the same and they must compete in the same global market? It seems that to escape capitalist logic, enterprise-level participation needs to be combined with democratic regulation of investment, like in Social Democratic visions before the 1980s.

Even if we develop new participatory practices that prove successful, and if they are combined with democratic economic decision-making on national or global levels, we face the dichotomy of local self-governance and centralized coordination—or participation and representation—that has historically been a key problem for economic democracy and democracy in general. Both left and right parties have always had problems in realizing their ideals of decentralizing power to ordinary citizens. Both groups have often viewed the economy as an apolitical sphere of factual knowledge, where power has rather been given to experts than the people. Leftist solutions in economic planning have drifted toward centralized bureaucracy governed by politicians, civil servants and trade unions, whereas right-wing ideals of economic freedom have resulted in managerialism and plutocracy controlled by capitalists and large corporations.

In recent decades, it has been common to view public bureaucracy as a bigger threat to democracy than private corporate power. This is understandable, as the former is viewed as a part of the 'political' sphere, where the need for democratic legitimation is evident, whereas the latter is a normal feature of the 'economic' sphere. Economic policy has for the past 40 years been increasingly based on the principle of free markets that were supposed to decentralize economic power and disperse wealth. However, the current phase of capitalism includes many centralized traits and entanglements of bureaucracy and plutocracy. In addition to concentration of wealth and power in transnational enterprises and investors, control of economic policy has been concentrated in 'neutral' experts in central banks and ministries of finance. Despite strong rhetoric that has persisted for decades, significant reforms that would increase citizen participation have been scarce in Western countries. This shows how persistent a problem the conflict between common and particular interests is. Seeking a balance between a comprehensive societal view and local concerns is delicate and seems to always require 'bureaucracy' in some form.

An even more difficult problem regarding democracy and its future is the dichotomy of facts and values. The strong tradition of conceiving the economy as a realm of objective knowledge illustrates a conceptual dilemma of democracy: The political sphere and therefore the legitimate scope of democracy are limited by anything that is defined as objective as opposed to values and matters of opinion. The belief 'we cannot vote about facts' is intuitively appealing, but it overlooks the process of how facts are formed. Both facts and values are based on beliefs, which are justified but often uncertain and potentially falsifiable. Besides values, political struggles often concern competing knowledge claims. Distinction between categories is useful in assessing the rational warrant of different beliefs, but if facts are mostly determined outside democracy in expert domains, a space for asymmetric power relations is opened. As the basis of democratic decision-making, we always need as objective and warranted knowledge as possible and experts to form and distribute it. However, the justifications, uncertainties and alternatives of knowledge should be communicated to citizens more clearly. This does not mean moving to radical relativism or a 'post-truth' era where anything goes. Instead, we should have a constant and more open discussion on the boundaries of democracy: Which issues are so decontested that they can be given to experts? When making democratic decisions, we should also be more aware of whether we are basing them on values or facts. For example, we can find some relatively 'objective' beliefs on how to promote economic growth, and the consequences of stronger and weaker growth. In contrast, the question of whether we should prioritize some other values and objectives than growth can ultimately be determined only by making normative judgments. For this task, democratic decision-making is constantly a desirable tool.

Notes

1. Jenny Andersson, *Between Growth and Security: Swedish Social Democracy from a Strong Society to a Third Way* (Manchester: Manchester University Press, 2006), 21–22; Kristina Boréus, *Högervåg: Nyliberalism och kampen om språket i svensk offentlig debatt 1969–1989* (Stockholm: Tiden, 1994), 316–318, 324.
2. For example, Jenny Andersson, *När framtiden redan hänt: Socialdemokratin och folkhemsnostalgin* (Stockholm: Ordfront, 2009), 27–30.
3. Niklas Olsen, *The Sovereign Consumer: A New Intellectual History of Neoliberalism* (Cham: Palgrave Macmillan, 2019), 7–11.
4. For example, Robert A. Dahl, *On Democracy* (New Haven & London: Yale University Press, 2000), 79.

5. Dahl, *On Democracy*, 173–178; Joseph Stiglitz, *The Price of Inequality* (New York and London: W.W. Norton, 2012), 148–172; David Schweickart, *After Capitalism* (Lanham: Rowman & Littlefield, 2002), 105–110; Wolfgang Streeck, *Buying Time: The Delayed Crisis of Democratic Capitalism* (London and New York: Verso, 2014); Colin Crouch, *Post-Democracy* (Cambridge: Polity Press, 2004).
6. For example, Jonathan D. Ostry, Prakash Loungani and Davide Furceri, "Neoliberalism: Oversold?" *Finance & Development* 53, 2 (2016). http://www.imf.org/external/pubs/ft/fandd/2016/06/ostry.htm.
7. *Global Warming of 1.5 °C. An IPCC Special Report.* (Geneva: World Meteorological Organization, 2018) https://www.ipcc.ch/sr15/.

References

Archival Sources

Central Archives for Finnish Business Records, Mikkeli (ELKA)
  Archive of the Central Committee of Finnish Industry
    Meeting minutes
  STK Archive
    Board meeting minutes
    Managing group minutes
The Archives of Salaried Employees, Helsinki
  STTK Archive
    STTK congress protocol 1981
The Labour Archives, Helsinki (TA)
  SAK Archive
    Board meeting minutes
    Congresses
  SDP Archive
    Parliamentary elections
The National Archives of Finland, Helsinki (KA)
  EVA Archive
    CEO's manuscripts
  Meeting minutes
  Employee Representation Committee's Archive
  Participation Systems Committee's Archive

I. Kärrylä, *Democracy and the Economy in Finland and Sweden since 1960*, Palgrave Studies in Political History,
https://doi.org/10.1007/978-3-030-80631-6

Published Sources

Aarnio, Aulis. "SDP:n periaateohjelma ja yhteiskunnan haasteet." *Sosialistinen aikakauslehti* 3/1984, 43–48.

Åberg, Carl Johan. "Att hamna fel." *Tiden* 3/1977, 182–185.

Abrahamsson, Bengt. *Exemplet Jugoslavien och den svenska debatten om löntagarstyre*. Stockholm: Almqvist & Wiksell, 1976.

Act on Cooperation within Undertakings. Säädös 725/1978. *Laki yhteistoiminnasta yrityksissä*. http://www.finlex.fi/fi/laki/alkup/1978/19780725?search%5Btype%5D=pika&search%5Bpika%5D=laki%20yhteistoiminnasta%20yrityksiss%C3%A4.

Act on Personnel Funds. Säädös 814/1989. *Henkilöstörahastolaki*. http://finlex.fi/fi/laki/alkup/1989/19890814?search%5Btype%5D=pika&search%5Bpika%5D=henkil%C3%B6st%C3%B6rahastolaki.

Act on Renewing the Act on Cooperation within Undertakings. Säädös 724/1988. *Laki yhteistoiminnasta yrityksissä annetun lain muuttamisesta*. http://finlex.fi/fi/laki/alkup/1988/19880724?search%5Btype%5D=pika&search%5Bpika%5D=724%2F1988.

Adler-Karlsson, Gunnar. *Funktionssocialism. Ett alternativ till kommunism och kapitalism*. Stockholm: Prisma, 1967.

Aftonbladet.

Alderin, Robert. "Varför Meidnerfond över huvud taget?" *Arbetsgivaren* 10/1978.

Arbetsgivaren.

Bergqvist, Jan. "Arbetarrörelsen och den ekonomiska makten." *Tiden* 9/1973, 546–555.

Bergström, Villy. "Stabiliseringspolitiken." *Tiden* 3/1977, 176–180.

Bergström, Villy and Lennart Låftman. "Misstag i fonddebatten." *Dagens Nyheter* 3 March 1987, 5.

Bildt, Carl. "Åldringens försvar för sitt verk." *Svenska Dagbladet* 22 April 1989, 3.

Bildt, Carl. *Den enda vägen*. Stockholm: Moderata samlingspartiet, 1994.

Bratt, Christian. "Tre skilda nivåer på medbestämmande." *Arbetsgivaren* 20 October 1977.

Bruun, Kettil and Antti Eskola (eds.). *Taloudellinen valta Suomessa*. Helsinki: Tammi, 1969.

Carlshamre, Nils. "Ernst Wigforss: Den osäkre ägardemokraten." *Medborgaren* 16/1964, 8.

Carlsson, Ingvar. "Handlingsviljan socialdemokratins främsta garanti." *Tiden* 2/1966.

Carlsson, Ingvar. "Ett nytt uppdrag för socialdemokratin!" *Tiden* 9/1985, 486–490.

Center Party of Finland. *Keskustapuolueen tavoitteet 1980-luvun alkupuoliskolle*. (1980). https://www.fsd.uta.fi/pohtiva/ohjelmalistat/KESKP/234.

Center Party of Finland. *Kestävän kehityksen ja vapaan ihmisen vuosikymmen. Suomen keskustan ohjelma 1990-luvulle.* (1990). http://www.fsd.uta.fi/pohtiva/ohjelmalistat/KESK/215.

Center Party of Finland. *Kestävän työllisyyden ja yrittäjyyden yhteiskunta.* Suomen Keskustan 65. puoluekokous, Jyväskylä 17.–19.6.1994. http://www.fsd.uta.fi/pohtiva/ohjelmalistat/KESK/246.

Center Party of Sweden. *Centerpartiets program.* Fastställt av centerpartiets riksstämma den 30 juni 1959. https://snd.gu.se/sv/vivill/party/c/p/1959.

Center Party of Sweden. *Valprogram för Centerpartiet.* Antaget vid Centerpartiets riksstämma i Visby 17–19 Juni 1968. https://snd.gu.se/sv/vivill/party/c/v/1968.

Center Party of Sweden. *Handlingsprogram för en utbyggd företagsdemokrati* (1969).

Committee report 1970: A3 *Yritysdemokratiakomitean mietintö.* Helsinki 1970.

Committee report 1972: A6. *Keskittymiskomitean mietintö.* Helsinki 1972.

Committee report 1974: 99. *Yritysdemokratian sovellutuskomitean raportti.* Helsinki 1974.

Committee report 1987: 40. *Tuottava osallistuminen uudistuvassa työelämässä.* Helsinki 1987.

Dagens Nyheter.

Digitala svenska dagstidningar. http://tidningar.kb.se/.

Edin, Per-Olof, Klas Eklund and Hans-Eric Holmqvist. *Detta är Steget! Förslag till löntagarfonder i ATP-systemet.* Stockholm: SAP, 1983.

Edlund, Sten. "Både lagstiftning och avtal behövs för att lösa § 32-problemen." *Fackföreningsrörelsen* 13/1971, 408–411.

Edlund, Sten. "Nej, vi kompromissade inte..." *Fackföreningsrörelsen* 6/1975, 16–17.

Efterord. In *Mitt i steget – Om ägande och inflytande inför 90-talet.* Stockholm: Tidens förlag, 1988.

Ekegren, Bo. *Frihet eller socialism?* Uppsala: Medborgarskolan, 1979.

Eklund, Klas. "Är Keynes verkligen död?" *Tiden* 8–9/1981, 503–513.

Eklund, Klas. "Den tredje vägen – och alternativet." *Tiden* 3/1985, 143–149.

Elinkeinoelämän valtuuskunta (EVA). *Minne menet hyvinvointiyhteiskunta?* Helsinki 1981.

Elvander, Nils. "Håller den fackliga solidariteten?" *Tiden* 9/1984, 536–544.

Elvytyksen linjat. Talouspoliittinen konferenssi 5.–6.9.1977. Helsinki: Valtion painatuskeskus, 1977.

Enström, Axel. "Hur beslut kommer till i ett storföretag." *Tiden* 10/1965, 603–608.

Ersman, Nina. "Kulmen på kampanjen för nyliberalismen." *Svenska Dagbladet* 17 November 1980, part 2, 1.

Expressen.

Fackföreningsrörelsen.
Färm, Göran. "En anpassning till liberalismen." *Aftonbladet* 23 July 1989, 2.
Faxén, Karl-Olof. "Produktivitet och företagsdemokrati." *Arbetsgivaren* 27 August 1971, 4.
Feldt, Kjell-Olof. "Arbete, sparsamhet och hushållning." *Tiden* 4/1980, 223–229.
Feldt, Kjell-Olof. "Löntagarägande och demokrati." *Tiden* 7/1980, 411–418.
Feldt, Kjell-Olof. "S-politiken offensiv mot nyliberalismen." *Tiden* 3/1985, 137–142.
Finnish National library's archive of digitized newspapers. https://digi.kansalliskirjasto.fi/sanomalehti/.
Finnish parliamentary documents 1985, 1989, 1990.
Finnish parliamentary proceedings 1960–1969, 1988, 1989.
Folkpartiet (FP). *Folkpartiets program*. Antaget vid landsmötet i Göteborg 1962. http://snd.gu.se/sv/vivill/party/fp/p/1962.
Folkpartiet. *Företagsdemokrati i utveckling* (1967).
Folkpartiet. *Demokrati och medinflytande* (1969).
Folkpartiet. *Socialliberal kurs*. Stockholm 1972. http://snd.gu.se/sv/vivill/party/fp/p/1972.
Folkpartiet. *Ny kurs för Sverige. Valmanifest inför valet 1985 antaget av Folkpartiets partistyrelse den l juni 1985*. http://snd.gu.se/sv/vivill/party/fp/v/1985.
Folkpartiet. *Valmanifest 88*. Stockholm 1988. https://snd.gu.se/sv/vivill/party/fp/v/1988.
Furåker, Bengt. "Staten som chef." In *Mitt i steget – Om ägande och inflytande inför 90-talet*. Stockholm: Tidens förlag, 1988.
Gardell, Bertil. "Starka krav på ökat inflytande från de anställda." *Fackföreningsrörelsen* 11/1967, 397–399.
Geijer, Arne. "Företagsdemokratin under 1970-talet." *Fackföreningsrörelsen* 4/1971, 99–102.
Greider, Göran. "Nystarta debatten om ekonomisk demokrati!" *Dalademokraten* 5 October 2016, 2.
Hagman, Lennart. "Årtiondet då vi gick med +++++." *Aftonbladet* 9 December 1989, 16–17.
Hammarström, Olle. "Vad den företagsdemokratiska försöksverksamheten gett – och vad den kan ge." *Tiden* 5/1973, 290–292.
Hansson, Per Albin. Speech in the parliament's second chamber, 18 January 1928 (Folkhemstalet). http://www.svenskatal.se/1928011-per-albin-hansson-folkhemstalet/.
Hautala, Arvo. "Yritysdemokratiakomitean mietintö SAK:n näkökulmasta." In *Yritysdemokratia: Demokratian yritys*, edited by Matti Parjanen. Helsinki: Kirjayhtymä, 1970.
Hedborg, Anna. "Jämlikhetsgruppens andra rapport." *Fackföreningsrörelsen* 20/1972, 8.

Helldén, Arne. "Återfinn den "lyckade" reformismen." *Tiden* 6/1983, 339–342.

Hellström, Mats. "Finns det en väg ut ur kapitalismen?" *Tiden* 4/1973, 213–214.

Helsingin Sanomat (HS).

Helsingin Sanomat Aikakone. https://www.hs.fi/aikakone/.

Hermansson, C.H. *Monopol och storfinans: De 15 familjerna*. 3rd edition. Stockholm: Rabén & Sjögren, 1971.

Hermansson, Jörgen. "Steget som kom bort: Om politisk framgång och misslyckande." In *Mitt i steget – Om ägande och inflytande inför 90-talet*. Stockholm: Tidens förlag, 1988.

Herrman, Elving. "Arbetsorganisation och företagsdemokrati." *Fackföreningsrörelsen* 13/1971, 412–415.

Hietala, Harri. *Paikallista sopimista koskeva selvitys*. Helsinki: Työ- ja elinkeinoministeriö, 2015.

Högerpartiet. *Högerpartiets principprogram*. Fastställt av Högerpartiets riksstämma den 4 juni 1956. http://snd.gu.se/sv/vivill/party/m/p/1956.

Högerpartiet. *Egendomsägande demokrati*. Stockholm, 1962.

Högerpartiet. *Konsten att fånga en miljon*. Stockholm, 1964. https://snd.gu.se/sv/vivill/party/m/v/1964.

Holmström, Barry. "I Norge förs den – demokratidebatten!" *Tiden* 2/1985, 98–102.

Iivari, Ulpu. "Sosialidemokratian asema vasemmiston murroksessa." *Sosialistinen aikakauslehti* 4/1990, 8–11.

International Movement for Monetary Reform. https://internationalmoneyreform.org/.

Isaksson, Anders. "SAP inför 80-talet: Ett parti utan inre kompass." *Tiden* 4/1983, 207–210.

Janérus, Inge. "Vildvuxen debatt om företagsdemokrati borde hyfsas från fackligt håll." *Fackföreningsrörelsen* 5/1966, 177.

Janérus, Inge. "Företagsnämndsarbetet – något bättre." *Fackföreningsrörelsen* 26/1968, 385–387.

Janérus, Inge. "Demokrati i företagen." *Fackföreningsrörelsen* 13/1971, 406–407.

Janérus, Inge. "Sopas §32 under mattan – eller avskaffas den?" *Fackföreningsrörelsen* 4/1975, 8–9.

Johansson, Sten. "En plädering för jämlikhetspolitik." *Tiden* 9/1967, 541–553.

Johansson, Sten. "Socialdemokratins roll i samhällsstrukturen." *Tiden* 3/1968, 144–152.

Jäminki, Olavi. "Pääomien ohjaus – yhdentekevääkö?" SA 2/1967, 43.

Kairamo, Aimo. *Tärkeintä on liike: Demokraattisen sosialismin edellytykset ja sosialidemokratian uudet tehtävät*. Helsinki: Tammi, 1989.

Karlsson, Jan O. "Lärdomar från oppositionsåren." *Tiden* 6/1982, 402–408.

Karlsson, Kalle. "Bred uppslutning viktig för ny saltsjöbadsanda." *SAF-tidningen* 13/1982, 3.

Karlsson, Kalle. "Fonderna slår hårdast mot de minsta företagen." *SAF-tidningen* 28/1982, 3.
Koivisto, Mauno (ed.). *Laajempaan kansanvaltaan*. Helsinki: Akateeminen sos. dem. yhdistys, 1960.
Koljonen, Niilo. *Työntekijä ja yritysdemokratia*. Helsinki: Tammi, 1966.
Lag (1976:580) om medbestämmande i arbetslivet https://www.riksdagen.se/sv/dokument-lagar/dokument/svensk-forfattningssamling/lag-1976580-om-medbestammande-i-arbetslivet_sfs-1976-580.
Laine, Jermu. "Kohti aktiivista elinkeinopolitiikkaa." *Sosialistinen aikakauslehti* 2/1968, 38–43.
Laine, Jermu. "1970-luvun talouspolitiikan ydinkysymyksiä." In *Talouspolitiikan ydinkysymyksiä*, edited by Martti Koivisto. Helsinki: Tammi, 1974.
Lappalainen, Heikki. "Mitä "yritysdemokratiauudistus" merkitsee?" *Ahjo* 27 September 1978, 8–9.
Larsson, Allan. "Mot en ny svensk modell?" In *Mot en ny svensk modell*, edited by Per Olof Edin, Olle Hammarström, Bengt KÅ Johansson, Allan Larsson and Björn Rosengren. Stockholm: Tidens debatt, 1988.
Larsson, Gudmund. "Systemskifte – nu framträder modellen." *Tiden* 7/1985, 390–408.
Larsson, Stig. "Deltagande demokrati." *Tiden* 4/1987, 232–238.
Lepage, Henri. *I morgon kapitalism*. Stockholm: Ratio, 1980.
Lifvendahl, Tove. "Socialismen var nära." *Svenska Dagbladet* 9 October 2016, 4.
Lindgren, Anne-Marie. "Vem skall bestämma?" *Tiden* 1/1987, 34–49.
Lindgren, Anne-Marie. "På många plan och i flera former." In *Mitt i steget – Om ägande och inflytande inför 90-talet*. Stockholm: Tidens förlag, 1988.
Lindholm, Berndt. "Den långsamma revolutionen." *Tiden* 7/1984, 394–400.
Lindroth, Bengt. "Vad felas Sverige?" *Tiden* 8/1980, 495–499.
Ljunggren, Olof. *SAFs uppgift. Speech at SAF congress 1980*. Stockholm: SAF, 1981.
LO (Landsorganisationen i Sverige). Congress protocol 1971, 1976, 1991.
LO. *Fackföreningsrörelsen och företagsdemokratin* (1961).
LO. *Kollektiv kapitalbildning genom löntagarfonder* (1976).
LO. *Solidariskt medbestämmande* (1976).
LO. *Det utvecklande arbetet* (1991).
LO. *Ägaransvar och ägarmakt* (2006).
LO-tidningen.
LO and SAP. *Löntagarfonder och kapitalbildning: Förslag från LO–SAPs arbetsgrupp* (1978).
Ludvigsson, Maria. "Vinstfrågan är vår tids löntagarfondsstrid." *Svenska Dagbladet* 20 September 2012, 4.
Lundström, Mats. "Bisamhällets politiska filosofi." *Tiden* 7/1985, 409–413.
Malm, Stig. "Visst begicks misstag." *Dagens Nyheter* 6 December 1993, 4.
Medborgaren.

Meidner, Rudolf, Anna Hedborg and Gunnar Fond. *Löntagarfonder*. Stockholm: Landsorganisation LO, 1975.

Moderata samlingspartiet. *Partiprogram i sammandrag* (1969). http://snd.gu.se/sv/vivill/party/m/p/1969.

Moderata samlingspartiet. *Ägandespridning – som vi ser det* (1978).

Moderata samlingspartiet. *Moderata Samlingspartiets idéprogram antogs vid 1978 års partistämma*. http://snd.gu.se/sv/vivill/party/m/p/1984.

Moderata samlingspartiet. *Valmanifest 1985. Framtid i frihet*. Stockholm 1985. http://snd.gu.se/sv/vivill/party/m/v/1985.

Moderata samlingspartiet. *Valmanifest 1988. Framtidens idéer – 20 punkter för ett bättre Sverige*. http://snd.gu.se/sv/vivill/party/m/v/1988.

Moderata samlingspartiet. *Framtidens idéer – Det bästa för Sverige. Valmanifest 1991*. http://snd.gu.se/sv/vivill/party/m/v/1991.

Moderata samlingspartiet. *Idé och handlingsprogram* (1993).

Molin, Rune. "Ge AP-fonderna frihet att köpa aktier." *Svenska Dagbladet* 31 May 1990, 11.

Myhrman, Johan. "Hur demokratibegreppet missbrukas." *Svenska Dagbladet* 19 May 1983, 2.

National Coalition Party. *Me luotamme ihmiseen ja vapauteen* (1956). https://www.fsd.uta.fi/pohtiva/ohjelmalistat/KOK/115.

National Coalition Party. *Kohti huomispäivän yhteiskuntaa*. Kansallisen kokoomuksen poliittinen toimintaohjelma 1966. https://www.fsd.uta.fi/pohtiva/ohjelmalistat/KOK/90.

National Coalition Party. *Kokoomuksen lähiajan tavoiteohjelma*. Hyväksytty Kokoomuksen puoluevaltuuston kokouksessa Tuusulassa 6.8.1972. https://www.fsd.uta.fi/pohtiva/ohjelmalistat/KOK/80.

National Coalition Party. *Työ- ja ammattiyhdistyspoliittinen ohjelma 1984*. https://www.fsd.uta.fi/pohtiva/ohjelmalistat/KOK/92.

National Coalition Party. *Kansallisen kokoomuksen vaaliohjelma eduskuntakaudeksi 1991–1995*. http://www.fsd.uta.fi/pohtiva/ohjelmalistat/KOK/932.

National Coalition Party. *Programme of Principles. Approved by the Party Conference on 11–13 June 1993*. http://www.fsd.uta.fi/pohtiva/ohjelmalistat/KOK/1033.

National Coalition Party. *Kansallinen Kokoomus Tavoiteohjelma 1995–1999*. Hyväksytty ylimääräisessä puoluekokouksessa 27.–28.8.1994 Espoo. http://www.fsd.uta.fi/pohtiva/ohjelmalistat/KOK/83.

Nicolin, Curt. *Företagandets uppgift. Speech at SAF congress 1980*. Stockholm: SAF, 1981.

Nicolin, Curt. "Mindre makt till herrarna." *Svenska Dagbladet* 11 September 1987.

Nicolin, Curt. "Företagen förtvinar." *Dagens Nyheter* 22 January 1990, 5.

Nicolin, Curt. "Välfärdspolitiken har kommit till vägs ände." *Svenska Dagbladet* 31 August 1990, 3.

Nicolin, Curt. "Marknadsekonomin måste utvecklas i Sverige." *Svenska Dagbladet* 3 August 1991, 3.

Nikula, Anneli. "Kilpailukykyä henkilöstöstrategialla." *Teollisuusviikko* 25 August 1983.

Nordling, Danne. "Meidners löntagarfonder ny väg till socialismen." *Arbetsgivaren* 30/1975, 6.

Nordling, Danne. *Fritt näringsliv eller fondsocialism*. Stockholm: SAF, 1977.

Öhman, Berndt. "Tiden är mogen för industriell demokrati." *Tiden* 3/1974.

Oikeusministeriö. *Kansalaisvaikuttamisen politiikkaohjelman loppuraportti* (2007).

Oikeusministeriö. *Demokratiapolitiikan suuntaviivat. Demokratiapoliittinen keskusteluasiakirja* (2009).

Oksanen, Heikki. "Mietintö taloudellisesta demokratiasta ja tuottavasta osallistumisesta." *Sosialistinen Aikakauslehti* 4/1987, 30–35.

Östergren, Bertil. "En intellektuell revolution." *Svenska Dagbladet* 4 November 1980, 2.

Rhenman, Eric. *Företagsdemokrati och företagsorganisation*. Stockholm: P. A. Norstedt & Söners Förlag, 1964.

Rhenman, Eric. *Industrial Democracy and Industrial Management*. London: Tavistock, 1968.

Palme, Olof. *Politik är att vilja*. Stockholm: Prisma, 1968.

Palme, Olof. "Ett demokratiskt genombrott." *Tiden* 7/1973, 393–397.

Palme, Olof. "Ett rejält nederlag för nyliberalismen." *Tiden* 8/1985, 429–436.

Palonen, Kari. "Sosialistien demokratiasta." *Nykypäivä* 4/1967, 35–36.

Pärnänen, Heikki. "Yritysdemokratia yrityksen teorian valossa." *Ekonomia* 8/1968, 284–286.

Pärnänen, Heikki. "Yritysdemokratia." *Teollisuuslehti* 6–7/1969, 166–169.

Pärnänen, Heikki. "Onko voiton maksimointi yrityksen päätavoite?" *Yritystalous* 13/1969, 22–23.

Pärnänen, Heikki. "Yritysdemokratia: Kenen osallistumista ja mihin?" in *Yritysdemokratia – demokratian yritys*, edited by Matti Parjanen. Helsinki: Kirjayhtymä, 1970.

Pärnänen, Heikki. "Heikki Pärnänen vastaa: STK:n yritysdemokratia-ajattelun arvostelua." *Teollisuuslehti* 4/1970, 128–129.

Paulsen, Roland. "Drömmen om utopin." *Dagens Nyheter* 2 April 2017, 53–55.

Pettersson, Eric. "Demokratin i företagen." *Fackföreningsrörelsen* 6/1964, 186–189.

Pettersson, Lars-Olof and Robert Björkenwall. "Löntagarfonder – och sedan?" *Tiden* 5–6/1984, 336–341.

Program of Kalevi Sorsa's II government, 1977. http://valtioneuvosto.fi/hallitusohjelmat/-/asset_publisher/60-paaministerin-kalevi-sorsan-ii-hallituksen-ohjelma.

Program of Harri Holkeri's government 30 April 1987. https://valtioneuvosto.fi/hallitusohjelmat/-/asset_publisher/64-paaministeri-harri-holkerin-hallituksen-ohjelma.

Program of Paavo Lipponen's first government, 1995. https://valtioneuvosto.fi/hallitusohjelmat/-/asset_publisher/66-paaministeri-paavo-lipposen-hallituksen-ohjelma.

Program of Juha Sipilä's first government. *Ratkaisujen Suomi. Pääministeri Juha Sipilän hallituksen strateginen ohjelma*. Hallituksen julkaisusarja 10/2015. https://valtioneuvosto.fi/hallitusohjelmat/-/asset_publisher/73-stubb-24-6-2014-29-5-2015-.

Puoskari, Pentti. "Haastavampi ohjelma – turvallisuusriski?" *Sosialistinen aikakauslehti* 2/1987, 22–25.

Puoskari, Pentti. *Liike ja linja*. Helsinki: Työväen sivistysliitto, 1989.

Raatikainen, Erkki. "Asenteista." *Sosialistinen aikakauslehti* 2/1967, 3–5.

Raatikainen, Erkki. "Järjellä ja sydämellä." *Sosialistinen aikakauslehti* 4/1968, 3–4.

Raatikainen, Erkki. "Aatteellisuuden paluu." *Sosialistinen aikakauslehti* 1/1969, 3–4.

Regeringens proposition 2001/02:80. *Demokrati för det nya seklet*. https://www.riksdagen.se/sv/dokument-lagar/dokument/proposition/demokrati-for-det-nya-seklet-prop-20010280_GP0380.

Ruin, Olof. "Dagens demokratidebatt." *Tiden* 7/1969, 413–419.

Saarikko, Arvo and Eero Voutilainen. *Johtaminen, yhteistoiminta ja yritysdemokratia*. Helsinki: Weilin + Göös, 1977.

SAF (Svenska Arbetsgivareförening). *Samarbetet i framtidens företag* (1965).

SAF. *SAF-kongressen sammanfattad* (1978).

SAF. *SAF kongressen 1980 sammanfattad* (1981).

SAF. *SAF Congress 1980: Reports, summaries.*

SAF-tidningen.

Sajari, Petri: "Rehn: Liittojen palkkasopimukset kallis virhe." *Helsingin Sanomat* 13 June 2015. https://www.hs.fi/kotimaa/art-2000002831575.html.

SAK (Suomen Ammattiliittojen Keskusjärjestö). *SAK:n yritysdemokratiatyöryhmän mietintö* (1969).

SAK Congress Protocol 1981, 1986.

SAK. *Taloudellinen demokratia ja palkansaajarahastot* (1985).

Sandkull, Bengt. "Medbestämmande utan inflytande." *Tiden* 9/1984, 545–551.

Sandlund, Maj-Britt. "Sverige borde kunna planera." *Tiden* 1/1965, 34–38.

Santalainen, Timo, Eero Voutilainen, Pertti Porenne and Hannes Nissinen: *Tulosjohtaminen*. Helsinki: Weilin + Göös, 1980.

SAP (Sveriges socialdemokratiska arbetareparti). *Program för Sveriges socialdemokratiska arbetareparti*. Stockholm 1897. https://snd.gu.se/sv/vivill/party/s/p/1897.

SAP. Congress protocols 1967, 1968, 1969, 1972, 1975, 1978, 1987, 1990.

SAP. *Valmanifest 1979*. http://snd.gu.se/sv/vivill/party/s/v/1979.

SAP. *Framtid för Sverige* (1981).

SAP. *Valmanifest*. Antaget av socialdemokratiska partistyrelsen den 9 augusti 1985. http://snd.gu.se/sv/vivill/party/s/v/1985.

SAP. *Ett rättvisare Sverige* (1987).

SAP. *Socialdemokraternas partiprogram*. Antaget på socialdemokraternas 31:a kongress 1990. https://snd.gu.se/sv/vivill/party/s/p/1990.

SAP. *Riktlinjer för nittiotalet. Antagna på Socialdemokraternas 31:a kongress* (1990).

SAP. *Till väljarna i höstens val. Valet gäller rättvisan* (1991). http://snd.gu.se/sv/vivill/party/s/v/1991.

SAP. *Valmanifest antaget av den socialdemokratiska partistyrelsen, 1994-08-19*. http://snd.gu.se/sv/vivill/party/s/v/1994.

SAP. *Partiprogram för Socialdemokraterna. Antaget vid partikongressen 2001*. https://snd.gu.se/sv/vivill/party/s/p/2001.

SAP and LO. *Program för aktiv näringspolitik* (1968).

SAP and LO. *Näringspolitiskt program* (1972).

SAP and LO. *Arbetarrörelsen och löntagarfonderna* (1981).

SAP, LO, SSKF and SSU. *Arbetarrörelsens efterkrigsprogram* (1944).

STK (Suomen Työnantajain Keskusliitto). *Laatupiirit Yhdysvalloissa* (1983).

Schager, Nils Henrik. "Regeringen och facket avvaktande till förslagen om löntagarfonder." *Arbetsgivaren* 26/1975.

SDP (Social Democratic Party of Finland). Congress protocols 1969, 1981, 1990.

SDP. *Sosialidemokratian suunta. SDP:n tienviitat 1980-luvulle*. Hyväksytty SDP:n 31. puoluekokouksessa v. 1978 Espoossa. https://www.fsd.uta.fi/pohtiva/ohjelmalistat/SDP/462.

SDP. *Periaateohjelma hyväksytty SDP:n 34. puoluekokouksessa Helsingissä 4.–7.6.1987*. https://www.fsd.uta.fi/pohtiva/ohjelmalistat/SDP/450.

SDP. *SDP:n tavoitteita 1990-luvulle -asiakirja* (1990).

SDP. *SDP:n työelämän uudistamisohjelma*. Hyväksytty puoluehallituksessa 11.6.1998. https://www.fsd.uta.fi/pohtiva/ohjelmalistat/SDP/478.

SDP. *Sosialidemokratian periaatteet*. Hyväksytty XXXVIII puoluekokouksessa Turussa 29.5.1999. http://www.fsd.uta.fi/pohtiva/ohjelmalistat/SDP/451.

Sigfrid, Karl. "Har läkarna "överlöner"?" *Svenska Dagbladet* 2 September 2016, 4.

Södersten, Bo. "Klarar sällan granskning." *Svenska Dagbladet* 30 November 1980, 3.

Sorsa, Kalevi. "Pääomavirtoja ohjattava – tuloja tasattava." *Sosialistinen aikakauslehti* 2/1970, 3–4.

Sorsa, Kalevi. "Tasa-arvo sosialidemokratian tavoitteena ja mittapuuna." *Sosialistinen aikakauslehti* 4/1970, 3–4.

Sorsa, Kalevi. "Sosialidemokratia 1970-luvulla." In *Käytännön sosialidemokratiaa*, edited by Pentti Holappa. Helsinki: Tammi, 1973.

Sorsa, Kalevi. "Luottavasti tulevaisuuteen – kunhan eväät uusitaan." *Sosialistinen aikakauslehti* 1/1991, 8–12.

Sosialistinen aikakauslehti.

SOU (Statens offentliga utredningar) 1968: 7. *Ägande och inflytande inom det privata näringslivet.*

SOU 1975: 1. *Demokrati på arbetsplatsen: Förslag till ny lagstiftning om förhandlingsrätt och kollektivavtal.*

SOU 1979: 8 *Löntagarna och kapitaltillväxten 1.*

SOU 1990: 44. *Demokrati och makt i Sverige.*

SOU 1993: 16. *Nya villkor för ekonomi och politik.*

SOU 2000: 1 *En uthållig demokrati.*

Suhonen, Daniel. "Vi ser en renässans för den demokratiska socialismen." *Dagens Nyheter* 26 March 2016, 6.

Sulkunen, Olavi. "Yritysdemokratiasta yhäkin selkiytymättömiä käsityksiä." *Palkkatyöläinen* 17 June 1971, 14.

Sulkunen, Olavi. "Kansalaisoikeudet työpaikoille!" *Palkkatyöläinen* 19 December 1988, 9.

Sundqvist, Ulf. "Byrokratia, herra vai renki." *Sosialistinen aikakauslehti* 1/1979, 3–4.

Suomen Sosialidemokraatti.

Sutinen, Teija. "Sdp:n Antti Lindtman vaatii radikaalia uudelleenajattelua työmarkkinoille: lisää tulospalkkausta, joka voisi joustaa myös alaspäin." *Helsingin Sanomat* 1 September 2018. https://www.hs.fi/politiikka/art-2000005811708.html.

Svegfors, Mats. "Den återupprättade idyllen." *Svenska Dagbladet* 4 August 1991, 2.

Svenska Dagbladet.

Sveriges Industriförbund and Svenska Arbetsgivareföreningen. *Företagsvinster, kapitalförsörjning, löntagarfonder. Rapport från en arbetsgrupp inom näringslivet* (1976).

Talousdemokratia ry. http://talousdemokratia.fi/.

Tehokas yritys.

Tehostaja.

Teollisuus.

Teollisuuslehti.

Teollisuusviikko.

Tham, Carl. "Idéer från vänster motar nyliberalism." *Tiden* 8/1985, 451–455.

Therborn, Göran (ed.). *En ny vänster.* Stockholm: Rabén & Sjögren, 1966.

Therborn, Göran. "Från konservatism till nya djärva mål." *Tiden* 8/1985, 456–460.

Thorsrud, Einar and Fred E. Emery. *Mot en ny bedriftsorganisasjon: Eksperimenter i industrielt demokrati: fra samarbeidsprosjektet LO/NAF.* Oslo: Tanum, 1969.

Tiden.

Tikka, Seppo. *Pehmeään politiikkaan.* Helsinki: Kirjayhtymä, 1979.

Tobisson, Lars. "Vinsttak steg mot socialism." *Svenska Dagbladet* 22 October 2017, 6.

Towns, Ann. "Demokrati i arbetslivet är en glömd fråga." *Bohusläningen* 15 March 2014, 2.

TVK (Toimihenkilö- ja virkamiesjärjestöjen keskusliitto). *Palkansaajarahastoista puheenollen!* (1984).

Työnantaja.

Vasemmistoliitto. *Ohjelma hyväksytty perustavassa kokouksessa Helsingissä 28.–29.4.1990.* https://www.fsd.uta.fi/pohtiva/ohjelmalistat/VAS/799.

Voutilainen, Eero. *Yritysdemokratia: Yhteistoimintaa yrityksessä.* Helsinki: Tietomies, 1974.

Voutilainen, Eero. "Tulospalkkiot olisivat yhteinen etu." Helsingin Sanomat 1 December 1987.

Wachtmeister, Tom. "Endast Sverige satsar på ökat statligt företagande." *Svenska Dagbladet* 1 August 1990, B6.

Waldenström, Erland. "Vad ont har småspararna gjort?" *Fackföreningsrörelsen* 27/1975, 10–11.

Westermark, Gunnar. ""Målstyrning i samverkan": Plan för ökat medinflytande." *Arbetsgivaren* 17 October 1969.

Widén, Leif. "Det geniala sättet att överta makten." *Svenska Dagbladet* 1 October 1987.

Wigforss, Ernst. *Ekonomisk demokrati.* Stockholm: Natur och kultur, 1948.

Wigforss, Ernst. *Kan dödläget brytas? Dagspolitik och utopi.* Stockholm: Tidens förlag, 1959.

Wigforss, Ernst. "Göteborgsprogrammet." In Ernst Wigforss, *Vision och verklighet* (Stockholm: Prisma, 1967), 19–25.

Wigforss, Ernst. "Utgångspunkter för industriell demokrati." In Ernst Wigforss, *Vision och verklighet* (Stockholm: Prisma, 1967), 26–32.

Wiio, Osmo A. "Yritysdemokratiasta." *Teollisuuslehti* 5/1967, 106–111.

Wiio, Osmo A. *Yritysdemokratia ja muuttuva organisaatio.* Helsinki: Weilin + Göös, 1970.

Yritystalous.

Literature

Alapuro, Risto. "Ulkoinen ja sisäinen: Suomen poliittisen kulttuurin pitkä linja." *Yhteiskuntapolitiikka* 75, 5 (2010): 528–537.

Albert, Michael and Robin Hahnel. *The Political Economy of Participatory Economics.* Princeton: Princeton University Press, 1991.

Andersson, Jenny. *Between Growth and Security: Swedish Social Democracy from a Strong Society to a Third Way*. Manchester: Manchester University Press, 2006.

Andersson, Jenny. *När framtiden redan hänt: Socialdemokratin och folkhemsnostalgin*. Stockholm: Ordfront, 2009.

Andersson, Jenny. *The Library and the Workshop: Social Democracy and Capitalism in the Knowledge Age*. Stanford: Stanford University Press, 2010.

Archer, Robin. *Economic Democracy: The Politics of Feasible Socialism*. Oxford: Oxford University Press, 1995.

Arrhenius, Gustaf. "Politisk och ekonomisk demokrati." In *Tillsammans: En fungerande ekonomisk demokrati*, edited by Bo Rothstein. Stockholm: SNS förlag, 2012.

Åsard, Erik. *LO och löntagarfondsfrågan: En studie i facklig politik och strategi*. Stockholm: Rabén & Sjögren, 1978.

Åsard, Erik. *Kampen om löntagarfonderna: Fondutredningen från samtal till sammanbrott*. Stockholm: Norstedt, 1985.

Aunesluoma, Juhana. *Vapaakaupan tiellä: Suomen kauppa- ja integraatiopolitiikka maailmansodista EU-aikaan*. Helsinki: Suomalaisen kirjallisuuden seura, 2011.

Atkinson, Anthony. *Inequality: What can be Done?* Cambridge (MA): Harvard University Press, 2015.

Bair, Jennifer. "Taking Aim at the New International Economic Order." In *The Road from Mont Pèlerin. The Making of the Neoliberal Thought Collective*, edited by Philip Mirowski and Dieter Plehwe, 347–385. Cambridge (MA): Harvard University Press, 2009.

Ban, Cornel. *Ruling Ideas: How Global Neoliberalism Goes Local*. Oxford and New York: Oxford University Press, 2016.

Belfrage, Claes and Magnus Ryner. "Renegotiating the Swedish Social Democratic Settlement: From Pension Fund Socialism to Neoliberalization." *Politics & Society* 37, 2 (2009): 257–287.

Bell, Daniel. *The End of Ideology: On the Exhaustion of Political Ideas in the Fifties*. New York: The Free Press, 1965.

Berggren, Henrik. *Underbara dagar framför oss: En biografi över Olof Palme*. Stockholm: Norstedts, 2010.

Bergholm, Tapio. *Sopimusyhteiskunnan synty I: Työehtosopimusten läpimurrosta yleislakkoon. Suomen Ammattiyhdistysten Keskusliitto 1944–1956*. Helsinki: Otava, 2005.

Bergholm, Tapio. *Sopimusyhteiskunnan synty II: Hajaannuksesta tulopolitiikkaan. SAK 1956–1969*. Helsinki: Otava, 2007.

Bergholm, Tapio. *Kohti tasa-arvoa: Tulopolitiikan aika I*. Helsinki: Otava, 2012.

Bergholm, Tapio. *Laatua ja vapaa-aikaa. Tulopolitiikan aika II: Suomen ammattiliittojen keskusjärjestö vuodesta 1977*. Helsinki: Suomalaisen kirjallisuuden seura, 2018.

Berman, Sheri. *The Social Democratic Moment: Ideas and Politics in the Making of Interwar Europe*. Cambridge (MA): Harvard University Press, 1998.

Berman, Sheri. *The Primacy of Politics: Social Democracy and the Making of Europe's Twentieth Century*. Cambridge: Cambridge University Press, 2006.

Bevir, Mark. *The Logic of the History of Ideas*. Cambridge: Cambridge University Press, 1999.

Biebricher, Thomas. "Neoliberalism and Democracy." *Constellations* 22, 2 (2015): 255–266.

Biebricher, Thomas. *The Political Theory of Neoliberalism*. Stanford: Stanford University Press, 2019.

Blyth, Mark. *Great Transformations: Economic Ideas and Institutional Change in the Twentieth Century*. Cambridge: Cambridge University Press, 2002.

Blyth, Mark. *Austerity: The History of a Dangerous Idea*. Oxford: Oxford University Press, 2013.

Boas, Taylor C. and Jordan Gans-Morse. "Neoliberalism: from New Liberal Philosophy to Anti-Liberal Slogan." *Studies in Comparative International Development* 44, 2 (2009): 145–152.

Bobbio, Norberto. *Democracy and Dictatorship: The Nature and Limits of State Power*. Cambridge: Polity Press, 1989.

Boltanski, Luc and Ève Chiapello. *The New Spirit of Capitalism*. London and New York: Verso, 2005 [1999].

Boréus, Kristina. *Högervåg: Nyliberalism och kampen om språket i svensk offentlig debatt 1969–1989*. Stockholm: Tiden, 1994.

Brenner, Robert. *The Economics of Global Turbulence*. London and New York: Verso, 2006.

Brown, Wendy. *Undoing the Demos: Neoliberalism's Stealth Revolution*. New York: Zone Books, 2015.

Bruun, Niklas, Pauli Kettunen and Ilkka Turunen. "Industriell demokrati i Norden: Introduktion till det finska delprojektet." In *Industriell demokrati i norden*, edited by Daniel Fleming. Lund: Arkiv Förlag, 1990.

Carlsson, Ingvar. *Så tänkte jag: Politik & dramatik*. Stockholm: Hjalmarson & Högberg, 2003.

Carrington, Damian. "'Historic Breakthrough': Norway's Giant Oil Fund Dives into Renewables." *The Guardian* 5 April 2019. https://www.theguardian.com/environment/2019/apr/05/historic-breakthrough-norways-giant-oil-fund-dives-into-renewables.

Castillo, Greg. *Cold War on the Home Front: The Soft Power of Midcentury Design*. Minneapolis: University of Minnesota Press, 2010.

Cerny, Philip G. *The Changing Architecture of Politics: Structure, Agency, and the Future of the State*. London: Sage, 1990.

Cerny, Philip G. "International Finance and the Erosion of Capitalist Diversity." In *Political Economy of Modern Capitalism*, edited by Colin Crouch and Wolfgang Streeck. London: Sage, 1997.

Childs, Marquis W. *This is Democracy: Collective Bargaining in Scandinavia*. New Haven: Yale University Press, 1938.

Christiano, Tom. "Democracy." In *The Stanford Encyclopedia of Philosophy*, edited by Edward N. Zalta (Spring 2015 Edition). https://plato.stanford.edu/archives/spr2015/entries/democracy/.

Conway, Martin. "Democracy in Western Europe after 1945." In *Democracy in Modern Europe: A Conceptual History*, edited by Jussi Kurunmäki, Jeppe Nevers and Henk te Velde. New York: Berghahn, 2018.

Cornelissen, Lars. "'How can the People be Restricted?': The Mont Pèlerin Society and the Problem of Democracy, 1947–1998." *History of European Ideas* 43, 5 (2017): 507–524.

Crouch, Colin. *Post-Democracy*. Cambridge: Polity Press, 2004.

Crouch, Colin. *The Strange Non-Death of Neoliberalism*. Cambridge: Polity Press, 2011.

Dahl, Robert A. *Preface to Economic Democracy*. Cambridge: Polity Press, 1985.

Dahl, Robert A. *Democracy and its Critics*. New Haven and London: Yale University Press, 1989.

Dahl, Robert A. *On Democracy*. New Haven & London: Yale University Press, 2000.

Dahlström, Edmund. *Klasser och samhällen: Teorier om social skiktning och social integration*. Stockholm: Prisma, 1971.

Dahrendorf, Ralf. *Class and Class Conflict in Industrial Society*. London: Routledge & Kegan, 1959.

Dalgaard, Niels. *Ved demokratiets grænse. Demokratisering af arbejdslivet i Danmark 1919–1994*. Copenhagen: Selskabet til Forskning i Arbejderbevægelsens Historie, 1995.

De Geer, Hans. *Från svenska modellen till Svenskt Näringsliv: Om SAF och den svenska arbetsmarknadens organisering under 1990-talet*. Stockholm: Ratio, 2007.

Diamond, Larry. *The Spirit of Democracy*. New York: Times Books, 2008.

Drucker, Peter F. *The Unseen Revolution: How Pension Fund Socialism Came to America*. New York: Harper & Row, 1976.

Dryzek, John S. *Democracy in Capitalist Times*. New York and Oxford: Oxford University Press, 1996.

Dunn, John. *Setting the People Free: The Story of Democracy*. London: Atlantic Books, 2005.

Edling, Nils. "The Primacy of Welfare Politics: Notes on the Language of the Swedish Social Democrats and their Adversaries in the 1930s." In *Multi-layered Historicity of the Present*, edited by Heidi Haggrén, Johanna Rainio-Niemi and

Jussi Vauhkonen, 125–135. Helsinki: Publications of the Department of Political and Economic Studies 8, 2013.

Edling, Nils. "Multiple Welfare States: Histories of a Keyword." In *Changing Meanings of the Welfare State: Histories of a Key Concept in the Nordic Countries.* Edited by Nils Edling. New York and Oxford: Berghahn, 2019.

Ehrenkrona, Olof. *Nicolin: En svensk historia*. Stockholm: Timbro, 1991.

Ekdahl, Lars. *Mot en tredje väg: En biografi över Rudolf Meidner. I. Tysk flyktning och svensk modell.* Lund: Arkiv förlag, 2001.

Ekdahl, Lars. "Svensk arbetarrörelse på den tredje vägen? Socialdemokratiska vägval under det "korta 1900-talet"." In *Kommunismen hot och löfte: Arbetarrörelsen i skuggan av Sovjetunionen 1917–1991*, edited by Håkan Blomqvist and Lars Ekdahl. Stockholm: Carlsson, 2002.

Ekdahl, Lars. *Mot en tredje väg: En biografi över Rudolf Meidner. II. Facklig expert och demokratisk socialist.* Lund: Arkiv förlag, 2005.

Ekdahl, Lars. "Den fackliga rörelsen mellan två modeller." In *Det långa 1990-talet: När Sverige förändrades*, edited by Anders Ivarsson Westerberg, Ylva Waldemarson and Kjell Östberg. Umeå: Boréa, 2014.

Ekman Jørgensen, Thomas. *Transformations and Crises: The Left and the Nation in Denmark and Sweden, 1956–1980.* New York and Oxford: Berghahn, 2008.

Englund, Peter and Vesa Vihriälä. "Financial Crisis in Finland and Sweden: Similar but not Quite the Same." In *The Great Financial Crisis in Finland and Sweden: The Nordic Experience of Financial Liberalization*, edited by Lars Jonung, Jaakko Kiander and Pentti Vartia, 71–89. Cheltenham and Northampton: Edward Elgar, 2009.

Eskola, Antti. "Sosiologian uudistuminen 1950-luvulla." In *Suomalaisen sosiologian historia*, edited by Risto Alapuro, Matti Alestalo and Elina Haavio-Mannila. Helsinki: WSOY, 1992.

Feldt, Kjell-Olof. *Alla dessa dagar – i regeringen 1982–1990.* Stockholm: Norstedt, 1991.

Fellman, Susanna. "Academic Patriots or Individualistic Entrepreneurs? Finnish Management in a Nordic Perspective." In *The Democratic Challenge to Capitalism: Management and Democracy in the Nordic Countries*, edited by Haldor Byrkjeflot, Sissel Myklebust, Christine Myrvang and Francis Sejersted. Bergen: Fagbokforlaget, 2001.

Foucault, Michel. *Discipline and Punish: The Birth of the Prison.* New York: Pantheon Books, 1977.

Fourcade-Gourinchas, Marion and Sarah L. Babb. "The Rebirth of the Liberal Creed: Paths to Neoliberalism in Four Countries." *The American Journal of Sociology*, 108, 3 (2002): 533–579.

Freeden, Michael. *Ideologies and Political Theory: A Conceptual Approach.* Oxford: Oxford University Press, 1996.

Freedom House. https://freedomhouse.org/.

Friberg, Anna. *Demokrati bortom politiken: En begreppshistorisk analys av demokratibegreppet inom Sveriges socialdemokratiska arbetareparti 1919–1939.* Stockholm: Atlas, 2012.

Fukuyama, Francis. "The End of History?" *National Interest*, Summer 1989, 3–18.

Georgi, Frank. *L'autogestion en chantier: Les gauches françaises et le « modèle » yougoslave (1948–1981).* Nancy: Arbre bleu, 2018.

Gilcher-Holtey, Ingrid. "Political Participation and Democratization in the 1960s: The Concept of Participatory Democracy and its Repercussions." In *Democracy in Modern Europe: A Conceptual History*, edited by Jussi Kurunmäki, Jeppe Nevers and Henk te Velde, 257–273. New York: Berghahn, 2018.

Gilljam, Mikael. *Svenska folket och löntagarfonderna: En studie i politisk åsiktsbildning.* Lund: Studentlitteratur, 1988.

Global Warming of 1.5 °C. An IPCC Special Report. Geneva: World Meteorological Organization, 2018. https://www.ipcc.ch/sr15/.

Glyn, Andrew. "Aspirations, Constraints, and Outcomes." In *Social Democracy in Neoliberal Times*, edited by Andrew Glyn. Oxford: Oxford University Press, 2002.

Glyn, Andrew. *Capitalism Unleashed: Finance Globalisation and Welfare.* Oxford: Oxford University Press, 2006.

Hadenius, Axel. *Medbestämmandereformen.* Stockholm: Almqvist & Wiksell, 1983.

Hahnel, Robin. *Economic Justice and Democracy: From Competition to Cooperation.* New York: Routledge, 2005.

Hancock, M. Donald, John Logue and Bernt Schiller (eds.). *Managing Modern Capitalism: Industrial Renewal and Workplace Democracy in the United States and Western Europe.* New York: Praeger, 1991.

Harris, Howell John. "Industrial Democracy and Liberal Capitalism, 1890–1925." In *Industrial Democracy in America: The Ambiguous Promise*, edited by Nelson Lichtenstein and Howell John Harris, 43–66. New York: Woodrow Wilson Center Press, 1993.

Harvey, David. *A Brief History of Neoliberalism.* Oxford and New York: Oxford University Press, 2005.

Hayek, Friedrich. *Studies in Philosophy, Politics and Economics.* New York: Simon & Schuster, 1967.

Heikkinen, Sakari and Seppo Tiihonen. *Hyvinvoinnin turvaaja: Valtiovarainministeriön historia 3.* Helsinki: Edita, 2010.

Held, David. *Models of Democracy.* 2nd edition. Stanford: Stanford University Press, 1996.

Hilson, Mary. *The International Co-operative Alliance and the Consumer Co-operative Movement in Northern Europe, c. 1860–1939.* Manchester: Manchester University Press, 2018.

Hinnfors, Jonas. *Reinterpreting Social Democracy: A History of Stability in the British Labour Party and Swedish Social Democratic Party.* Manchester University Press, Manchester 2006.

Hirschman, Albert O. *The Rhetoric of Reaction: Perversity, Futility, Jeopardy.* Cambridge, MA and London: Belknap/Harvard University Press, 1991.

Hobsbawm, Eric. *Age of Extremes: The Short Twentieth Century 1914–1991.* London: Abacus, 1995.

Holmén, Janne. "Den demokratiska skolan: Om likvärdighet och delaktighet 1960–2020." In *Demokratins drivkrafter: Kontext och särdrag i Finlands och Sveriges demokratier 1890–2020*, edited by Henrik Meinander, Petri Karonen and Kjell Östberg. Helsinki: Svenska litteratursällskapet i Finland, 2018.

Holmström, Barry. "The Judicialization of Politics in Sweden." *International Political Science Review* 15, 2 (1994): 153–164.

Hugemark, Agneta. *Den fängslande marknaden: Ekonomiska experter om välfärdsstaten.* Lund: Arkiv, 1994.

Hulkko, Kustaa and Jorma Pöysä. *Vakaa markka: Teot ja tarinat.* Jyväskylä: Atena, 1998.

Hyvärinen, Matti. "Valta." In *Käsitteet liikkeessä: Suomen poliittisen kulttuurin käsitehistoria*, edited by Matti Hyvärinen, Jussi Kurunmäki, Kari Palonen, Tuija Pulkkinen and Henrik Stenius. Tampere: Vastapaino, 2003.

Ifversen, Jan. "About Key Concepts and How to Study Them." *Contributions to the History of Concepts* 6, 1 (2011): 65–88.

Irving, Sean. "Limiting Democracy and Framing the Economy: Hayek, Schmitt and Ordoliberalism." *History of European Ideas* 44, 1 (2018): 113–127.

Iversen, Torben. "The Choices for Scandinavian Social Democracy in Comparative Perspective." In *Social Democracy in Neoliberal Times*, edited by Andrew Glyn. Oxford: Oxford University Press, 2002.

Jessop, Bob. "Post-Fordism and the State." In *Post-Fordism: A Reader*, edited by Amin Ash, 251–279. Oxford: Blackwell, 1994.

Jessop, Bob. *The State: Past, Present, Future.* Cambridge: Polity Press, 2015.

Johansson, Anders L. and Lars Magnusson. *LO – 1900-talet och ett nytt millennium.* Stockholm: Atlas, 2012.

Johansson, Joakim. *SAF och den svenska modellen: En studie av uppbrottet från förvaltningskorporatismen 1982–91.* Doctoral dissertation, Uppsala University 2000.

Johnsen, Thore and Ole Gjølberg. "Management of the Norwegian Oil Fund: The Challenges and Costs of Being Ethical." *Beta* 01 (2009): 1–26.

Jonung, Lars, Jaakko Kiander and Pentti Vartia. "The Great Financial Crisis in Finland and Sweden: The Dynamics of Boom, Bust and Recovery, 1985–2000." In *The Great Financial Crisis in Finland and Sweden: The Nordic Experience of Financial Liberalization*, edited by Lars Jonung, Jaakko Kiander and Pentti Vartia. Cheltenham and Northampton: Edward Elgar, 2009.

Judt, Tony. *Postwar: A History of Europe since 1945*. London: Penguin, 2005.

Julkunen, Raija. *Työprosessi ja pitkät aallot*. Tampere: Vastapaino, 1987.

Julkunen, Raija. *Suunnanmuutos: 1990-luvun sosiaalipoliittinen reformi Suomessa*. Tampere: Vastapaino, 2001.

Jyränki, Antero. "Kansanedustuslaitos ja valtiosääntö 1906–2005." In *Eduskunnan muuttuva asema: Suomen eduskunta 100 vuotta*, edited by Antero Jyränki and Jaakko Nousiainen. Helsinki: Edita, 2006.

Kantola, Anu. *Markkinakuri ja managerivalta: Poliittinen hallinta Suomen 1990-luvun talouskriisissä*. Helsinki: Loki-kirjat, 2002.

Kantola, Anu. "Unholy Alliances: Competitiveness as a Domestic Strategy." In *National Policy-Making: Domestication of Global Trends*, edited by Pertti Alasuutari and Ali Qadir. London and New York: Routledge, 2014.

Kantola, Anu and Johannes Kananen. "Seize the Moment: Financial Crisis and the Making of the Finnish Competition State." *New Political Economy* 18, 6 (2013): 811–826.

Kari, Markus. *Suomen rahoitusmarkkinoiden murros 1980-luvulla: Oikeushistoriallinen tutkimus*. Helsinki: Into, 2016.

Karlsson, Sten O. *Det intelligenta samhället: En omtolkning av socialdemokratins idéhistoria*. Stockholm: Carlssons, 2001.

Kauppinen, Liisa. "Yrityksissä yleistyy nyt vanha palkitsemistapa, joka tekee työntekijöistä sijoittajia." *Helsingin Sanomat* 1 July 2019. https://www.hs.fi/talous/art-2000006159032.html.

Kettunen, Pauli. *Poliittinen liike ja sosiaalinen kollektiivisuus: Tutkimus sosialidemokratiasta ja ammattiyhdistysliikkeestä Suomessa 1918–1930*. Helsinki: Suomen historiallinen seura, 1986.

Kettunen, Pauli. *Suojelu, suoritus, subjekti: Työsuojelu teollistuvan Suomen yhteiskunnallisissa ajattelu- ja toimintatavoissa*. Helsinki: Suomen historiallinen seura, 1994.

Kettunen, Pauli. *Työjärjestys: Tutkielmia työn ja tiedon poliittisesta historiasta*. Helsinki: Tutkijaliitto, 1997.

Kettunen, Pauli. *Kansallinen työ: Suomalaisen suorituskyvyn vaalimisesta*. Helsinki: Yliopistopaino, 2001.

Kettunen, Pauli. "Yhteiskunta." In *Käsitteet liikkeessä: Suomen poliittisen kulttuurin käsitehistoria*, edited by Matti Hyvärinen, Jussi Kurunmäki, Kari Palonen, Tuija Pulkkinen and Henrik Stenius. Tampere: Vastapaino, 2003.

Kettunen, Pauli. "The Tension between the Social and the Economic." In *The Road to Prosperity: An Economic History of Finland*, edited by Jari Eloranta, Jukka Jalava and Jari Ojala, 285–313. Helsinki: Suomalaisen Kirjallisuuden Seura, 2006.

Kettunen, Pauli. *Globalisaatio ja kansallinen me: Kansallisen katseen historiallinen kritiikki*. Tampere: Vastapaino, 2008.

Kettunen, Pauli. "The Transnational Construction of National Challenges: The Ambiguous Nordic Model of Welfare and Competitiveness." In *Beyond Welfare State Models: Transnational historical perspectives on social policy*, edited by Pauli Kettunen and Klaus Petersen. Cheltenham: Edward Elgar, 2011.

Kettunen, Pauli: *Historia petollisena liittolaisena: Näkökulmia työväen, työelämän ja hyvinvointivaltion historiaan*. Helsinki: Työväen historian ja perinteen tutkimuksen seura, 2015.

Kettunen, Pauli. *Työväenkysymyksestä henkilöstöpolitiikkaan: Liiketoiminnan sosiaalinen ulottuvuus – tapaus Partek*. Helsinki: Työväen historian ja perinteen tutkimuksen seura, 2018.

Kiander, Jaakko. *Laman opetukset: Suomen 1990-luvun kriisin syyt ja seuraukset*. Helsinki: Government Institute for Economic Research, 2001.

Kiander, Jaakko. "1930-luvun pulakausi ja 1990-luvun talouskriisi: Talouspolitiikan ja taloudellisen ajattelun vertailua." In *Lamakirja: Näkökulmia 1990-luvun talouskriisiin ja sen historiallisiin konteksteihin*, edited by Helena Blomberg, Matti Hannikainen and Pauli Kettunen. Turku: Kirja-Aurora, 2002.

Kiander, Jaakko and Pentti Vartia. *Suuri lama: Suomen 1990-luvun kriisi ja talouspoliittinen keskustelu*. Helsinki: Taloustieto, 1998.

Knudsen, Herman. *Employee Participation in Europe*. London: Sage, 1995.

Kocka, Jürgen. "Introduction." In *Capitalism: The Reemergence of a Historical Concept*, edited by Jürgen Kocka and Marcel van der Linden. London and New York: Bloomsbury Academic, 2016.

Koroma, Johannes. *Suomalaisten hyvinvointia rakentamassa: Teollisuuden keskusliiton historia*. Helsinki: Suomalaisen kirjallisuuden seura, 2015.

Korpi, Walter. *The Working Class in Welfare Capitalism: Work, Unions and Politics in Sweden*. London: Routledge & Kegan Paul, 1978.

Koselleck, Reinhart. "Introduction and Prefaces to the Geschichtliche Grundbegriffe." *Contributions to the History of Concepts* 6, 1 (2011) [1972]: 1–37.

Koselleck, Reinhart. "Social History and Begriffsgeschichte." In *History of Concepts: Comparative Perspectives*, edited by Iain Hampsher-Monk, Karin Tilmans and Frank van Vree. Amsterdam: Amsterdam University Press, 1998.

Kosonen, Pekka. *Pohjoismaiset mallit murroksessa*. Tampere: Vastapaino, 1998.

Kuisma, Markku. *Kylmä sota, kuuma öljy: Neste, Suomi ja kaksi Eurooppaa 1948–1979*. Porvoo: WSOY, 1997.

Kuisma, Markku. *Valtion yhtiöt: Nousu ja tuho*. Helsinki: Siltala, 2016.

Kujala, Antti. *Paperiliiton historia 1906–2005: Paperiteollisuuden työmarkkinasuhteet ja suomalainen yhteiskunta*. Helsinki: Paperiliitto Ry, 2006.

Kuokkanen, Anna. *Johtamisen ihmissuhdekoulukunta Suomessa: Työntekijäkeskeiset johtamisopit suomalaisen työelämän muutoksessa*. Helsinki: Työterveyslaitos, 2015.

Kurunmäki, Jussi. "'Nordic Democracy' in 1935: On the Finnish and Swedish Rhetoric of Democracy." In *Rhetorics of Nordic Democracy*, edited by Jussi Kurunmäki and Johan Strang. Helsinki: Finnish Literature Society, 2010.

Kurunmäki, Jussi and Johan Strang. "Introduction: 'Nordic Democracy' in a World of Tensions." In *Rhetorics of Nordic Democracy*, edited by Jussi Kurunmäki and Johan Strang. Helsinki: Finnish Literature Society, 2010.

Kurunmäki, Jussi, Jeppe Nevers and Henk te Velde. "Introduction." In *Democracy in Modern Europe: A Conceptual History*, edited by Jussi Kurunmäki, Jeppe Nevers and Henk te Velde, 1–11. New York: Berghahn, 2018.

Kyntäjä, Timo. *Tulopolitiikka Suomessa: Tulopoliittinen diskurssi ja instituutiot 1960-luvulta 1990-luvun kynnykselle*. Helsinki: Gaudeamus, 1993.

Kärenlampi, Paavo. *Taistelu kouludemokratiasta: Kouludemokratian aalto Suomessa*. Helsinki: Suomen Historiallinen Seura, 1999.

Kärrylä, Ilkka. "Kansallinen etu demokratian rajoituksena: Suomalaisten työnantajien retoriikka 1960- ja 1970-lukujen yritysdemokratiakeskustelussa." *Historiallinen aikakauskirja* 114, 4 (2016): 445–457.

Kärrylä, Ilkka. "A Cautionary Tale: Reception of the Swedish Wage-Earner Fund Debate in Finland." *Työväentutkimus* 34 (2020): 21–37.

Kärrylä, Ilkka. "National Interest as a Limit to Democracy: The Rhetoric of Finnish and Swedish Employers in the Debates on 'Enterprise Democracy' during the 1960s and 1970s," in *Nationalism and Democracy in the Welfare State*. Edited by Pauli Kettunen, Saara Pellander and Miika Tervonen. Cheltenham: Edward Elgar, 2022 [forthcoming].

Kärrylä, Ilkka. "Concepts, Beliefs and their Constellations: A Proposal for Analytical Categories in the Study of Human Thought." *Contributions to the History of Concepts* 17 (2022) [forthcoming].

Kääriäinen, Seppo. *Sitä niittää, mitä kylvää: Keskustan strategiset valinnat 1964–2001*. Jyväskylä: Gummerus, 2002.

Lappalainen, Heikki. "Yritysdemokratiasta YT-lakiin: Yritysdemokratiakeskustelu Suomessa 1970-luvulla." *Työelämän tutkimus* 1, 2 (2003): 158–161.

Lavelle, Ashley. *The Death of Social Democracy: Political Consequences in the 21st Century*. Farnham: Ashgate, 2008.

Lewin, Leif. *Planhushållningsdebatten*. Stockholm: Almqvist & Wiksell, 1967.

Lichtenstein, Nelson and Howell John Harris (eds.). *Industrial Democracy in America: The Ambiguous Promise*. New York: Woodrow Wilson Center Press, 1993.

Lilja, Kari. *Työntekijöiden osallistuminen hallintoon teollisuusyrityksissä: Tutkimus työnantajapuolen toiminnan kehityksestä*. Helsinki: Helsingin kauppakorkeakoulun julkaisuja B-22, 1977.

Lilja, Kari. "Henkilöstöhallinnon ammattikäytännön kehityspiirteitä Suomessa." *Hallinnon tutkimus* 16, 3 (1987): 185–194.

Lindberg, Henrik Malm and Stig-Björn Ljunggren. *Från jämlikhet till effektivitet: Om lärande socialdemokrati under 1980-talet*. Stockholm: Hjalmarson & Högberg, 2014.

Lindvall, Johannes. *The Politics of Purpose: Swedish Macroeconomic Policy after the Golden Age*. Gothenburg: Gothenburg University, 2004.

Lindvall, Johannes and Bo Rothstein. "Sweden: The Fall of the Strong State." *Scandinavian Political Studies* 29, 1 (2006): 47–63.

Lipponen, Paavo. *Järki voittaa: Suomalainen identiteetti globalisaation aikakaudella*. Helsinki: Otava, 2008.

Lipponen, Paavo. *Muistelmat 1*. Helsinki: WSOY, 2009.

Ljunggren, Stig-Björn. *Folkhemskapitalismen: Högerns programutveckling under efterkrigstiden*. Stockholm: Tidens förlag, 1992.

Logue, John. "Democratic Theory and Atheoretical Democracy: Reflections on Building Democratic Enterprises in the American Economy." In *Managing Modern Capitalism: Industrial Renewal and Workplace Democracy in the United States and Western Europe*, edited by M. Donald Hancock, John Logue and Bernt Schiller. New York: Praeger, 1991.

Lukes, Steven. "The Grand Dichotomy of the Twentieth Century." In *Cambridge History of 20th Century Political Thought*, edited by Terence Ball and Richard Bellamy. Cambridge: Cambridge University Press, 2003.

Lundberg, Bengt. *Jämlikhet? Socialdemokratin och jämlikhetsbegreppet*. Lund: Dialog, 1979.

Lundberg, Urban. *Juvelen i kronan: Socialdemokraterna och den allmänna pensionen*. Stockholm: Hjalmarson & Högberg, 2003.

Lundh, Christer. *Den svenska debatten om industriell demokrati 1919–1924: 1. Debatten i Sverige*. Lund: Studentlitteratur, 1987.

Lundh, Christer. *Den svenska debatten om industriell demokrati 1919–1924: 2. Utländska inspirationskällor*. Lund: Studentlitteratur, 1989.

Lundh, Christer. *Spelets regler: Institutioner och lönebildning på den svenska arbetsmarknaden 1850–2000*. Stockholm: SNS förlag, 2002.

Magnusson, Lars. *Sveriges ekonomiska historia*. Stockholm: Norstedts, 2010.

Mair, Peter. *Ruling the Void: The Hollowing of Western Democracy*. London and New York: Verso, 2013.

Majander, Mikko. "SDP:n ensimmäinen periaate- ja puolueohjelma Forssan ohjelman merkitys Suomen kehittämisessä." In *Vasemmiston tulevaisuus*, edited by Pirjo Alijärvi, Hildur Boldt, Ismo Kainulainen and Katri Söder. Helsinki: Into, 2014.

Mansner, Markku. *Suomalaista yhteiskuntaa rakentamassa: Suomen Työnantajain Keskusliitto 1940–1956*. Helsinki: Teollisuuden kustannus, 1984.

Mansner, Markku. *Suomalaista yhteiskuntaa rakentamassa: Suomen Työnantajain Keskusliitto 1956–1982*. Helsinki: Teollisuuden kustannus, 1990.

Mansner, Markku. *Suomalaista yhteiskuntaa rakentamassa: Suomen työnantajain keskusliitto 1980–1992*. Helsinki: Elinkeinoelämän keskusliitto EK, 2005.

Marklund, Carl. "Sharing Values and Shaping Values: Sweden, 'Nordic Democracy' and the American Crisis of Democracy." In *Rhetorics of Nordic Democracy*, edited by Jussi Kurunmäki and Johan Strang. Helsinki: Finnish Literature Society, 2010.

Marttila, Jouko. *Hillitty markkinatalous: Kokoomuksen ja SDP:n talouspoliittinen lähentyminen ja hallitusyhteistyö 1980-luvulla*. Jyväskylä: Docendo, 2016.

Mattila, Aarne. *Kunnat työmarkkinapolitiikassa: Kunnallinen työmarkkinalaitos 1970–2000*. Helsinki: Kunnallinen työmarkkinalaitos, 2000.

Meidner, Rudolf. *Spelet om löntagarfonder*. Stockholm: Atlas, 2005.

Meinander, Henrik. "Det långa 1900-talet." In *Demokratins drivkrafter: Kontext och särdrag i Finlands och Sveriges demokratier 1890–2020*, edited by Henrik Meinander, Petri Karonen and Kjell Östberg. Helsinki: Svenska litteratursällskapet i Finland, 2018.

Mickelsson, Rauli. *Samanlaiset ja erilaiset puolueet: Retoriikka- ja diskurssianalyyttinen tutkimus kokoomuslaisten ja sosiaalidemokraattien jäsenlehdissä ilmaisemista käsityksistä omista puolueistaan vuosina 1965–1995*. Turku: University of Turku, 1999.

Milanovic, Branko. *Global Inequality: A New Approach for the age of Globalization*. Cambridge, MA: Belknap Press of Harvard University Press, 2016.

Mill, John Stuart. *Principles of Political Economy with Some of their Applications to Social Philosophy*. Kitchener: Batoche, 2001 [1848].

Mirowski, Philip. "Postface: Defining Neoliberalism." In *The Road from Mont Pèlerin: The Making of the Neoliberal Thought Collective*, edited by Dieter Plehwe and Philip Mirowski. Cambridge, MA and London: Harvard University Press, 2009.

Mirowski, Philip. *Never Let a Serious Crisis Go to Waste: How Neoliberalism Survived the Financial Meltdown*. London and New York: Verso, 2013.

Montgomery, David. "Industrial Democracy or Democracy in Industry? The Theory and Practice of the Labor Movement, 1870–1925." In *Industrial Democracy in America: The Ambiguous Promise*, edited by Nelson Lichtenstein and Howell John Harris. New York: Woodrow Wilson Center Press, 1993.

Moschonas, Gerassimos. *In the Name of Social Democracy: The Great Transformation: 1945 to Present*. London and New York: Verso, 2002.

Moyn, Samuel. *The Last Utopia: Human Rights in History*. Cambridge, MA: Belknap Press of Harvard University Press, 2010.

Moyn, Samuel. *Not Enough: Human Rights in an Unequal World*. Cambridge, MA: Belknap Press of Harvard University Press, 2018.

Mudde, Cas and Cristóbal Rovira Kaltwasser. "Populism: Corrective *and* Threat to Democracy." In *Populism in Europe and the Americas: Threat or Corrective for Democracy?* edited by Cas Mudde and Cristóbal Rovira Kaltwasser. Cambridge: Cambridge University Press, 2012.

Mudge, Stephanie L. *Leftism Reinvented: Western Parties from Socialism to Neoliberalism.* Cambridge, MA: Harvard University Press, 2018.

Müller, Jan-Werner. *Contesting Democracy: Political Ideas in Twentieth Century Europe.* New Haven and London: Yale University Press, 2011.

Müller, Jan-Werner. *What is Populism?* Philadelphia: University of Pennsylvania Press, 2016.

Müller-Jentsch, Walther. "Formation, Development and Current State of Industrial Democracy in Germany." *Transfer: European Review of Labour and Research* 22, 1 (2016): 45–62.

Mykkänen, Juri. "Kuka päättää hyvinvointimallin tulevaisuudesta?" In *Kilpailuvaltion kyydissä: Suomen hyvinvointimallin tulevaisuus*, edited by Johannes Kananen. Helsinki: Gaudeamus, 2017.

Nevalainen, Pasi and Ville Yliaska. "From State-owned Smokestacks to Post-industrial Dreams: The Finnish Government in Business, 1970–2010." *Business History* 62 (2020). https://doi.org/10.1080/00076791.2020.1842874.

Nilsson, Torbjörn. *Mellan arv och utopi: Moderata vägval under hundra år, 1904–2004.* Stockholm: Santérus, 2004.

Nilsson, Torbjörn. *Hundra år av svensk politik.* Malmö: Gleerups, 2009.

Nilsson, Torbjörn. "Nyliberalismens spöke och Moderaternas politik." In *Det långa 1990-talet: När Sverige förändrades*, eited by Anders Ivarsson Westerberg, Ylva Waldemarson and Kjell Östberg. Umeå: Boréa, 2014.

Okkonen, Ville. *Peruskoulua vastaan: Yksityisoppikoulut ja yhteiskuntajärjestys 1966–1975.* Doctoral dissertation. University of Turku 2017.

Olsen, Gregg M. *The Struggle for Economic Democracy in Sweden.* Aldershot and Brookfield: Avebury, 1992.

Olsen, Niklas. "A Second-Hand Dealer in Ideas: Christian Gandil and Scandinavian Configurations of European Neoliberalism, 1945–1970." In *Re-inventing Western Civilisation: Transnational Reconstructions of Liberalism in Europe in the Twentieth Century*, edited by Hagen Schulz-Forberg and Niklas Olsen. Newcastle upon Tyne: Cambridge Scholars Publishing, 2014.

Olsen, Niklas. *The Sovereign Consumer: A New Intellectual History of Neoliberalism.* Cham: Palgrave Macmillan, 2019.

Östberg, Kjell. *1968 – när allting var i rörelse.* Stockholm: Prisma, 2002.

Östberg, Kjell. *När vinden vände: Olof Palme 1969–1986.* Stockholm: Leopard, 2009.

Östberg, Kjell. "Politikens förändrade villkor." In *Det långa 1990-talet: När Sverige förändrades*, edited by Anders Ivarsson Westerberg, Ylva Waldemarson and Kjell Östberg. Umeå: Boréa, 2014.

Östberg, Kjell. "När ingen längre kokar kaffe – eller vad har hänt folkrörelsepartierna?" In *Demokratins drivkrafter: Kontext och särdrag i Finlands och Sveriges demokratier 1890–2020*, edited by Henrik Meinander, Petri Karonen and Kjell Östberg. Helsinki: Svenska litteratursällskapet i Finland, 2018.

Ostry, Jonathan D., Prakash Loungani and Davide Furceri. "Neoliberalism: Oversold?" *Finance & Development* 53, 2 (2016). http://www.imf.org/external/pubs/ft/fandd/2016/06/ostry.htm.

Outinen, Sami. *Sosiaalidemokraattien tie talouden ohjailusta markkinareaktioiden ennakointiin: Työllisyys sosiaalidemokraattien politiikassa Suomessa 1975–1998*. Helsinki: Into, 2015.

Outinen, Sami. "From Steering Capitalism to Seeking Market Acceptance: Social Democrats and Employment in Finland, 1975–1998." *Scandinavian Journal of History* 42, 4 (2017): 389–413.

Paavonen, Tapani. "Talouden kehitys ja talouspolitiikka hyvinvointivaltion kaudella." In *Eduskunta hyvinvointivaltion rakentajana: Suomen eduskunta 100 vuotta*, edited by Tapani Paavonen and Olli Kangas. Helsinki: Edita, 2006.

Paavonen, Tapani. *Vapaakauppaintegraation kausi: Suomen suhde Länsi-Euroopan integraatioon FINN-EFTAsta EC-vapaakauppaan*. Helsinki: Suomalaisen kirjallisuuden seura, 2008.

Palonen, Kari. "Demokratiapolitiikka – demokratian epäpolitisointia. Reunahuomautuksia oikeusministeriön keskusteluasiakirjaan "Demokratiapolitiikan suuntaviivat"." *Politiikka* 51, 2 (2009): 146–150.

Peck, Jamie. *Constructions of Neoliberal Reason*. Oxford: Oxford University Press, 2010.

Peck, Jamie. "Explaining (with) Neoliberalism." *Territory, Politics, Governance* 1, 2 (2013): 132–157.

Pekkarinen, Jukka. "Keynesianism and the Scandinavian Models of Economic Policy." In *The Political Power of Economic Ideas: Keynesianism across Nations*, edited by Peter A. Hall. Princeton: Princeton University Press, 1989.

Pekkarinen, Jukka and Juhana Vartiainen. *Suomen talouspolitiikan pitkä linja*. Helsinki: WSOY, 1993.

Perelman, Chaïm and Lucie Olbrechts-Tyteca. *The New Rhetoric: A Treatise on Argumentation*. Notre Dame and London: University of Notre Dame Press, 1969.

Piketty, Thomas. *Capital in the Twenty-First Century*. Cambridge, MA: Belknap Press of Harvard University Press, 2014.

Plehwe, Dieter. "Introduction." In *The Road from Mont Pèlerin: The Making of the Neoliberal Thought Collective*, edited by Dieter Plehwe and Philip Mirowski. Cambridge, MA and London: Harvard University Press, 2009.

Polanyi, Karl. *The Great Transformation: The Political and Economic Origins of Our Time*. Boston: Beacon Press, 1971 [1944].

Pontusson, Jonas. *The Limits of Social Democracy: Investment Politics in Sweden*. Ithaca: Cornell University Press, 1992.

Pontusson, Jonas and Sarosh Kuruvilla. "Swedish Wage-earner Funds: An Experiment in Economic Democracy." *Industrial and Labor Relations Review* 45, 4 (1992): 779–791.

Pontusson, Jonas and Peter Swenson. "Labor Markets, Production Strategies, and Wage Bargaining Institutions: The Swedish Employer Offensive in Comparative Perspective." *Comparative Political Studies* 29, 2 (1996): 223–250.

Popper, Karl. *The Open Society and its Enemies*. London: Routledge, 2002 [1945].

Przeworski, Adam. *Capitalism and Social Democracy*. Cambridge: Cambridge University Press, 1985.

Przeworski, Adam. "How Many Ways Can Be Third?" In *Social Democracy in Neoliberal Times*, edited by Andrew Glyn. Oxford: Oxford University Press, 2002.

Puhakka, Sirpa. *Vasemmistoliiton synty*. Helsinki: Into, 2015.

Puoskari, Pentti. *Väärää politiikkaa suuren muuton vuosina? Virolaisen ja Paasion hallitusten elinkeino- ja rakennepolitiikka 1964–1968*. Joensuu: University of Eastern Finland, 2013.

Rentola, Kimmo. *Vallankumouksen aave: Vasemmisto, Beljakov ja Kekkonen 1970*. Helsinki: Otava, 2005.

Rinta-Tassi, Osmo. *Kansanvaltuuskunta punaisen Suomen hallituksena*. Helsinki: Opetusministeriö, 1986.

Rodgers, Daniel T. *Work Ethic in Industrial America 1850–1920*. Chicago and London: University of Chicago Press, 1978.

Rodgers, Daniel T. *Age of Fracture*. Cambridge, MA & London: Belknap Press of Harvard University Press, 2011.

Rogers, Joel and Wolfgang Streeck (eds.). *Works Councils: Consultation, Representation, and Cooperation in Industrial Relations*. Chicago and London: University of Chicago Press, 1995.

Rogers, Joel and Wolfgang Streeck. "The Study of Works Councils: Concepts and Problems." In *Works Councils: Consultation, Representation, and Cooperation in Industrial Relations*, edited by Joel Rogers and Wolfgang Streeck. Chicago and London: University of Chicago Press, 1995.

Rose, Nikolas. *Powers of Freedom: Reframing Political Thought*. Cambridge: Cambridge University Press, 1999.

Rothstein, Bo. "Ekonomisk demokrati? Reflexioner kring en borttappad diskussion." In *Tillsammans: En fungerande ekonomisk demokrati*, edited by Bo Rothstein, 9–28. Stockholm: SNS förlag, 2012.

Ryner, J. Magnus. *Capitalist Restructuring, Globalisation and the Third Way: Lessons from the Swedish Model*. London and New York: Routledge, 2002.

Saari, Juho. "Suomalainen konsensus: Korpilammen konferenssi (-77) käännekohtana." *Yhteiskuntapolitiikka* 75, 5 (2010): 469–485.

Sassoon, Donald. *One Hundred Years of Socialism: The West European Left in the Twentieth Century*. London: Fontana Press, 1996.

Savtschenko, Ritva. *Kompuroiden korporatismissa: Eheytyneen SAK:n ristipaineet suomalaisessa korporatismissa 1968–1978*. Doctoral dissertation, University of Helsinki 2015.

Sayer, Andrew. *Why We Can't Afford the Rich*. Bristol: Policy Press, 2015.

Schäfer, Joachim. *Från tillväxt till trygghet: Tio års debatt om strukturpolitikens mål och medel*. Stockholm: Almqvist & Wiksell, 1984.

Schiller, Bernt. *"Det förödande 70-talet": SAF och medbestämmandet 1965–1982*. Stockholm: Arbetsmiljöfonden, 1988.

Schiller, Bernt "Workplace Democracy: The Dual Roots of Worker Participation." In *Managing Modern Capitalism: Industrial Renewal and Workplace Democracy in the United States and Western Europe*, edited by M. Donald Hancock, John Logue and Bernt Schiller. New York: Praeger, 1991.

Schulz-Forberg, Hagen. "Laying the Groundwork: The Semantics of Neoliberalism in the 1930s." In *Re-inventing Western Civilisation: Transnational Reconstructions of Liberalism in Europe in the Twentieth Century*, edited by Hagen Schulz-Forberg and Niklas Olsen, 13–39. Newcastle upon Tyne: Cambridge Scholars Publishing, 2014.

Schulz-Forberg, Hagen and Bo Stråth. *The Political History of European Integration: The Hypocrisy of Democracy-through-market*. Abingdon & New York: Routledge, 2010.

Schweickart, David. *After Capitalism*. Lanham: Rowman & Littlefield, 2002.

Sejersted, Francis. "Capitalism and Democracy: A Comparison between Norway and Sweden." In *The Democratic Challenge to Capitalism: Management and Democracy in the Nordic Countries*, edited by Haldor Byrkjeflot, Sissel Myklebust, Christine Myrvang and Francis Sejersted. Bergen: Fagbokforlaget, 2001.

Sejersted, Francis. *The Age of Social Democracy: Norway and Sweden in the Twentieth Century*. Princeton: Princeton University Press, 2011 [2005].

Siisiäinen, Martti. *Suomalainen protesti ja yhdistykset*. Helsinki: Tutkijaliitto, 1990.

Simonson, Birger. *Arbetarmakt och näringspolitik: LO och inflytandefrågorna 1961–1982*. Stockholm: Arbetsmiljöfonden, 1988.

Sjöberg, Stefan. *Löntagarfondsfrågan – En hegemonisk vändpunkt: En marxistisk analys*. Uppsala: Universitetstryckeriet, 2003.

Skinner, Quentin. *Visions of Politics I: Regarding Method*. Cambridge: Cambridge University Press, 2002.

Slobodian, Quinn. *Globalists: The End of Empire and the Birth of Neoliberalism*. Cambridge, MA: Harvard University Press, 2018.

Smolander, Jyrki. *Suomalainen oikeisto ja "kansankoti": Kansallisen Kokoomuksen suhtautuminen pohjoismaiseen hyvinvointivaltiomalliin jälleenrakennuskaudelta konsensusajan alkuun*. Helsinki: Suomalaisen kirjallisuuden seura, 2000.

Soikkanen, Hannu. *Kohti kansanvaltaa 1: Suomen Sosialidemokraattinen puolue 75 vuotta, 1899–1937*. Helsinki: Suomen Sosialidemokraattinen puolue, 1975.

Soikkanen, Hannu. *Kohti kansanvaltaa 3: SDP 1944–1952*. Helsinki: Suomen Sosialidemokraattinen puolue, 1991.

Stedman Jones, Daniel. *Masters of the Universe: Hayek, Friedman, and the Birth of Neoliberal Politics*. Princeton: Princeton University Press, 2012.

Stenlås, Niklas. *Den inre kretsen: Den svenska ekonomiska elitens inflytande över partipolitik och opinionsbildning 1940–1949*. Lund: Arkiv, 1998.

Stiglitz, Joseph. *The Price of Inequality*. New York and London: W.W. Norton, 2012.

Strang, Johan. "Why 'Nordic Democracy?': The Scandinavian Value Nihilists and the Crisis of Democracy," in *Rhetorics of Nordic Democracy*, edited by Jussi Kurunmäki and Johan Strang. Helsinki: Finnish Literature Society, 2010.

Streeck, Wolfgang. "Works Councils in Western Europe: From Consultation to Participation." In *Works Councils: Consultation, Representation, and Cooperation in Industrial Relations*, edited by Joel Rogers and Wolfgang Streeck. Chicago and London: University of Chicago Press, 1995.

Streeck, Wolfgang. *Buying Time: The Delayed Crisis of Democratic Capitalism*. London and New York: Verso, 2014.

Stråth, Bo. *Folkhemmet mot Europa: Ett historiskt perspektiv på 90-talet*. Stockholm: Tiden, 1993.

Stråth, Bo. *Mellan två fonder: LO och den svenska modellen*. Stockholm: Atlas, 1998.

Stråth, Bo. "Nordic Capitalism and Democratisation." In *The Democratic Challenge to Capitalism: Management and Democracy in the Nordic Countries*, edited by Haldor Byrkjeflot, Sissel Myklebust, Christine Myrvang and Francis Sejersted. Bergen: Fagbokforlaget, 2001.

Stråth, Bo. "När var demokratin?" *Historisk tidsskrift* 95, 2 (2016): 269–291.

Svensson, Torsten. *Marknadsanpassningens politik: Den svenska modellens förändring 1980–2000*. Uppsala: Statsvetenskapliga föreningen, 2001.

Swenson, Peter A. *Capitalists against Markets: The Making of Labor Markets and Welfare States in the United States and Sweden*. Oxford: Oxford University Press, 2002.

Tarkka, Jukka. *Uhan alta unioniin: Asennemurros ja sen unilukkari Eva*. Helsinki: Otava, 2002.

Teivainen, Teivo. *Enter Economism, Exit Politics: Experts, Economic Policy and the Damage to Democracy*. London and New York: Zed Books, 2002.

Teivainen, Teivo. *Yritysvastuun umpikuja*. Helsinki: Kalevi Sorsa -säätiö, 2013.

Therborn, Göran. *The Killing Fields of Inequality*. Cambridge: Polity Press, 2013.

Therborn, Göran. *Kapitalet, överheten och alla vi andra: Klassamhället i Sverige – Det rådande och det kommande*. Lund: Arkiv, 2018.

Tilton, Tim. *The Political Theory of Swedish Social Democracy*. Oxford: Oxford University Press, 1990.

Timonen, Sakari. *Paikallisen sopimisen käänne*. Helsinki: Työsuojelurahasto, 2000.

Tingsten, Herbert. *Från idéer till idyll: Den lyckliga demokratien*. Stockholm: Norstedts, 1966.

Tobisson, Lars. *Löntagarfonder: Så nära men ändå inte.* Stockholm: Dialogos, 2016.

Torngren Wartin, August: "Att kartlägga terrängen: Medarbetarägandets olika skepnader." In *Tillsammans: En fungerande ekonomisk demokrati*, edited by Bo Rothstein, 47–67. Stockholm: SNS förlag, 2012.

Trägårdh, Lars (ed.). *Civilt samhälle kontra offentlig sektor.* Stockholm: SNS förlag, 1995.

Tuomala, Matti. *Markkinat, valtio ja eriarvoisuus.* Tampere: Vastapaino, 2019.

Turunen, Ilkka. "Ammattiyhdistysutopia." In *Kansa liikkeessä* edited by Risto Alapuro, Ilkka Liikanen, Kerstin Smeds and Henrik Stenius. Helsinki: Kirjayhtymä, 1987.

Turunen, Ilkka. "Arbete, produktion och demokrati: De finländska produktionskommittéernas historia." In *Industriell demokrati i norden*, edited by Daniel Fleming. Lund: Arkiv, 1990.

Van Horn, Rob and Philip Mirowski. "The Rise of the Chicago School of Economics and the Birth of Neoliberalism." In *The Road from Mont Pèlerin: The Making of the Neoliberal Thought Collective*, edited by Dieter Plehwe and Philip Mirowski. Cambridge, MA and London: Harvard University Press, 2009.

Vandekerckhove, Wim. "What Managers Do: Comparing Rhenman and Freeman." *Philosophy of Management* 8, 3 (2009): 25–35.

Vares, Vesa. *Suomalaiskansallinen kokoomus: Kansallisen kokoomuspuolueen historia 1944–1966.* Helsinki: Edita, 2008.

Vares, Vesa. *Korpivaellukselta vallankahvaan: Kansallisen kokoomuspuolueen historia 1966–1987.* Jyväskylä: Docendo, 2017.

Vartiainen, Matti and Christina Sweins. *Henkilöstörahastot Suomessa: Toimivuus ja kannustevaikutukset.* Helsinki: Työministeriö, 2002.

Venugopal, Rajesh. "Neoliberalism as a Concept." *Economy and Society* 14, 2 (2015): 165–187.

Vesikansa, Jarkko. *Laman taittaja: Raimo Sailas ja kolme talouskriisiä.* Helsinki: Otava, 2016.

Vestermark Køber, Jesper. *Et spørgsmål om nærhed: Nærdemokratibegrebets historie i 1970'ernes Danmark.* Doctoral dissertation, University of Copenhagen, 2017.

Viktorov, Ilja. *Fordismens kris och löntagarfonder i Sverige.* Stockholm: Stockholm University, 2006.

Vivekanadan, B. *Global Visions of Olof Palme, Bruno Kreisky and Willy Brandt: International Peace and Security, Co-operation and Development.* Basingstoke: Palgrave Macmillan, 2016.

Westerberg, Rikard. "The Alternative: How Nordic Business Interest Associations Attempted to Formulate an Ideological Programme, 1945–1975." *Scandinavian Journal of History* 2018, https://doi.org/10.1080/03468755.2018.1532316.

Westerberg, Rikard. *Socialists at the Gate: Swedish Business and the Defense of Free Enterprise, 1940–1985*. Stockholm: Stockholm School of Economics, 2020.

Whyman, Philip. "An Analysis of Wage-Earner Funds in Sweden: Distinguishing Myth from Reality." *Economic and Industrial Democracy* 25, 3 (2004): 411–445.

Whyte, Jessica. *The Morals of the Market: Human Rights and the Rise of Neoliberalism*. London and New York: Verso, 2019.

Wuokko, Maiju. *Markkinatalouden etujoukot: Elinkeinoelämän valtuuskunta, Teollisuuden keskusliitto ja liike-elämän poliittinen toiminta 1970–1980-lukujen Suomessa*. Helsinki: Helsingin yliopisto, 2016.

Wuokko, Maiju. "Business in the Battle of Ideas, 1945–1991: Conclusions from the Finnish Case." *Scandinavian Economic History Review* 65, 3 (2017): 279–293.

Yliaska, Ville. *Tehokkuuden toiveuni: Uuden julkisjohtamisen historia Suomessa 1970-luvulta 1990-luvulle*. Helsinki: Into, 2014.

Yliaska, Ville. "New Public Management as a Response to the Crisis of the 1970s: The Case of Finland, 1970–1990." *Contemporary European History* 24, 3 (2015): 435–459.

Index[1]

A
Adler-Karlsson, Gunnar, 34
Ahlström, Krister, 219
Ahmavaara, Pekka, 223
Aho, Esko, 268, 279, 282
Albåge, Lars-Gunnar, 106
Allardt, Erik, 79
Andersson, Jenny, 11, 32, 47, 187, 194, 195, 197, 234
Austria, 27
Autonomy, 80, 97–100, 163, 174, 224, 263, 276, 309, 310

B
Bauer, Otto, 48
Bergström, Villy, 138
Bernstein, Eduard, 26, 225
Bevir, Mark, 10, 193, 195, 197, 282, 307, 309
Bildt, Carl, 237, 258, 274, 275, 278, 279, 285
Blair, Tony, 181, 284
Blyth, Mark, 166, 167
Bohman, Gösta, 58, 186
Boldt, Peter, 141, 142
Boltanski, Luc, 35, 163
Boréus, Kristina, 196, 197
Brandt, Willy, 267
Bretton Woods system, 30, 184
Bureaucracy, 34, 35, 50, 53, 179, 191, 192, 211, 225, 229, 265, 266, 310, 322

C
Callaghan, James, 162
Capitalism, 4, 8, 9, 12, 24, 28, 30, 32, 34–37, 56, 83, 101, 122, 134, 148, 161–164, 168, 174, 178, 179, 185, 188, 193, 195, 196,

[1] Note: Page numbers followed by 'n' refer to notes.

I. Kärrylä, *Democracy and the Economy in Finland and Sweden since 1960*, Palgrave Studies in Political History,
https://doi.org/10.1007/978-3-030-80631-6

211–217, 223, 225, 226, 229, 230, 235, 252–254, 256, 264, 266, 270, 271, 274, 280, 284–290, 308, 312–318, 320–322
Carlsson, Ingvar, 228, 229, 267, 270, 285
Carter, Jimmy, 162
Center Party, 41, 42, 44, 51, 54, 55, 58, 79, 85, 92, 126, 134, 135, 144, 180, 182, 184, 189, 258, 279, 280, 292
Chiapello, Ève, 35, 163
Civil society, 55, 56, 59, 253, 269, 276–278, 280, 293, 308
Clinton, Bill, 284
Codetermination, 27, 52, 76, 78–88, 91, 92, 100, 102–107, 127, 141, 149, 150, 185, 190, 193, 199, 227, 234, 263, 266, 270, 271
Cold War, 1, 8, 307, 314
Collective bargaining, 2, 12, 23, 24, 27, 29, 32, 76, 90, 105, 147, 218, 219, 221, 269
Collective decision-making, 8, 253, 314, 317
Collective ownership, 2, 3, 12, 26, 30, 42, 119–150, 169, 171, 172, 190, 199, 236, 267, 273, 287, 310
Collectivism, 6, 219, 229, 231, 236–237, 265, 273, 277, 313, 320
Common good, 11, 107, 134, 173, 175–179, 219, 223, 224, 312, 315, 316
Communism, 1, 13, 25, 29, 30, 75, 86, 99, 141, 146, 150, 165, 229, 253, 263
Competitiveness, 11, 31, 49, 95, 98, 101, 103, 106, 128, 132, 134, 136, 139, 140, 165, 166, 169, 173, 175, 176, 179, 181, 182, 186, 189, 218, 221–223, 230, 231, 238, 239, 252, 254, 259, 268, 271, 277, 281–285, 292, 294, 308, 312
Conservatives, 13, 14, 27, 54–56, 59, 129, 148, 178, 197, 215, 236, 274, 308
Consultation, 4, 24, 77, 81, 83, 85–87, 89–91, 95, 97, 101, 106, 308, 310
Consumers, 8, 85, 132, 164, 176, 177, 228, 231–233, 235, 264, 270, 274, 277, 279, 286–288, 316
Cooperation, 3, 6, 24, 27, 32, 33, 58, 75–107, 122, 132, 135, 136, 139–142, 144, 146, 149, 150, 164, 165, 167–174, 183, 185, 199, 217, 218, 220–223, 235, 237–239, 251, 267–269, 272, 275, 277, 287, 289, 293, 312, 317, 319–321
Cooperatives, 24, 42, 126, 129, 190, 227, 230, 232, 271, 310
Corporate governance, 89, 90, 92, 172, 190, 222, 226, 238–240, 293
Corporatism, 28, 29, 167, 280, 290
Counter-concepts, 26, 83, 86, 100, 178, 191, 224, 236, 253, 277

D

Dahlström, Edmund, 79
Dahrendorf, Ralf, 79
Decentralization, 50–53, 85, 130, 167, 189–193, 199, 220, 231, 265, 266, 278, 280, 281, 308, 310
Democratization, 2, 12, 24, 26, 27, 30, 32–37, 41, 43, 44, 46, 51,

53, 57, 75–77, 79, 80, 82–85, 87, 88, 91, 93, 98, 100, 120, 122, 124, 125, 127–129, 139, 141, 150, 161–199, 211–217, 222–224, 226, 227, 230, 231, 233, 251–294, 308, 310, 312
Denmark, 37, 92, 105, 119, 148
Deregulation, 57, 217, 237
Drucker, Peter, 40

E

Economic democracy, 2–5, 7, 9, 11, 23–26, 28–30, 36–38, 41–44, 46, 49, 51, 55, 56, 58, 59, 86, 119–150, 164, 169–172, 176, 182, 184, 189–193, 195, 197–199, 211–241, 252, 256, 259, 267, 269, 271–273, 280, 283, 286–294, 307–310, 313, 316–322
Economic growth, 11, 27, 32–34, 42, 43, 47, 49, 50, 77, 101, 120, 122, 124, 163, 170, 178, 185, 187, 194, 198, 211, 214, 226, 234, 237, 254, 272, 277, 283, 284, 287, 288, 312, 321, 323
Economic planning, 2, 6, 12, 25, 29–34, 38–45, 49, 51, 52, 55, 59, 77, 124, 170, 190, 252, 254, 287, 288, 322
Economics, 6, 9, 30, 162, 164, 292, 312
Economic sphere, 5, 7, 26, 107, 132, 169, 170, 177, 199, 257, 266, 274, 280, 314, 316
Edin, Per-Olof, 136
Edlund, Sten, 86
Efficiency, 11, 45, 47, 48, 50, 58, 77, 80, 84, 93–96, 98–102, 104, 106, 107, 132–134, 141, 143, 145, 169, 173–175, 187, 220, 222, 223, 229, 252, 259, 266, 276, 288, 308, 312, 315, 318
Ekdahl, Lars, 128, 188, 193, 255, 272, 285
Ekegren, Bo, 177
Eklund, Klas, 186, 187, 215
Employment, 6, 27, 30–33, 38–40, 44–47, 49, 94, 98, 102, 122, 124, 127, 137, 139, 141, 143, 166, 175, 181–183, 185, 195, 196, 198, 213–215, 217, 218, 221, 222, 225, 226, 228, 231–235, 238–240, 252, 254, 258, 266, 270, 275, 281, 283–285, 289, 291, 309, 321
Enterprise democracy, 2–4, 10–14, 37, 38, 41–44, 51, 52, 75–107, 125, 129, 131–134, 139, 150, 163, 169–174, 183, 184, 189, 190, 192, 193, 199, 218, 222, 223, 225, 235, 236, 238–240, 251, 252, 254, 256, 261, 263, 268, 280, 281, 286, 290, 291, 293, 307, 308, 310, 311, 315, 319, 321
Equality, 11, 26, 30, 36, 38, 40, 44–47, 49, 84, 85, 93, 98, 99, 107, 124, 141, 190, 194, 220, 231, 255, 261, 262, 270, 287, 294, 309, 318
Erlander, Tage, 40, 265
Eskilsson, Sture, 131, 136
Europe, 25, 27, 32, 37, 56, 76, 77, 119, 129, 213, 214, 218, 260, 262, 263, 267, 273, 274, 276, 280
European Union, 270, 276, 281, 283–285
EVA, 13, 140, 164, 165, 167, 170, 171, 212, 213

F

Fälldin, Thorbjörn, 126, 134, 135, 184, 186
Färm, Göran, 270
Faxén, Karl-Olof, 96
Feldt, Kjell-Olof, 128, 136, 186, 187, 215, 217, 268
Finland, v, 3, 9–14, 15n2, 22n70, 24, 28, 29, 31–33, 36, 37, 41–44, 48–50, 52, 54–56, 59, 60n5, 62n23, 62n25, 62n26, 62n28, 63n32, 64n50, 65n58, 75–81, 83, 86, 87, 89–102, 104–107, 108n1, 108n8, 113n90, 119, 139–144, 146–150, 154n69, 158n136, 158n139, 159n165, 159n167, 160n184, 163–165, 167–172, 174–176, 178–183, 185, 186, 188–192, 198, 201n15, 204n55, 211–213, 216–223, 227, 235, 237–241, 245n52, 248n126, 249n133, 249n140, 251, 252, 254, 257–266, 268, 269, 274, 276, 279–287, 289, 290, 292–294, 294n2, 299n83, 304n180, 304n182, 307–311, 313–315, 317, 319, 320
Flexibility, 146, 163, 173, 183, 218–221, 238, 239, 259, 263, 267, 269, 277, 283, 285, 287, 294, 312
Fond, Gunnar, 120, 123
Fordism, 162, 173
Foucault, Michel, 10, 179, 195
France, 24, 30, 34, 119, 129, 198, 211, 217
Freedom, 5, 30, 33, 53, 56–58, 94, 95, 99, 133, 134, 175–178, 197, 214, 219, 224, 228, 231, 237, 252, 253, 257, 261, 270, 273, 274, 276–278, 280, 290, 314–318, 322
Freedom of choice, 228, 280, 290
Free markets, 5–7, 30, 59, 130, 162, 168, 178, 195, 199, 233, 253, 263, 272, 278, 281, 309, 311, 312, 314, 317, 322
Friedman, Milton, 6, 7, 215
Fukuyama, Francis, 253, 274
Functional socialism, 34, 45, 46, 48, 125, 141, 148, 149, 232, 285, 319
Furåker, Bengt, 233

G

Geijer, Arne, 100, 122
Germany, 25, 27, 47, 105, 119, 123, 217, 284
Giesecke, Curt-Steffan, 87, 165
Globalization, 5, 211, 216, 270, 278, 290, 318, 320, 321
Gorbachev, Mikhail, 211, 253
Great Depression, 6, 27, 30, 185
Green Party, 13, 284
Gunnarsson, Olle, 85
Gustafsson, Jukka, 146
Gyllenhammar, Pehr, 135

H

Hämäläinen, Niilo, 90, 100
Hammarström, Olle, 101
Hansson, Per Albin, 26
Hästö, Stig, 97, 143, 171
Hautala, Arvo, 86
Hayek, Friedrich, 6, 7, 59, 164, 165, 215
Heckscher, Gunnar, 59
Hedborg, Anna, 98, 120, 123
Helldén, Arne, 227
Hermansson, Carl-Henrik, 37
Hermansson, Jörgen, 233
Hetemäki, Päiviö, 94

Holkeri, Harri, 238–240, 251, 262
Holmberg, Yngve, 58, 129
Human capital, 168, 234, 235, 288
Human rights, 253, 261, 265, 269, 286

I

Ideational constellations, 11, 59, 107, 147, 148, 169, 195, 196, 240, 252, 270, 281, 288, 312
Ideology, 6, 9, 11, 13, 26, 31, 32, 47, 55, 56, 96, 134, 149, 150, 169, 178, 194, 196, 253, 255, 261, 281
Ihalainen, Lauri, 220, 268
Iivari, Ulpu, 261
Individual freedom, 6, 7, 55, 59, 177, 199, 224, 253, 262, 264, 265, 273, 277–279, 309, 314, 315, 317
Individualism, 144, 191, 212, 219, 226–235, 265, 267
Industrial democracy, 2, 5, 9–13, 23–25, 27–29, 32, 37, 46, 76–78, 81, 82, 87, 307
Industrial policy, 11, 12, 38–48, 58, 84, 125, 133, 186, 230, 272, 288
Inequality, 9, 36, 140, 145, 188, 211, 233, 255, 264, 268, 286, 291, 318, 320
Inflation, 6, 33, 49, 137–139, 161, 162, 165, 166, 176, 180–182, 184–186, 189, 194, 196, 198, 211, 214, 221, 231, 254, 259, 262, 268, 275, 277, 281, 285
Information society, 162, 173, 181, 185, 218, 228
Innovation, 50, 56, 181, 277, 280, 288, 320
Intellectual history, 3, 6, 10, 307
Internationalization, 103, 161, 166, 196, 226, 264, 269, 272, 287, 309
International Monetary Fund, 6, 32, 162, 180, 216, 319
Interwar period, 28–30

J

Jakobson, Max, 167, 170, 212, 213
Janérus, Inge, 91
Johansson, Göran, 272
Johansson, Sten, 45

K

Kairamo, Aimo, 225
Kanerva, Ilkka, 146
Kantola, Anu, 260
Kari, Markus, 281
Karjalainen, Ahti, 44
Karleby, Nils, 30, 34
Kekkonen, Urho, 31, 44, 56
Ketola, Eino, 262
Kettunen, Pauli, 48, 104, 179, 182, 224, 256, 261
Kevätsalo, Kimmo, 102
Keynes, John Maynard, 187, 225, 260
Keynesianism, 5, 6, 30, 31, 55, 56, 162, 178, 184, 185, 187, 188, 194, 195, 198, 217, 226
Kiander, Jaakko, 258
Kiljunen, Kimmo, 261, 262
Knowledge economy, 181
Knowledge society, 234, 288
Koivisto, Mauno, 42, 189, 238
Koselleck, Reinhart, 9

L

Labor market policy, 27, 33, 42, 150, 167, 275
Labor market relations, 23, 27–29, 143
Låftman, Lennart, 138
Laine, Jermu, 43, 49

Larsson, Allan, 221
Left Alliance, 263, 283, 284
Legitimation, 47, 95, 100, 120, 122, 124, 142, 144, 163, 172, 175, 179, 219, 223, 257, 280, 282, 309, 314–316, 322
Lepage, Henri, 168
Liberal democracy, 9, 143, 253, 254, 286, 320
Liberalism, 6, 7, 56, 58, 59, 129, 134, 178, 270, 274, 279, 315
Liberalization, 5, 12, 138, 139, 149, 211, 216–218, 234, 251–294, 310
Lindbeck, Assar, 275
Lindgren, Anne-Marie, 231–233
Lindvall, Johannes, 195, 281
Lipponen, Paavo, 283, 284
Ljunggren, Olof, 178
Ljunggren, Stig-Björn, 194
LO, 3, 13, 38, 77, 78, 84–86, 90–92, 98, 100, 102, 103, 120, 122–128, 130, 132–136, 138, 140, 146, 147, 149, 166, 194, 214, 219, 228, 229, 231, 235, 236, 267, 269–272, 285, 289, 310

M

Malm Lindberg, Henrik, 194
Malm, Stig, 229, 230, 270, 272
Market economy, 5, 43, 45, 46, 48, 54–59, 93, 101, 127, 131, 133, 140, 141, 147, 149, 164–169, 171, 175–179, 188, 190, 199, 226–235, 237, 240, 253, 262, 265, 266, 273, 274, 277, 280, 281, 287, 288
Marketization, 6, 7, 252, 253, 273, 275, 280, 281, 290
Marttila, Jouko, 281
Marx, Karl, 45, 48
Maslow, Abraham, 79
Meidner, Rudolf, 33, 120, 122–125, 127, 128, 130, 131, 134, 136, 187
Middle-class, 41, 56, 180, 211, 212, 227, 255, 263
Miettunen, Martti, 180
Mill, John Stuart, 24
Mitterrand, François, 217
Mixed economy, 32, 137, 141, 190, 223, 262, 288
Moderates, 55, 58, 134, 135, 137, 147, 177, 178, 186, 214, 236, 237, 274–280, 283, 286
Mont Pèlerin society (MPS), 6, 164
Myrdal, Alva, 36
Myrdal, Hans-Göran, 132

N

National Coalition Party (NCP), 44, 54–56, 144–146, 238, 239, 279, 280, 284, 285, 292
National interest, 48, 94, 95, 97, 98, 100, 107, 134, 175, 179, 181, 222, 259, 308, 309, 313, 315
Nationalization, 27, 31, 38, 42, 43, 45, 133, 190, 235, 267
Near democracy, 50, 52, 85, 215, 227, 266, 276, 280, 311
Neoliberalism, 5–8, 166, 168, 178, 179, 188, 197, 214, 215, 228, 238, 255, 313, 315
Neoliberalization, 7, 188, 215, 217, 252, 253, 281, 313
Netherlands, 28
New Left, 35–38, 52, 54, 77, 79, 83, 84, 86, 99, 100, 163, 266, 308
Nicolin, Curt, 131, 167, 175, 178, 236, 273

Nordic countries, 2, 3, 7, 24, 26, 28, 31, 95, 164, 168, 240, 253, 290, 293
Nordic democracy, 27
Nordling, Danne, 131, 133
Norway, 37, 92, 105, 141, 190

O

OECD, 6, 162, 181, 216, 217, 319
Oil crisis, 49, 103, 130, 139, 161, 184
Oligarchy, 26, 55, 86, 191, 224, 308
Olsen, Gregg, 25
Olsen, Niklas, 6, 233, 316
Owner democracy, 56–58, 129, 148, 169, 236, 268, 271, 273, 274, 277, 308, 310–311, 317, 318

P

Paasio, Rafael, 44, 165
Palme, Olof, 40, 45, 46, 51, 52, 75, 125, 136, 149, 191, 214, 217, 229, 257, 267, 310
Palmstierna, Erik, 25
Parliamentarism, 1, 2, 24, 26, 167, 189
Pärnänen, Heikki, 96, 97, 102
Participation, 2, 35, 37, 41, 47, 51, 52, 58, 80–83, 86, 91, 93, 95, 96, 98, 106, 107, 143, 144, 147, 163, 169–175, 179, 191, 192, 196, 199, 218, 220, 222, 225, 228, 230, 238, 251, 253, 261, 265, 266, 268, 269, 271, 276, 279, 287, 293, 308, 310, 312, 317, 321, 322
Participatory democracy, 4, 50, 52, 224, 227, 292, 320
Peasant Union, 27, 33, 54
Pekkanen, Matti, 144, 147
Pension funds, 34, 39, 40, 46, 49, 56, 122, 127, 130, 236, 267, 270, 271, 273, 289–291, 310
People's capitalism, 56–58, 129, 141, 144, 146–150, 169, 274, 293, 308, 310
People's home, 26, 214, 264
Persson, Göran, 285, 286
Peterson, Thage, 185
Piketty, Thomas, 9
Planned economy, 4, 31, 50, 56, 58, 80, 121, 125, 133, 165, 166, 185, 188, 190, 223, 233, 253, 265, 267
Plato, 260
Polanyi, Karl, 163
Political sphere, 5, 257, 314, 323
Politicization, 4, 45, 132, 167, 177
Pontusson, Jonas, 148
Popper, Karl, 195, 196
Post-Fordism, 162, 181, 218
Postmodernism, 212
Postwar era, 3, 10, 15, 32, 55, 119, 176, 187, 278
Private ownership, 8, 46, 48, 55, 58, 59, 80, 95, 126, 133, 171, 224, 236, 237, 265, 273, 275, 277, 317
Private-sector, 38, 258, 283, 284
Privatization, 183, 228, 231, 237, 280, 281, 284, 285, 290
Production committees, 3, 76–78, 81, 89, 105
Property-owning democracy, 56–58
Proudhon, Pierre-Joseph, 23
Public debt, 42, 162, 163, 185, 198, 213, 258, 275, 276, 280, 284, 311
Public sector, 34, 143, 149, 150, 162, 164, 166, 170, 175, 178, 186, 188, 189, 194, 198, 211–215, 227, 228, 231, 237, 239, 258–268, 270, 273, 275, 280, 281, 283, 290

Public services, 163, 178, 227, 228, 231, 235, 252, 257, 264, 265, 280, 290, 292
Puoskari, Pentti, 225, 226

R

Raatikainen, Erkki, 43, 45
Randell, Seppo, 79
Reagan, Ronald, 6, 168, 198
Redistribution, 26, 124, 140, 141, 161, 169, 171, 187, 190, 214, 224, 227, 266, 312
Reformism, 26, 35, 46, 148, 192, 193, 224, 226, 227, 234, 253
Regulation, 7, 30, 34, 38, 51, 59, 88, 101, 150, 161, 163, 178, 185, 191, 195, 213, 216, 218, 225, 229, 231, 232, 256, 257, 277, 285, 287, 288, 291–293, 309, 311, 313, 314, 319–321
Rehn, Olli, 280
Rehn-Meidner model, 33, 121, 187
Relativism, 212, 323
Representation, 1, 5, 8, 39, 76, 77, 81, 88–92, 104, 190–192, 220, 222, 226, 237–240, 285, 293, 310, 312, 314, 322
Rhenman, Eric, 82–84, 87, 91, 94, 95, 97, 99, 291
Ruin, Olof, 52
Rule of law, 5, 7, 276
Ryner, J. Magnus, 195–197, 255

S

SAF, 13, 77, 82–84, 87, 88, 91–94, 96, 102, 106, 129–133, 135, 136, 140, 145, 164–166, 172, 175, 176, 178, 218, 235, 236, 269, 276, 317
Sailas, Raimo, 260
SAK, 13, 86, 89–92, 99, 100, 104, 105, 140–142, 145, 219, 220, 222, 223, 239, 268, 269, 282, 283
SAP, 13, 23, 25–27, 29, 30, 35, 36, 38, 40, 42, 45–48, 51, 53, 84, 85, 102, 125–128, 130, 135, 136, 148, 184–189, 193–195, 214, 215, 217, 224, 227–231, 233, 236, 237, 256, 264–267, 270–272, 283, 285, 287–289, 310
Schröder, Gerhard, 284
Schumpeter, Joseph, 181, 182, 185, 230, 259, 288, 313
SDP, 13, 29, 36, 41, 43, 44, 49, 104, 105, 139–142, 145, 165, 172, 180, 182, 183, 186, 189–192, 224, 225, 238, 261, 262, 264–266, 279, 282–284, 286–289, 292, 310
Second World War, 1, 29, 55, 76, 161, 289, 307
Self-governance, 4, 25, 27, 55, 58, 81, 83, 192, 194, 224–227, 231, 322
Sipponen, Kauko, 213
Skinner, Quentin, 10
Skogh, Göran, 106
Social choice economy, 56
Social democracy, 13, 26, 32, 45, 47, 53, 188, 190, 194, 225, 229, 234, 251–257, 261, 264, 286
Socialism, 4, 9, 12, 26, 30, 32, 40, 47, 52, 55, 56, 58, 122, 129–135, 142, 147, 164, 170, 171, 188–190, 192, 194, 197, 199, 212, 215, 223–225, 231, 232, 236, 237, 252–254, 260, 261, 263, 267, 273, 274, 284, 286–289, 311, 313, 319–321
Socialization, 25, 29–34, 43, 45–50, 122, 124, 133, 170, 190, 197, 225, 236, 237, 267

Social market economy, 32, 56, 280
Social reforms, 27, 30, 32, 33, 38, 43, 55, 56, 124, 170, 175, 187, 188, 196, 221, 226, 265, 286, 319
Social security, 27, 45, 100, 161, 188, 226, 266, 268, 279, 285
Somerto, Pentti, 218
Sorsa, Kalevi, 44, 50, 140, 144, 165, 180–183, 185, 191, 192, 217, 219, 222, 223, 262, 282
Soviet Union, 36, 42, 170, 211, 253
Stagflation, 161, 195, 211
Stagnation, 103, 104, 161, 184, 277
State-owned enterprises, 30, 31, 34, 39, 42, 43, 45, 49, 55, 58, 78, 183, 277, 284, 285, 291, 309
State ownership, 254, 291
Stiglitz, Joseph, 9
Stimulation, 162, 180, 183, 184, 187, 194, 236, 282, 283
STK, 13, 80, 83, 87, 89, 91, 94, 96, 97, 102, 142–144, 146, 171–173, 175, 179, 218–220, 239, 292
Sträng, Gunnar, 184
Stråth, Bo, 150, 166, 194, 195, 228, 269, 270
Structural renewal, 38, 44, 183, 241, 283
STTK, 13, 142
Sulkunen, Olavi, 99
Sundqivst, Ulf, 191
Suominen, Ilkka, 238
Sweden, 3–5, 9–14, 16n13, 18n27, 22n70, 23–43, 45, 47–50, 52–59, 61n11, 61n15, 61n20, 62n23, 62n26, 64n39, 64n44, 64n45, 66n64, 68n91, 70n143, 70n147, 75–84, 86–89, 91–95, 98, 100–107, 108n1, 119–123, 126, 127, 129, 130, 132–134, 136–150, 153n51, 154n70, 156n98, 156n108, 156n109, 157n110, 160n175, 163–172, 174–179, 182–187, 189–196, 198, 199, 200n4, 202n25, 202n29, 211–221, 224, 227–231, 235–237, 244n32, 246n84, 252, 254–260, 262, 263, 267–269, 271–276, 279–281, 283–285, 287–290, 292–294, 296n16, 296n21, 297n32, 303n156, 307–311, 313–315, 317, 319, 320, 323n1

T

TCO, 13, 92, 102, 135
Thatcher, Margaret, 6, 168, 198
Therborn, Göran, 35, 83, 99, 215
Think tanks, 13, 164–166, 170, 181, 212
Third way, 122, 180–189, 215, 274
Thorsrud, Einar, 83
Tiivola, Mika, 170
Tikka, Seppo, 192
Timbro, 13, 166
Trade unions, 3, 13, 24, 29, 32, 33, 37, 75, 79, 84, 86, 90, 92, 98–102, 104, 105, 107, 123, 126, 130, 133, 134, 137, 141, 143, 146, 167, 170, 187, 191, 194, 213, 219, 221–223, 228, 229, 231, 252, 254, 260, 261, 268, 270, 272, 287, 308–310
TVK, 13, 142

U

Undén, Östen, 34
Unemployment, 33, 39, 100, 107, 136, 139, 162, 163, 185, 189, 194, 213–215, 221, 255, 258, 259, 268, 271, 275, 277, 279, 284, 290, 292, 320

United Kingdom, 6, 24, 284
United States, 6, 14, 23–25, 40, 47, 129, 161, 162, 164, 217, 284

V
Value hierarchies, 11, 101, 223, 255, 308
Vesikansa, Jarkko, 260, 281
Viinanen, Iiro, 279
Viinanen, Pertti, 222
Viktorov, Ilja, 120, 149
Voutilainen, Eero, 87, 220

W
Wachtmeister, Tom, 273
Wage-earner funds, 3, 11, 12, 119, 120, 122–128, 131, 133–144, 146–150, 166, 171, 172, 185, 190, 193, 195, 199, 220, 222, 227, 229, 230, 234, 236, 237, 255, 256, 267, 275, 289, 293, 310
Wage-earners, 3, 40, 52, 53, 98, 99, 119, 123, 128, 129, 134, 138–142, 162, 191, 192, 222, 226, 230, 231, 233, 235, 236, 238, 263, 264, 268, 287, 289
Waldenström, Erland, 130, 131, 133, 144, 145
Welfare state, 27, 35, 36, 55, 56, 58, 85, 102, 149, 167, 175, 186, 195, 212, 214, 224, 226, 228, 229, 254–256, 258, 261, 264, 270, 271, 276, 283–285, 292
Westerberg, Bengt, 214
Westholm, Carl-Johan, 176
Whyman, Philip, 139
Wigforss, Ernst, 23, 25, 30, 48, 121, 167, 289
Wiio, Osmo, 83
Working hours, 176, 218, 219, 221, 238, 263, 266, 268, 269, 271, 277, 288, 290
Works councils, 25, 27, 32, 76–78, 81, 84, 85, 88, 90–92, 103, 174, 308

The manufacturer's authorised representative in the EU is Springer Nature Customer Service Centre GmbH, Europaplatz 3, 69115 Heidelberg, Germany. If you have any concerns regarding our products, please contact ProductSafety@springernature.com

Printed and bound by CPI Group (UK) Ltd, Croydon, CR0 4YY
22/09/2026
02221066-0016